Applied
Mathematica®

Getting Started,
Getting It Done

William T. Shaw
Jason Tigg

Addison-Wesley Publishing Company
Reading, Massachusetts • Menlo Park, California
New York • Don Mills, Ontario
Wokingham, England • Amsterdam • Bonn
Sydney • Singapore • Tokyo • Madrid
San Juan • Milan • Paris

Anscombes Quartet (Chapter 15) is adapted with permission from the American Statistician. Copyright (1973) by the American Statistical Association. All rights reserved. Material from *Numerical Recipes in C, The Art of Scientific Computing*, by W. H. Press, B. R. Flannery, S. A. Teukolsky, and W. T. Vetterling is used with permission from Cambridge University Press.

This book was reproduced by Addison-Wesley from text and illustration files supplied by the authors.

Library of Congress Cataloging-in-Publication Data

Shaw, William T.
    Applied Mathematica : getting started, getting it done / by William T. Shaw and Jason Tigg.
       p.   cm.
    Includes bibliographical references and index.
    ISBN 0–201–54217–X
    1. Mathematica (Computer file)   2. Mathematics—Data processing.
  I. Tigg, Jason. II. Title.
  QA76.95.S52 1994   93-13908
  510′.285′5369—dc20   CIP

1 2 3 4 5 6 7 8 9 10-MA-97969594

Preface

How to Use This Book

This book has been designed to be used by professionals, educators, and students in applied mathematics and the applied sciences. It explores *Mathematica* by *using Mathematica* to solve useful applied problems; it grew out of our experiences in mathematical and *Mathematica* consultancy and from our teaching other people how to use *Mathematica*. As such, it is organized along particular lines.

The book is divided into four parts. Part One is introductory in nature and helps you get off to a quick start using the *Mathematica* system. It also covers points that are assumed by Parts Two through Four of the book.

The division into Parts Two and Three for the main expository material reflects our experience in seeing the different ways that people use *Mathematica*. Part Two is about how to use *Mathematica* as a data analysis and visualization system. It therefore covers the various stages of the data analysis process, starting with the importation of data and then dealing with data organization, processing, analysis, and visualization in two, three, or more dimensions. These data could have come from outside *Mathematica* and could be in essentially any form, or they could have been created by a model entirely within the *Mathematica* system.

The principles of modeling within *Mathematica* are discussed in Part Three, which is a self-contained exposition of how to program with *Mathematica*. The text begins with a clear explanation of simple user-defined functions and progresses through a general discussion of the structure of *Mathematica*. We first discuss the different styles of programming; we then explain how to optimize your code through efficient coding, how to use the *Mathematica* compiler, and how to communicate with other programs by using the MathLink system. The material of Part Three may be used in conjunction with that of Part Two.

To give substance to the expository material and to supplement the examples given in Parts Two and Three, we have included in Part Four a number of case studies that explore and apply *Mathematica* to particular areas. These case studies span a wide range of applications, from serious data analysis with robust regression theory, through a maximum entropy data analysis, to a just-for-fun exploration of the Mandelbrot set using MathLink to create a movie. They cover detailed coding issues (such as in digital image processing) and aspects of packaging (as in probabilistic system assessment). The examples are drawn from fields as diverse as engineering, finance, environmental modeling, and image processing, and there are also numerous problems in applied mathematics.

History

We began using *Mathematica* in our work several years ago, soon after it first appeared in the United Kingdom. After we had used it in a variety of applications, we set up our company, Oxford System Solutions, at the end of 1990. We were grateful for the encouragement of Wolfram Research in the early days of our company, and we had a great deal of fun showing off their product with them at trade shows and mathematics conferences. Building on the experience that we gained in applying the system, we began providing *Mathematica* training courses in mid-1991, offering two full-day courses, "Introduction to *Mathematica*" and "Graphics and Data Visualization with *Mathematica*." These courses have since evolved and been joined by courses in programming, in data analysis, and in case study analysis. In all our work with *Mathematica*, we have had in mind applied problems, and many of the people whom we have taught have needed to find the solutions to problems in the applied sciences. Many of the excellent books already available for *Mathematica* cover in detail pure and recreational mathematics, but our experience suggested that there was a need for a book for professionals doing work in the applied sciences. In this book we provide such a resource.

Acknowledgments

We begin by apologizing to anyone who has been left out of the acknowledgments that follow. William Shaw wishes to first thank his parents for generally getting him going and then thank his wife, Dr. Dinah Parums, pathologist extraordinaire, supplier of endless moral support, financial support, and computer equipment, without whom much of this work would definitely not have existed. Jason Tigg thanks his parents for both financial support and much encouragement over the past 25 years and his sister Alison for the same reasons and moreover for the gift of the juggling bags. Support and encouragement have been forthcoming from many current and now-departed staff at Wolfram Research, and we thank in particular Stephen Wolfram, Conrad Wolfram, Paul Abbott, Helen Jenkins, Pippa Russell, Jon McCloone, Scott May, Shawn Sheridan, and Glenn Sholebo. In fact, we thank all the developers because this book would not exist without their diverse contributions. The success of the training courses has rested on contributions from several people at Oxford Brookes University, including Marjorie Hoek, Karen Mount, Barbara Roberts, Andy Woods, and Angela Talbot. Our ideas about *Mathematica* have also evolved as a result of the contributions of all those people who have attended our courses. We thank Dave Jehan for the Holmium information and his general enthusiasm for the project. Our computer equipment has been supplied by Noah computers of Oxford — in our view the world's best Apple dealer — and Lofgren computers, also of Oxford. Our writing of the book has been greatly facilitated by our use of the Textures typesetting system by Blue Sky Research. We also are grateful to Peter Gordon of Addison-Wesley for sharing our enthusiasm sufficiently to encourage us to proceed with this project and to Helen Goldstein, Juliet Silveri, and the Addison-Wesley production staff for organizing us and helping us get over the multitude of problems that may arise with a techno-book such as this one. The prose of this book has been corrected ruthlessly by our editors, Lyn Dupré and Jean Peck, whose heroic efforts we wish to acknowledge fulsomely. We are also grateful to our four anonymous reviewers for their subtle blend of constructive and carping criticism.

About the Authors

William Shaw is the founder and principal consultant of Oxford System Solutions (OSS). OSS is a consultancy providing mathematical problem-solving capabilities to government, industry, and commerce: Its consultants have a total of 16 years of experience in the application of mathematics to pure and applied problems. *Mathematica* features strongly in these activities, and several years of its use have shown it to be an indispensable tool for analytical, semianalytical, and numerical modeling in both business and academic applications. Jason Tigg is in the final stages of completing a D. Phil. in theoretical particle physics at Oxford University in which he made extensive use of *Mathematica* to simplify complex integration problems. Formerly with OSS, he is now with Merrill Lynch Europe Ltd. After he earned a D. Phil. in mathematics at Oxford, William Shaw carried out research and teaching at Cambridge University and M.I.T.; he now combines his consultancy work with teaching applied mathematics at Balliol College, Oxford.

About the Electronic Supplement

Parts of this book, including longer code segments, are available as item number 0205-366 from *MathSource*^{TM}. *MathSource* is an on-line archive of *Mathematica*-related materials contributed by Wolfram Research and *Mathematica* users around the world. You can obtain this material from *MathSource* in three ways:

Electronic Mail

To have materials sent to you automatically by electronic mail, send the single-line email message:
```
Send 0205-366
```
to the *MathSource* server at
```
MathSource@wri.com
```
For more information about *MathSource*, send the message:
```
HelpIntro
```

Anonymous FTP

MathSource is also accessible via anonymous ftp at `MathSource.wri.com`.

Direct Dialup

You can also direct dialup to *MathSource* with a modem to 217-398-1898 (U.S. number).

Communication with OSS

OSS welcomes any comments, criticism, or statements of error regarding the contents of this book. You can contact us for these or any other reasons; feel free to do so. We provide regular training courses in *Mathematica*, as well as offer consultancy services in *Mathematica* work and more general mathematical modeling. We are always willing to discuss how we may be able to help you or your organization.

Oxford System Solutions
The Magdalen Centre
Oxford Science Park
Oxford OX4 4GA
United Kingdom
Telephone +44 [0]865 784270
Facsimile +44 [0]865 784004

Contents

Part Two
MANAGING DATA WITH *Mathematica*

Part Three
MODELING WITH *Mathematica*

Part Four
CASE STUDIES

PART ONE

Introduction to *Mathematica*

CHAPTER ONE

Getting a Quick Start

This chapter contains explanations of topics that you need to understand in order to make sense of the later chapters of this book and to use *Mathematica* effectively. We strongly recommend that you read this chapter first, whether you are a new or a relatively experienced user.

1.1 Kernels and Front Ends

In dealing with a computer and a software system, you should first establish how to communicate with the computer and the software. *Mathematica* is divided into two pieces: The actual calculations are done by a *computational kernel*, but you communicate through a *front end*. The kernel and the front end may be running either on the same computer or on different computers linked by some kind of network.

This book is not oriented toward any particular front end, but it focuses for the most part on capabilities of the Version 2.1 kernel and the packages that are standard with Version 2.1. Some remarks on new features of Version 2.2 are included where there is an effect on the subjects covered by this book. We shall not cover all the possible front ends that are available. Our own use of *Mathematica* is on systems running a NoteBook front end. NoteBooks are available for Macintosh, Windows 3.x computers, and NeXT systems, and, as of this writing, a generic X Windows system is in the final stages of development and testing. We strongly prefer to use NoteBook-based front ends. The NoteBook files are just text files and can be exchanged among all systems that presently support them. Most of the concepts that we shall discuss are independent of the computer system and front end being used.

When you obtain *Mathematica*, please consult the installation instructions to learn how to install and start the program. Installation is particularly dependent on your choice of computer system, and you may need the help of a system manager if you work in a networked UNIX environment or run a system such as a Macintosh front end to a Cray computer. However, starting the program takes one of two forms for the systems with which we are familiar :

1. UNIX systems: Type "math" at a terminal prompt. Preferably, you should enter this prompt from a window with scrolling enabled. For example, on a SUN computer, a *command tool* window is a good choice, running under OpenWindows 2 or 3.
2. Macintosh, Windows, or NeXT systems: Double-click the *Mathematica* icon in the Finder/Windows program manager/Next display. *Mathematica* will start up, will display the version number, and will issue dire warnings about software piracy.

We are now ready to do a few simple calculations.

1.2 The Four Pillars of *Mathematica*

It has become a tradition to begin all sessions of *Mathematica* with the simplest possible calculation! Type "2+2" into the system. Do not enter the quotation marks; type only the expression within them. Enter the calculation. Entering depends a little on the system: On a Macintosh, you can use the Enter key or Shift + Return; on a Windows computer, you can use Shift + Return or Insert. We shall use the word "Enter" to denote the generic operation of asking *Mathematica* to execute a calculation, irrespective of how the particular system behaves. With the default settings on most systems, *Mathematica* labels both your input and its output with numbers:

In[1]:=   2+2

Out[1]=   4

Now enter the command `Expand[(x + 2 y)^2]`:

In[2]:=   `Expand[(x + 2 y)^2]`

Out[2]= $x^2 + 4 x y + 4 y^2$

The *Mathematica* function `Expand` carries out a basic expansion of the expression that you supply as an argument. Here we are evaluating $(x+2y)^2 = (x+2y)*(x+2y) = x^2+4xy+y^2$. Whenever we present an example such as this one, the expressions that you should enter are set in bold-faced type.

Enter the following sequence of statements. When you enter the commands given in bold-faced type, they will acquire `In[n]:=` labels, although you may find that your numbers get out of step with ours. Do not worry about that — it will happen if you have to repeat something. Also, if you make a mistake, you should correct it. How you correct expressions will depend on what editing facilities you have available. In the worst case, you will have to type in these commands again!

In our first example, we use the `N` function to ask for the numerical value of `Pi` (π) with 100-digit precision:

In[3]:=   `N[Pi, 100]`

Out[3]=   3.141592653589793238462643383279502884197169399375105820974
9445923078164062862089986280348253421170668

In our second example, we introduce the `Plot` operation. In the simplest application of `Plot`, it is necessary to supply only a function and a range to produce a default graph of the function. The range for the plot is given as a *Mathematica* list structure. Such lists are always indicated by curly brackets {...}. Here, and elsewhere in this book, we have suppressed the `Out` statement for a graphic:

In[4]:=   `Plot[x^2, {x, -3, 3}]`

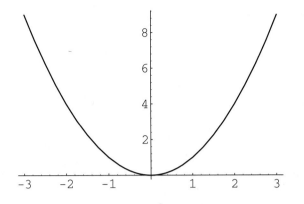

In our third example, note the colon and semicolon. We shall discuss the meaning of this punctuation later in this chapter. For now, we just want you to see *Mathematica* operating in a simple programming example. We first define a function f that computes the cube of its argument; then we apply f twice to an argument y:

```
In[5]:=    f[x_] := x^3;
           f[f[y]]
```

```
Out[5]=    9
           y
```

In the last of our series of initial examples, you should create the object data by use of the Table command. Like Plot, Table takes a function and a range as its arguments, but this time we obtain a table of values of the function over the given range. Here the object data is a list of pairs of integers and their squares:

```
In[6]:=    data = Table[{i, i^2}, {i, 0, 10}]
```

```
Out[6]=    {{0, 0}, {1, 1}, {2, 4}, {3, 9}, {4, 16}, {5, 25}, {6, 36},
           {7, 49}, {8, 64}, {9, 81}, {10, 100}}
```

To reference the third element of the list that you have just created, you enter the following:

```
In[7]:=    data[[3]]
```

```
Out[7]=    {2, 4}
```

You should appreciate that in *Mathematica* graphics, there is a close analogy between functions such as Plot, which can be applied to functions, and related functions such as ListPlot, which can be applied to data in an appropriate list format:

```
In[8]:=    ListPlot[data]
```

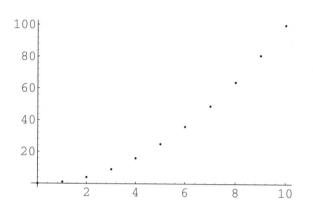

1.2.1 Remarks

In the few examples in Section 1.2, we actually covered the four basic areas of *Mathematica*:

1. Numerical calculations: We asked for the numerical value of π to 100 decimal places.
2. Symbolic or algebraic calculations: We asked for the expansion of $(x + 2y)^2$.
3. Graphics: We asked for plots of a function and also of a table of numbers.
4. Programming: We defined a function and asked for it to be applied iteratively to a variable.

We shall explore each of these areas in more detail later. Right now, we need to do groundwork on understanding how *Mathematica* works.

From here on, the expressions that you enter may be a little longer, so, if you make a mistake, you will not want to have to keep retyping your input. We recommend that you immediately consult your *Mathematica* documentation for your specific system to see how best to edit material.

1.3 Basic Operations

Mathematica is a system that uses commands expressed as text. As in any such system, effective communication relies on using the language appropriately. New users often experience problems when using the *Mathematica* language. A few key points remembered now will save you a great deal of frustration later. In this section, we look at the basics of *Mathematica* syntax.

1.3.1 Creation of Correct *Mathematica* Input

A quick inspection of our first few examples will show that we need to understand how *Mathematica* reads expressions, especially those using different types of brackets: [ ], ( ), { }. In normal written work, people tend to use square brackets [ ], round brackets or parentheses ( ), and curly brackets or braces { } more or less interchangeably. To ensure that the computer understands unambiguously what we mean, we must introduce conventions. Although they may seem fussy to you, taking the time to follow them is a small price to pay for the benefits that will soon become apparent.

Arguments of functions are always enclosed in square brackets. This rule applies just as much to algebraic functions such as Expand[ ] as it does to built-in graphics functions such as Plot[ ], which take another function and some ranges as a minimum set of arguments, as well as to user-defined functions such as f[ ], as given in Section 1.2.

When we wish to group together expressions so that we can apply a subsequent operation to the entire group, we use parentheses. For example, (x + 2 y)^2 means "the square of $x + 2y$." Note that this distinction gives f[x + 2 y] and f(x + 2 y) two different meanings and also that we have acquired the freedom to use a space between adjacent quantities to denote multiplication. If you wish, you can explicitly type an asterisk * to denote multiplication.

Note that there are occasions when you do not need to use round brackets for grouping since the usual rules of precedence apply. For example, x^2 + 3 means $x^2 + 3$, and not x^{2+3}. You may find it helpful to use brackets anyway, to remove any potential ambiguity.

Curly brackets { } and double square brackets [[ ]] are also used in *Mathematica* with list structures. This topic is important, so let's spend time on it now.

1.3.2 Lists in *Mathematica*

In dealing with data or tables of values, we shall employ the concept of a *list*. Lists are indicated by curly brackets. We have already used a list in our example for the structure data. Let's simplify this list by redefining it as a simple list of squares:

In[9]:=   `data = Table[i^2, {i, 0, 10}]`

Out[9]=   `{0, 1, 4, 9, 16, 25, 36, 49, 64, 81, 100}`

Now we have a simple one-dimensional list. We frequently need to refer to particular elements of such a list or to index elements of the list by their position in the list. We can do so by using the fourth type of bracketing, double square brackets. If we want the fourth element of this list, we enter the following:

In[10]:= `data[[4]]`

Out[10]= `9`

Output truncation and suppression

Our list data is short, so there is no disadvantage in having *Mathematica* output the full result. If you are working with large data sets, however, you will almost certainly not want to see the results at each stage. It may sometimes be desirable to suppress large results of purely symbolic operations. In the first of the following operations, the data set bigdata is created without being displayed at all; the semicolon is the key ingredient for suppressing output completely. Then, we give two different ways of generating the default short form:

In[11]:=   `bigdata = Table[i^2, {i, 0, 1000}];`

In[12]:=   `Short[bigdata]`

Out[12]=   `{0, 1, 4, 9, 16, 25, 36, <<991>>, 996004, 998001, 1000000}`

In[13]:=   `bigdata // Short`

Out[13]=   `{0, 1, 4, 9, 16, 25, 36, <<991>>, 996004, 998001, 1000000}`

Indexation, listability, and back-reference

The need to index a list such as our list `data` is common. In written mathematics, there are standard index notations. If we had an object *data* and we wished to refer to its *i*th element, we would refer to the element $data_i$ or possibly $data^i$. In *Mathematica*, such referencing is implemented by the use of double square brackets. For example, suppose that we wanted a new list consisting of each of the first three members of `data` multiplied by the member after it. We could create this new list with

In[14]:=   `newlist = Table[data[[i]] data[[i+1]], {i, 1, 3}]`

Out[14]=   `{0, 4, 36}`

This last command introduces a couple of other new ideas. The `Table` command is useful for generating new lists, and we can see how another subsidiary list, {i, 1, 3}, is used to indicate the range of values of the index. Our lists may well be generated within *Mathematica* by use of the `Table` command, or they may be generated outside *Mathematica*, imported, and then manipulated by the use of a `Table` command to become a graphical object. By the way, do not use the `Table` command to apply functions to each element of a list on its own. For example, to generate the list of squares of each element, we apply

In[15]:=   `data^2`

Out[15]=   `{0, 1, 16, 81, 256, 625, 1296, 2401, 4096, 6561, 10000}`

This example illustrates a powerful feature: Many functions in *Mathematica* — including, if you wish, those you construct yourself — can be applied to lists automatically.

In carrying out such a sequence of calculations, we want to avoid typing where possible. At any point, we can refer back to the results of previous calculations by typing a percent sign, immediately followed by the number of the output corresponding to the result. A special shorthand for the last computed result is %; %% denotes the next-to-last result:

In[16]:=   `%`

Out[16]=   `{0, 1, 16, 81, 256, 625, 1296, 2401, 4096, 6561, 10000}`

To obtain the fourth element of the list generated in output 16, you can use the following (be sure to replace the 16 by your own output number if you are not working through these commands in sequence or if you have repeated an input):

In[17]:=   `%16[[4]]`

Out[17]= 81

Indices are used elsewhere. If we want to use the concept of a vector, we use a list, and each element of the list corresponds to the components of the vector with respect to a particular basis. A simple example is the use of a list such as {1, 2, 1} to denote the vector with component 1 in the x-direction, 2 in the y-direction, 1 in the z-direction.

Arrays, matrices, and lists of lists

Next up from a list in the conceptual hierarchy is a *list of lists*. We use this idea in several ways. Here is an example of a list of lists:

In[18]:= Lol = {{1, 2, 1, 2}, {4, 3, 4, 3}, {7, 8, 9, 10}}

Out[18]= {{1, 2, 1, 2}, {4, 3, 4, 3}, {7, 8, 9, 10}}

One use to which we put such an object is easily demonstrated:

In[19]:= MatrixForm[Lol]

Out[19]=
```
1    2    1    2
4    3    4    3
7    8    9    10
```

So, *Mathematica* uses lists of lists to represent matrices. We can ask about the dimensions of this matrix:

In[20]:= Dimensions[Lol]

Out[20]= {3, 4}

We use a list of lists to represent any two-dimensional array of numbers. It could be an array for plotting, or a matrix, or a rank 2 tensor. You should be careful about the distinction between matrix multiplication and list operations. *Mathematica* uses a period to denote multiplication of matrices. We define a simple square matrix to make the point:

In[21]:= SmLol = {{1, 2}, {3, 4}}

Out[21]= {{1, 2}, {3, 4}}

In[22]:= SmLol.SmLol

Out[22]= {{7, 10}, {15, 22}}

The operation of squaring the matrix should not be confused with the operation of squaring each element of the matrix:

In[23]:= SmLol^2

Out[23]= {{1, 4}, {9, 16}}

Use of Flatten and Partition

We may wish to convert between a list and a list of lists:

In[24]:= `Lolasalist = Flatten[Lol]`

Out[24]= {1, 2, 1, 2, 4, 3, 4, 3, 7, 8, 9, 10}

In[25]:= `Partition[Lolasalist, 4]`

Out[25]= {{1, 2, 1, 2}, {4, 3, 4, 3}, {7, 8, 9, 10}}

Note that each sublist is of length 4; the second argument of `Partition` refers to the length of the resulting sublists, rather than to the number of such sublists.

Other simple list operations

Various other standard operations can be carried out. We demonstrate these operations by example, starting with the standard operation that allows us to transpose a matrix:

In[26]:= `Transpose[Lol]`

Out[26]= {{1, 4, 7}, {2, 3, 8}, {1, 4, 9}, {2, 3, 10}}

In[27]:= `MatrixForm[Transpose[Lol]]`

Out[27]= 1   4   7

2   3   8

1   4   9

2   3   10

In[28]:= `Lol[[1]]`

Out[28]= {1, 2, 1, 2}

In[29]:= `Transpose[Lol][[1]]`

Out[29]= {1, 4, 7}

In[30]:= `Lol[[1, 2]]`

Out[30]= 2

Mathematica uses a straightforward translation of matrix notation. The three sublists making up `Lol` are just the rows of the matrix. `Lol[[1]]` denotes the first row, while `Lol[[1, 2]]` denotes the element in the first row and the second column. `Lol[[i, j]]` is the element that would be denoted in many mathematical books as Lol_{ij}.

In graphical operations, we shall frequently be dealing with lists and lists of lists. We shall sometimes have to deal with higher-order objects too. A list of lists of lists can easily arise as a two-dimensional array of vectors. Such objects can also be used to denote rank 3 tensors, with the obvious generalization to rank k. We shall have need to perform rearrangements on such higher-order structures; such reorderings should be undertaken with great care and in keeping with Chapter 3.

1.3.3 Standard Kernel Functions

Mathematica contains hundreds of functions within its standard kernel, and hundreds more are available in the packages. We have already observed that arguments of functions must be enclosed in square brackets. We shall illustrate the generic behavior of *Mathematica* functions by considering one function: FactorInteger. We have deliberately chosen this function because it is probably the simplest *Mathematica* function that exhibits all the key features of most *Mathematica* functions. As its name suggests, it gives the prime factors of an integer, together with the powers to which they are raised. Like the names of all built-in functions, its name begins with a capital letter; like many such functions, further capitals in its name indicate new words.

We can find out how FactorInteger works by questioning *Mathematica* about it. We do so by prefixing the function name by a question mark:

In[31]:=   ?FactorInteger

     FactorInteger[n] gives a list of the prime factors of the integer

     n, together with their exponents.

For example, we can ask for

In[32]:=   FactorInteger[200]

Out[32]= {{2, 3}, {5, 2}}

This result means that the number 200 can be written as $2^3 * 5^2$, and you can use *Mathematica* to verify this result:

In[33]:=   2^3 5^2

Out[33]= 200

Like many *Mathematica* functions, FactorInteger has options, which have default values that are applied when no explicit options are specified. We can ask about the options easily:

In[34]:=   Options[FactorInteger]

Out[34]= {FactorComplete -> True, GaussianIntegers -> False}

For example, if you happen to be interested in factorization into complex numbers of the form $m + i\,n$, with m and n integers, you set the GaussianIntegers option to True:

In[35]:=   FactorInteger[200, GaussianIntegers -> True]

Out[35]= {{-I, 1}, {1 + I, 6}, {1 + 2 I, 2}, {2 + I, 2}}

Whether or not you are interested in this particular option to this function, it is important that you understand that options are often vital for controlling the results of applying *Mathematica* functions.

We can obtain more complete information about a function by using a stronger inquiry:

In[36]:=   ??FactorInteger

```
FactorInteger[n] gives a list of the prime factors
    of the integer n, together with their exponents.

Attributes[FactorInteger] = {Listable, Protected}

Options[FactorInteger] =
  {FactorComplete -> True,
   GaussianIntegers -> False}
```

The function FactorInteger, in common with many other standard functions, has an attribute Listable. This powerful feature allows standard functions to be applied to a list without any need for loops. This feature applies as much to simpler functions, such as Sin, as it does to FactorInteger:

In[37]:= `FactorInteger[{2, 9, 21}]`

Out[37]= `{{{2, 1}}, {{3, 2}}, {{3, 1}, {7, 1}}}`

In[38]:= `Sin[{1, 4, Pi}]`

Out[38]= `{Sin[1], Sin[4], 0}`

Unless you are interested in number theory or cryptography, the particular function FactorInteger may not be one that you wish to use. However, you may be interested in factorization generally. You can ask *Mathematica* what functions it has that contain the word Factor by using the * (asterisk) wild card. If you want functions that just begin with Factor, you use Factor*. Here we use *Factor* to get functions with names containing Factor:

In[39]:= `?*Factor*`

```
DampingFactor      FactorInteger       FactorTerms
Factor             FactorList          FactorTermsList
FactorComplete     FactorSquareFree    NProductExtraFactors
Factorial          FactorSquareFreeList NProductFactors
Factorial2
```

In Sections 1.3.4 through 1.3.8, we shall explore other functions that illustrate special capabilities of *Mathematica*. We conclude this section by pointing out that under some NoteBook front ends and on DOS systems, there are a couple of other useful tricks. Some *Mathematica* names are extremely long. Such names avoid ambiguity, but they can be irritating when you are entering commands. *Complete Selection* and *Make Template* are two useful tools (located in the pulldown menus) that help you to enter long or complicated functions. *Complete Selection* allows you to type the first few characters of a function name and to have *Mathematica* type the rest. *Make Template* creates a template for a function, complete with dummy arguments. The details of how these two functions are implemented depend on which computer system and which version of *Mathematica* that you are using, and you must consult your front-end documentation to see whether and how the tools work on your system.

1.3.4 Exact and High-Precision Computation

With most computer languages, you are restricted to certain levels of precision in the values of numbers. You are not thus restricted with *Mathematica*. You should try the following series of inputs, which begin by applying the Factorial function that we discovered with our ?*Factor* query:

```
In[40]:=  Factorial[69]
Out[40]=  1711224524281413113724683388812728390922705448935203693936480409
             23257279754140647424000000000000000000
```

```
In[41]:=  % // N
Out[41]=               98
          1.71122 10
```

```
In[42]:=  N[%%, 23]
Out[42]=                             98
          1.7112245242814131137247 10
```

Note the use of % to refer to the last output and the use of %% to refer to the next-to-last output. The first result is exact; the second is approximate and has a default precision; the last has a specified precision of 23 digits. Note that like the Short qualifier, expr //N is just the same as N[expr].

Now consider the following:

```
In[43]:=  (31/10)^100
Out[43]=  1368262370896645160067849227020097517311854200306072083894003612
             08970492284104921593558152840939371764513984884825007414238204
             24077813256592898608001 /

          10000000000000000000000000000000000000000000000000000000000000000
             00000000000000000000000000000000000000000
```

```
In[44]:=  3.1^100
Out[44]=            49
          1.36826 10
```

This example highlights an important assumption made by *Mathematica*. *Mathematica* will produce exact results as a default, often leaving expressions in symbolic form, even though you are dealing purely with numbers. Numerical approximations will result only if you ask for them. Note that asking may be explicit, as when you say N[expr], or implicit, as when you entered 3.1^100. Numbers with explicit decimal points are treated as approximate. Using such a number can trigger unexpected results. The following example illustrates this point as well as others.

Let's consider the solution of a quadratic equation by using the Solve function. In its simplest form, Solve takes two arguments: The first is an equation to be solved; the second is the variable for which you wish to solve. Note the use of == within Solve. The double equals sign is used to denote equality, rather than assignment, for which = or := is used (we shall discuss assignment in more detail in Section 1.4):

```
In[45]:=  Solve[x^2 + x + 11/10 == 0, x]
Out[45]=           -10 + 2 I Sqrt[85]              -10 - 2 I Sqrt[85]
          {{x -> ------------------},  {x -> ------------------}}
                         20                           20
```

Let's consider the form of this answer from several points of view. First, we can just apply the N operator to see the numerical form of the result:

In[46]:=   N[%]

Out[46]=   {{x -> -0.5 + 0.921954 I}, {x -> -0.5 - 0.921954 I}}

Suppose now that we specify the equation in a slightly different way, replacing 11/10 by 1.1:

In[47]:=   Solve[x^2 + x + 1.1 == 0, x]

Out[47]=   {{x -> -0.5 - 0.921954 I}, {x -> -0.5 + 0.921954 I}}

Mathematica treats the equation as a nonexact expression, and it supplies a numerical approximation to the result immediately.

New users of *Mathematica* are often frustrated by the form in which Solve and related functions return results. When you use *Mathematica* to solve equations for variables, the result is returned not as a value, but rather as a substitution rule or, as in the example just presented, as a list of substitution rules. To obtain the values of the variables, you must ask for the variable *given* given the result of Solve. The word "given" is denoted in *Mathematica* by /. (slash dot):

In[48]:=   x /. %

Out[48]=   {-0.5 - 0.921954 I, -0.5 + 0.921954 I}

1.3.5 Elementary Symbolic Computation

We begin this section by doing simple algebra. We make use of yet another function, Factor, which factors expressions. Enter all the following statements and execute each one in turn.

Begin by creating the following simple cubic expression involving y (note that *Mathematica* has its own ideas about the order of terms in polynomials — do not be put off by this ordering):

In[49]:=   y^3 + 3 y

Out[49]= $$3 y + y^3$$

Next, add 3 y^2 to this last result:

In[50]:=   % + 3 y^2

Out[50]= $$3 y + 3 y^2 + y^3$$

Then, add 1 to this last result and Factor it:

In[51]:=   Factor[% + 1]

Out[51]= $$(1 + y)^3$$

Undo the effects of Factor by using the Expand function:

In[52]:= Expand[%]

Out[52]=
$$1 + 3 y + 3 y^2 + y^3$$

Assign x to be this new cubic in y:

In[53]:= x = %

Out[53]=
$$1 + 3 y + 3 y^2 + y^3$$

Now, Solve the equation for this cubic to be zero, making use of x as a convenient shorthand for the cubic expression:

In[54]:= Solve[x == 0, y]

Out[54]= {{y -> -1}, {y -> -1}, {y -> -1}}

Assign a value to y, without displaying the result, and ask for the value of x:

In[55]:= y = 2;
x

Out[55]= 27

Then, Clear the value of y and ask again for the value of x:

In[56]:= Clear[y];
x

Out[56]=
$$1 + 3 y + 3 y^2 + y^3$$

You should appreciate from this little session the use of Factor, Expand, Solve, and Clear in a simple algebraic exercise. You may find it helpful to repeat this sequence of operations with different expressions. Do not use polynomials of degree greater than 4 unless they are simple. *Mathematica* knows how to solve all quadratic, cubic, and quartic equations exactly, but Solve will only cope symbolically with higher-order polynomials if it can spot simple factors and reduce the degree to 4 or less. It is a good idea to use Clear frequently so that you do not cause problems simply by trying to define expressions that conflict with earlier definitions. Clear your assignments of x and y now:

In[57]:= Clear[x, y]

Thus far in this section, we have considered polynomial expressions. *Mathematica* can carry out a variety of algebraic manipulations on rational expressions. The following sequence of operations illustrates the more useful common functions. *Warning*: If you execute this next command without the application of Clear to x and y, *Mathematica* will go into an internal loop and will complain about exceeding its recursion depth. You can wait for *Mathematica* to sort itself out, or you can abort the calculation. You can abort with Control-C under the UNIX operating system, with command "." on a Macintosh, or with ALT "." under Windows. NoteBook front ends also support menu-driven interrupts, so you can interrupt or abort the calculation from the Action menu.

Begin by creating the following simple rational expression involving x and y:

```
In[58]:=  y = 1/(x^2 - 4) - 1/(x - 2)

Out[58]=       1              1
          -(------) +  -------
            -2 + x             2
                         -4 + x
```

The Together function literally places all terms together over a common denominator:

```
In[59]:=  u = Together[y]

Out[59]=        -1 - x
          -----------------
          (-2 + x) (2 + x)
```

You can, at any time, isolate the current numerator and denominator of an expression:

```
In[60]:=  Numerator[u]

Out[60]=  -1 - x

In[61]:=  Denominator[u]

Out[61]=  (-2 + x) (2 + x)
```

You can also target an expansion to a part of an expression:

```
In[62]:=  ExpandDenominator[u]

Out[62]=  -1 - x
          -------
                2
          -4 + x
```

With rational, rather than polynomial, expressions, it may help to separate out the top and bottom parts for manipulation. In many cases, you will find Expand, Factor, and their relatives sufficient. There is a do-it-all simplification function called Simplify, which we are not overly fond of. Often, it will straighten everything out just the way you want it, but Simplify can have unpredictable results and can get into lengthy internal machinations before changing an expression to one that is not quite what you wanted. It is usually more effective to develop a slightly bigger *Mathematica* vocabulary and to apply various operations selectively.

The following worked example will illustrate a few more selective operations. We begin by introducing an algebraic expression stuff:

```
In[63]:=  stuff = (x^2 - 4) (x - 3)^2/((x - 2)(x - 4)(x - 6))

Out[63]=              2          2
            (-3 + x)   (-4 + x )
          ---------------------------
          (-6 + x) (-4 + x) (-2 + x)
```

In[64]:= Expand[stuff]

Out[64]=
```
              -36                         24 x
- - - - - - - - - - - - - - - - - - - +  - - - - - - - - - - - - - - - - - - - - - - - +
(-6 + x) (-4 + x) (-2 + x)     (-6 + x) (-4 + x) (-2 + x)


                  2                              3
                5 x                            6 x
- - - - - - - - - - - - - - - - - - - - - -  -  - - - - - - - - - - - - - - - - - - - - - - - - +
(-6 + x) (-4 + x) (-2 + x)     (-6 + x) (-4 + x) (-2 + x)


                  4
                 x
- - - - - - - - - - - - - - - - - - - - - -
(-6 + x) (-4 + x) (-2 + x)
```

Note that Expand has targeted the numerator. If you wish to expand all parts of an expression, then you should use ExpandAll:

In[65]:= ExpandAll[stuff]

Out[65]=
```
              -36                              24 x
- - - - - - - - - - - - - - - - - - - +  - - - - - - - - - - - - - - - - - - - - - - +
                   2    3                          2    3
    -48 + 44 x  -  12 x  + x        -48 + 44 x  -  12 x  + x


                  2                              3
                5 x                            6 x
- - - - - - - - - - - - - - - - - - - - - -  -  - - - - - - - - - - - - - - - - - - - - - +
                   2    3                          2    3
    -48 + 44 x  -  12 x  + x        -48 + 44 x  -  12 x  + x


                  4
                 x
- - - - - - - - - - - - - - - - - - - - -
                   2    3
    -48 + 44 x  -  12 x  + x
```

In[66]:= Together[%]

Out[66]=
```
          2    3
18 - 3 x - 4 x  + x
- - - - - - - - - - - - - - - - - -
              2
    24 - 10 x + x
```

The Apart function is great for doing partial fractions:

In[67]:= Apart[%]

Out[67]=
```
       36        3
6 +  - - - - -  -  - - - - - + x
     -6 + x     -4 + x
```

```
In[68]:=  Factor[%]
```

```
Out[68]=          2
          (-3 + x)  (2 + x)
          ------------------
          (-6 + x) (-4 + x)
```

You may have noticed that the numerator and denominator of stuff had a common factor of (x - 4). It can be canceled with the Cancel function:

```
In[69]:=  Cancel[stuff]
```

```
Out[69]=          2
          (-3 + x)  (2 + x)
          ------------------
          (-6 + x) (-4 + x)
```

Another useful pair of operations are Collect and Coefficient. The following example should make their use clear:

```
In[70]:=  Clear[x, y];
          otherstuff = (2 x + 3)^2 (x + y)^2
```

```
Out[70]=         2       2
          (3 + 2 x)  (x + y)
```

```
In[71]:=  Expand[otherstuff]
```

```
Out[71]=    2       3       4                2        3        2
          9 x  + 12 x  + 4 x  + 18 x y + 24 x  y + 8 x  y + 9 y  +

                  2      2 2
            12 x y  + 4 x  y
```

```
In[72]:=  Collect[%, x]
```

```
Out[72]=    4       2    3                2                   2
          4 x  + 9 y  + x  (12 + 8 y) + x  (9 + 24 y + 4 y ) +

                         2
            x (18 y + 12 y )
```

So, Collect[expr, x] literally collects together terms with the same power of x. We can pick out the coefficients by

```
In[73]:=  Coefficient[Expand[otherstuff], x^2]
```

```
Out[73]=                  2
          9 + 24 y + 4 y
```

This type of operation can be useful in doing perturbation theory, and it can also be used with the Series function, which we shall discuss in Section 1.3.6.

Substitutions are a common requirement in manipulation. We can do substitutions temporarily or permanently. Temporary substitution is achieved by use of the "given" qualifier /., together with a substitution rule of the form expr1 -> expr2, for replacing expr1 by expr2:

```
In[74]:=  otherstuff /. x -> 3 y
```
$$Out[74]= 16\ y^2\ (3\ +\ 6\ y)^2$$

```
In[75]:=  otherstuff
```
$$Out[75]= (3\ +\ 2\ x)^2\ (x\ +\ y)^2$$

A substitution that is both immediate and permanent, at least until there is an application of Clear, is effected by an assignment with the equals sign:

```
In[76]:=  x = 3 y
```
```
Out[76]=  3 y
```

```
In[77]:=  otherstuff
```
$$Out[77]= 16\ y^2\ (3\ +\ 6\ y)^2$$

1.3.6 Calculus

Differentiation and integration work in a straightforward way. There are various notations for differentiation, of which the D operator is perhaps the most flexible:

```
In[78]:=  D[x^n, x]
```
$$Out[78]= n\ x^{-1\ +\ n}$$

```
In[79]:=  Integrate[%, x]
```
$$Out[79]= x^n$$

Partial differentiation works too. You supply a function of several variables and the variable with respect to which you wish to differentiate:

```
In[80]:=  D[x^3 y^2 + x^2, y]
```
$$Out[80]= 2\ x^3\ y$$

Integration with respect to y will reverse this operation up to an arbitrary function of x:

```
In[81]:=  Integrate[%, y]
```
$$Out[81]= x^3\ y^2$$

Mixed and multiple derivatives are also supported. For example, to differentiate just once with respect to x and to y, you should apply the following:

```
In[82]:=  D[x^3 y^2 + x^2, y, x]
```
$$Out[82]= 6\ x^2\ y$$

You can specify higher derivatives by supplying the number of differentiations as part of a list. For example, to compute

$$\frac{\partial^5 f}{\partial x^3 \partial y^2}$$

with $f = x^3 y^2 + x^2$, you carry out the following:

```
In[83]:=  D[x^3 y^2 + x^2, {x, 3}, {y, 2}]

Out[83]=  12
```

Of course, differentiation is defined by a limiting procedure. *Mathematica* can take limits explicitly. Formulas such as the following can be used to introduce calculus from first principles:

```
In[84]:=  Limit[((x + h)^3 - x^3)/h, h -> 0]
Out[84]=      2
          3 x
```

```
In[85]:=  Limit[Sin[x]/x, x -> 0]
Out[85]=  1
```

Mathematica also knows how to use Taylor's theorem through the Series command. The use of Series generates a certain type of expression truncated by an "O" expression. These series can be manipulated according to the usual rules of asymptotic series or can be converted to a normal form (without an "O"):

```
In[86]:=  Series[Sin[x], {x, 0, 5}]
Out[86]=         3     5
                x     x             6
          x  -  -- +  --- + O[x]
                6     120
```

```
In[87]:=  %^2
Out[87]=          4       6
           2     x     2 x            7
          x   -  -- +  ---- + O[x]
                 3      45
```

```
In[88]:=  Normal[%]
Out[88]=          4       6
           2     x     2 x
          x   -  -- +  ----
                 3      45
```

When carrying out integrals, you may be reassured that the result is correct if you can differentiate it and recover your starting point. This area is one where we have found that Simplify works well. You may find it useful to work through the following example with several different choices of function. Try to use both Simplify and the other manipulation functions to check that differentiation gives back the function you started with. Consider the integration of $1/(1 - x^3)$ first as an indefinite integral:

```
In[89]:=  Integrate[1/(1 - x^3), x]
```

```
Out[89]=       1 + 2 x
          ArcTan[-------]                                    2
                 Sqrt[3]    Log[-1 + x]   Log[1 + x + x ]
          --------------- - ----------- + ---------------
             Sqrt[3]             3               6
```

```
In[90]:=  D[%, x]
```

```
Out[90]=      -1              1 + 2 x                  2
          ---------- + -------------- + ------------------
          3 (-1 + x)          2                        2
                       6 (1 + x + x )          (1 + 2 x)
                                         3 (1 + ----------)
                                                     3
```

```
In[91]:=  Simplify[%]
```

```
Out[91]=     1
          ------
              3
          1 - x
```

For definite integration, you must supply a list giving the lower and upper limits of the integration variable:

```
In[92]:=  Integrate[1/(1 - x^3), {x, 2, 4}]
```

```
Out[92]=            5
             ArcTan[-------]                3/2
                    Sqrt[3]    ArcTan[3   ]   Log[3]   Log[7]   Log[21]
          -(---------------) + ------------- - ------ - ------ + -------
              Sqrt[3]             Sqrt[3]         3        6        6
```

1.3.7 Simple Differential Equations

The subject of differential equations is huge. *Mathematica* is a useful tool for treating certain differential equations. The facility for solving ordinary differential equations is well developed. The symbolic solver DSolve can treat a large class of equations and has a syntax similar to that of Solve, except that you tell DSolve about both the independent variable and the dependent variable:

```
In[93]:=  DSolve[y''[x] + y[x] == 0, y[x], x]
```

```
Out[93]=  {{y[x] -> C[2] Cos[x] - C[1] Sin[x]}}
```

If you give appropriate initial conditions, the arbitrary constants are removed:

```
In[94]:=  DSolve[{y'[x] + x y[x] == 0, y[0] == 1}, y[x], x]
```

```
Out[94]=                 2
                      -x /2
          {{y[x] -> E      }}
```

If you wish to check that this result is indeed a solution of the given equation, it helps first to implement the substitution rule. We set Y to be y[x] given the solution of the differential equation; furthermore, since DSolve returns a list of solutions, we extract the first and only element of this list as the required solution:

```
In[95]:=   Y = (y[x] /. %)[[1]]

Out[95]=        2
           -x /2
          E
```

```
In[96]:=   D[Y, x] + x Y

Out[96]=  0
```

1.3.8 Standard Numerical Functions

Sometimes, *Mathematica* cannot do integrals symbolically. In such cases, numerical integration is available. The following example demonstrates the syntax. The range of integration is specified as it is with definite symbolic integration:

```
In[97]:=   NIntegrate[Sin[Sin[z]], {z, 0, 2}]

Out[97]=  1.24706
```

Let's spend a little time on this particular function. You should be careful not to use NIntegrate too cavalierly. First, suppose that you have an integration over a finite range of a function that has no singularities within the range or at the endpoints. NIntegrate will give good answers with all the default settings unless the function is highly oscillatory. Try the following inputs. You should appreciate that numerical integration may require your assistance:

```
In[98]:=   Integrate[Sin[x]^2, {x, 0, 2}]

Out[98]=        Sin[4]
           1 - ------
                 4
```

```
In[99]:=   N[%, 20]

Out[99]=  1.18920062382698206284
```

```
In[100]:= NIntegrate[Sin[x]^2, {x, 0, 2}]

Out[100]= 1.1892
```

```
In[101]:= Integrate[Sin[200 x], {x, 0, 2}]

Out[101]=   1     Cos[400]
           --- - --------
           200     200
```

```
In[102]:= N[%]

Out[102]= 0.00762648
```

In[103]:= `NIntegrate[Sin[200 x], {x, 0, 2}]`

> `NIntegrate::ncvb:`
>
>> `NIntegrate failed to converge to prescribed accuracy after 7`
>>
>> `recursive bisections in x near x = 0.132813.`

Out[103]= `0.00762648`

Mathematica may have warned you of trouble. Sometimes, you get such a warning even when the answer is sufficiently accurate for your purposes. The way to deal with this problem is to adjust some of the settings for `NIntegrate` by setting various options. We saw how to use options in Section 1.3.3: You add various settings to a function. `NIntegrate` has several options that we can reveal by using the `Options` function:

In[104]:= `Options[NIntegrate]`

Out[104]= `{AccuracyGoal -> Infinity, Compiled -> True, GaussPoints -> Automatic,`

   `MaxRecursion -> 6, Method -> Automatic, MinRecursion -> 0,`

   `PrecisionGoal -> Automatic, SingularityDepth -> 4,`

   `WorkingPrecision -> 19}`

We get a list of options and their default settings. We can change these settings easily. For example, the kernel has no lack of confidence in returning a result when you increase the amount of repeated subdivision of the range of integration:

In[105]:= `NIntegrate[Sin[200 x], {x, 0, 2}, MaxRecursion -> 10]`

Out[105]= `0.00762648`

We saw how to solve a quadratic in Section 1.3.4. *Mathematica* can cope analytically with all polynomials up to degree 4. For degree 5 and above, a numerical approach usually is required:

In[106]:= `NSolve[x^5 + x^2 + 1 == 0, x]`

Out[106]= `{{x -> -1.19386}, {x -> -0.15459 - 0.828074 I},`

   `{x -> -0.15459 + 0.828074 I}, {x -> 0.751519 - 0.784616 I},`

   `{x -> 0.751519 + 0.784616 I}}`

`NSolve` and its symbolic counterpart can also be used to solve sets of equations with several variables:

In[107]:= `NSolve[{x^2 + y == 0, y^3 - x == 2}, {x, y}]`

Out[107]= {{x -> -0.921067 - 0.453263 I, y -> -0.642916 - 0.834971 I},

　　　　　　{x -> -0.921067 + 0.453263 I, y -> -0.642916 + 0.834971 I},

　　　　　　{x -> 1.02362 + 0.639381 I, y -> -0.638991 - 1.30897 I},

　　　　　　{x -> 1.02362 - 0.639381 I, y -> -0.638991 + 1.30897 I},

　　　　　　{x -> -0.102554 - 1.13685 I, y -> 1.28191 - 0.233176 I},

　　　　　　{x -> -0.102554 + 1.13685 I, y -> 1.28191 + 0.233176 I}}

When DSolve does not work, you still have the option of trying a purely numerical solution to a differential equation by using NDSolve. This function returns an interpolating function, rather than a traditional table of values. This choice of output has advantages. For example, you can ask for the value of the solution anywhere in the solution range. As usual, use of the /. construction allows the extraction of numerical values:

In[108]:= Clear[x, y, t]

In[109]:= NDSolve[{x'[t] == y[t],
　　　　　　　　y'[t] == -4.0*x[t] - 0.1*y[t],
　　　　　　　　x[0] == 1, y[0] == 1},
　　　　　　　　{x, y}, {t, 10}]

Out[109]= {{x -> InterpolatingFunction[{0., 10.}, <>],

　　　　　　y -> InterpolatingFunction[{0., 10.}, <>]}}

In[110]:= {x[2], y[2]} /. %

Out[110]= {{-0.951532, 0.793324}}

1.4 User-Defined Functions

There are many ways to construct your own functions within *Mathematica*, and this diversity is one of the strengths of *Mathematica* as a programming environment. For now, we shall focus on functions defined by a formula. The key ingredient is to identify independent variables by use of the underscore. The use of := (rather than just =) is an example of delayed (rather than immediate) assignment. We shall also give an example of how this choice can make a difference. The subjects of evaluation and the role of underscores are discussed in detail in Chapter 10.

Suppose that you wish to define a function that in standard mathematical notation might be given by $h[x, y] = x/y^2$. You enter the definition in *Mathematica* as follows:

In[111]:= h[x_, y_] := x/y^2

In[112]:= h[1, 2]

Out[112]= 1
　　　　　-
　　　　　4

You can now ask about your function:

In[113]:= ?h

Global`h

h[x_, y_] := x/y^2

If you wish to clear the definition, you just enter

In[114]:= Clear[h]

In[115]:= ?h

Global`h

If you wish to remove the symbol h completely, you use Remove:

In[116]:= Remove[h]

New users often are confused by the use of := as opposed to =. You use = when you wish to effect immediate evaluation, and you use := when you wish to evaluate the function only when it is called. The best way to illustrate the difference is to construct two functions, each of which adds a random number between −0.5 and +0.5 to a given argument (note that *Mathematica* gives a result when you ask for immediate evaluation):

In[117]:= addrandone[x_] := x + Random[] - 0.5

In[118]:= addrandtwo[x_] = x + Random[] - 0.5

Out[118]= -0.247022 + x

Now consider evaluating each of these functions twice on the same value:

In[119]:= {addrandone[0], addrandone[0]}

Out[119]= {0.0492387, 0.403692}

In[120]:= {addrandtwo[0], addrandtwo[0]}

Out[120]= {-0.247022, -0.247022}

The function addrandtwo is not that random! To make the example more interesting, you should construct two random walks based on these two functions. We introduce one of a number of cunning *Mathematica* functions that facilitate certain types of construction. The function NestList takes as its arguments a function, a starting value, and the number of times it is to be applied successively, as in the following example:

In[121]:= NestList[Sin, x, 3]

Out[121]= {x, Sin[x], Sin[Sin[x]], Sin[Sin[Sin[x]]]}

Using NestList, you can construct your random walks easily. This command is a good place to suppress the output — unless you enjoy looking at hundreds of numbers!

In[122]:= walkone = NestList[addrandone, 0, 1000];

In[123]:= walktwo = NestList[addrandtwo, 0, 1000];

In[124]:= `ListPlot[walkone, PlotJoined -> True]`

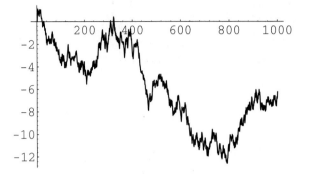

In[125]:= `ListPlot[walktwo, PlotJoined -> True]`

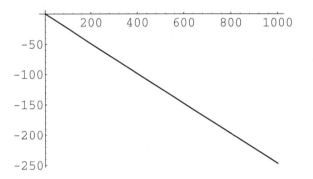

In the first case, you obtain a new random number each time; in the second case, the same random number is subtracted over and over again, yielding a disappointing "random" walk.

1.5 Pure Functions

This section contains absolutely vital material and must not be omitted on a first reading!

Pure functions are extremely important in *Mathematica* and shall be used extensively throughout this book. It is vital that you obtain a thorough grasp of their use before you attempt to use the rest of this book. The following examples should make pure functions clear. Consider first the random walk that you have just created. So, what is the problem with this example? The point is that you have had to create the function `addrandone`, which you probably will never use again. Its name is of considerably less significance than its behavior. *Mathematica* provides you with another method of performing this operation without creating an unwanted or irrelevantly named function along the way. Furthermore, matters are arranged such that pure functions work elegantly with objects such as NestList. We shall begin our discussion of pure functions by looking at several simpler examples; then we shall return to the random walk.

There is, as usual, more than one way to dispose of names in defining functions. Consider a simple function that is designed to square a number. We have already seen the notation:

```
In[126]:= g[x_] := x^2;
          g[3]
```

```
Out[126]= 9
```

The function Function allows us to specify this example in a different way. In its simplest form, Function takes its first argument and maps that argument to the second, where the formula is specified:

```
In[127]:= Function[w, w^2]
```

```
Out[127]=              2
          Function[w, w ]
```

```
In[128]:= %[4]
```

```
Out[128]= 16
```

This is an example of a *pure function*, but such functions are usually written more economically. You can recognize the economic forms by the & sign at their end and by the # sign that refers to the argument of the function. The function that squares an argument can be written as follows (the parentheses are superfluous in this particular expression, but in an expression involving several pure functions, they prevent ambiguity):

```
In[129]:= (#^2 &)
```

```
Out[129]=   2
          #1   &
```

Note that *Mathematica* returns #1. The appearance of the "1" is an indication that pure functions of many variables are possible. Consider the following:

```
In[130]:= %[3]
```

```
Out[130]= 9
```

```
In[131]:= (Cos[#] + # &)
```

```
Out[131]= Cos[#1] + #1 &
```

You should experiment with a few pure functions of your own. Pure functions with more than one argument also are allowed. We distinguish various arguments by appending their position in the square brackets to the #:

```
In[132]:= (#1 + #2^2 &)[a,b]
```

```
Out[132]=     2
          a + b
```

How would you re-create your random walk using pure functions? Here is one answer:

```
In[133]:= NestList[(# + Random[] - 0.5 &), 0, 1000];
In[134]:= ListPlot[%]
```

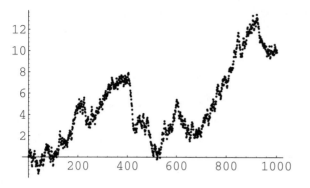

We can often write *Mathematica* programs much more efficiently by using pure functions, especially in constructions involving lists. Here are two examples that introduce the important functions Map and Select. In the first example, we take a pure function that cubes its argument, and then we literally Map this function onto a list:

```
In[135]:= Map[(#^3 &), {1, 2, 3, 4, 5}]
Out[135]= {1, 8, 27, 64, 125}
```

In the second example, we introduce the Select function. Select[list, test] returns those elements of list for which test is True:

```
In[136]:= Select[{1, 2, 3, 4, 5}, (# > 2 &)]
Out[136]= {3, 4, 5}
```

If you have been using *Mathematica* for some time without making use of such pure functions, you should ask yourself, for example, how you would carry out the operation of selecting those elements of a list that satisfy some condition. The previous construction using Select and a pure function is, we believe, the most economical way to achieve this goal.

Finally, we remark that the function ListPlot, a graphical function that takes a list as its main argument, has much in common with the function FactorInteger with which we commenced our discussion of functions: Its name is multiword capitalized, and it has an option setting PlotJoined, which defaults to False. The principal differences are that ListPlot does not have the attribute Listable, and it does have many more options. You might want to examine them using ?, ??, and Options. ListPlot cannot have the attribute Listable, as explained in Section 9.1.

1.6 The Packages

Mathematica comes with a great deal of documentation, which you should examine. The three main points of reference are the following:

1. *Mathematica, A System for Doing Mathematics by Computer*, S. Wolfram [27]
2. "Guide to Standard *Mathematica* Packages," Wolfram Research [25]
3. Your system-specific user guide

We emphasize the packages documentation, the second item. Our experience in teaching people how to use *Mathematica* indicates that this source is underused. Many useful operations are available in packages, yet many people neglect to consult them. We have heard people say that *Mathematica* cannot handle useful statistics, or plot surfaces defined on irregular grids, or put proper legends on graphs. All these capabilities are available in packages; you just need to find them.

There are several ways of loading a package. We prefer to use the Needs function because it handles accidental attempts to load a package twice. (Some packages are not designed to be loaded twice.) For example, suppose that you wish to load a package to do basic descriptive statistics. You might imagine that *Mathematica* already knows about the Variance function in statistics — you can check with the following:

```
In[137]:= ?Variance
```

Information::notfound: Symbol Variance not found.

You can enhance the kernel by loading the relevant package with a Needs command:

```
In[138]:= Needs["Statistics`DescriptiveStatistics`"]
```

```
In[139]:= ?Variance
```

Variance[list] gives the variance of the entries in list. Division by n-1

(rather than n) is used, giving an unbiased estimate of the population

variance (use VarianceMLE[list] for a maximum likelihood estimate).

This function and many others have been added to the system. There are several other statistics packages; Section 5.6 gives a list of where to find them and where they are discussed in this book. If you are interested in data analysis, you will use these packages extensively.

If you consult the packages documentation, you will see that packages are grouped into various topics, such as statistics or calculus. Sometimes, they add completely new capabilities to the system, identified by new functions. Some packages enhance the capabilities of existing kernel functions. The standard form of DSolve cannot handle the following example (at least with the Version 2.1 kernel):

```
In[140]:= DSolve[x y''[x] + (1 - x^2) y'[x] - x y[x] == 0, y[x], x]
```

```
Out[140]=                              2
          DSolve[-(x y[x]) + (1 - x ) y'[x] + x y''[x] == 0, y[x], x]
```

To use the enhanced DSolve, we load the appropriate package and try again:

```
In[141]:= Needs["Calculus`DSolve`"]
```

```
In[142]:= DSolve[x y''[x] + (1 - x^2) y'[x] - x y[x] == 0, y[x], x]
```

Out[142]=

$$\{\{y[x] \to \frac{E^{x^2/4} \; BesselI[0, \frac{x^2}{4}] \; C[1]}{Sqrt[Pi]} + \frac{E^{x^2/4} \; BesselK[0, \frac{-x^2}{4}] \; C[2]}{Sqrt[Pi]}\}\}$$

The number of available packages grows with each release of *Mathematica*. We conclude this introduction by looking at a package that became available with Version 2.2 of *Mathematica*:

In[143]:= `Needs["Calculus`PDSolve1`"]`

In addition to adding new functions, this package further extends `DSolve`. Here is a simple example, where we require the solution of the following partial differential equation:

$$\frac{\partial z}{\partial t} + l * z + v * \frac{\partial z}{\partial x} = 0$$

In[144]:= `DSolve[D[z[t, x], t] + 1*z[t, x] + v*D[z[t, x], x] == 0,`
`z[t, x], {t, x}]`

Out[144]=

$$\{\{z[t, x] \to \frac{C[1][-(t \; v) + x]}{E^{l \; t}}\}\}$$

Mathematica supplies us with a rule, as usual, and we can extract the result given this substitution rule:

In[145]:= `z[t, x] /. %`

Out[145]=

$$\{\frac{C[1][-(t \; v) + x]}{E^{l \; t}}\}$$

The result now involves an arbitrary function of one variable, and we can specify it to be any function we want. Here we choose a Gaussian function and finally label the result Z:

In[146]:= `Z[x_, t_, 1_, v_] = %[[1]] /.  C[1][p_] -> Exp[-p^2]`

Out[146]=

$$E^{-(l \; t) \; - \; (-(t \; v) \; + \; x)^2}$$

We plot the result for two sample values of t, with 1 = v = 1:

In[147]:= `Plot[{Z[x, 0, 1, 1], Z[x, 1, 1, 1]}, {x, -3, 3}]`

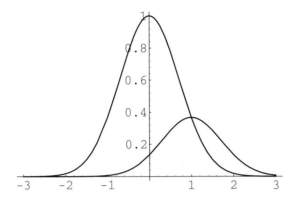

1.7 Summary

In this chapter, we have covered the basic operation of *Mathematica*, and we have introduced several structures that we shall use freely throughout this book. We advise you to take the time now to experiment a little. A good plan is to consider a few of the examples that we have presented and to vary them. You can do so by varying the functions used, by adding or changing option settings, or by changing the parameters (of a plot, for example).

Where should you turn next? If you need to analyze data within *Mathematica*, you should go straight to Chapter 2, where the process of importing data is discussed. Graphics fans may wish to skip to Chapters 4 or 6. Programming fanatics may wish to dive in at Chapter 8. The book is structured so that you can take various paths through it depending on your interests. Several chapters contain expanded discussions of material in this first chapter. The index is the best guide to all the material, but a few pointers may be helpful here. If you are interested in statistics generally, then you may wish to consult Sections 5.2, 5.3, and 5.6 and Chapters 15, 17, and 18. Differential equations are touched on again in Section 5.7 and are discussed from a transform point of view in Chapter 16. Examples of integral equations are given in Chapter 14. An extensive discussion of built-in and user-defined functions and evaluation is given in Chapters 9 and 10.

PART TWO

Managing Data with *Mathematica*

CHAPTER TWO

Importing Data into *Mathematica*

This chapter explains how to import data into *Mathematica*. We assume that the data are in the form of a text or binary file on a disk available to the computer system. They may have been typed in, created by another program in FORTRAN or C, downloaded from a spreadsheet, or dumped from a database. If live access to a structured database is required, MathLink should be used in conjunction with appropriate libraries supplied by the database vendor. See Chapters 14 and 19 for a discussion of MathLink.

2.1 Locating a Data File

Users who are new to *Mathematica* often have difficulty in persuading *Mathematica* to load their data files. In this section, we describe which directories *Mathematica* searches by default, as well as what to do when your file is not stored in one of these directories.

If you wish to keep file management simple, but rather messy, you can just put your data into the directory where the *Mathematica* program resides. *Mathematica* will always find it there, and you can proceed straight to Section 2.2. However, if you wish to be more organized, you will need to understand the remaining parts of this section.

2.1.1 Where *Mathematica* Looks for Files

You can use double exclamation points, !!, to view the contents of a data file from within a NoteBook or terminal front end. Imagine that you have created a small data file (or, indeed, go ahead and create one in text format with any word processor) called `sample1.dat` and have placed it in a directory somewhere on the hard disk or another medium on your computer system. In principle, to display its contents, you give the following command:

```
In[1]:=    !!sample1.dat

General::noopen: Can't open sample1.dat.
```

Unfortunately, unless you have thought ahead about where *Mathematica* might look for this file, *Mathematica* will be unable to find the file because it does not know where the file is stored. In fact, *Mathematica* searches only a few directories before giving up — you can see which directories these are with the command `$Path`. Try entering this command on your machine now. Different machines use different syntax to denote directory structure, so we give here typical results of issuing the command immediately after starting *Mathematica* on three popular systems. On our Macintosh, there is a directory called Macintosh on the volume Macintosh HD; on our PC, the *Mathematica* directory is a subdirectory on drive C:

In[2]:= $Path

Macintosh

Out[2]=   {Macintosh HD:Mathematica:Packages,
    Macintosh HD:Mathematica:Packages:Startup}

PC

Out[2]=   {.,C:Mathematica \Packages \, C: \Programs \Mathematica \
    Packages \StartUp \}

UNIX

Out[2]=   {.,~, /usr/local/math/Install/Preload, /usr/local/math/Startup,
    /usr/local/math/Packages}

On both PCs and UNIX systems, a period denotes the current directory. If the file that you want to access is not in one of the listed directories or in the *Mathematica* directory itself, it will not be found. *Mathematica*'s response to this situation again depends on what type of machine you are using. On a Macintosh, you will be prompted to help find the file; when you have done so, the file's location will be appended to the search path. On PCs and UNIX systems, you simply will be informed that the file cannot be found.

2.1.2 How to Tell *Mathematica* to Look Elsewhere

There are two ways to solve the problem of *Mathematica*'s inability to locate your file. The first is to refer to files that are not on the search path by giving both their name and location. We have stored the file sample1.dat in a subdirectory datfiles of the book directory on the volume data of our Macintosh, as well as in appropriate directories on PCs and UNIX systems. To display the file contents, you enter commands such as:

Macintosh

In[3]:=   !!data:book:datfiles:sample1.dat

PC

In[3]:=   !!C: \data \book \datfiles \sample1.dat

UNIX

In[3]:=   !!/home/tigg/book/sample1.dat

```
1
4
9
16
25
```

The response reveals that `sample1.dat` contains the squares of the first five integers, each on a separate line. The drawback of this method is that it is entirely temporary. When you try to access the file subsequently, using just its name, you will face your original problem because the search path has not been changed.

So, if you wish to make frequent use of the files in a given directory, it makes more sense to add the name of the directory to your search path, which is the second method. To use this method for your directory `datfiles` on, for example, a Macintosh computer, you enter

In[4]:=   `$Path = Append[$Path,"Data:Book:datfiles:"]`

Out[4]=   `{Macintosh HD:Mathematica:Packages,`

            `Macintosh HD:Mathematica:Packages:StartUp,`

            `Data:Book:datfiles:}`

For the moment, you may want to regard this command simply as a trick for making your programs load. What we have done is taken the list of strings given by `$Path` and appended a string giving the path (in the language of our particular computer system) to our data file. Subsequently, we can refer to the file `sample1.dat` by just its name:

In[5]:=   `!!sample1.dat`

```
1
4
9
16
25
```

We strongly recommend that you modify the `$Path` variable if you are working with many data files; the modification saves a great deal of typing and reduces mistakes and consequent frustration. If your file is exceedingly long, you may want to display only the first few lines on the screen, perhaps to remind yourself of the format in which the data are stored. We describe a method for performing this operation in Section 2.3.

2.2 Importing the Contents of a Data File

Mathematica is clever at reading in and processing data, as well as at visualizing the results. However, the first stage in this procedure — namely, reading in the data — can present particular problems because data may be stored in many different formats. In this section, we present techniques that will allow you to tackle even the most uncooperative data file! Our first investigations focus on text data separated by simple spaces or new lines.

2.2.1 Numerical Data

The file `sample1.dat` contained a list of numbers only. We can read these numbers into *Mathematica* with the `ReadList` command:

In[6]:= `ReadList["sample1.dat", Number]`

Out[6]= `{1, 4, 9, 16, 25}`

Notice that the second argument of `ReadList` tells *Mathematica* what type of data we are reading — in this case, the type is `Number`. In `sample1.dat`, the numbers were stored one number per line. There are other possibilities, as the following (rather contrived) example demonstrates:

In[7]:= `!!messydata`

```
12.0        56

   123           142        87

   -20
```

In[8]:= `ReadList["messydata",Number]`

Out[8]= `{12., 56, 123, 142, 87, -20}`

Structured numerical data

Sometimes, your data file may contain a structure that is lost when you read it in as one large list of numbers. For instance, you may have a file containing experimental data points in pairs — for example, *y* as a function of *x*. The file `experim.dat` is such a file:

In[9]:= `!!experim.dat`

```
1.00    1.23
2.00    2.09
3.00    3.32
4.00    4.52
5.00    5.87
```

Ideally, we would like to read these data into *Mathematica* as a list of *x*, *y* values — in other words, as a list of lists. There are several ways in which we can achieve this goal. The first is to use `ReadList` in the same way we have done already and then to partition the result using the `Partition` function:

In[10]:= `data = ReadList["experim.dat",Number]`

Out[10]= `{1., 1.23, 2., 2.09, 3., 3.32, 4., 4.52, 5., 5.87}`

In[11]:= `Partition[data,2]`

Out[11]= `{{1., 1.23}, {2., 2.09}, {3., 3.32}, {4., 4.52}, {5., 5.87}}`

Alternatively, we can achieve the same result in a single step by telling `ReadList` to read in the data in pairs of numbers:

In[12]:= `ReadList["experim.dat",{Number,Number}]`

Out[12]=   {{1., 1.23}, {2., 2.09}, {3., 3.32}, {4., 4.52}, {5., 5.87}}

A third method is to let *Mathematica* sort out the structure of the file itself, assuming that each line contains a new record entry (this method also requires Version 2.0 or later of the kernel):

In[13]:=   `ReadList["experim.dat",Number,RecordLists -> True]`

Out[13]=   {{1., 1.23}, {2., 2.09}, {3., 3.32}, {4., 4.52}, {5., 5.87}}

If each record in your data file contains so many numbers that a record does not fit onto a single line, then the third method will not work. Furthermore, filling in the list of {Number, Number, ... , Number} in the second method becomes tedious. However, you can use the `Table` command to do the job for you:

In[14]:=   `ReadList["experim.dat",Table[Number,{2}]]`

Out[14]=   {{1., 1.23}, {2., 2.09}, {3., 3.32}, {4., 4.52}, {5., 5.87}}

As we shall see, these data are now in the correct format to be plotted, as discussed in Chapter 4, or to be fitted to a function by a suitable method, such as least squares, as discussed in Chapter 5.

Data elements not separated by spaces

Sometimes, a file may contain data separated by characters other than spaces. In the following file, entries on the same line are separated by commas:

In[15]:=   `!!comma.dat`
             1.2E2, 3.4E2, 433

             67.45466E1, 0.003456E5, 12353E-2

             123, 456, 789

The simplest way to read this file into *Mathematica* is to use the `RecordLists` facility, telling *Mathematica* that records may be separated by either a comma or a newline character ("\n"):

In[16]:=   `ReadList["comma.dat",Number,RecordLists -> True,`
             `          RecordSeparators -> {"\n",","}]`

Out[16]=
                                                                    12353
             {{120.}, {340.}, {433}, {674.547}, {345.6}, {-----}, {123},
                                                                     100

             {456}, {789}}

Then, to get rid of the unnecessary curly brackets — that is, the two-dimensional list — we flatten this list:

In[17]:=   `Flatten[%]`

Out[17]=
                                              12353
             {120., 340., 433, 674.547, 345.6, -----, 123, 456, 789}
                                               100

You may be puzzled by the sudden appearance of the "fraction" in the last two outputs. An important *Mathematica* convention is that numbers are treated as exact unless they contain a decimal point. Thus, 12353E-2 is treated as 12353/100. The Number type applies to approximate or exact numbers. If you wish to treat all your data as approximate real numbers, use Real instead of Number:

```
In[18]:=  Flatten[ReadList["comma.dat",Real,RecordLists -> True,
                 RecordSeparators -> {"\n",","}]]

Out[18]=  {120., 340., 433., 674.547, 345.6, 123.53, 123., 456., 789.}
```

Some packages — notably spreadsheets — separate data items with tab marks. This format presents no problem for ReadList since tabs are treated like one or more spaces.

2.2.2 Mixed Numerical and Textual Data

Data files frequently contain both numbers and text. The following file contains a list of examination results for a group of students:

```
In[19]:=  !!examres
          Alison  80

          Jason   22

          William 65

          Dinah   94
```

Here we have a list of records, each containing a word and a number. We must supply *Mathematica* with this information if we are to read in the data:

```
In[20]:=  ReadList["examres",{Word,Number}]

Out[20]=  {{Alison, 80}, {Jason, 22}, {William, 65}, {Dinah, 94}}
```

Files are not always so simple to read. Consider the following file of values of gross domestic product (GDP) per capita for various countries:

```
In[21]:=  !!GDP.dat
          Australia       14083

          France          17004

          United States   19815

          Spain            8668
```

Clearly, we want to read in the file as a list of records of the form {*Country Name, GDP value*}. However, if we use the same instruction as for the examination results, we get an error:

```
In[22]:=  ReadList["GDP.dat",{Word,Number}]

          Read::readn: Syntax error reading a real number from GDP.dat.
```

Out[22]=   {{Australia, 14083}, {France, 17004}, {United, EndOfFile}}

The problem is caused by the space between the words "United" and "States." *Mathematica* does not treat the combination as a single word — as clearly it should not do in general — because a single space is normally used to denote a word separation. In this case, it is more useful to classify a double space as a word separator, a technique that solves the problem (in the following there are two spaces between the quotation marks):

In[23]:=   `ReadList["GDP.dat",{Word,Number}, WordSeparators -> "  "]`

Out[23]=   {{Australia, 14083}, {France, 17004}, {United States, 19815},

{Spain, 8668}}

In general, more drastic measures may be necessary. The method we have just used would still have failed if there had been more than one space between the words "United" and "States" or, as is more likely, if only a single space had been left between a country name and its GDP value. The following file of company data illustrates several problems:

In[24]:=   `!!company`

```
A very big company    - MEGACORP    10000000        20000

Arnie's Amazing Gadgets 100000    20

One man band                 20000 1
```

It is clear that the structure of each entry is a name followed by two numbers. What follows is one way to read it in as such. For now, unless you are familiar with the components of the following functions, you may wish to regard them as another set of useful tricks. The first function that we define takes a list of strings, adds a space to each one using the Map function, and then joins them together with StringJoin:

In[25]:=   `merge[list_List] := StringJoin[ Map[StringJoin[#," "]&,list] ]`

In[26]:=   `merge[{"join","this","list"}]`

Out[26]=   `join this list`

Next, we make a function that takes a list of strings whose last two members are numbers in string form and converts these last two strings into numbers:

In[27]:=   `conv[list_List] := {merge[Drop[list,-2]],ToExpression[list[[-2]]],`
`                            ToExpression[list[[-1]]]}`

In[28]:=   `conv[{"text","followed","by","two","numbers","1","2"}]`

Out[28]=   {text followed by two numbers , 1, 2}

Finally, we can read in the company data, treating each record as a list of words, and then convert the last two words of each record into numbers:

In[29]:=   `Map[conv, ReadList["company",Word,RecordLists -> True]]`

Out[29]=   {{A very big company - MEGACORP , 10000000, 20000},

{Arnie's Amazing Gadgets , 100000, 20},

{One man band , 20000, 1}}

The preceding example was complex, but it allowed us to handle a layout that was unstructured. Other cases may be best treated by the use of different methods. Consider the following file:

In[30]:=   !!compsectors

```
MegaDrug Inc          121      DRU       3456

GigaPills United      321      DRU       12789

Shoes and Socks Inc 278       FW        1100
```

If it were not for the single space after Inc in the third line, we could handle this file by setting the WordSeparators to two spaces, as before. As things stand, it makes sense to exploit the fixed length of each element of the file and to introduce the Character type (an approach that is analogous to the use of format statements in FORTRAN, such as A19):

In[31]:=   u = Map[Drop[#, -1]&, ReadList["compsectors",
              {StringJoin[Table[Character, {19}]],
              Number, Word, Number, Character}]]

Out[31]=   {{MegaDrug Inc   , 121, DRU, 3456},

{GigaPills United   , 321, DRU, 12789},

{Shoes and Socks Inc, 278, FW, 1100}}

In this example, we have included the extra Character at the end to prevent newline characters from being confused with the first letter of the subsequent company name. We dropped this character after the data were read in by mapping Drop[#, -1] onto the data.

2.2.3 Nonuniform Data

Data files frequently come with more information than the formatted data. Often, some text is included at the head of the file — for example, a description of the file's contents or the date on which the file was written. All the examples so far have concerned data that have the same format throughout the entire data file. Of course, not all data have a consistent format. In the remaining subsections of Section 2.2, we describe how to read in a file whose format is not uniform.

Skipping header text

The file power.dat contains some header information before the data:

In[32]:= `!!power.dat`

```
World Power Consumption for the Year 1988
(Breakdown in percentages)

Nuclear         6
Hydroelectric   6
Coal            28
Gas             20
Petroleum       40
```

We cannot use `ReadList` alone to read in this information because the structure of the data is not uniform. Instead, we should read in the first three lines (including the blank line) separately and then apply `ReadList` to the remaining lines of the file. First, we must open a stream to the file so that we can read from it at our leisure:

In[33]:= `inline = OpenRead["power.dat"]`

Out[33]= `InputStream[power.dat, 16]`

Then, we use the `Read` command to read in three lines from the file:

In[34]:= `Read[inline,{String,String,String}]`

Out[34]= `{World Power Consumption for the Year 1988,`

   `(Breakdown in percentages), }`

We use `String` as an input data type to refer to the entire contents of a given line. Once we have read in the first three lines, the data follow a structured pattern that can be handled by `ReadList`:

In[35]:= `ReadList[inline,{Word,Number}]`

Out[35]= `{{Nuclear, 6}, {Hydroelectric, 6}, {Coal, 28}, {Gas, 20},`

   `{Petroleum, 40}}`

It is important to remember to use the name of the input stream (`inline`, in this example), rather than the name of the file, when we apply `ReadList` to our partially read file. Finally, we must not forget to close the stream:

In[36]:= `Close[inline]`

Out[36]= `power.dat`

Reading in selected data items

Of course, we can define our own function that acts in the same way as `ReadList`, but that first drops a number of lines to be specified by the user. To understand how `Module` works, you should refer to Section 10.4 (the after `opts` in the function definition is two underscore characters):

```
In[37]:=  dropread[dropno_Integer,filename_String,opts___]:=
          Module[{inline,result},
              inline = OpenRead[filename];
              Read[inline,Table[String,{dropno}]];
              result = ReadList[inline,opts];
              Close[inline];
              result]
```

Suppose that we want to drop the first five lines of the file power.dat and to read in the rest as a list of words and numbers. The command would be

```
In[38]:=  dropread[5,"power.dat",{Word,Number}]
```

```
Out[38]=  {{Coal, 28}, {Gas, 20}, {Petroleum, 40}}
```

This function allows complete control not only over where we start reading the data file, but also over how many data items we subsequently read in. We just supply this number as the final argument:

```
In[39]:=  dropread[5,"power.dat",{Word,Number},2]
```

```
Out[39]=  {{Coal, 28}, {Gas, 20}}
```

ReadList gives us similar control over the number of data items (which is why it works for our function).

2.2.4 Database Records

A typical database consists of many records, each with several structured fields. In this section, we show how *Mathematica* can be used to read selected data items from each record in a file. Our example file database contains a fictional set of data for a group of people:

```
In[40]:=  !!database
          Name:            Charles Peter Dingleberry III
          Height:          1.80 m
          Weight:          82 kg
          Date of Birth:   3 June 1934

          Name:            Maria Smith
          Height:          1.62 m
          Weight:          63 kg
          Date of Birth:   5 August 1964

          Name:            Elliot Percy
          Height:          1.51 m
          Weight:          97 kg
          Date of Birth:   21 December 1960
```

Extracting an element from a record

Suppose that we are interested in compiling a list of the weights of the people in our database. We need to create a function that will read in a record and extract the weight from that record. This function should operate as follows: First, it should skip lines 1 and 2, which contain irrelevant information. Then, it should read in the third line as a list of the form {*"Weight:"*, *Number,"kg"*}, from which the second element is extracted. Finally, it should skip to the beginning of the next record (which takes three jumps, rather than two, since the Read statement did not move us onto a new line). The code for this function is as follows:

```
In[41]:=  extractweight[stream_] :=
Module[{weight},
    Skip[stream,String,2];
    weight = Read[stream,{Word,Number,Word}];
    If[weight === EndOfFile, ,weight = weight[[2]]];
    Skip[stream,String,3];
    weight]
```

We have included a test to see whether the file has ended so that we do not try to extract the weight if it has. To see this function in action, we must first open the database for reading:

```
In[42]:=  dbase = OpenRead["database"]
```

```
Out[42]=  InputStream[database, 86]
```

Now we can extract the weights:

```
In[43]:=  extractweight[dbase]
```

```
Out[43]=  82
```

```
In[44]:=  extractweight[dbase]
```

```
Out[44]=  63
```

```
In[45]:=  extractweight[dbase]
```

```
Out[45]=  97
```

If we try to read another weight, we obtain an EndOfFile message:

```
In[46]:=  extractweight[dbase]
```

```
Out[46]=  EndOfFile
```

So, this point is probably a good one at which to close the file!

```
In[47]:=  Close[dbase]
```

```
Out[47]=  database
```

Reading data from the entire database

In general, we will not know how many elements there are in a database file. Using the EndOfFile condition, we can get *Mathematica* to step through the file until it reaches the end. We can append the weights to a list as we go, and we can print out this list when the end of the file is reached. Once again, we can package all the instructions in a function:

```
In[48]:=  weightread[filename_String] :=
          Module[{weightlist = {},dbase,weight},
              dbase = OpenRead["database"];
              While[!((weight = extractweight[dbase]) === EndOfFile),
                  AppendTo[weightlist,weight]];
              Close[dbase];
              weightlist]

In[49]:=  weightread["database"]

Out[49]=  {82, 63, 97}
```

Searching for a keyword in a file

As is usually the case with *Mathematica*, there is more than one way to tackle the database problem. We know that each occurrence of a weight value is preceded by the word "Weight:." We can get *Mathematica* to search through the database for occurrences of this word using the Find command. Unfortunately, this function subsequently moves the stream position to the beginning of the next line. We must skip back a sufficient number of characters (we used 10) to move the stream pointer before the weight value, which can then be read into the weight list:

```
In[50]:=  weightsearch[filename_String] :=
          Module[{weightlist = {},dbase,weight},
              dbase = OpenRead["database"];
              While[!(Find[dbase,"Weight:"] === EndOfFile),
                  SetStreamPosition[dbase,StreamPosition[dbase]-10];
                  weight = Read[dbase,Number];
                  weightlist = Append[weightlist,weight];];
              Close[dbase];
              weightlist]

In[51]:=  weightsearch["database"]

Out[51]=  {82, 63, 97}
```

2.3 Inspecting a Data File

Throughout this chapter, we have made frequent use of double exclamation points to display the contents of a file. This approach may be far from ideal when the data file is long. You may want to inspect just the first few lines of the file, perhaps to see in what format the data have been stored. When you are dealing with a database, you may want to view just a single entry, rather than the whole file. In this section, we describe techniques for selectively viewing lines from a file.

2.3.1 Displaying the First Few Lines

It is relatively easy to define a function that displays only the first lines from a file. The function should open the data file, read in and print out a specified number of lines, and then close the data file:

```
In[52]:=  inspect[filename_String,lines_Integer]:=
          Module[{indata},
              indata = OpenRead[filename];
              Do[Print[Read[indata,String]],{lines}];
              Close[indata];]
```

In Section 2.2.4, we accessed a file called database. We can use our inspect function to look at the first three lines of this file:

```
In[53]:=  inspect["database",3]

          Name:          Charles Peter Dingleberry III
          Height:        1.80 m
          Weight:        82 kg
```

2.3.2 Choosing Which Lines to Display

A simple extension of the function that we defined in Section 2.3.1 allows us to select a line at which to start our inspection. We just skip through the unwanted lines:

```
In[54]:=  inspect1[filename_String,startline_Integer,lines_Integer]:=
          Module[{indata},
              indata = OpenRead[filename];
              Skip[indata,String,startline];
              Do[Print[Read[indata,String]],{lines}];
              Close[indata];]
```

To display the second entry in the database, we want to read four lines, starting from line 5:

```
In[55]:=  inspect1["database",5,4]

          Name:          Maria Smith
          Height:        1.62 m
          Weight:        63 kg
          Date of Birth: 5 August 1964
```

2.3.3 Determining the Number of Entries in a File

We can count the number of lines in a file using ReadList:

```
In[56]:=  Length[ReadList["database",String]]

Out[56]=  14
```

Frequently, a knowledge of the quantity of records in a database is more important than is a knowledge of the number of lines that the database possesses. For our database, each record includes one occurrence of the string "Name:." To determine the number of records, all we have to do is to count the number of lines containing this string:

```
In[57]:=  dbase = OpenRead["database"];
          Length[FindList[dbase,"Name:"]]
```

Out[57]=   3

In[58]:=   Close[dbase];

We can define a function that counts the number of lines that contain a particular string in a data file:

In[59]:=   ```
howmany[filename_String,keyword_String]:=
Module[{dbase,lines},
    dbase = OpenRead[filename];
    lines = Length[FindList[dbase,keyword]];
    Close[dbase];
    lines]
```

To see how many people have the name "Smith," we enter

*In[60]:=*    howmany["database","Smith"]

*Out[60]=*    1

## 2.4  Searching Directories

In Section 2.1, we described how to tell *Mathematica* where a particular file is located. To find out this information yourself, you probably left *Mathematica* and used a file manager to move around directories, and to display their contents. However, in Version 2.0 or later of *Mathematica*, it is possible to perform this operation without ever leaving the comfort of your NoteBook interface.

### 2.4.1  Setting the Directory and Listing File Names

*Mathematica* possesses sophisticated directory-handling and file-handling capabilities. Let's start by displaying the name of the current directory:

*In[61]:=*    Directory[]

*Out[61]=*    Data:Book:datfiles

If we set the directory to datfiles, we can list the files that are stored there:

*In[62]:=*    ```
SetDirectory["Data:Book:datfiles:"];
FileNames[]
```

Out[62]=   {comma.dat, company, database, experim.dat, GDP.dat,

    messydata, power.dat, sample1.dat, tab.dat, examres}

Remember that directory syntax varies from machine to machine (see Section 2.1.1). Using wild cards, we can select all files whose names end with the string ".dat":

In[63]:=   FileNames["*.dat"]

Out[63]=   {comma.dat, experim.dat, GDP.dat, power.dat, sample1.dat,

    tab.dat}

2.4.2 Inspecting a Group of Files

In Section 2.3, we described a function `inspect` that inspected the first few lines of a file. Using this function, we can define a new function to display both the name of a file and its first three lines:

```
In[64]:=  getinfo[filename_String] :=
          Module[{},
              Print["Filename: ",filename," \n"];
              inspect[filename,3];
              Print[" \n"];]
```

```
In[65]:=  getinfo["examres"]
```

```
Filename: examres

Alison   80
Jason    22
William  65
```

Now we can inspect a group of files in a directory by mapping this function onto a list of their names:

```
In[66]:=  Map[getinfo,FileNames["*.dat"]];
```

```
Filename: comma.dat

1.2E2, 3.4E2, 433
67.45466E1, 0.003456E5, 12353E-2
123, 456, 789
```

```
Filename: experim.dat

1.00    1.23
2.00    2.09
3.00    3.32
```

```
Filename: GDP.dat

Australia       14083
France          17004
United States   19815
```

```
Filename: power.dat

World Power Consumption for the Year 1988
(Breakdown in percentages)
```

```
Filename: sample1.dat

1
4
9
```

2.5 Reading Binary Files

All the files that we have dealt with in this chapter have been ASCII files; that is, they only contain text characters. Storing data in ASCII files is inefficient. Consider the integer 234. In a text file, this number will take up three characters (or 3 bytes), whereas the same number could be stored in a single unsigned byte (which has a range from 0 to 255). Needless to say, for large data files, the second storage technique, called *binary*, is employed.

Mathematica possesses facilities for both reading in and writing to binary files in the package `Utilities`BinaryFiles`:

In[67]:= `Needs["Utilities`BinaryFiles`"]`

We shall use the commands defined in the `BinaryFiles` package to write the following data file to the binary file `data.bin`:

In[68]:= `data = Table[{i,N[Sin[i]],i^2},{i,1,5}]`

Out[68]= `{{1, 0.841471, 1}, {2, 0.909297, 4}, {3, 0.14112, 9},`

`{4, -0.756802, 16}, {5, -0.958924, 25}}`

In[69]:= `outline = OpenWriteBinary["data.bin"];`
`WriteBinary[outline,data]`
`Close[outline];`

When we ask our computer for information about `data.bin` (which you can do on a Macintosh computer by selecting the file and selecting *Get Info* from the *File* menu), we find that it is 60 bytes long. Compare this with the ASCII method, which consumes 166 bytes:

In[70]:= `outline = OpenWrite["data.asc"];`
`Write[outline,data]`
`Close[outline];`

The 60 bytes for the binary file breaks down as follows: 5 records that each contain 12 bytes — 2 bytes each for the integers i and i^2 and 8 bytes for the real number `N[Sin[i]]`. We can use a variant of the `ReadList` command, known as `ReadListBinary`, to pull the data back into *Mathematica*. As usual, we must specify the data types that we are reading in. The 2-byte (signed) integers come under the category `Int16`, whereas the 8-byte real number is categorized as a `Double`:

In[71]:= `ReadListBinary["data.bin",{Int16, Double, Int16}]`

Out[71]= `{{1, 0.841471, 1}, {2, 0.909297, 4}, {3, 0.14112, 9},`

`{4, -0.756802, 16}, {5, -0.958924, 25}}`

2.5.1 Random Access to Binary Files

It is particularly simple to randomly access a binary file. *Random access* refers to the facility of starting to read from a chosen point in a file without having to read through all the earlier entries (as is done in sequential access). Since we know that each record in data.bin is 12 bytes long, we know the exact byte position of any record. For example, to read in the second record, we enter

```
In[72]:=  inline = OpenReadBinary["data.bin"];
```

```
In[73]:=  SetStreamPosition[inline,12];
          ReadBinary[inline,{Int16, Double, Int16}]
```

```
Out[73]=  {2, 0.909297, 4}
```

Similarly, the third record starts at byte 24:

```
In[74]:=  SetStreamPosition[inline,24];
          ReadBinary[inline,{Int16, Double, Int16}]
```

```
Out[74]=  {3, 0.14112, 9}
```

```
In[75]:=  Close[inline]
```

```
Out[75]=  data.bin
```

2.6 Summary

In this chapter, we have demonstrated several methods for reading data into *Mathematica* from a file. First, we explained how to help *Mathematica* to locate your file. Next, we showed how to read in well-formatted data with the help of the ReadList command. In the real world, data files frequently are not formatted well, but they can still be read into *Mathematica*. We considered several examples of nonuniformly formatted data files and demonstrated that, with suitable ingenuity, you can tackle them all adequately. Then, we showed how you can inspect a portion of a data file by using similar techniques, and we used the directory-handling capabilities of *Mathematica* to scan the header information from all the files in a particular directory. Finally, we showed how you can access data in binary format.

CHAPTER THREE

Organizing Information in *Mathematica*

In Chapter 2, we explored several ways to import data into *Mathematica*. In many cases, we were able to carry out basic rearrangements of the data at the same time that we imported them. Frequently, however, we will need to perform certain types of reorganization after we have imported the data. This chapter explains how we organize a variety of basic and useful structures. We begin by looking at one-dimensional list structures, and then we move on to lists of lists and higher-dimensional structures.

3.1 Organizing Simple Lists

In this section, we consider *simple lists*, which, by definition, are one-dimensional. We show how data can be stored in such structures and subsequently manipulated. The manipulation processes that we look at include adding and dropping data elements, simple set operations, selection by various criteria, and elementary numerical operations.

3.1.1 Basic Operations

To explore *Mathematica*'s capabilities, we begin by defining a few standard one-dimensional list structures:

```
In[1]:=    numlist = {4.2, 1.1, 2, 5, 3, 4.2, 7};
           othernum = {1.1, 7, 8, 9, 10};
           namelist = {Ethan, Dylan, Bill, Piers};
           mixedlist = Join[numlist, namelist]

Out[1]=    {4.2, 1.1, 2, 5, 3, 4.2, 7, Ethan, Dylan, Bill, Piers}
```

The Join operation simply joins together two or more lists. In mixedlist, the two lists had no elements in common. If we apply Join to numlist and othernum, we can compare the result with the result of the Union operation, which, in addition to discarding duplicates, carries out a sort:

```
In[2]:=    Join[numlist, othernum]

Out[2]=    {4.2, 1.1, 2, 5, 3, 4.2, 7, 1.1, 7, 8, 9, 10}

In[3]:=    Union[numlist, othernum]

Out[3]=    {1.1, 2, 3, 4.2, 5, 7, 8, 9, 10}
```

Other logical operations on pairs of lists also are supported:

In[4]:=   `Intersection[numlist, othernum]`

Out[4]=   `{1.1, 7}`

In[5]:=   `Complement[numlist, othernum]`

Out[5]=   `{2, 3, 4.2, 5}`

This second operation selects those elements that are in `numlist` but are not in `othernum`. `Union` can also be applied to a single list, as can the `Sort` operation:

In[6]:=   `Union[numlist]`

Out[6]=   `{1.1, 2, 3, 4.2, 5, 7}`

In[7]:=   `Sort[numlist]`

Out[7]=   `{1.1, 2, 3, 4.2, 4.2, 5, 7}`

Various other rearrangements of the list as a whole can be performed. If, for example, you have imported or created data back to front, you can turn them around with `Reverse`:

In[8]:=   `Reverse[numlist]`

Out[8]=   `{7, 4.2, 3, 5, 2, 1.1, 4.2}`

3.1.2 Rotate Operations and Their Applications

One class of functions with a surprising number of applications includes the `RotateLeft` and `RotateRight` operations, as shown in the following examples:

In[9]:=   `numlist`

Out[9]=   `{4.2, 1.1, 2, 5, 3, 4.2, 7}`

In[10]:=   `RotateLeft[numlist]`

Out[10]=   `{1.1, 2, 5, 3, 4.2, 7, 4.2}`

In[11]:=   `RotateRight[numlist]`

Out[11]=   `{7, 4.2, 1.1, 2, 5, 3, 4.2}`

In[12]:=   `RotateRight[numlist, 2]`

Out[12]=   `{4.2, 7, 4.2, 1.1, 2, 5, 3}`

These cyclical operations have a great deal of power. Not only can you perform cyclical permutations in group theory, but also if you have any kind of periodic data, as you often do in applied mathematics, you can use these operations to shift the origin in a natural way. You can also use them to construct discrete forms of differential operators. We shall return to this topic many times, but the basic idea is simple. (If you are not interested in solving Laplace's equation or related diffusive problems, skip this discussion and move on to Section 3.1.3.)

Suppose that we have a simple list and that we wish to construct the discrete form of the Laplace operator:

$$\nabla^2 = \frac{d^2}{dx^2}$$

Given data y_i defined at points x_i with constant separation h, $(\nabla^2 y)_i$ is given by:

$$(\nabla^2 y)_i = \frac{y_{i-1} - 2y_i + y_{i+1}}{h^2}$$

This difference scheme is implemented naturally by the use of Rotate operations. The following function Laplace takes a list and a step size as arguments; if the latter is omitted, it defaults to 1:

```
In[13]:=  Laplace[data_, step_:1] :=
          (RotateRight[data] - 2 data + RotateLeft[data])/step^2

In[14]:=  Laplace[numlist]

Out[14]=  {-0.3, 4., 2.1, -5, 3.2, 1.6, -5.6}
```

Here is a pair of more interesting examples. Let's construct some periodic data and some polynomial data:

```
In[15]:=  periodata = Table[N[Sin[2 Pi i/15]], {i, 1, 15}]
          polydata = Table[i^2 + 3 i - 2, {i, 1, 6}]

Out[15]=  {0.406737, 0.743145, 0.951057, 0.994522, 0.866025, 0.587785, 0.207912,
           -0.207912, -0.587785, -0.866025, -0.994522, -0.951057, -0.743145,
           -0.406737, 0}

Out[15]=  {2, 8, 16, 26, 38, 52}

In[16]:=  Laplace[periodata, N[2 Pi/15]]

Out[16]=  {-0.400824, -0.732342, -0.937232, -0.980065, -0.853437, -0.579241,
           -0.204889, 0.204889, 0.579241, 0.853437, 0.980065, 0.937232, 0.732342,
                                -18
           0.400824, -3.39857 10    }

In[17]:=  Laplace[polydata]

Out[17]=  {56, 2, 2, 2, 2, -64}
```

In the first case, the Laplacian has given us approximately minus the original data set, as it should, since $\nabla^2 \sin x = -\sin x$. In the second case, the calculation demonstrates that the second differences of a quadratic are constant. Note, in the latter case, that only the interior values of the list have significance. This case is one of many where we may wish to drop the end or other elements of a list, so we discuss it next.

3.1.3 List Droppings: Selection by Position

First we remind ourselves of numlist. Then we consider certain truncated lists, which we can identify by elements that are dropped or by elements that are retained. This can take two forms, depending on whether we identify the elements by their position or by their values. Let's first consider identification by position within the list:

```
In[18]:=  numlist
Out[18]=  {4.2, 1.1, 2, 5, 3, 4.2, 7}

In[19]:=  Rest[numlist]
Out[19]=  {1.1, 2, 5, 3, 4.2, 7}

In[20]:=  Drop[numlist, 1]
Out[20]=  {1.1, 2, 5, 3, 4.2, 7}

In[21]:=  Drop[numlist, -1]
Out[21]=  {4.2, 1.1, 2, 5, 3, 4.2}

In[22]:=  Drop[numlist, -3]
Out[22]=  {4.2, 1.1, 2, 5}

In[23]:=  Take[numlist, 2]
Out[23]=  {4.2, 1.1}

In[24]:=  Take[numlist, -2]
Out[24]=  {4.2, 7}
```

Both `Drop` and `Take` can have a pair of numbers as second arguments. For example, if we wish to retain elements 2 through 5, we can say

```
In[25]:=  Take[numlist, {2, 5}]
Out[25]=  {1.1, 2, 5, 3}
```

We can also accomplish the retention of particular elements by direct indexing with the `Range` function, which we prefer since this approach generalizes easily to nested lists:

```
In[26]:=  Range[3]
Out[26]=  {1, 2, 3}

In[27]:=  Range[2, 5]
Out[27]=  {2, 3, 4, 5}

In[28]:=  numlist[[Range[2, 5]]]
Out[28]=  {1.1, 2, 5, 3}
```

As an application, if we wish our Laplace operator to act on nonperiodic data, we can restrict it to act on the interior by removing the two endpoint elements. Removing the ends gives a better second-difference operator on sequences:

```
In[29]:=  LaplaceInterior[data_List, step_:1] :=
             Take[Laplace[data, step], {2, -2}]
```

In[30]:=   `LaplaceInterior[polydata]`

Out[30]=   {2, 2, 2, 2}

3.1.4 The Addition of Elements to Lists

We have explored how to remove certain elements from lists. Now we consider how to add elements to lists. In Section 3.1.1, we saw how `Join` and `Union` were used for adding one list to another. Other functions enable us to add single elements. Clearly, we may consider adding them to the beginning of the list, to the end of the list, or to some position within the list. First we recall our list of names, `namelist`:

In[31]:=   `namelist`

Out[31]=   {Ethan, Dylan, Bill, Piers}

We have the following three functions:

In[32]:=   `Prepend[namelist, "Joe"]`

Out[32]=   {Joe, Ethan, Dylan, Bill, Piers}

In[33]:=   `Append[namelist, "Joe"]`

Out[33]=   {Ethan, Dylan, Bill, Piers, Joe}

In[34]:=   `Insert[namelist, "Joe", 2]`

Out[34]=   {Ethan, Joe, Dylan, Bill, Piers}

People often make one or both of two mistakes in the use of these functions. The first mistake is to swap the list and the element being added. You should use `Prepend` in the form "`Prepend` to the list `namelist` (argument 1) the element `Joe` (argument 2)" rather than "`Prepend` `Joe` to `namelist`." Although the latter construction is perhaps more natural, these functions do not work that way!

The second error is to assume that `namelist` is actually updated. If you ask for the value of `namelist` after having executed any of the previous three commands, you will see that `namelist` is unaffected:

In[35]:=   `namelist`

Out[35]=   {Ethan, Dylan, Bill, Piers}

If we require that our list be updated, we can always resort to force:

In[36]:=   `namelist = Prepend[namelist, "Joe"]`

Out[36]=   {Joe, Ethan, Dylan, Bill, Piers}

Mathematica also allows us to do the updating automatically through use of the forms `PrependTo` and `AppendTo`. Here is an example of `AppendTo`:

In[37]:=   `AppendTo[namelist, "Janet"]`

Out[37]=   {Joe, Ethan, Dylan, Bill, Piers, Janet}

In[38]:=   namelist

Out[38]=   {Joe, Ethan, Dylan, Bill, Piers, Janet}

The functions Append, AppendTo, and other insertion functions can be used to build up useful list structures by iterative methods. A particular application of their use is given in Chapter 15, where we consider techniques for robust regression.

3.1.5 Selection by Value and Filtering

The functions Drop and Take remove or retain, respectively, elements identified by position within a list. We can also consider identifying elements by the form that they take. A full treatment of this topic, which will allow you, for example, to manage the selection of symbolic objects matching particular patterns, will be given in Chapter 9. For now, we shall consider relatively simple numerical operations, such as screening a list for elements above a certain value. (The discussion immediately following makes use of the concept of a pure function. If you have not yet read Section 1.5 regarding pure functions, we advise you to do so before you read the remainder of this section.)

Select[list, test] gives the elements in the list for which the test returns the value True. We begin our investigation of this function by recalling our numerical list and selecting from it those elements that have a value strictly greater than 3:

In[39]:=   numlist

Out[39]=   {4.2, 1.1, 2, 5, 3, 4.2, 7}

In[40]:=   Select[numlist, (# > 3 &)]

Out[40]=   {4.2, 5, 4.2, 7}

This use of Select is how we filter data to satisfy certain criteria. We can build up more complicated tests involving, for example, several inequalities. If we wish to select those elements between 3 and 5 (inclusive of the endpoints), we can apply either of the following operations to numlist:

In[41]:=   Select[numlist, (# >= 3 && # <= 5 &)]

Out[41]=   {4.2, 5, 3, 4.2}

In[42]:=   Select[numlist, (3 <= # <= 5 &)]

Out[42]=   {4.2, 5, 3, 4.2}

In this last pair of operations, we have introduced three new ideas. "Greater than or equal to" is represented by the shorthand >=. We have also combined two tests with a logical AND operation, shortened to &&. The inequalities can be combined into one statement if you wish to avoid explicit use of an AND operation. If we wished to have those elements of the list that are either less than 3 or greater than 5, we would invoke the logical OR by using the || notation:

In[43]:=   Select[numlist, (# < 3 || # > 5 &)]

Out[43]=   {1.1, 2, 7}

When managing purely numerical data, you will probably most often want to use Select with simple inequalities such as those considered here. However, this investigation shows only the "tip of the iceberg" of what is possible. We shall discuss string-based selections in Section 3.1.7, and we shall examine general symbolic filtering in Chapter 9. Our immediate goal is to understand how to generalize the examples we have just considered, where we grouped data into subgroups with numerical values lying in particular ranges, to the more useful problem of grouping data into multiple regions and performing frequency counts. A treatment of grouping requires us to go beyond what is in the basic *Mathematica* kernel and to explore the contents of the DataManipulation package.

3.1.6 Grouping and Data Manipulation

Thus far in this chapter, we have discussed only kernel functions. There are a few commonplace operations, not represented by kernel functions, that are available in the DataManipulation package in the Statistics package area. You may not necessarily want to do any statistics, but this package contains useful basic operations such as data grouping. We shall begin by loading the package into *Mathematica* using the loading commands discussed in Section 1.6. (note that Chapter 13 will discuss package contexts and will explain the syntax in more detail):

In[44]:=   Needs["Statistics`DataManipulation`"]

To test that we have loaded this package properly, as well as to find out what functions have been added, we inquire about functions within this new context. The following incantation does the trick:

In[45]:=   ?Statistics`DataManipulation`*

BinCounts	ColumnTake	Ordering
BinLists	CumulativeSums	QuantileForm
BooleanSelect	DropNonNumeric	RangeCounts
CategoryCounts	DropNonNumericColumn	RangeLists
CategoryLists	Frequencies	RowJoin
ColumnDrop	LengthWhile	TakeWhile
ColumnJoin		

We will not discuss every function in this package, and a discussion of some functions (those relating to re-reorganizing higher-dimensional lists) will be deferred to the end of this chapter. Our immediate goal is to understand grouping and frequency counts. The lists that we have used so far are too trivial to do justice to this package, so we will invent some. You should create a data set by executing the following command. (Since we are about to invoke random sampling, be aware that for the remainder of this section, the detailed numerical results that you obtain will not be the same as ours! However, the principles should be clear.)

We create 1000 numbers, randomly chosen from the interval 0 to 10, by executing the following command:

In[46]:=   randdata = Table[Random[Real, {0, 10}], {i, 1, 1000}];

Just how random are these data? Although we are not discussing graphics yet, we cannot resist taking a quick look at our data:

```
In[47]:=  ListPlot[randdata]
```

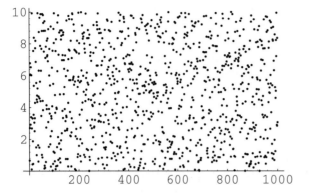

We can obtain a better understanding of our data by reducing them to more manageable proportions. A common operation is to group, or *bin*, the data. The function BinCounts does the job for uniform bins, while RangeCounts allows you to give a detailed description of the intervals. Let's first consider ten equal-sized bins, from 0 to 10, in steps of 1. The function BinCounts computes the number of elements of data in each interval or *bin*:

```
In[48]:=  BinCounts[randdata, {0, 10, 1}]

Out[48]=  {117, 97, 86, 101, 91, 106, 105, 91, 108, 98}
```

Let's next consider one large bin from 0 to 5 and then five other bins from 5 to 10. In this particular example, the endpoints are unnecessary, but more generally they could be used to quantify the size of the tails of a data set:

```
In[49]:=  RangeCounts[randdata, {0, 5, 6, 7, 8, 9, 10}]

Out[49]=  {0, 492, 106, 105, 91, 108, 98, 0}
```

If, rather than just counting the number of elements in each bin, you want to extract those elements in one or more particular bins (this extraction is the generalization of Select that we require), you should use BinLists and RangeLists. In the following example, we use BinLists with a smaller bin size and look at the contents of the first bin:

```
In[50]:=  BinLists[randdata, {0, 10, 0.1}][[1]]

Out[50]=  {0.0256091, 0.0420122, 0.00523281, 0.0875525, 0.0814658, 0.0809081,

          0.0753309, 0.0552022, 0.0134153, 0.0342341, 0.00593815, 0.000270723}
```

If you cannot wait to do a bar chart (histogram) based on these examples, you may wish to turn to Section 4.4.1.

It is appropriate to use Bin or Range when the data take continuous values. If they only take a finite number of discrete values and you wish to count the number of times that each value is attained, then you should use the Frequencies function. We illustrate its use by constructing a list of random integers from 0 to 10 inclusive; the Frequencies function returns a list of pairs of the form {*frequency, value*}:

```
In[51]:=   intdata = Table[Random[Integer, {0, 10}], {i, 1, 1000}];
```

```
In[52]:=   Frequencies[intdata]
```

```
Out[52]=   {{88, 0}, {81, 1}, {76, 2}, {106, 3}, {82, 4}, {105, 5}, {89, 6}, {88, 7},

           {87, 8}, {100, 9}, {98, 10}}
```

3.1.7 Selection Using String Criteria

To select a subgroup of a data list, we must define a criterion by which to select. For example, the following function tests a string to see whether it matches the word "John":

```
In[53]:=   johntest[name_String] := If[name == "John", True, False];
           johntest["John"]
```

```
Out[53]=   True
```

```
In[54]:=   johntest["Peter"]
```

```
Out[54]=   False
```

Suppose that we have a list consisting of a first name and surname in that order. We can now test to see whether the first name is John:

```
In[55]:=   fullname1 = {"John","Saunders"};
           johntest[fullname1[[1]]]
```

```
Out[55]=   True
```

```
In[56]:=   fullname2 = {"Peter","John"};
           johntest[fullname2[[1]]]
```

```
Out[56]=   False
```

In the following example, we use johntest to select all the Johns in a list:

```
In[57]:=   namelist = {{"John","Smith"},{"Albert","Einstein"},{"John","Kennedy"}}
```

```
Out[57]=   {{John, Smith}, {Albert, Einstein}, {John, Kennedy}}
```

```
In[58]:=   Select[namelist, johntest[ #[[1]] ]&]
```

```
Out[58]=   {{John, Smith}, {John, Kennedy}}
```

In fact, when using pure functions, we do not need to define a function johntest at all:

```
In[59]:=   Select[namelist, (#[[1]] == "John" &)]
```

```
Out[59]=   {{John, Smith}, {John, Kennedy}}
```

Similarly, we can select rapidly all people with surname "Einstein":

```
In[60]:=   Select[namelist, (#[[2]] == "Einstein" &)]
```

```
Out[60]=   {{Albert, Einstein}}
```

We can define conditions on numerical values in a similar way. The function `reallyold` decides whether an age qualifies as being really old:

```
In[61]:=   reallyold[age_Integer] := If[age > 80, True, False];
           reallyold[34]
```

```
Out[61]=   False
```

```
In[62]:=   reallyold[101]
```

```
Out[62]=   True
```

We can then extract all the really old people from a data list:

```
In[63]:=   agelist = {{"John","Smith",85},{"Jason","Tigg",24},{"Old","Man",98}};
           Select[agelist, reallyold[ #[[3]] ]& ]
```

```
Out[63]=   {{John, Smith, 85}, {Old, Man, 98}}
```

Multiple tests are also possible — as && does with numerical operations, && denotes a logical AND. The following condition selects all really old people called John:

```
In[64]:=   Select[agelist, ( #[[3]] > 80   &&   #[[1]] == "John"  &)   ]
```

```
Out[64]=   {{John, Smith, 85}}
```

3.2 Organizing Lists of Lists

The organization of lists of lists, lists of lists of lists, and even higher-dimensional structures requires considerably more care and concentration than the manipulation of simple lists. To describe adequately the various operations that are possible, we introduce several standard list structures and a few standard means of visualizing them. First, we define our standard list of lists `stdlol`:

```
In[65]:=   stdlol = {{1, 2, 3, 4}, {5, 6, 7, 8}, {9, 10, 11, 12}};
```

Our standard way of viewing this object is as a matrix, for which there is a built-in kernel function `MatrixForm` with the property that it displays such a list in ordinary matrix notation. We define our own function `Viewlol`, which sets a few parameters to control the layout:

```
In[66]:=   Viewlol[data_] :=
           MatrixForm[data, TableSpacing -> {0, 1},
           TableAlignments -> {Right, Right, Right, Right}]
```

```
In[67]:=   Viewlol[stdlol]
```

```
Out[67]=   1  2   3  4
           5  6   7  8
           9 10  11 12
```

To explain higher-dimensional objects, we work with a standard $3 \times 3 \times 3$ list of lists of lists:

```
In[68]:=   stdlolol = {{{1, 2, 3}, {4, 5, 6}, {7, 8, 9}},
              {{a, b, c}, {d, e, f}, {h, j, k}},
              {{P, Q, R}, {S, T, U}, {V, W, X}}}
Out[68]=   {{{1, 2, 3}, {4, 5, 6}, {7, 8, 9}}, {{a, b, c}, {d, e, f}, {h, j, k}},
              {{P, Q, R}, {S, T, U}, {V, W, X}}}
```

Our standard method for viewing such an object is as an array of matrices, for which we introduce a function Viewlolol to produce a standard layout:

```
In[69]:=   Viewlolol[data_] :=
           Map[MatrixForm[#, TableSpacing -> {0, 1}]&, data]

In[70]:=   Viewlolol[stdlolol]
Out[70]=   {1 2 3,  a b c,  P Q R}
            4 5 6   d e f   S T U
            7 8 9   h j k   V W X
```

3.2.1 Operations That Change the Depth of Nesting

The first operations that we consider are those that destroy or create nesting in list structures. The functions that destroy nesting are Flatten and its relatives. First, we apply Flatten to our standard lists (we are giving the resulting lists the names flaone, flatwo, to flafive — you should do so too if you wish to see how to undo each operation to recover the original structure):

```
In[71]:=   flaone = Flatten[stdlol]
Out[71]=   {1, 2, 3, 4, 5, 6, 7, 8, 9, 10, 11, 12}
```

How many levels of nesting does Flatten destroy? If you apply it to stdlolol, you will see that it destroys all levels:

```
In[72]:=   flatwo = Flatten[stdlolol]
Out[72]=   {1, 2, 3, 4, 5, 6, 7, 8, 9, a, b, c, d, e, f, h, j, k, P, Q, R, S, T, U,
              V, W, X}
```

Greater control is obtained by the use of an optional second argument to Flatten. If we wish to remove just the top level of nesting, we supply the value 1:

```
In[73]:=   flathree = Flatten[stdlolol, 1]
Out[73]=   {{1, 2, 3}, {4, 5, 6}, {7, 8, 9}, {a, b, c}, {d, e, f}, {h, j, k},
              {P, Q, R}, {S, T, U}, {V, W, X}}
```

A common mistake is to imagine that if you use 2 instead of 1 as the second argument, you will flatten just at the second level. In fact, Flatten[data, n] flattens the top n levels in a list, as the following example makes clear:

```
In[74]:=   Flatten[stdlolol, 2]
Out[74]=   {1, 2, 3, 4, 5, 6, 7, 8, 9, a, b, c, d, e, f, h, j, k, P, Q, R, S, T, U,
              V, W, X}
```

If we want to flatten stdlolol only at the second level, we merely map Flatten onto stdlolol:

```
In[75]:=  flafour = Map[Flatten, stdlolol]
Out[75]=  {{1, 2, 3, 4, 5, 6, 7, 8, 9}, {a, b, c, d, e, f, h, j, k},
          {P, Q, R, S, T, U, V, W, X}}
```

These examples have covered all the basic Flatten possibilities for lists up to depth 3. To secure detailed control over the level at which you flatten a list with nesting depth 4 or greater, you should use the level control available in Map, together with the depth control available in Flatten. There are many possibilities once you get to this level of nesting, so we give just one example where we remove an intermediate level of nesting on a list of depth 4 (it is possible, by one or more applications of operations of this type, to control precisely what levels of nesting are removed on a list of arbitrary depth):

```
In[76]:=  stdlololol = {{{{a, b}, {c, d}}, {{e, f}, {g, h}}},
                        {{{A, B}, {C, D}}, {{E, F}, {G, H}}}};
In[77]:=  Dimensions[stdlololol]
Out[77]=  {2, 2, 2, 2}
In[78]:=  flafive = Map[Flatten[#, 1]&, stdlololol, 1]
Out[78]=  {{{a, b}, {c, d}, {e, f}, {g, h}}, {{A, B}, {C, D}, {E, F}, {G, H}}}
```

If, for some reason, our lists are insufficiently nested, then we can fix that too. In fact, our experience is that people tend to use ReadList just to generate a list of depth 1 or perhaps 2, and then they impose additional structure within *Mathematica*. Addition of nesting is a common requirement. We add further structure into a list by using the Partition function. We illustrate its use by seeing how our original standard lists can be recovered from the set flaone to flafive.

Partition[data, n] partitions the data into sublists of length n. For example, to recover stdlol from flaone, we partition flaone into sublists of length 4:

```
In[79]:=  Partition[flaone, 4]
Out[79]=  {{1, 2, 3, 4}, {5, 6, 7, 8}, {9, 10, 11, 12}}
```

Two applications are needed to restore flatwo to its original state. We note that the intermediate stage is flathree. The composition of two applications of Partition illustrates that we must work out from the innermost levels:

```
In[80]:=  flatwo
Out[80]=  {1, 2, 3, 4, 5, 6, 7, 8, 9, a, b, c, d, e, f, h, j, k, P, Q, R, S, T, U,
          V, W, X}
In[81]:=  Partition[flatwo, 3]
Out[81]=  {{1, 2, 3}, {4, 5, 6}, {7, 8, 9}, {a, b, c}, {d, e, f}, {h, j, k},
          {P, Q, R}, {S, T, U}, {V, W, X}}
In[82]:=  Partition[%, 3]
```

Out[82]=   {{{1, 2, 3}, {4, 5, 6}, {7, 8, 9}}, {{a, b, c}, {d, e, f}, {h, j, k}},
             {{P, Q, R}, {S, T, U}, {V, W, X}}}

Just as we obtained flafour by mapping Flatten, we restore it by a corresponding Map of Partition. The same type of operation restores the original nesting to flafive:

In[83]:=   flafour

Out[83]=   {{1, 2, 3, 4, 5, 6, 7, 8, 9}, {a, b, c, d, e, f, h, j, k},
             {P, Q, R, S, T, U, V, W, X}}

In[84]:=   Map[Partition[#, 3]&, flafour]

Out[84]=   {{{1, 2, 3}, {4, 5, 6}, {7, 8, 9}}, {{a, b, c}, {d, e, f}, {h, j, k}},
             {{P, Q, R}, {S, T, U}, {V, W, X}}}

In[85]:=   flafive

Out[85]=   {{{a, b}, {c, d}, {e, f}, {g, h}}, {{A, B}, {C, D}, {E, F}, {G, H}}}

In[86]:=   Map[Partition[#, 2]&, flafive]

Out[86]=   {{{{a, b}, {c, d}}, {{e, f}, {g, h}}},

             {{{A, B}, {C, D}}, {{E, F}, {G, H}}}}

3.2.2 Symmetry Operations on Data

You may find, from time to time, that even though you have figured out how to read in data and have decided on and imposed the kind of list structure that you want for them, your lists are still not quite right for your purposes. Suppose, for example, that you had taken part in an experiment to gather some type of numerical information (soil pH value will do) from a field. Maybe the person who gathered some data for you started at the north–west corner of the field, rather than the south–west corner as you thought she would, and gathered data in north–south strips, rather than west–east strips. You want to impose your original organizational plan on the data. You do so by using a set of symmetry operations.

We begin by reminding ourselves of our original standard list of lists, viewed as a matrix:

In[87]:=   Viewlol[stdlol]

Out[87]=   1 2 3 4
             5 6 7 8
             9 10 11 12

To reflect the data in a horizontal line, we Reverse them:

In[88]:=   Viewlol[Reverse[stdlol]]

Out[88]=   9 10 11 12
             5 6 7 8
             1 2 3 4

To reflect the data in a vertical line, we map Reverse onto them:

```
In[89]:=  Viewlol[Map[Reverse, stdlol]]
Out[89]=   4  3  2  1
           8  7  6  5
          12 11 10  9
```

We can compose these two operations to obtain a rotation of 180 degrees:

```
In[90]:=  rotdata = Reverse[Map[Reverse, stdlol]];
          Viewlol[rotdata]
Out[90]=  12 11 10  9
           8  7  6  5
           4  3  2  1
```

To reflect the data in a line down the leading diagonal, we Transpose them:

```
In[91]:=  Viewlol[Transpose[stdlol]]
Out[91]=   1  5  9
           2  6 10
           3  7 11
           4  8 12
```

To reflect the data in a line down the other diagonal, we can, for example, Transpose our rotated data:

```
In[92]:=  Viewlol[Transpose[rotdata]]
Out[92]=  12  8  4
          11  7  3
          10  6  2
           9  5  1
```

To rotate the data through just 90 degrees, we simply compose Transpose and Reverse. Note the order of these two operations — swapping it rotates the data the other way!

```
In[93]:=  Viewlol[Transpose[Reverse[stdlol]]]
Out[93]=   9  5  1
          10  6  2
          11  7  3
          12  8  4
```

Purists may argue that these observations are all applications of trivial group theory (which is true), but we have found it convenient to list these operations in this visual form in order to provide a quick recipe list for carrying out all the standard transformations on the data treated as a *rigid* array.

Of course, many other symmetry operations are possible if we imagine that our data no longer have a rigid organization. We can imagine swapping two rows or two columns or carrying out a cyclical permutation operation either horizontally or vertically. These further operations are certainly of interest in group theory, but we have never found it necessary to apply such operations to correct a difficulty with data. We shall have cause to apply cyclical permutations to lists of lists, which will be discussed in the context of Laplace-type operators for image processing (Chapter 21) and the solution of partial differential equations (Section 5.7).

The possible symmetry transformations on a more deeply nested structure are clearly more extensive. We shall not itemize them all, but instead we shall focus on the building blocks for common operations. For those of you familiar with tensor analysis, let's imagine that the object stdlolol is a tensor s_{ijk}, which could be represented in *Mathematica* by the element stdlolol[[i, j, k]]:

```
In[94]:=  Viewlolol[stdlolol]
Out[94]=  {1 2 3, a b c, P Q R}
           4 5 6  d e f  S T U
           7 8 9  h j k  V W X
```

The operation, which, in tensor terms, corresponds to defining an object $t_{ijk} = s_{jik}$, is as follows:

```
In[95]:=  t = Transpose[stdlolol];
          Viewlolol[t]
Out[95]=  {1 2 3, 4 5 6, 7 8 9}
           a b c  d e f  h j k
           P Q R  S T U  V W X
```

We can obtain $u_{ijk} = s_{ikj}$ by mapping Transpose:

```
In[96]:=  u = Map[Transpose, stdlolol];
          Viewlolol[u]
Out[96]=  {1 4 7, a d h, P S V}
           2 5 8  b e j  Q T W
           3 6 9  c f k  R U X
```

More generally, we obtain permutations of the index structure by supplying a permutation as a second argument to Transpose. For example, to swap just the first and third index, thus defining $v_{ijk} = s_{kji}$, we set the following:

```
In[97]:=  v = Transpose[stdlolol, {3, 2, 1}];
          Viewlolol[v]
Out[97]=  {1 a P, 2 b Q, 3 c R}
           4 d S  5 e T  6 f U
           7 h V  8 j W  9 k X
```

You may find the relationship easier to understand if you consider a few sample values:

```
In[98]:=  {v[[3, 3, 1]], stdlolol[[1, 3, 3]]}
Out[98]=  {9, 9}
```

We can perform cyclical permutations of the indices (not to be confused with cyclical rotation of data within a list) by supplying other permutations such as {2, 3, 1}, {3, 1, 2}.

We end this discussion by illustrating the various ways in which Reverse can be used at different levels:

```
In[99]:=  Viewlolol[stdlolol]
Out[99]=  {1 2 3,  a b c,  P Q R}
           4 5 6   d e f   S T U
           7 8 9   h j k   V W X
```

We can apply `Reverse` at the topmost level to reverse the order of the main blocks:

```
In[100]:= Viewlolol[Reverse[stdlolol]]
Out[100]= {P Q R,  a b c,  1 2 3}
           S T U   d e f   4 5 6
           V W X   h j k   7 8 9
```

We can apply `Reverse` at the next level down to reverse the positions of the rows, while retaining the order of the main blocks:

```
In[101]:= Viewlolol[Map[Reverse[#]&, stdlolol]]
Out[101]= {7 8 9,  h j k,  V W X}
           4 5 6   d e f   S T U
           1 2 3   a b c   P Q R
```

We can apply `Reverse` only at the lowest level to keep the positions of the rows and main blocks intact, while reversing the order of elements within each row (note the form of the level specification for `Map`):

```
In[102]:= Viewlolol[Map[Reverse[#]&, stdlolol, {2}]]
Out[102]= {3 2 1,  c b a,  R Q P}
           6 5 4   f e d   U T S
           9 8 7   k j h   X W V
```

If we forget to treat the level specification as a list, then `Map` applies to both levels, reversing rows and columns within each main block:

```
In[103]:= Viewlolol[Map[Reverse[#]&, stdlolol, 2]]
Out[103]= {9 8 7,  k j h,  X W V}
           6 5 4   f e d   U T S
           3 2 1   c b a   R Q P
```

3.2.3 Further Applications of the DataManipulation Package

You may have observed that there is a degree of asymmetry in the way that *Mathematica* treats matrix structures as a list of lists. Given the structure `stdlol`, which we view as a matrix s_{ij}, we can refer directly to the ith row by `stdlol[[i]]`, and we can delete or insert rows by using `Drop` or `Take`, respectively, just as we did for a simple list:

```
In[104]:= stdlol
Out[104]= {{1, 2, 3, 4}, {5, 6, 7, 8}, {9, 10, 11, 12}}
In[105]:= stdlol[[2]]
Out[105]= {5, 6, 7, 8}
```

```
In[106]:= Drop[stdlol, 1]
```
```
Out[106]= {{5, 6, 7, 8}, {9, 10, 11, 12}}
```
```
In[107]:= Take[stdlol, {1, 2}]
```
```
Out[107]= {{1, 2, 3, 4}, {5, 6, 7, 8}}
```

If you wish to perform corresponding operations on columns, you can always Transpose the data first, carry out the required operation, and then Transpose them back. Suppose that we wish to delete the second column from stdlol:

```
In[108]:= Viewlol[Transpose[Drop[Transpose[stdlol], {2}]]]
```
```
Out[108]= 1  3  4
          5  7  8
          9 11 12
```

This approach can become tedious, and only one forgotten Transpose will cause problems. The DataManipulation package introduces functions that allow you to work with columns directly. If you have not already loaded the DataManipulation package into your current *Mathematica* session, load it now:

```
In[109]:= Needs["Statistics`DataManipulation`"]
```

The following operations illustrate the ideas, all of which are simple shorthand notations, for a Transpose, row operation, Transpose, sandwich:

```
In[110]:= Viewlol[ColumnDrop[stdlol, {2}]]
```
```
Out[110]= 1  3  4
          5  7  8
          9 11 12
```

```
In[111]:= Column[stdlol, 2]
```
```
Out[111]= {2, 6, 10}
```

```
In[112]:= Viewlol[ColumnTake[stdlol, 3]]
```
```
Out[112]= 1  2  3
          5  6  7
          9 10 11
```

The best way to select contiguous submatrices in a list of any nesting depth is to use indexing in conjunction with a Range statement. For example, the best way to extract the submatrix consisting of rows 2 and 3 and columns 2 through 4 is as follows:

```
In[113]:= stdlol[[Range[2, 3], Range[2, 4]]]
```
```
Out[113]= {{6, 7, 8}, {10, 11, 12}}
```

```
In[114]:= Viewlol[%]
```
```
Out[114]= 1  2  3
          5  6  7
          9 10 11
```

3.3 Summary

In this chapter, we have considered all the list management operations that we have found to be useful in organizing data within *Mathematica*. You can reorganize simple lists in various ways, and you can drop or add elements. You can refer to elements of lists by position or by value, and you can apply selection criteria using both numerical and string qualities. The DataManipulation package adds many useful functions, especially for grouping data. You can reorganize lists of lists and higher-dimensional structures in several additional ways. The most important techniques include changing the depth of nesting by using commands such as Flatten and Partition, and operations to Transpose or Reverse the data.

At this stage, if you have read Chapters 2 and 3, you should be able to import an arbitrary data set into *Mathematica* and to organize it into a list structure suitable for further analysis.

CHAPTER FOUR

Visualizing Data in Two Dimensions

Chapter 2 explained how to import data into *Mathematica*, and Chapter 3 how to organize those data into suitable lists. At this stage, you may wish to create a graphic or to process your data further. This chapter explains how to create two-dimensional graphics, and Chapter 6 explains various constructions for higher-dimensional graphics. If you wish to process your data further before plotting, turn to Chapter 5.

In *Mathematica* graphics, there is a close, but not an exact, symmetry between operations, such as Plot, for plotting functions and operations, such as ListPlot, for plotting data. A good basic rule is to remember that anything you can do with Plot, at least in generic cases, you can also do with ListPlot, and vice versa. There are exceptions, and we shall highlight those that experience has taught us are important. However, even the exceptions can be forced into line. If you have a set of data, you can always turn it into a function by interpolation; if you have a function, you can always make data by sampling it! Interpolation is explained in Chapter 5.

Our emphasis is on data visualization. Other books give a thorough discussion of function plotting; for the most part, we shall focus on the analogous list-plotting operations. For completeness, however, let's begin by taking a quick look at functions.

4.1 Plotting Functions

To plot a function of one variable, you can use the Plot function:

```
In[1]:=    Plot[ Sin[x], {x, -6 Pi, 6 Pi} ]
```

The `Plot` function has a multitude of options. The following example demonstrates several possibilities:

```
In[2]:=    Plot[{2 Exp[-x^2], Sin[x]}, {x,-3,3},
               PlotStyle -> {Thickness[0.007],
                            {Thickness[0.007],Dashing[{0.02,0.02}]}},
               PlotLabel -> FontForm["Gaussian Function and Sine Wave\n"
                            ,{"Times-Bold",10}],
               PlotRegion -> {{0.05, 0.95}, {0.05, 0.95}},
               GridLines -> Automatic,
               Background -> GrayLevel[0.9],
               PlotRange -> {{-3,3},{-1.5,2.5}},
               Ticks -> {{-3,-1.5,1.5,3},Automatic}]
```

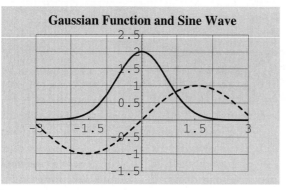

An explanation of the previous example may be useful. Since we wanted to plot two functions simultaneously, we supplied them to `Plot` in the form of a list with two entries: `{2 Exp[-x^2], Sin[x]}`. The second argument `{x,-3,3}` is just the normal range of x-values over which the function is to be plotted. To distinguish the two graphs from each other, we used the `PlotStyle` option to generate different line styles: For the Gaussian function, we selected an unbroken line of thickness 0.007 (slightly thicker than the default value); for the sine wave, we used a dashing line with equally spaced black and white marks. The `FontForm` command allowed us to display the plot label in bold-faced type, rather than in the plain default setting. A useful trick is to add, as shown in the code, a newline command `\n` at the end of the title. The default positioning, in our view, leaves the title rather close to the plot, and the dummy extra line gives the title an appropriate position. Setting `GridLines` to `Automatic` told *Mathematica* to superimpose a grid on the graph, using its own discretion to determine the quantity and positioning of the grid lines. We chose to display the entire graph on a light-gray background (`GrayLevel[0]` = black, `GrayLevel[1]` = white), and we chose a plot range of $-3 < x < 3$, $-1.5 < y < 2.5$. Finally, we have overridden the automatic tick marks on the x-axis and forced marks at $x = -3, -1.5, 1.5$, and 3. We allowed *Mathematica* to determine the positioning of the ticks on the y-axis. We will discuss the use of `PlotRange` and `PlotRegion` in Section 4.2.2.

For a complete exposition of the options available, consult S. Wolfram's book [27] or investigate `Options[Plot]`. Many of the options will emerge during our discussion of `ListPlot` in Section 4.2.

4.2 Plotting Data

Since data are stored in lists in *Mathematica*, the function used to plot data is called `ListPlot`.

4.2.1 Creation of a Default Plot

In this example, we generate a list of the first ten cubes and then plot them on a graph:

```
In[3]:=   cubedata = Table[i^3,{i,1,10}]
```

```
Out[3]=   {1, 8, 27, 64, 125, 216, 343, 512, 729, 1000}
```

```
In[4]:=   ListPlot[cubedata]
```

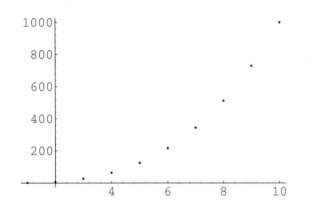

4.2.2 Customization of the Output

`ListPlot` has the same set of options as does `Plot`, so we have a great deal of control over the presentation of the output:

```
In[5]:=   pretty =
          ListPlot[cubedata,
                  PlotLabel -> FontForm["The Cubes\n",{"Helvetica-Bold",14}],
                  Background -> GrayLevel[0.8], PlotStyle -> PointSize[0.04],
                  PlotRange -> {-50, 1050},
                  PlotRegion -> {{0.05, 0.95}, {0.05, 0.95}},
                  GridLines -> {{1,2,3,4,5,6,7,8,9,10}, Automatic},
                  AxesOrigin -> {1,0},
                  AxesLabel -> {FontForm["n",{"Courier-Bold",10}],
                              FontForm["n^3",{"Courier-Bold",10}]}]
```

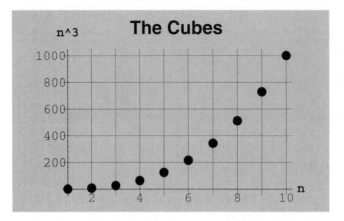

We have given the plot the name pretty because we want to use it again in Section 4.2.3. We have used several options to create pretty. Probably the most useful option here is PlotStyle -> PointSize[0.04], which has produced points larger than the default size (which is small when you have only a small data set). If you use this option, you will see that points near the edge of the plot range can be clipped. You can overcome this problem by expanding the PlotRange slightly. If you use a colored background, you may also find that your plot is uncomfortably close to the edge of the colored region. The PlotRegion setting allows you to control the proportion of the background that is taken up by the actual plot. The full region has the default setting PlotRange -> {{0, 1}, {0, 1}}, and we have compressed the plot slightly to give a reasonable border. Note that we have again added a newline command to the title. A discussion of the other options was given in Section 4.1.

4.2.3 Creation of Line Plots from Data

It is frequently useful to join the data points with lines. Again, there is an option to achieve this effect:

In[6]:=   ListPlot[cubedata, PlotJoined -> True, PlotStyle -> Thickness[0.008]]

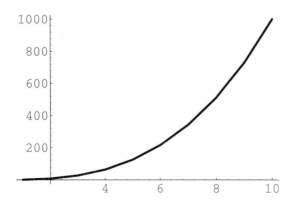

We can superimpose this line on top of the pretty picture using the Show command:

In[7]:= `Show[pretty,%, PlotRange -> {{0.75, 10.25}, {-50, 1050}}]`

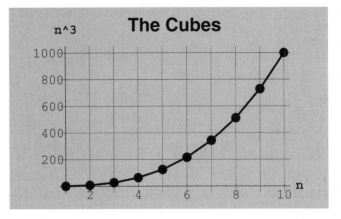

The order of the arguments given to this Show command is important. If we had typed Show[%, pretty], all the custom tailoring would have been lost. *Mathematica* pulls this information out of the first graphics object in the Show command.

4.2.4 Plotting Several Data Sets Simultaneously

Suppose that we generate a second set of data:

In[8]:= `gaussdata = Table[ N[1000 Exp[-i/5]] ,{i,1,10}]`

Out[8]= `{818.731, 670.32, 548.812, 449.329, 367.879, 301.194, 246.597, 201.897, 165.299, 135.335}`

How is it possible to display these data at the same time as the text data? Unlike in Plot, there is no facility within ListPlot to display multiple graphs (this failure is one of those rare asymmetries that we mentioned in the introduction to this chapter):

In[9]:= `ListPlot[{cubedata,gaussdata}]`

```
ListPlot::lpn:
    {{1, 8, 27, 64, 125, 216, 343, 512, 729, 1000}, <<1>>}
      is not a list of numbers or pairs of numbers.
```

Out[9]= `ListPlot[{{1, 8, 27, 64, 125, 216, 343, 512, 729, 1000},`
`          {818.731, 670.32, 548.812, 449.329, 367.879, 301.194, 246.597,`
`          201.897, 165.299, 135.335}}]`

There are two ways to solve this problem. The first involves plotting the data sets individually (we have turned off the output for this stage) and then showing them simultaneously (remembering to switch the display back on):

In[10]:= `pic1 = ListPlot[cubedata, PlotStyle -> PointSize[0.02],`
`                  DisplayFunction -> Identity];`

```
In[11]:=  pic2 = ListPlot[gaussdata, PlotStyle -> PointSize[0.04],
                          DisplayFunction -> Identity];
In[12]:=  Show[pic1,pic2,DisplayFunction -> $DisplayFunction]
```

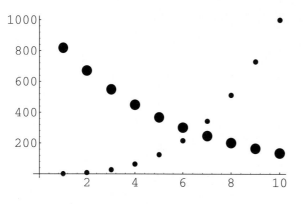

A second and much better method is to use the MultipleListPlot package:

```
In[13]:=  Needs["Graphics`MultipleListPlot`"]
In[14]:=  MultipleListPlot[cubedata,gaussdata, PlotJoined -> True]
```

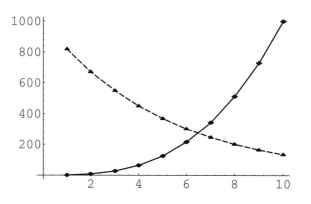

This plot is visually much better than the previous one. *Mathematica* has displayed both the points and the lines for each data set and has used different point and line styles to distinguish the two. Of course, you are free to choose the styles yourself: All the relevant information is contained in the Wolfram Research report "Guide to Standard *Mathematica* Packages" [25]. We shall return to the use of MultipleListPlot in Section 4.3.3, when we discuss the addition of legends in conjunction with the use of line styles.

4.2.5 Paired Data

Thus far, we have plotted one-dimensional lists of data. Under such circumstances, *Mathematica* gives each point an x-value equal to its position in the list. Your data may come in the form of $\{x, y\}$ pairs. You can also use `ListPlot` on such lists:

In[15]:= `xydata = {{0,1},{1.5,3},{3,2},{4,4},{7,1}};`

In[16]:= `ListPlot[xydata,PlotStyle -> PointSize[0.04], PlotRange -> {0, 5}]`

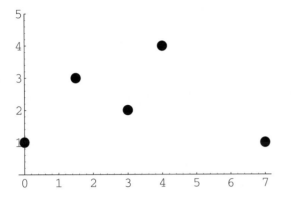

Data with errors

In experimental sciences, an individual datum frequently has three numbers associated it: an x-value and a y-value and the error in the y-value. There is a facility for displaying such data sets in the `Graphics` package:

In[17]:= `Needs["Graphics`Graphics`"];`
`datawitherrors = {{0,1,1},{1.5,3,1.3},{3,2,0.5},{4,4,1},{7,1,1.5}};`
`ErrorListPlot[datawitherrors]`

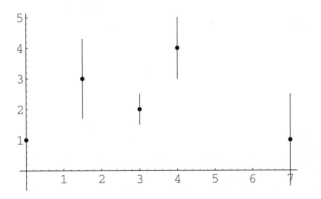

Unfortunately, the usual options available with the family of `Plot` functions are not currently available with `ErrorListPlot`. You can overcome this deficiency by using `Show` with two graphs, with and without the error bars, or by using overlay primitives with `Epilog`.

4.3 Labeling Graphs

Your plots will probably need labeling with additional information. In this section, we consider the most common requirements.

4.3.1 Simple Text Labels

We have already used *Mathematica* to include axis labels on graphs and to give a graph an overall title. Here we describe how to position a general text label on a graph. Consider the following data:

```
In[18]:=    nearlylineardata = {{1,1},{2,2},{3,3},{4,9},{5,5},{6,6}};
            ListPlot[nearlylineardata, PlotStyle -> PointSize[0.04],
            PlotRange -> {0, 10}]
```

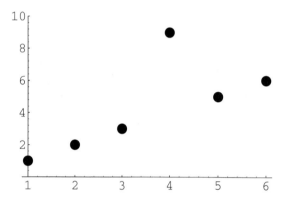

One of the data points is clearly off the main trend, so we might like to label it as such. We can create a text label containing the string "Bad Point ->" and place it at a suitable coordinate. The coordinates of the odd point are {3.7, 9}. We can use the offset {1, 0} to arrange that the text be positioned with its right end at {3.7, 9}:

```
In[19]:=    bad = Text["Bad Point ->  ",{3.7, 9}, {1, 0}];
```

We then include this graphical element as an Epilog to the plot. The arguments to Epilog take the form of graphics primitives. In Sections 4.6 and 4.7, we shall give some other examples of how to use primitives such as Text, Point, and Line, either on their own or in conjunction with ListPlot. For now, you need only appreciate that Text is a primitive to which you supply an expression with coordinates for its position, together with optional offset and direction parameters. We generally prefer to leave the direction as horizontal, which is the default, because that is more readable. We shall introduce other graphics primitives, in the context of Epilog, as we proceed. Here is our first use of Epilog:

```
In[20]:=    ListPlot[nearlylineardata,
            PlotStyle -> PointSize[0.04], Epilog -> bad]
```

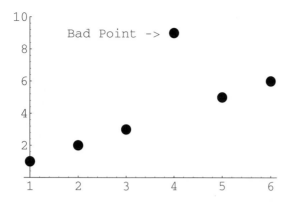

4.3.2 Greek Letters

We can use the Text primitive described in Section 4.3.1 to position text in many different typefaces, including Greek characters. If you use Text in conjunction with other primitives, such as Line, you can build up more complicated Epilogs. In the following example, we build up a fraction with Greek letters as the legend. The Line primitive takes as its argument a list of $\{x, y\}$ pairs, when applied in two-dimensional plots:

```
In[21]:=  Plot[2(1-x)/(1+x),{x,0,5},
          AxesLabel -> {FontForm["x",{"Symbol",10}],""},
          Epilog -> {Text[FontForm["2(1-x)",{"Symbol",10}],{4,1.6}],
          Text[FontForm["(1+x)",{"Symbol",10}],{4.08,1.1}],
          Line[{{3.8,1.35},{4.3,1.35}}], Line[{{3.0,1.35},{3.4,1.35}}]}]
```

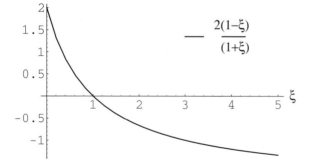

Warning: This example will not work if your computer does not support the symbolic font set.

Unfortunately, positioning labels such as this one is a matter of trial and error. If your axis labels must contain a mixture of Greek and normal text, you have to use this method, and not the AxesLabel option. Alternatively, you can export the graphics to a standard drawing package and include the labels from there (see Chapter 7).

4.3.3 Legends

The package `Graphics`Legend`` enables you to include a legend on a graph. It may take you a while to get used to this package, but it is capable of delivering most standard legends. This package is most definitely not symmetrical in the way it can be used with `Plot` and `ListPlot`. Its operation takes a simple form with `Plot` as applied to functions, as we shall explain. Its operation with `ListPlot`, in our view, is considerably more involved: This area is one where a strong case can be made for converting your data into functions so that you can make use of the simple form of legend.

We shall first explain the package's use with `Plot`. Then we shall consider data in the form of two lists, converting them to a pair of functions and using `Plot` again. We shall introduce the general form of the legend operation by looking at a `ParametricPlot` involving parametric functions. Then we shall show how to use `MultipleListPlot` with the `Legend` package. Those of you who have used point-and-click plotting packages may possibly find these operations rather involved. However, they are well worth the effort — first, because graphics should be properly labeled, and second, because this system is capable of generating interesting and eye-catching special effects. We shall illustrate this second property later by using a well-known historic data set (see Section 4.7).

Let's load the `Legend` package and construct a plot of two functions complete with legend. The operation of this package with `Plot` is very simple since the package merely adds some extra options to `Plot`. If we supply just a list of strings to the new option `PlotLegend`, then a default legend is created with the strings attached to the line styles that we have created.

```
In[22]:=  Needs["Graphics`Legend`"]

In[23]:=  Plot[{4 Exp[-x^2],3(1-x^2)},{x,-1,1},
              PlotRange -> {Automatic,{-4,4}},
              PlotStyle -> {AbsoluteThickness[1],
              {AbsoluteThickness[0.5], AbsoluteDashing[{4,4}]}},
              PlotLegend -> {"Theory","Expt"}]
```

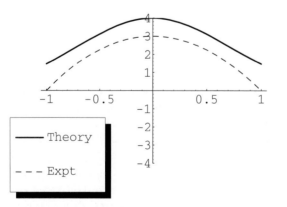

Warning: When setting plot attributes, such as line thickness or dashing, to be used in conjunction with the Legend package, it is vital that you use absolute values. Otherwise, the attributes given in the legend box will not match up with those on the main part of your plot. The units for absolute measures are printers' points — that is, 1/72 inch or one dot width on a typical monitor. Failure to observe this rule can lead to great frustration — the legend just will not look correct.

Now we consider a pair of data sets. Note that these data are created in numerical form. We then create two functions corresponding to interpolated forms of each data set and use Plot to view them. This time, we add a few more options to the legend in order to control both the position and the appearance of the legend:

```
In[24]:=  dataone = Table[N[{2 Pi i/20, Sin[2 Pi i/20]}], {i, 0, 40}];
          datatwo = Table[N[{2 Pi i/20, Cos[2 Pi i/20]}], {i, 0, 40}];

In[25]:=  fnone = Interpolation[dataone];
          fntwo = Interpolation[datatwo];

In[26]:=  Plot[{fnone[x], fntwo[x]}, {x, 0, 4 Pi},
            PlotStyle -> {
              {AbsoluteThickness[1], RGBColor[0, 0, 1]},
              {AbsoluteThickness[1], AbsoluteDashing[{4,4}]}},
            PlotLegend -> {" Sindata"," Cosdata"},
            LegendPosition -> {1.2, 0},
            LegendShadow -> {0, 0},
            LegendSize -> {1, 0.5},
            LegendLabel -> FontForm["Key", {"Helvetica",12}]]
```

The most important parts of these settings determine the position and size of the legend. You must understand that they use a coordinate system unrelated to the coordinates of the data that you are plotting. The coordinate system used is such that the center of the main graphic is at {0, 0} and the longest side of the graphic runs from −1 to +1. The LegendPosition relates to the bottom left corner of the legend box. Thus, to place the legend to the right of the main graphic, with its lower edge on the central horizontal line through the graphic, we used the coordinates {1.2, 0}. The rest of the options control the offset of the shadow box, the overall size of the legend box (in the same coordinates), and the type style of the legend title.

Note also the use of `AbsoluteThickness` and `AbsoluteDashing` to force the lines within the legend to have *precisely* the same attributes as those within the main plot.

Remember that the simple form of legend works only for `Plot`. There are other routines for plotting functions, and for these you must use the more general `ShowLegend` function. `ShowLegend` takes the form `ShowLegend[Plot, Legend Prescription]`. To stop the graphic from being drawn twice, we use `DisplayFunction -> Identity`, within the `Plot`, to suppress the plot from being drawn first without the legend.

As an example, we show the use of `ShowLegend` with `ParametricPlot`:

```
In[27]:=  ShowLegend[
            ParametricPlot[{{s, s^2}, {Sin[s], Sin[2 s]}}, {s, -2 Pi, 2 Pi},
              PlotStyle -> {{AbsoluteThickness[1]},
              {AbsoluteThickness[2], RGBColor[1, 0, 0]}}},
              DisplayFunction -> Identity],
            {{{Graphics[{AbsoluteThickness[1],
                      Line[{{-0.05, 0}, {0.05,0}}]}], " y = x^2"},
              {Graphics[{AbsoluteThickness[2], RGBColor[1, 0, 0],
                      Line[{{-0.05, 0}, {0.05,0}}]}], "BowTie"}},
            LegendPosition -> {0.7, 0.15}}]
```

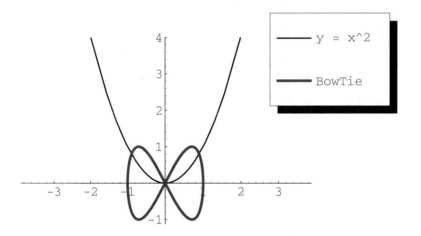

`LegendPrescription` has the syntax {{{*primitives, text*}, . . .{*primitives, text*}}, *Options*}: In our example, we have given just two lists of the form {*primitives, text*}, with one option relating to `LegendPosition`. Our earlier remarks about coordinate systems apply equally here.

One deficiency of this last sequence of commands is that we have duplicated entries. There is the flexibility, if you need it, to put independent graphics information in the legend; in most cases, however, you will probably want the exact same styles of line. Let's make a standard set of styles suitable for plots of up to four data sets. We are not necessarily saying these styles are the most appropriate or tasteful! Note the use of `AbsoluteDashing` and `AbsoluteThickness`. If you try to use `Thickness` and `Dashing`, the fact that they are relative variables will cause irritating discrepancies between your plot and your legend.

We have also automated the creation of the legend from your text strings by the use of our `makelegend` function. If there are more variables than styles, the styles are used periodically. In what follows, we show the use of our standard styles and lines in semiautomatic fashion, followed by their use with the `makelegend` function. We have suppressed the output in the first case:

```
In[28]:=  stdstyles = {{AbsoluteThickness[1]},
          {AbsoluteDashing[{5, 5, 5, 5}], AbsoluteThickness[1]},
          {RGBColor[1, 0, 0], AbsoluteThickness[1]},
          {RGBColor[0, 0, 1], AbsoluteThickness[1]}};
          stdline = Line[{{-1, 0}, {1,0}}];
```

```
In[29]:=  makelegend[data_List, styles_List, line_] :=
          Module[{len, baseprims, outlist},
          len = Length[data];
          lenstyles = Length[styles];
          baseprims = Map[Graphics, Map[Append[#, stdline]&, stdstyles]];
          outlist = {};
          Do[outlist = Append[outlist, {baseprims[[1]], data[[i]]}];
          baseprims = RotateLeft[baseprims],
          {i, 1, len}];
          outlist]
```

Here is the semiautomatic form:

```
In[30]:=  ShowLegend[
              ParametricPlot[{{Sin[s], Sin[2 s]}, {Sin[s], Sin[3 s]},
              {Sin[s], Sin[4 s]}, {Sin[s], Sin[5 s]}},
              {s, - Pi/2,  Pi/2},
              PlotStyle -> stdstyles,
              DisplayFunction -> Identity],
          {{{Graphics[{stdstyles[[1, 1]], stdline}], " Sin[2 s]"},
          {Graphics[{stdstyles[[2, 1]], stdline}], " Sin[3 s]"},
          {Graphics[{stdstyles[[3, 1]], stdstyles[[3, 2]], stdline}], " Sin[4 s]"},
          {Graphics[{stdstyles[[4, 1]], stdstyles[[4, 2]], stdline}], " Sin[5 s]"}},
          LegendPosition -> {1.2, -0.3},
          LegendSize -> {0.7, 0.6}}]
```

Here is the automatic form:

```
In[31]:=  ShowLegend[
            ParametricPlot[{{Sin[s], Sin[2 s]}, {Sin[s], Sin[3 s]},
            {Sin[s], Sin[4 s]},{Sin[s], Sin[5 s]}},
            {s, - Pi/2,  Pi/2},
            PlotStyle -> stdstyles,
            DisplayFunction -> Identity],
            {makelegend[{"Sin[2 s]", "Sin[3 s]", "Sin[4 s]", "Sin[5 s]"},
            stdstyles, stdline],
            LegendPosition -> {1.2, -0.3},
            LegendSize -> {0.7, 0.6}}]
```

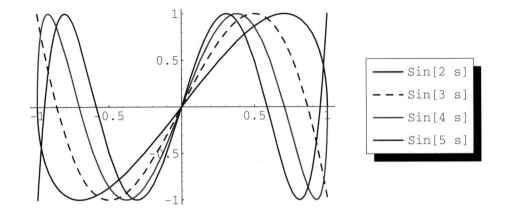

Combining MultipleListPlot and Legend

One of the more important tasks in data visualization is to take several data series and to produce a single properly labeled plot containing all the series. The tools for doing this task are the MultipleListPlot and Legend packages used together. We begin by reloading the MultipleListPlot package and by re-creating the data we used earlier in our first look at MultipleListPlot. In our view, the easiest way of using these packages together is to create afresh standard dot shapes and line styles as primitives and to use a variant of the package's MakeSymbol option to create the appropriate point styles:

In[32]:=
```
Needs["Graphics`MultipleListPlot`"];
gaussdata = Table[ N[1000 Exp[-i/5]] ,{i,1,10}];
cubedata = Table[i^3,{i,1,10}];
```

We have found that the MultipleListPlot package does not support the setting of attributes in plot symbols since the standard function MakeSymbol does not appear to be able to cope with attributes. If you wish to use MultipleListPlot with the Legend package, you will find this frustrating. The most economical solution that we have found to this problem is to use the following variant of the MakeSymbol command. This allows you to add attributes to the Line primitives that are being used, and it defaults to a fine line of AbsoluteThickness[0.1]:

In[33]:=
```
NewMakeSymbol[{a_, Line[x_]}] :=
    Module[{yugh, y}, y = Line[(Scaled[#1, yugh] & ) /@ x];
      y = y /. yugh -> #1; Evaluate[{a, y}]&]

NewMakeSymbol[Line[x_]] :=
NewMakeSymbol[{AbsoluteThickness[0.1], Line[x]}]
```

In[34]:=
```
diamond = RegularPolygon[4, 0.02];
star = RegularPolygon[5, 0.02, {0, 0}, 0, 2];
```

First we plot the graph without the legend (note the use of NewMakeSymbol):

In[35]:=
```
MultipleListPlot[gaussdata, cubedata,
DotShapes -> {NewMakeSymbol[diamond], NewMakeSymbol[star]}]
```

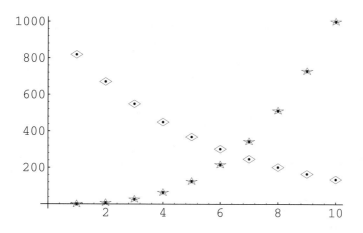

Now we plot it with the legend added by use of ShowLegend:

In[36]:= ```
ShowLegend[
  MultipleListPlot[gaussdata, cubedata,
    DotShapes -> {NewMakeSymbol[diamond], NewMakeSymbol[star]},
    DisplayFunction -> Identity],
  {{{Graphics[diamond], " gaussdata"},
  {Graphics[star], " cubedata"}},
  LegendPosition -> {1.2, -0.25}}]
```

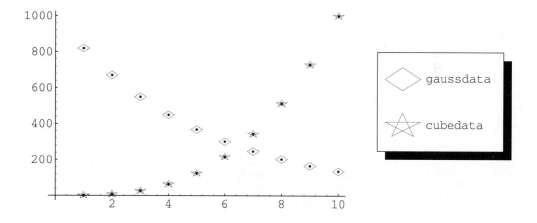

## 4.3.4 Changing the TickMarks in a ListPlot

When *Mathematica* plots a one-dimensional set of data, it allocates an *x*-value to each data point, corresponding to that data point's position in the list. It is this number that appears on the horizontal axis, and it may be far from ideal. If the data represent monthly figures, it is much more informative to label the axis by the initials of the month:
```

```
In[37]:=  ListPlot[{1,3,2,3,2,4},
                  Ticks -> { {{1,"Jan"},{2,"Feb"},{3,"Mar"},{4,"Apr"},
                             {5,"May"}},Automatic},
                  PlotStyle -> PointSize[0.03],
                  PlotRange -> {{0,5},Automatic},
                  PlotLabel -> "Monthly Figures"
                  ]
```

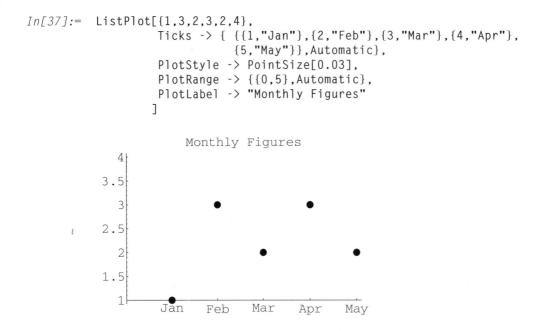

4.4 Creating Bar Charts and Pie Charts

In Version 2.1 of *Mathematica*, the facilities for drawing bar charts and pie charts have been extended greatly. We consider the two in turn.

4.4.1 Bar Charts

The command to draw bar charts is stored in the Graphics package:

```
In[38]:=  Needs["Graphics`Graphics`"]
```

The simplest operation that we can perform is to display a list of data:

```
In[39]:=  BarChart[{1,4,3,4,2}]
```

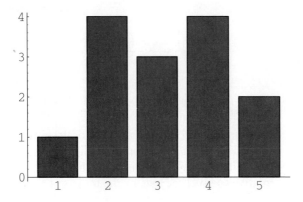

As usual, a multitude of facilities exist for customizing the output to your liking. The following example makes use of just a few of these facilities:

```
In[40]:=  barshading[x_] := GrayLevel[x/5]

In[41]:=  BarChart[{3,2,4,2,1,5,4,2,3},
              BarLabels -> {"J","F","M","A","M","J","J","A","S"},
              BarStyle -> barshading,
              BarSpacing -> -0.2,
              Background -> GrayLevel[0.9],
              PlotLabel -> FontForm["Monthly Data\n",
                                    {"Helvetica-Bold",12}],
              PlotRegion -> {{0.05, 0.95}, {0.05, 0.95}}  ]
```

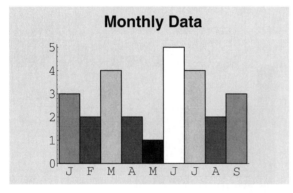

Several of the options that we have used here are the same as those for the Plot function. We have overridden the default numbering of the x-axis with the initial letters of the relevant months and have inserted a negative space between the bars to make them line up with one another. The shading of the bars is determined by the barshading function operating on their height.

Grouped data

Consider the following file of grouped data:

```
In[42]:=  !!companydata
```

Year	Company A	Company B	Company C
1990	100000	200000	150000
1991	130000	150000	160000
1992	200000	170000	150000
1993	220000	180000	130000

Using the techniques developed in Chapter 2, we can read in this data as the following list:

```
In[43]:=   companydata = {{"Year","Company A","Company B","Company C"},
                          {1990,100000,200000,150000},
                          {1991,130000,150000,160000},
                          {1992,200000,170000,150000},
                          {1993,220000,180000,130000}};
```

The data are clearly grouped, and we would like our bar chart to reflect this fact. In the first instance, we shall group the data by year. The syntax for displaying grouped data is BarChart[{data1},{data2}...], which is unfortunate since we would like to use the function in the form BarChart[{{data1},{data2}...}]. We do so by defining a new function:

```
In[44]:=   ourbarchart[{x___},opts___] := BarChart[x,opts]
```

```
In[45]:=   ourbarchart[Map[Rest,Rest[companydata]],
                   BarStyle -> Table[GrayLevel[x/3],{x,0,3}],
                   BarLabels -> Rest[companydata[[1]] ]    ]
```

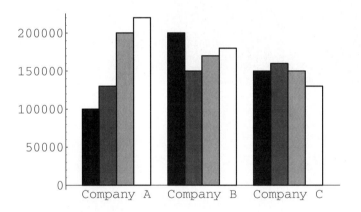

Alternatively, by simply transposing the data list, we can use exactly the same command to group the data by year. We have also included a key to the shading:

```
In[46]:=   transposedata = Transpose[companydata]
```

```
Out[46]=   {{Year, 1990, 1991, 1992, 1993},
            {Company A, 100000, 130000, 200000, 220000},
            {Company B, 200000, 150000, 170000, 180000},
            {Company C, 150000, 160000, 150000, 130000}}
```

```
In[47]:=   key = {Text["Company A",{7,150000}],
                  Text["Company B",{7,130000}],
                  Text["Company C",{7,110000}],
                  {GrayLevel[0],Rectangle[{5.6,145000},{5.9,155000}]},
                  {GrayLevel[1/3],Rectangle[{5.6,125000},{5.9,135000}]},
                  {GrayLevel[2/3],Rectangle[{5.6,105000},{5.9,115000}]} };
```

```
In[48]:=  ourbarchart[Map[Rest,Rest[transposedata]],
              BarStyle -> Table[GrayLevel[x/3],{x,0,2}],
              BarLabels -> Rest[transposedata[[1]] ],
              Epilog -> key, PlotRange -> {{0,8},Automatic}]
```

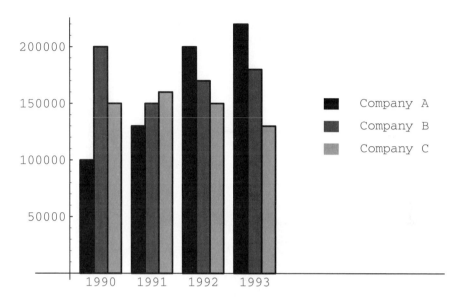

The Epilog facility, as well as graphics primitives such as the rectangles in the previous example, are described in more detail in Chapter 5 and Section 4.6, respectively.

4.4.2 Pie Charts

The functions for displaying pie charts are also stored in Graphics`Graphics`. Simple pie charts are easy to create:

```
In[49]:=  PieChart[{1,2,2,3}]
```

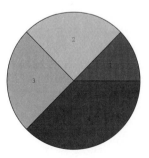

We can produce some interesting visualization effects with minimal effort. For instance, we define here a function that operates on the company data we used earlier and shows the market breakdown by company for a given year (we have chosen to highlight Company A's share by exploding the slice):

```
In[50]:=  market[year_Integer] := PieChart[
            Rest[Select[companydata,#[[1]] == year &][[1]] ],
            PieExploded -> {1},
            PieLabels -> Map[FontForm[#,{"Helvetica-Bold",12}]&,{"A","B","C"}],
            PieStyle -> {GrayLevel[0.4],GrayLevel[0.6],GrayLevel[0.8]},
            PlotLabel -> FontForm[ToString[year], {"Helvetica-Bold",12}],
            DisplayFunction -> Identity]
```

Now we can produce an array of pie charts:

```
In[51]:=  Show[GraphicsArray[Partition[Table[market[year],{year,1990,1993}],2]],
            DisplayFunction -> $DisplayFunction]
```

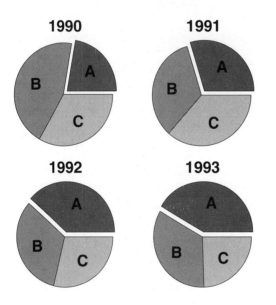

4.5 Including Insets in Graphs

In Section 4.4, we described how to define your own visualization tools using basic graphics primitives. You can also use these primitives to place an inset in a graph. In this section, we generate experimental data whose visualization could benefit from such an inset, which we then supply.

4.5.1 Generating Experimental Data

Here we generate data that are the sum of two peaked functions with added noise:

```
In[52]:=  exptdata = Table[{x,1/((x-10)^2 + 0.1) + 1/((x-13)^2+0.5)
                    + 0.3 Random[]}, {x,0,20,0.1}];
```

```
In[53]:=  maingraph =
          ListPlot[exptdata, PlotJoined -> True, PlotRange -> All,
           PlotLabel -> FontForm["Spectral Data - main peak subtracted in inset\n",
           {"Helvetica-Bold",10}], Background -> GrayLevel[0.8],
           PlotRegion -> {{0.05, 0.95}, {0.05, 0.95}}]
```

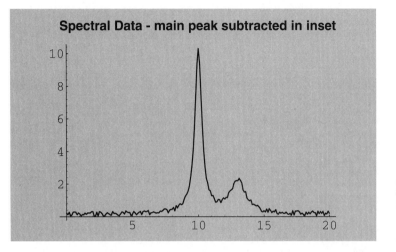

Suppose that we are interested in the smaller peak. By using a suitable fitting procedure, we can subtract out the larger peak:

```
In[54]:=  smallpeak = Map[{#[[1]],#[[2]] - 1/((#[[1]]-10)^2+0.1)}&,
                       exptdata];
```

```
In[55]:=  ListPlot[smallpeak, PlotJoined -> True, PlotRange -> All]
```

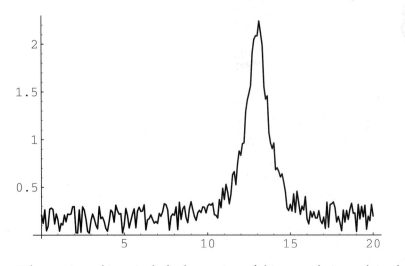

What we intend is to include the portion of this second picture lying between $x = 10$ and $x = 16$ as an inset in the first graph.

4.5.2 Drawing Your Own Graph!

First we extract from the `smallpeak` data list the items that we want to plot:

In[56]:=   `insetdat = Take[smallpeak,{101,161}];`

We can plot them using `ListPlot`:

In[57]:=   `insetgraph = ListPlot[insetdat, PlotJoined -> True,`
`DefaultFont -> {"Courier", 8}, Frame -> True]`

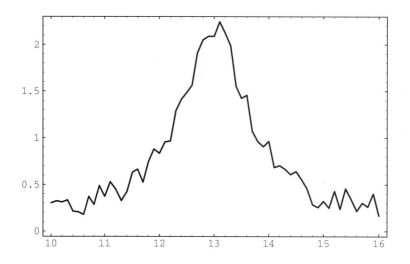

In[58]:=   `Show[Graphics[{Rectangle[{0,0}, {1, 1}, maingraph],`
`Rectangle[{0.6,0.4}, {0.9, 0.9}, insetgraph]} ]]`

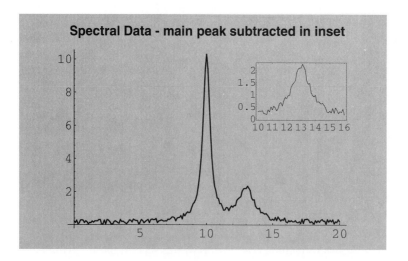

4.6 Building Your Own Visualization Tools

In this section, we explore the use of graphics primitives to build up a custom plot.

4.6.1 Limits to *Mathematica*'s Built-in Functions

Inevitably, there is a limit to what you can achieve using *Mathematica*'s own plotting functions. If necessary, you can write your own functions that make use of *graphics primitives*, which are simple graphical objects such as straight lines and rectangles. Let's consider an example to demonstrate their use.

We have the following data file containing information on GDP growth rates for various South American countries, averaged over the years 1965 to 1980 and 1980 to 1988:

```
In[59]:=   !!SouthAmerica.dat
           COUNTRY    1965-1980   1980-1988

           Argentina     3.5         -0.9
           Bolivia       4.5         -1.1
           Brazil        9.0          2.4
           Chile         1.9          2.1
           Colombia      5.6          3.3
           Ecuador       8.7          2.0
           Paraguay      6.9          2.5
           Peru          3.9          0.7
           Uruguay       2.4         -0.5
           Venezuela     3.7          0.9
```

It would be useful if we could plot the data for each country as a bar chart on a map of South America. It is not a surprise to find that there is no built-in function that achieves this purpose, so we shall have to make our own. We do not have to start exactly from square 1 because there is a package to draw maps of countries. First, we need to read this package into *Mathematica*:

```
In[60]:=   Needs["Miscellaneous`WorldPlot`"]
```

```
In[61]:=   southamerica = WorldPlot[SouthAmerica, WorldToGraphics -> True]
```

By using the option WorldToGraphics -> True, we have forced *Mathematica* to produce a conventional Graphics output rather than the default type, which is called World-Graphics for this function. This forced conversion will allow us to superimpose our own graphics primitives on the output.

4.6.2 Graphics Primitives

Mathematica produced the map in Section 4.6.1 by using a set of polygon primitives. We can create a single simple polygon as follows:

In[62]:=   `Show[Graphics[ Polygon[{{0,0},{2,0},{4,2},{-2,2},{0,0}}]]]`

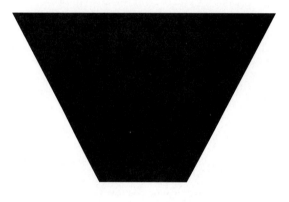

We can change the shading by specifying a GrayLevel of a value between 0 and 1 (0 = black, 1 = white). To draw just the outline of the polygon, we can use the Line function:

In[63]:=   `Show[Graphics[Line[{{0,0},{2,0},{4,2},{-2,2},{0,0}}]]]`

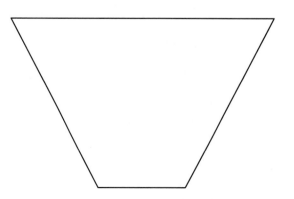

To create the picture of South America, *Mathematica* has converted the outline of each country into a rough polygon and has stored the coordinates of each vertex. Let's take a look at these data:

```
In[64]:=  WorldData["Ecuador"]
Out[64]=  {{{-202, -4820}, {-121, -4786}, {-139, -4855}, {-62, -4855},

            {86, -4729}, {86, -4729}, {-6, -4517}, {-6, -4517},

            {-300, -4742}, {-266, -4829}, {-202, -4822}}}
```

To include our data on the map, we shall create two rectangle primitives for each country and shall display them in the center of that country. Obviously, we need a function that gives us the coordinates of the center of any named country. We shall take an average of the coordinates of the vertices specifying the country — an adequate definition for most country shapes:

```
In[65]:=  Mean[x_List] := Apply[Plus,x]/Length[x];
          countrycenter[country_String] :=
           Reverse[N[Map[Mean,Transpose[WorldData[country][[1]]] ]]];
          countrycenter["Ecuador"]
Out[65]=  {-4745.55, -102.909}
```

We have reversed the result because `WorldData` is, rather unconventionally, in the form of $\{y, x\}$ pairs.

4.6.3 Placing a Bar Chart on the Map

We want to define a function that will operate on a list such as `{"Ecuador",8.7,2.0}` and that will produce a graphics primitive with two differently shaded rectangles centered on the country. The first rectangle will have a height proportional to 8.7, and the second rectangle will have a height proportional to 2.0 (it is a matter of trial and error to deduce the proportionality constant — it will depend on the range of your data values):

```
In[66]:=  rect[data_List] :=
          Module[{coords,r1,r2},
            coords = countrycenter[data[[1]] ];
            r1 = {GrayLevel[0], Rectangle[coords-{100,0},coords+{0,70 data[[2]]}]};
            r2 = {GrayLevel[0.5], Rectangle[coords,coords+{100,70 data[[3]]}]};
            Graphics[{r1,r2}] ];
          ecuador = rect[{"Ecuador",8.7,2.0}]
```

Now we can superimpose these two rectangles on the map of South America:

```
In[67]:=  Show[southamerica,ecuador]
```

It is a simple matter to include the data on all the other countries as well. First, we use the techniques of Chapter 2 to read in the file. We use the `dropread` function, as defined in Section 2.2.3:

In[68]:=   `GDPlist = dropread[2,"SouthAmerica.dat",{Word,Number,Number}]`

Out[68]= `{{Argentina, 3.5, -0.9}, {Bolivia, 4.5, -1.1},`
`{Brazil, 9., 2.4}, {Chile, 1.9, 2.1}, {Colombia, 5.6, 3.3},`
`{Ecuador, 8.7, 2.}, {Paraguay, 6.9, 2.5}, {Peru, 3.9, 0.7},`
`{Uruguay, 2.4, -0.5}, {Venezuela, 3.7, 0.9}}`

Next, we map our `rect` function onto every member of this list:

In[69]:=   `bars = Map[rect,GDPlist]`

Finally, we display this set of graphics on the map:

In[70]:=   `Show[southamerica,bars]`

Notice that the function for determining the center of a country has not worked well for Peru, whose data are spilling over into Brazil. We can easily fix this problem:

```
In[71]:=  countrycenter["Peru"]

Out[71]=  {-4406.62, -486.962}

In[72]:=  countrycenter["Peru"] = {-4500,-650}

Out[72]=  {-4500, -650}
```

4.6.4 Finishing Touches

The final touch in our map-drawing exercise is to include a key and a title, again using graphics primitives (remember to reevaluate the bars list to center the Peru data):

```
In[73]:=  key = Graphics[{
            Text["1965-1980 %",{-3200,-2800},{-1,0}],
           Text["1980-1988 %",{-3200,-3000},{-1,0}],
           {GrayLevel[0],Rectangle[{-3350,-2850},{-3250,-2750}]},
           {GrayLevel[0.5],Rectangle[{-3350,-3050},{-3250,-2950}]},
           Text[FontForm["GDP - Annual average growth rate",
               {"Courier-Bold",10}],{-5400,1400},{-1,0}]}];
          Show[{southamerica,bars,key}]
```

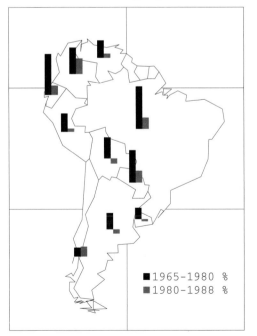

4.7 Exploring an Historic Data Set

To tie together all that we have discussed in this chapter, we shall consider a well-known data set. We wish to illustrate

1. Effective use of built-in functions
2. Effective use of the packages, when necessary
3. Effective use of graphics primitives and programming, when necessary

We shall start by giving data already in *Mathematica* format. One of the more interesting lessons of history (not learned, apparently) is the importance of the weather in conducting military campaigns in Russia. During the winter of 1812, the French army returned from Moscow. The temperature on various dates is given by the following list, each element of which has the form {{yyyy, mm, dd}, temp}. The temperature is on the Reaumur scale (on which the boiling point of water is at 80 degrees above zero on the scale and the freezing point is at zero):

```
In[74]:=  tempdata = {{{1812,10,18},  0},{{1812,10,24},  0},{{1812,11, 9}, -9},
          {{1812,11,14},-21},{{1812,11,25},-11},{{1812,11,28},-20},
          {{1812,12, 1},-24},{{1812,12, 6},-30},{{1812,12, 7},-26}};
```

4.7.1 Using Just the Built-in Functions

We can plot the temperature data tempdata as a function of observation point by extracting the temperature readings:

```
In[75]:=  temps = Map[#[[2]]&, tempdata]
```

```
Out[75]=  {0, 0, -9, -21, -11, -20, -24, -30, -26}
```

Then we use a standard ListPlot with a few options to tidy up:

```
In[76]:=  ListPlot[temps, DefaultFont -> {"Helvetica", 12}, PlotJoined -> True,
          AxesOrigin -> {1,0}, PlotRange -> {{1, 9}, {-30, 0}},
          Frame -> True, RotateLabel -> False,
          FrameLabel -> {"Observation Point", "Deg R",
          "Temperature on Napoleon's Return from Moscow", " "}]
```

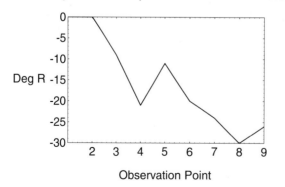

4.7.2 Adding Functionality via Packages

We can get more information into our chart if we make use of the date data to have our horizontal axis represent the time. *Mathematica* contains a calendar package that allows us to compute, for example, elapsed time:

```
In[77]:=  Needs["Miscellaneous`Calendar`"]
```

To define the dates, we first extract the dates from our combination series:

```
In[78]:=  dates = Map[#[[1]]&, tempdata]
Out[78]=  {{1812, 10, 18}, {1812, 10, 24}, {1812, 11, 9}, {1812, 11, 14},
          {1812, 11, 25}, {1812, 11, 28}, {1812, 12, 1}, {1812, 12, 6},
          {1812, 12, 7}}
```

The function that we need is `DaysBetween`, which we can use to calculate days elapsed since the army left Moscow:

```
In[79]:=  ?DaysBetween
          DaysBetween[{y1,m1,d1}, {y2,m2,d2}, cal] gives the number of days
             between the dates {y1, m1, d1} and {y2, m2, d2} in calendar cal.
             The default calendar is the usual American calendar.
In[80]:=  dayseps = Map[DaysBetween[#, dates[[1]] ]&, dates]
Out[80]=  {0, 6, 22, 27, 38, 41, 44, 49, 50}
```

We now construct a new list of pairs {*elapsed days*, *temp*}:

```
In[81]:=  plottemp = Transpose[{dayseps, temps}]
Out[81]=  {{0, 0}, {6, 0}, {22, -9}, {27, -21}, {38, -11}, {41, -20}, {44, -24},
          {49, -30}, {50, -26}}
```

Finally, we can plot `plottemp` with a more sensible *x*-axis:

```
In[82]:=  ListPlot[plottemp,
            DefaultFont -> {"Helvetica", 12},
            PlotJoined -> True,
            AxesOrigin -> {0,0},
            PlotRange -> All,
            Frame -> True,
            RotateLabel -> False,
            FrameLabel -> {"Elapsed Days", "Deg R",
            "Temperature on Napoleon's Return from Moscow", " "}]
```

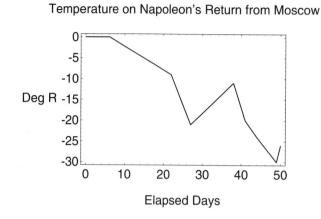

Temperature on Napoleon's Return from Moscow

4.7.3 Adding the Fate of the Army

Now we wish to fold in some information — the number of soldiers in the main column:

```
In[83]:=  armydata = {
          {{1812,10,18},100000},{{1812,10,24},  96000},
          {{1812,11, 1},  87000},{{1812,11, 4},  87000},
          {{1812,11, 4},  55000},{{1812,11, 9},  55000},
          {{1812,11, 9},  37000},{{1812,11,14},  37000},
          {{1812,11,14},  24000},{{1812,11,19},  24000},
          {{1812,11,19},  20000},{{1812,11,25},  20000},
          {{1812,11,25},  50000},{{1812,11,28},  50000},
          {{1812,11,28},  28000},{{1812,12, 6},  12000},
          {{1812,12, 7},   8000}};
```

We turn the calculation of elapsed time into a procedure, which also has the option of rescaling the data:

```
In[84]:=  Elapsify[datedata_, yscale_] :=
          Module[{dates, values, days},
          dates =  Map[#[[1]]&, datedata];
          values = Map[#[[2]]&, datedata];
          days =   Map[DaysBetween[#, dates[[1]] ]&, dates];
          Transpose[{days, values/yscale}]]
```

We can generate a new series of pairs of the form {*elapsed days, soldiers in 1000s*}:

```
In[85]:=  elapsedarmy = Elapsify[armydata, 1000]
Out[85]=  {{0, 100}, {6, 96}, {14, 87}, {17, 87}, {17, 55}, {22, 55}, {22, 37},
          {27, 37}, {27, 24}, {32, 24}, {32, 20}, {38, 20}, {38, 50}, {41, 50},
          {41, 28}, {49, 12}, {50, 8}}
```

One point you should have appreciated is that while Plot can handle a list of several functions, ListPlot cannot handle several data series. One way to solve this problem is to load the package that is designed for this case. At the same time, load the package for making legends:

In[86]:= Needs["Graphics`MultipleListPlot`"];
Needs["Graphics`Legend`"]

The MultipleListPlot package opens up some interesting possibilities. In particular, if you want, you can define your own plot symbols, which can be fun. For example, let's represent the number of soldiers by a gun image and the temperature by a snowflake. This point is a convenient one for us to take a further look at the concept of a graphics primitive.

We give data for our simple snowflake as a collection of lines in a hexagonal pattern (some experimentation or a bit of fiddling with graph paper might help you here):

In[87]:= snowflake = Line[{{0,0},{0,0.025},{0,0},{Sqrt[3]/80,0.0125},{0,0},
{Sqrt[3]/80,-0.0125},{0,0},{0,-0.025},{0,0},
{-Sqrt[3]/80,-0.0125},{0,0},{-Sqrt[3]/80, 0.0125},{0,0}}];

We also give the coordinates of a simple gun shape:

In[88]:= gundata = {{-0.0375,0.005},{0.0375,0.005},{0.0375, 0.},
{0.,0.},{0.,-0.005},{-0.0125, -0.005},
{-0.0125, 0.},{-0.0375, -0.0125},{-0.0375, 0.005}};

We rotate these coordinates by 45 degrees and make them into a graphics object:

In[89]:= gun = Line[Map[Dot[N[{{1/Sqrt[2], -1/Sqrt[2]},
{1/Sqrt[2], 1/Sqrt[2]}}], #]&, gundata]];

To see what these objects look like, we show them in a graphics environment:

In[90]:= Show[Graphics[{gun, snowflake}],
AspectRatio -> Automatic]

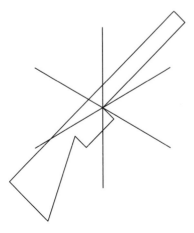

Now for the graph — note the use of NewMakeSymbol, as defined in Section 4.3.3.

```
In[91]:=   ShowLegend[
           MultipleListPlot[
             plottemp, elapsedarmy,
             DotShapes -> {NewMakeSymbol[snowflake],NewMakeSymbol[gun]},
             PlotRange -> {{-4, 55}, {-40, 120}}, PlotJoined -> True,
             LineStyles ->{{AbsoluteThickness[1], Dashing[{0.01,0.02}]},
             {AbsoluteThickness[1], Dashing[{0.01,0.01}]} },
             PlotLabel -> FontForm["Napoleon's Return from Moscow",
             {"Helvetica-Bold", 18}],
             AxesLabel -> {"Days Elapsed", " "},
             DisplayFunction -> Identity],
           {Graphics[If[#==1, snowflake, gun]]&,
           2, "Soldiers [1000s]", "Temp [Deg R]",
           LegendPosition -> {0.0, 0.15},
           LegendSize ->{1, 0.15}}]
```

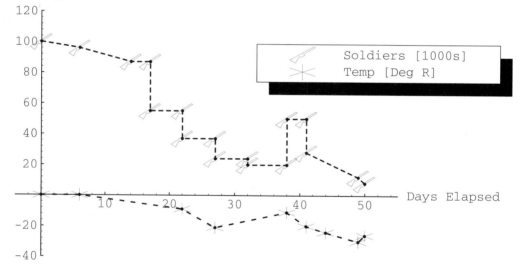

Note that MultipleListPlot does not require that you fiddle with primitives. It comes with a handy set of default line styles and symbols that you can use as is. Some charts, however, do need the power of primitives, as we shall see next.

4.7.4 Minard's Chart and Full Use of Primitives

So far, so good. In E. Tufte's book [24], there is a combination of data map and time series drawn by the French engineer Charles Joseph Minard in 1861! Can we draw a similar map with *Mathematica*? We just need to understand how to make full use of graphical primitives.

First, we define various lists giving the temperature, a title, some key cities and labels, the strength of the army, the main rivers, and so on:

```
In[92]:=   TempData = {{0.955, 0.306, 0},{0.885, 0.304, 0},{0.7, 0.259, -9},
           {0.612, 0.228, -21},{0.433, 0.177, -11},{0.372, 0.17, -20},
           {0.316, 0.201, -24}, {0.279, 0.181, -30},{0.158, 0.195, -26}};

In[93]:=   TitleData = {{0.5,0.45, "Napoleon's Russian Campaign of 1812"}};
           PointData = {{0.965,0.396, "Moscow"}};
           TextData = {{0.98, 0.085, "0"}, {0.98, 0.026, "-30"},
            {0.111, 0.1502, "R. Niemen"}, {0.37, 0.20, "R. Berezina"},
            {0.5,0.015,"Temperature in degrees Reaumur - return march"},
            {0.1, 0.22, "422,000"},{0.9, 0.38, "100,000"},{0.04, 0.175, "10,000"},
            {0.4, 0.4, "Strength of army = approximate thickness of track"},
            {0.4, 0.38, "Return marches shown in black"}};

In[94]:=   StrengthData = {
           {{0.142, 0.238, 50000, 1},{0.257, 0.331, 50000, 1},{0.312, 0.326, 50000, 1},
           {0.312, 0.326, 33000, 1},{0.392, 0.318, 33000, 0}},{{0.392, 0.318, 30000, 0},
           {0.433, 0.177, 30000, 0}},{{0.105, 0.242, 22000, 1},{0.111,0.351, 22000, 1}},
           {{0.103, 0.353, 6000, 0},{0.0916,0.193, 6000, 0}},{{0.0565, 0.23, 422000,1},
           {0.105, 0.242, 422000, 1},{0.105, 0.242, 400000, 1},{0.181, 0.234, 400000, 1},
           {0.181, 0.234, 340000, 1},{0.333, 0.273, 257000, 1},{0.476, 0.288, 175000, 1},
           {0.595, 0.250, 145000, 1},{0.704, 0.290, 136000, 1},{0.789, 0.368, 127000, 1},
           {0.84 , 0.355, 127000, 1},{0.84,  0.355, 100000, 1},{0.856, 0.349, 100000, 1},
           {0.955, 0.4  , 100000, 1}},{{0.965, 0.382,100000, 0},{0.953, 0.374, 100000, 0},
           {0.945, 0.312, 100000, 0},{0.932, 0.302,  98000, 0},{0.838, 0.326,  87000, 0},
           {0.768, 0.296,  87000, 0},{0.768, 0.296,  55000, 0},{0.7,   0.259,  55000, 0},
           {0.7  , 0.259,  37000, 0},{0.612, 0.228,  37000, 0},{0.612, 0.228,  24000, 0},
           {0.511, 0.209,  24000, 0},{0.511, 0.209,  20000, 0},{0.433, 0.177,  20000, 0},
           {0.433, 0.177,  50000, 0},{0.390, 0.162,  50000, 0},{0.380, 0.164,  50000, 0},
           {0.380, 0.164,  28000, 0},{0.316, 0.201,  22000, 0},{0.279, 0.181,  22000, 0},
           {0.248, 0.191,  14000, 0},{0.158, 0.195,   8000, 0},{0.125, 0.193,   8000, 0},
           {0.125, 0.193,   4000, 0},{0.0916,0.193,   4000, 0},{0.0916,0.193, 10000, 0},
           {0.0682,0.193, 10000, 0}}};

In[95]:=    RiverData = {{{0.39, 0.123}, {0.39, 0.131}, {0.388, 0.135}, {0.388, 0.14},
           {0.382, 0.144}, {0.382, 0.152}, {0.378, 0.156}, {0.38, 0.17}, {0.376, 0.17},
           {0.378, 0.177}, {0.374, 0.187}, {0.376, 0.195}, {0.372, 0.199}, {0.366, 0.199},
           {0.357, 0.203}, {0.349, 0.214}}, {{0.513, 0.123}, {0.513, 0.133}, {0.511, 0.138},
           {0.509, 0.15}, {0.517, 0.166}, {0.517, 0.181}, {0.509, 0.185}, {0.511, 0.195},
           {0.509, 0.199}, {0.511, 0.207}, {0.513, 0.212}, {0.522, 0.226}, {0.536, 0.23},
           {0.548, 0.23}, {0.55, 0.234}}, {{0.0702, 0.121}, {0.0712, 0.13}, {0.076, 0.134},
           {0.077, 0.142}, {0.0721, 0.148}, {0.0673, 0.153}, {0.0653, 0.156}, {0.0692,
           0.161}, {0.0721, 0.165}, {0.0712, 0.169}, {0.0692, 0.173}, {0.0692, 0.175},
           {0.0712, 0.179}, {0.076, 0.184}, {0.076, 0.191}, {0.0702, 0.202}, {0.0692,
           0.212}, {0.0682, 0.218}, {0.0624, 0.222}, {0.0575, 0.224}, {0.0546, 0.23},
           {0.0575, 0.238}, {0.0585, 0.245}, {0.0585, 0.251}, {0.0546, 0.255}, {0.0546,
           0.259}, {0.0507, 0.265}, {0.0507, 0.271}, {0.0448, 0.275}, {0.039, 0.276},
```

```
            {0.0331, 0.275}, {0.0292, 0.277}, {0.0292, 0.283}, {0.0292, 0.287}, {0.0224,
            0.286}, {0.0175, 0.281}, {0.0146, 0.278}, {0.0107, 0.278}, {0.00487, 0.278}},
          {{0.847, 0.363}, {0.847, 0.365}, {0.847, 0.371}, {0.844, 0.374}, {0.843, 0.379},
            {0.841, 0.381}, {0.833, 0.382}, {0.830, 0.383}, {0.828, 0.383}, {0.825, 0.383},
            {0.822, 0.383}, {0.821, 0.385}, {0.817, 0.386}, {0.814, 0.388}, {0.813, 0.392},
            {0.811, 0.394}, {0.809, 0.397}, {0.807, 0.4}, {0.804, 0.402}, {0.804, 0.405},
            {0.802, 0.407}, {0.798, 0.411}, {0.794, 0.415}}};
```

In[96]:=   ```
          BoxData = {{{0, 0.121},{1.05, 0.121},{1.05, 0}, {0, 0}, {0, 0.121}},
          {{0, 0.121}, {1.05, 0.121}, {1.05, 0.474}, {0, 0.474}, {0, 0.121}}};
          ```

Next, we enlist help from the ghost of Minard by loading a package:

*In[97]:=*   ```
          Needs["Minard`"]
          ```

What is `Minard` in *Mathematica*?

In[98]:=   ```
          ?Minard
          ```

```
          Minard.m is a package for producing thematic maps in the style of C. J. Minard
```

We have defined the following function using standard *Mathematica* conventions!

In[99]:=   ```
          NapoleonicMarchOnMoscowAndBackAgainPlot[StrengthData, TempData,
            RiverData, BoxData, TitleData, PointData, TextData]
          ```

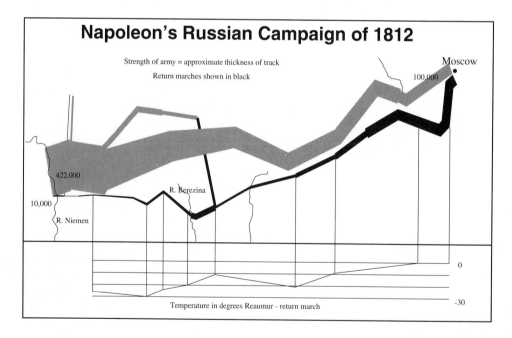

The `Minard` package is listed after the summary for this chapter. In each case, we map suitable primitives onto data sets; the production of the track of the army is a little more subtle since it is necessary to join up polygons without gaps. Depending on your Postscript interpreter and screen renderer, you may need to modify the font names to obtain good results (for printed output we find modifying "Times" to "Times-Roman" helps).

4.8 Summary

In this chapter, we have explained how to use *Mathematica* to produce a variety of plots. When producing a plot, you should first see whether you can achieve your goal by using standard *Mathematica* kernel functions such as Plot, ListPlot, and their relatives. Do not forget to exploit the generic symmetry between Plot and ListPlot operations and to take advantage of the host of options that can be revealed by using the Options command. If you cannot achieve the desired results with standard goals using kernel functions, remember that there are many packages that add common requirements. In particular, you will find that the Graphics`Graphics`, Graphics`Legend`, and Graphics`MultipleListPlot` packages solve most standard problems. If all else fails, you can build up any graphic you want by using primitives such as Point, Line, Polygon, and Text in a Show[Graphics[...primitives]] construction.

Listing of Minard Package

```
BeginPackage["Minard`"]

Minard::usage = "Minard.m is a package for producing thematic maps
in the style of C. J. Minard"

ProcessTemp::usage = "ProcessTemp[list] computes the graphics primitives to be
associated with a list of elements of the form {x, y, temp}"

stuff::usage = "stuff[list] computes the
graphics primitives to be associated with a list of elements of the form {x, y,
strength}"

ProcessStrength::usage = "ProcessStrength[list] computes the graphics primitives
to be associated with a list of elements of the form {{x1, y1, strength1},... ...,
{xn, yn, strengthn}}"

ProcessRivers::usage = "ProcessRivers[list] computes the graphics primitives to
be associated with a list of river coordinates"

ProcessPoints::usage = "ProcessPoints[list] computes the graphics primitives to
be associated with a list of city or other point coordinates"

ProcessTitle::usage = "ProcessTitle[location, title] computes the graphics
primitives to be associated with the title"

ProcessBoxes::usage = "ProcessBoxes[list] computes the graphics primitives to be
associated with a list of box coordinates"

ProcessText::usage = "ProcessText[list] computes the graphics primitives to be
associated with a list of coordinates and associated text"

NapoleonicMarchOnMoscowAndBackAgainPlot::usage =
"NapoleonicMarchOnMoscowAndBackAgainPlot[strengthlist, templist,
riverdatalist, boxdatalist, titledatalist, pointdatalist, textdatalist]
```

shows the thematic chart associated with the strength temperature, river, box,
title, point and text lists, in the style of C. J. Minard."

```
Begin["`Private`"]

ProcessTemp[tdata] :=
Module[{tprimlist, coords = Array[coordarr, 100], numb, k,
temprules, firstx, lastx},
temprules = {0, -10, -20, -30};
firstx = First[tdata][[1]];
lastx = Last[tdata][[1]];
tprimlist = Map[({Thickness[0.001], Line[{{firstx,
0.0916 + 0.00188333*#},
{lastx, 0.0916 + 0.00188333*#}}]})&, temprules];
numb = Length[tdata];
Do[
coords[[k]] = {tdata[[k, 1]], 0.0916 + tdata[[k,3]]*0.0018833}
,{k, 1, numb}];
Do[
tprimlist = Append[tprimlist,
{Thickness[0.001], Line[{tdata[[k, Range[2]]] , coords[[k]]} }]];
,{k, 1, numb}];
Do[
tprimlist = Append[tprimlist,
{Thickness[0.001], Line[{coords[[k]] , coords[[k+1]]} }]];
,{k, 1, numb-1}];
tprimlist]

stuff[sd] := Module[{k, m, primlist,pca, pcb, pcc, pcd,
scale, dir = Array[dirarr, 100],
rotdir = Array[rotdirarr, 100],
l = Array[larr, 100],
avevec = Array[avevecarr, 100]},
scale = 10500000;
primlist = { };
k = Length[sd];
Do[(dir[[m]] = sd[[m+1, Range[2] ]] - sd[[m, Range[2] ]];
l[[m]] = Sqrt[dir[[m, 1]]^ 2 + dir[[m, 2]]^ 2]),
{m, 1, k-1}];
Do[
If[l[[m]] $>$ 0.0001,
rotdir[[m]] = {-dir[[m, 2]], dir[[m, 1]]}/l[[m]],
rotdir[[m]] = {-dir[[m+1, 2]], dir[[m+1, 1]]}/l[[m+1]]],
{m, 1, k-1}];
avevec[[1]] = rotdir[[1]];
avevec[[k]] = rotdir[[k-1]];
Do[
avevec[[m]] =
(rotdir[[m]] + rotdir[[m-1]])/(1 +
rotdir[[m,1]]*rotdir[[m-1,1]]
+ rotdir[[m,2]]*rotdir[[m-1,2]]), {m, 2, k-1}];
Do[
pca = sd[[m,Range[2]]] - sd[[m,3]]*avevec[[m]]/scale;
pcb = sd[[m+1,Range[2]]] - sd[[m+1,3]]*avevec[[m+1]]/scale;
pcc = sd[[m+1,Range[2]]] + sd[[m+1,3]]*avevec[[m+1]]/scale;
pcd = sd[[m,Range[2]]] + sd[[m,3]]*avevec[[m]]/scale;
u = {If[sd[[m, 4]] == 1,
RGBColor[1,57129/65535,37232/65535],
RGBColor[0,0,0]],
```

```
Polygon[{pca, pcb, pcc, pcd}]];
primlist = Append[primlist, u],
{m, 1, k-1}];
primlist]


ProcessStrength[data] :=
Module[{strengthprims, str, len, v},
strengthprims = {};
len = Length[data];
Do[
(strengthprims =
Append[strengthprims, stuff[data[[v]]]]),
{v, 1, len}];
strengthprims ]

ProcessTitle[titledata] :=
Text[FontForm[titledata[[1, 3]],{"Helvetica-Bold", 14}],
 {titledata[[1, 1]], titledata[[1, 2]]}]

ProcessPoints[pointdata]:=
Map[({Point[Drop[#, -1]], Text[FontForm[Last[#], {"Times",   8}],
Drop[#, -1]+{0.01,0.01}, {0, -1}]})&, pointdata]

ProcessText[textdata] :=
Map[(Text[FontForm[Last[#], {"Times",   8}], Drop[#, -1], {0, -1}])&,  textdata]

ProcessRivers[riverdata] :=
Map[({RGBColor[0, 0, 1], Thickness[0.001],
Line[#]}&), riverdata]

ProcessBoxes[boxdata] :=
Map[({RGBColor[0, 0, 0], Thickness[0.002], Line[#]}&), boxdata]

NapoleonicMarchOnMoscowAndBackAgainPlot[sdata, tdata, riverdata,
boxdata, titledata, pointdata, textdata] :=
Show[Graphics[
{ProcessStrength[sdata],
 ProcessTemp[tdata],
 ProcessRivers[riverdata],
 ProcessBoxes[boxdata],
 ProcessTitle[titledata],
 ProcessPoints[pointdata],
 ProcessText[textdata]}
]]

End[]

EndPackage[]
```

Processing Information in *Mathematica*

Chapters 2 and 3 explained how to import data into *Mathematica* and how to organize them into a suitable list structure for further processing or visualization. At this stage, you may wish to work with the data in various ways. If plotting a graph is your next goal, then you should turn to Chapter 4 on data visualization in two dimensions or Chapter 6 on data visualization in three or more dimensions. If you wish to process your data, then you will need to know various simple facts about how to do data processing in *Mathematica*. This chapter explains how to perform several commonplace operations. We also describe several constructions in applied mathematics that make use of list-processing operations similar to those needed for data analysis. We make use of the two-dimensional graphical constructions described in Chapter 4.

5.1 Application of Functions

The application of functions to data is straightforward in *Mathematica*. There is no need to write DO loops, as in FORTRAN, or to manipulate columns of data and dialog boxes, as in spreadsheets. All relevant functions have the attribute Listable:

In[1]:= Attributes[Log]

Out[1]= {Listable, Protected}

Thus, if we want to take logs to the base 10 of some data, all we have to do is the following:

In[2]:= mydata = {1, 2, 3, 4, 5, 6, 7};
Log[10, mydata]

Out[2]=
$$\left\{0, \ \frac{\text{Log}[2]}{\text{Log}[10]}, \ \frac{\text{Log}[3]}{\text{Log}[10]}, \ \frac{\text{Log}[4]}{\text{Log}[10]}, \ \frac{\text{Log}[5]}{\text{Log}[10]}, \ \frac{\text{Log}[6]}{\text{Log}[10]}, \ \frac{\text{Log}[7]}{\text{Log}[10]}\right\}$$

Often, however, you may want to force numerical operation, as here:

In[3]:= N[Log[10, mydata]]

Out[3]= {0, 0.30103, 0.477121, 0.60206, 0.69897, 0.778151, 0.845098}

If your data are nested and you wish to apply functions to particular components, then, as discussed in Chapter 3, the Map function is the appropriate tool. In the following, to take logarithms of just the second component, we map Log onto the second component:

```
In[4]:=   data = {{1,4},{2,3},{4,3},{7,6},{10,11}};
          Map[{#[[1]], N[Log[10, #[[2]]]]}&, data]
```

```
Out[4]=   {{1, 0.60206}, {2, 0.477121}, {4, 0.477121}, {7, 0.778151},
             {10, 1.04139}}
```

If you wish to generate a standard series, do not forget to use `Table` (or `Range` for arithmetic progressions). If you want to generate a series of numbers from 0 to 7, in steps of 0.5, you can enter `Range[0,7,0.5]` or you can enter the following (once the series is created, it is easy to sum that series):

```
In[5]:=   stddata = Table[x, {x, 0, 7, 0.5}]
```

```
Out[5]=   {0, 0.5, 1., 1.5, 2., 2.5, 3., 3.5, 4., 4.5, 5., 5.5, 6., 6.5, 7.}
```

```
In[6]:=   Apply[Plus, stddata]
```

```
Out[6]=   52.5
```

We have already discussed binning and frequency counts in Chapter 3. Other common data-processing operations are running sums and products. There are many ways of calculating these lists. Here are two methods for defining a `RunningSum` that avoid DO loops! (You can obtain running products by replacing + by * where the former appears.)

```
In[7]:=   RunningSum[k_Integer, data_List] := 0 /; k <= 0;
          RunningSum[k_Integer, data_List] := data[[1]] /; k == 1;
          RunningSum[k_Integer, data_List] :=
          RunningSum[Length[data], data] /; k > Length[data]
          RunningSum[k_Integer, data_List] :=
          RunningSum[k-1, data] + data[[k]] /; k > 1 && k <= Length[data]
```

```
In[8]:=   OtherRunningSum[k_Integer, data_List] :=
            Which[k <= 0, 0, k >= Length[data], Apply[Plus, data], True,
              Apply[Plus, Take[data, k]]]
```

```
In[9]:=   Table[RunningSum[k, stddata], {k, 1, Length[stddata]}]
```

```
Out[9]=   {0, 0.5, 1.5, 3., 5., 7.5, 10.5, 14., 18., 22.5, 27.5, 33., 39.,
             45.5, 52.5}
```

```
In[10]:=  Table[OtherRunningSum[k, stddata], {k, 1, Length[stddata]}]
```

```
Out[10]=  {0, 0.5, 1.5, 3., 5., 7.5, 10.5, 14., 18., 22.5, 27.5, 33., 39.,
             45.5, 52.5}
```

In fact, there is a still more elegant way of obtaining such a structure — by using the `FoldList` command. You can think of `FoldList` as being a generalization of `NestList` that allows functions to take more than one argument:

```
In[11]:=  FoldList[f, x, {a, b, c}]
```

```
Out[11]=  {x, f[x, a], f[f[x, a], b], f[f[f[x, a], b], c]}
```

You may use `FoldList` with the functions `Times` and `Plus` to achieve the desired result, setting $x = 1$ and $x = 0$, respectively, and dropping the first element of the resulting list, with `Rest`:

```
In[12]:=  FoldList[Times, x, {a, b, c}]

Out[12]=  {1, a, a b, a b c}

In[13]:=  Rest[FoldList[Plus, 0, stddata]]

Out[13]=  {0, 0.5, 1.5, 3., 5., 7.5, 10.5, 14., 18., 22.5, 27.5, 33., 39.,
          45.5, 52.5}
```

5.2 Linear Regression

The Fit command fits a linear combination of functions of your choice to a set of data. Consider the following list and simple plot:

```
In[14]:=  data = {{1,4},{2,3},{4,3},{7,6},{10,11}};
          ListPlot[data, PlotStyle -> PointSize[0.03]]
```

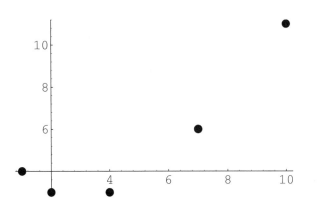

We can fit these data to a quadratic equation of the form $y = a + bx + cx^2$ (that is, we can find the values of the parameters a, b, and c) by giving Fit the list $\{1, x, x^2\}$. This input tells *Mathematica* that the functions to be fitted are a constant term, x, and x^2:

```
In[15]:=  Fit[data, {1,x,x^2}, x]
                                        2
Out[15]=  4.58964 - 1.00648 x + 0.165925 x
```

We can superimpose this fitted function on top of the list data:

```
In[16]:=  Show[
            ListPlot[data,
              PlotStyle -> PointSize[0.03],
             DisplayFunction -> Identity],
            Plot[ 4.58964 - 1.00648 x + 0.165925 x^2, {x,1,10},
            DisplayFunction -> Identity],
            DisplayFunction -> $DisplayFunction]
```

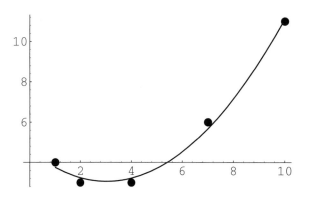

In the preceding example, setting `DisplayFunction` to `Identity` switched off the display while the individual plots were being drawn. Alternatively, you can use `Epilog` to add the points, as is demonstrated next. This use of `Epilog` is similar to that discussed in Section 4.3 of Chapter 4. We are not limited to just polynomial fits — `Fit` can perform a least-squares fit to any linear combination of functions:

```
In[17]:=  f[x_] = Fit[data,{1,Exp[x],Sin[x]},x]
Out[17]=                   x
          3.61957 + 0.000354056 E  + 0.625486 Sin[x]
In[18]:=  Plot[ f[x], {x,1,10}, PlotRange -> All,
          Epilog -> Map[{PointSize[0.03], Point[#]}&, data] ]
```

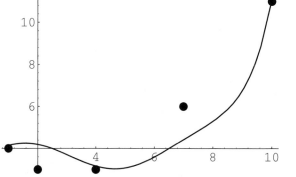

There are two circumstances when the `Fit` command is inappropriate. The first occurs when the function that we want to fit to is not linear in the unknown parameters. In this case, it is necessary to use the `NonlinearFit` package described in Section 5.3. The second circumstance occurs when the data contain a few outlying points that a least-squares fit will weight too heavily. A more robust fitting process must then be used. We describe such a method in the case study of Chapter 15.

Even when `Fit` is appropriate, we may wish to extract more information about the fitting process. A package exists to do just that; we shall discuss it next. We shall also describe how to do standard plots suitable for use with Fit.

5.2.1 A Full Regression Analysis and Visualization

In what follows, we perform a fit to a function of the form

$$ax \exp^{-bx}$$

by taking logs. Furthermore, we import a package that will allow us to do a much more sophisticated analysis. We begin by importing the package, creating some data, and plotting them:

```
In[19]:=  Needs["Statistics`LinearRegression`"]

In[20]:=  noisydata = Table[{x, 3.1 x Exp[-2.1 x] +
            0.05 (Random[ ]-0.5)}, {x, 0.02, 2, 0.02}];

In[21]:=  plotone = ListPlot[noisydata, PlotRange -> {0, 0.8},
            PlotStyle -> {RGBColor[1, 1, 0]},
            Background -> RGBColor[0,0,1],
            DefaultColor -> RGBColor[1, 1, 1],
            PlotLabel -> FontForm["Fit to Critical Damping",
            {"Helvetica", 12}],
            PlotRegion -> {{0.05, 0.95}, {0.05, 0.95}}]
```

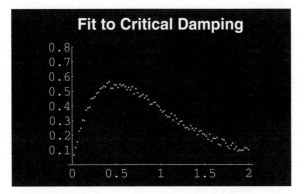

To use Fit, we need to turn the problem into one where the function to be fitted is linear in the unknown parameters. We can also use the considerably more extensive output available via the use of the Regress function:

```
In[22]:=  lnd = Map[{#[[1]], Log[#[[2]]]}&, noisydata];

In[23]:=  Fit[lnd, {1, Log[x], x}, x]

Out[23]=  1.10464 - 2.07616 x + 0.979436 Log[x]

In[24]:=  analysis = Regress[lnd, {1, Log[x], x}, x]
```

Out[24]= {ParameterTable ->

	Estimate	SE	TStat	PValue,
1	1.10464	0.0323274	34.1702	0
Log[x]	0.979436	0.0169247	57.87	0
x	-2.07616	0.0270704	-76.6949	0

RSquared -> 0.985245, AdjustedRSquared -> 0.984941,
EstimatedVariance -> 0.00482238,
ANOVATable ->

	DoF	SoS	MeanSS	FRatio	PValue}
Model	2	31.2346	15.6173	3238.5	0
Error	97	0.467771	0.00482238		
Total	99	31.7023			

We can also take over manual control of the output of Regress. Here we just extract the function and the corresponding predicted response (the output has been truncated):

In[25]:= analysis = Regress[lnd, {1, Log[x], x}, x,
OutputControl -> NoPrint,
OutputList -> {BestFit, PredictedResponse}]

Out[25]= {BestFit -> 1.10464 - 2.07616 x + 0.979436 Log[x],

PredictedResponse ->

{-2.76846, -2.13109, -1.77549, -1.53525, -1.35822, -1.22117,
 -1.11171, -1.02245, -0.94861, -0.886939, -0.835112,
 . . .
 -2.18026, -2.21142, -2.24269, -2.27406, -2.30554, -2.33712,
 -2.3688}}

We then convert the PredictedResponse back to the original functional form:

In[26]:= pred = Exp[PredictedResponse] /. analysis;

In[27]:= fitfn = Exp[BestFit] /. analysis

Out[27]= 1.10464 - 2.07616 x + 0.979436 Log[x]
E

Now we are in a position to calculate the residuals with respect to the original functional form:

In[28]:= errors = Transpose[{Transpose[noisydata][[1]], pred - Transpose[noisydata][[2]]}];

Next, we move on to the visualization of the results. We construct plots of the fitted function, and we show them with the original data:

In[29]:= plottwo =
           Plot[fitfn, {x, 0, 2},
           PlotStyle -> {{Thickness[0.007], RGBColor[1, 0, 0]}},
           Background -> RGBColor[0,0,1],
           DefaultColor -> RGBColor[1, 1, 1]]

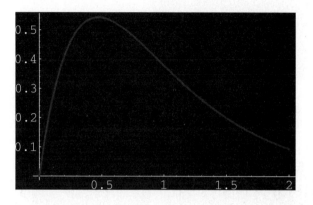

In[30]:= cp = Show[plotone, plottwo]

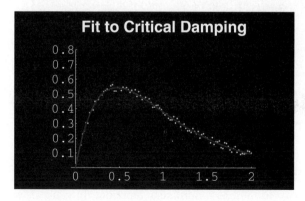

Then, we construct a plot of the residuals, and we insert it into our composite plot by using the Rectangle function:

In[31]:= plotthree = ListPlot[errors,
           PlotStyle -> {PointSize[0.015], RGBColor[1, 1, 1]},
           Background -> RGBColor[0,0,1],
           DefaultColor -> RGBColor[1, 1, 1],
           PlotLabel -> "Residuals"]

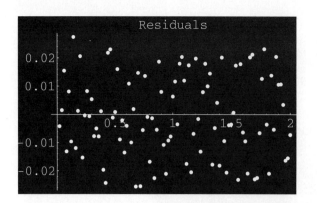

```
In[32]:=   Show[Graphics[{Rectangle[{0, 0}, {1, 1}, cp],
              Rectangle[{0.55, 0.45}, {0.95, 0.9}, plotthree]}]]
```

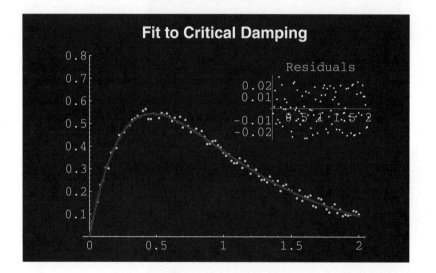

5.3 Nonlinear Regression

It is frequently necessary to fit data to a nonlinear function. In general, we cannot use the Fit command unless we happen on a transformation to reduce the problem to one linear in unknown parameters. For example, suppose that we generate data that are the sum of two Lorentzian functions, with added noise:

```
In[33]:=   exptdata = Table[{x,1/((x-10)^2 + 0.1)
                        + 1/((x-13)^2+0.5)
                        + 0.3 Random[]}, {x,0,20,0.1}];
```

```
In[34]:=   ListPlot[exptdata, PlotJoined -> True, PlotRange -> All]
```

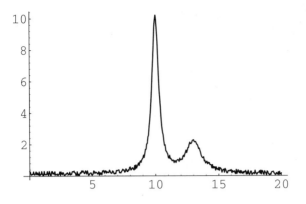

If these data had been generated experimentally, we might need to fit them to a function of the form

$$a + \frac{b}{(x-c)^2 + d} + \frac{e}{(x-f)^2 + g} \quad .$$

There exists a package to do this fitting with *Mathematica* using the Levenberg-Marquardt method.

In[35]:= `Needs["Statistics`NonLinearFit`"]`

Due to the large number of parameters to be fitted, the process takes some time. You might want to set the option `ShowProgress` to `True` before you try this example to assure yourself that *Mathematica* is actually doing something. Because we are fitting two functions of the same type (Lorentzians), we must break the symmetry by specifying start values for certain parameters — the default is to set them all to 1. We have chosen to tell *Mathematica* that the two peaks are centered close to the points $x = 11$ and $x = 14$:

In[36]:=
```
NonlinearFit[
           exptdata,
           a + b/((x-c)^2+d) + e/((x-f)^2+g),
           x,
           {a,b,{c,11},d,e,{f,14},g}
         ]
```

Out[36]= `{a -> 0.154491, b -> 0.991441, c -> 10.0003, d -> 0.0989602,`
`    e -> 1.0389, f -> 13.0029, g -> 0.515265}`

These results for the parameters are very close to the values that we used to generate the data. The parameter a has come from the noise, which we distributed randomly between 0 and 0.3 and which therefore had an average value of 0.15. Once we have fitted the peaks, it might be nice to subtract out the large peak and to plot what is left in an inset to highlight the smaller peak. We described a method for doing this subtraction in Chapter 4.

As a second illustration of nonlinear fit, we consider a common exercise in data analysis — to fit a sum of exponentials to a data set. As before, we make up test data, here containing two components, one of which decays much more rapidly than does the other:

In[37]:= `expodata = Table[{x, 2.1 Exp[-3.2 x] + 4.0 Exp[-100 x]},`
`        {x, 0, 2, 0.01}];`

In[38]:= `ListPlot[Drop[Log[expodata], 1], PlotRange -> All]`

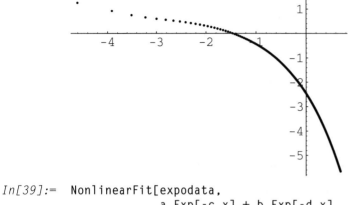

In[39]:= `NonlinearFit[expodata,`
`              a Exp[-c x] + b Exp[-d x],`
`              x,`
`              {a,b,c,d}]`

Out[39]= `{a -> 4., b -> 2.1, c -> 100., d -> 3.2}`

You need to be much more careful when using `NonlinearFit` than when using `Fit`. The package makes use of iterative methods and may give an answer that is of no use. If you set `ShowProgress` to `True`, you will gain considerable insight into the process so that you can spot problems with the convergence. Other options may be revealed in the usual way. We have found that increasing `MaxIterations` is often useful:

In[40]:= `Options[NonlinearFit]`

Out[40]= `{MaxIterations -> 30, Method -> LevenbergMarquardt,`
`     ShowProgress -> False, Weights -> Automatic,`
`     WorkingPrecision -> 19, AccuracyGoal -> 1, PrecisionGoal -> 3}`

5.4 Interpolation

In the file `height.dat`, we have stored data on the height of the water in a reservoir as a function of time. You should create such a file or create a list of the form `heightdata`:

In[41]:= `!!height.dat`

```
Day number        Height of Reservoir
                       in meters

        0                 10.5
        5                  7.4
       10                  6.5
       20                  8.0
       25                  8.4
       30                  7.6
```

To read in these data to *Mathematica*, we recall the `dropread` function from Chapter 2:

```
In[42]:=   dropread[dropno_Integer,filename_String,opts__]:=
           Module[{inline,result},
               inline = OpenRead[filename];
               Read[inline,Table[String,{dropno}]];
               result = ReadList[inline,opts];
               Close[inline];
               result]
```

```
In[43]:=   heightdata =  dropread[3,"height.dat",{Number,Number}]
```

```
Out[43]=   {{0, 10.5}, {5, 7.4}, {10, 6.5}, {20, 8.}, {25, 8.4}, {30, 7.6}}
```

We can see that the height readings were taken every 5 days but that the reading corresponding to day 15 is missing. Using interpolation, we can define a function that will take these data and give us an estimate to the height at any time between day 0 and day 30:

```
In[44]:=   height[x_] := Interpolation[heightdata][x]
```

This function evaluates to the known values when they are known:

```
In[45]:=   height[10]
```

```
Out[45]=   6.5
```

Elsewhere, the data are interpolated to provide an estimate of the height:

```
In[46]:=   height[15]
```

```
Out[46]=   7.03333
```

We can plot the data points and the interpolation function simultaneously:

```
In[47]:=   Plot[Evaluate[height[x]],{x,0,30}, Epilog ->
           Map[{PointSize[0.03], Point[#]}&, heightdata]]
```

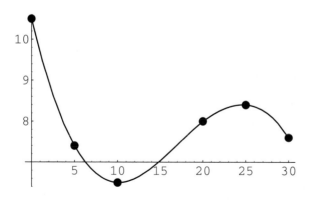

The default interpolation method is cubic spline (which means that we obtain the curve between any two points by fitting a cubic equation to these points and their next neighbors). It is possible to change this method, but we do not recommend that you do so unless you have good reason. Interpolation has one option, which is the order of the polynomial. If we set it to unity, we obtain piecewise linear interpolation:

```
In[48]:=  lheight[x_] := Interpolation[heightdata,
          InterpolationOrder -> 1][x]
In[49]:=  Plot[Evaluate[lheight[x]],{x,0,30}, Epilog ->
          Map[{PointSize[0.03], Point[#]}&, heightdata]]
```

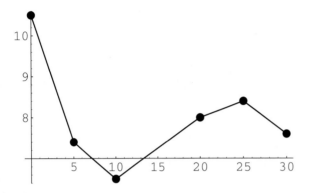

5.5 Fourier Analysis

This section is devoted to the subject of discrete Fourier transforms. Given a finite list of n numbers $a_1 \ldots a_n$, the Fourier transform can be represented by another list of n elements. The expression for the general element of this list f_m is

$$f_m = \frac{1}{\sqrt{n}} \sum_{j=1}^{n} e^{2\pi i (m-1)j/n} a_j \ .$$

From this definition, we expect that the Fourier transform of the list 1, 2, 3 should be given by

```
In[50]:=  N[{(1 + 2 + 3),
          (1 + 2 Exp[2 I Pi/3] + 3 Exp[4 I Pi/3]),
          (1 + 2 Exp[4 I Pi/3] + 3 Exp[4 I Pi/3])}/Sqrt[3]]
Out[50]=  {3.4641, -0.866025 - 0.5 I, -0.866025 - 2.5 I}
```

This expectation is correct:

```
In[51]:=  Fourier[{1,2,3}]
Out[51]=  {3.4641 + 0. I, -0.866025 - 0.5 I, -0.866025 + 0.5 I}
```

5.5.1 Signal Processing

A frequent use of Fourier transforms is to filter noisy signals. The noise is generally of high frequency and is easily removed when we have a description of the signal in frequency space:

```
In[52]:=  noisysound = Table[Cos[x]+Sin[2 x] + 0.3 Random[],
                         {x,0,6,0.01}];
```

```
In[53]:=  ListPlot[noisysound, PlotJoined -> True]
```

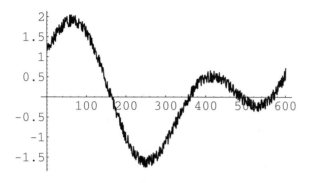

We can look at the profile of this function in frequency space by taking the Fourier transform and making a ListPlot of the absolute values of the complex numbers in this list. In the following example we have cyclically rotated the data so that the interesting information resides in the middle of the list, and we have zoomed in on the two peaks:

```
In[54]:=  ListPlot[Abs[RotateRight[Fourier[noisysound],300]],
                PlotJoined -> True,
                PlotRange -> {{280,320},All}];
```

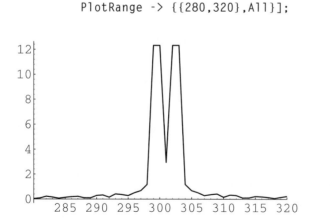

A simple filtering procedure is to Chop any element in the Fourier transform whose absolute value is less than a certain threshold — for instance 0.5:

```
In[55]:=  filtereddata = Chop[Fourier[noisysound],0.5];
```

We can then inverse Fourier transform these data and have a look at them:

```
In[56]:=  ListPlot[Chop[InverseFourier[filtereddata]],
                PlotJoined -> True]
```

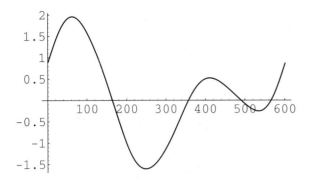

The second use of Chop was to remove the small imaginary components of the inverse transform caused by unavoidable numerical inaccuracy. If you believe that you know what frequencies are important, note that you can also use Fit with trigonometric functions. In the case study of Chapter 21, two-dimensional Fourier transforms are used to process digital images.

5.6 Statistical Analysis

The range of statistical tools that *Mathematica* supplies is extremely comprehensive. We have discussed some of these tools already, and some are treated in detail elsewhere in this book. The packages available are as follows (we indicate for reference the chapter and/or section in this book where the main discussion of each takes place):

Statistics Package	Where Discussed
ConfidenceIntervals	Here
ContinuousDistributions	Chapter 18
DataManipulation	Chapter 3
DescriptiveStatistics	Chapter 18
DiscreteDistributions	Here
HypothesisTests	Here
InverseStatisticalFunctions	Here
LinearRegression	Chapter 5, Section 5.2
MovingAverage	Chapter 17
NonlinearFit	Chapter 5, Section 5.3
NormalDistribution	Chapter 18

In Chapter 3, we explored various aspects of data manipulation; in particular, we considered the functions for obtaining bin counts and frequency counts for grouped and ungrouped data. In this chapter, we considered linear and nonlinear regression in Sections 5.2 and 5.3, respectively. You should also consult Chapter 15 for a discussion of robust regression. Chapter 17 discusses the analysis of time series and includes a simple application of the MovingAverage package. Chapter 18 is a detailed case study on the application of methods of probabilistic system assessment (PSA). You should read this chapter even if you do not plan to do probabilistic modeling since we will not duplicate the discussion contained therein of several important packages. In particular, the DescriptiveStatistics package contains basic functions such as Mean, Median, and Variance, and random sampling from normal and other continuous distributions is discussed there. In this section, we shall fill in a few gaps and touch on the contents of the other packages.

We shall need to use several packages in this section, so you should load them all right now:

```
In[57]:=  Needs["Statistics`Master`"];
          Needs["Graphics`Graphics`"];
```

One package with a rather bizarre status, in our view, is the InverseStatistical-Functions package. If you want to know values of the inverse error, gamma, and beta functions, by all means go ahead and use the package directly. However, if you wish to construct random samples from distributions, which construction, in principle, is facilitated by a knowledge of such functions, then you should use the generalized Random function defined in the NormalDistribution and ContinuousDistributions packages. The definitions there sometimes override those given in InverseStatisti-calFunctions, in particular for the normal distribution, and we shall see shortly why it is a good idea to not make direct use of the InverseStatisticalFunctions package directly.

To demonstrate statistical commands, we shall need data. As we generate some normal data, we will illustrate why we should not use the inverse error function. We have chosen to generate a list of 100 numbers that are normally distributed with mean 0 and variance 1. *Warning*: This takes time — the following command will give you an idea of how long it will take to generate each value on your computer:

```
In[58]:=  scale = N[Sqrt[2]];
```

```
In[59]:=  Timing[ scale*InverseErf[0.95] ]
```

```
Out[59]=  {2. Second, 1.95996}
```

The 100 data points on our machine take about 3 minutes to generate. You can cut down the number to speed up the calculations. The following commands both generate normally distributed data (these commands are simple examples of techniques used in Monte Carlo simulations, and such commands will be used extensively in Chapter 18):

```
In[60]:=  normaldata = Timing[Map[InverseErf, Table[Random[Real, {-1, 1}],{100}]]];
          normaldata[[1]]
```

```
Out[60]=  158.45 Second
```

```
In[61]:=  fastnormaldata = Timing[Table[Random[NormalDistribution[0,1]], {100}]];
          fastnormaldata[[1]]
```

```
Out[61]=  1.13333 Second
```

To see what the data look like, we do a simple bar chart, with unit-sized bins centered on the integers:

```
In[62]:=   BarChart[BinCounts[fastnormaldata[[2]],{-3.5, 3.5, 1}],
           PlotRange -> All,
           BarLabels -> {"-3", "-2", "-1", "0", "1", "2", "3"}]
```

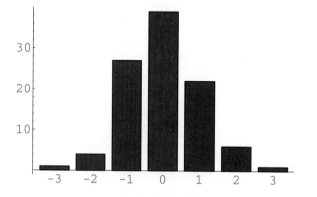

To save typing, we now relabel the data (taking the opportunity to scale properly the sample generated from InverseErf and to remove redundant precision) and use both random samples:

```
In[63]:=   ndata = fastnormaldata[[2]];
           mdata = N[scale*normaldata[[2]], 6];
```

5.6.1 Confidence Intervals for Estimated Parameters

We can calculate the mean of one of our samples from Section 5.6 in an obvious fashion:

```
In[64]:=   Mean[ndata]
Out[64]=   -0.0178212
```

The ConfidenceIntervals package allows us to give confidence intervals for the mean of the population from which ndata are drawn:

```
In[65]:=   MeanCI[ndata]
Out[65]=   {-0.222191, 0.186549}
```

These default to 95 percent confidence intervals, but this interval may be changed, as can whether you assume knowledge of the population variance, by use of Options:

```
In[66]:=   Options[MeanCI]
Out[66]=   {ConfidenceLevel -> 0.95, KnownStandardDeviation -> None,
           KnownVariance -> None}
```

To see how this interval is calculated, we illustrate the corresponding manual calculation by calling up several other useful functions. Note that we have 100 sample points, so Sqrt[100] = 10 gives the conversion from standard deviation to standard error of the mean:

In[67]:= StandardDeviation[ndata]

Out[67]= 1.02998

In[68]:= StandardErrorOfSampleMean[ndata]

Out[68]= 0.102998

If we had had a large sample, we would have multiplied this standard error by the ubiquitous factor of 1.96, an approximation to the 95 percent confidence intervals for the standard normal distribution:

In[69]:= Quantile[NormalDistribution[0,1], (0.95 + 1)/2]

Out[69]= 1.95996

Since we are not dealing with a large sample, it is better to use the following:

In[70]:= Quantile[StudentTDistribution[99], (0.95 + 1)/2]

Out[70]= 1.98422

Thus, for example, the lower end of the interval is just

In[71]:= -0.017821 - 1.98422*0.102998

Out[71]= -0.222192

Sometimes, you may want to calculate confidence intervals based on known parameters, rather than on those estimated from the sample. You can do this directly by using functions such as the following. The first example is another way of doing the calculation done by MeanCI, where we have inserted the mean and its standard error, together with the sample size; the second example shows what happens with the ordinary normal distribution — we obtain 1.96, as expected:

In[72]:= StudentTCI[-0.017821, 0.102998, 99,
           ConfidenceLevel -> 0.95]

Out[72]= {-0.222191, 0.186549}

In[73]:= NormalCI[0, 1, ConfidenceLevel -> 0.95]

Out[73]= {-1.95996, 1.95996}

We can carry out an analogous series of estimates for population variances:

In[74]:= Variance[ndata]

Out[74]= 1.06085

In[75]:= VarianceCI[ndata]

Out[75]= {0.817809, 1.43161}

Since we have two samples, we can also make comparisons between them. First, we can calculate differences between the means and give confidence intervals for them. As well as giving an optional pair of variances, we can just state that the variances are equal. We may also give confidence intervals for the ratio of the variances:

```
In[76]:=  Mean[mdata] - Mean[ndata]

Out[76]=  0.0836804

In[77]:=  MeanDifferenceCI[mdata, ndata]

Out[77]=  {-0.196114, 0.363475}

In[78]:=  VarianceRatioCI[mdata, ndata]

Out[78]=  {0.603885, 1.33392}

In[79]:=  Variance[mdata]

Out[79]=  0.952132
```

5.6.2 Hypothesis Testing

If we formulate hypotheses about the underlying population, we can test these hypotheses based on a sample. The output of such a test is a *p*-value, this value being the probability that the sample estimate is as extreme as it is given that the hypothesis about the value of the parameter is true. For example, let's test the hypothesis that our data came from a distribution with mean 0. The function MeanTest returns the *p*-value. It defaults to carrying out a one-sided test, but we can force a two-sided test with an option:

```
In[80]:=  MeanTest[ndata, 0, TwoSided -> True]

Out[80]=  TwoSidedPValue -> 0.862985
```

It is therefore very likely that ndata came from a distribution with mean 0. We can extract more detailed information by asking for a full report. Let's ask for the probability that the data came from a population with mean unity, and suggest a significance level for application of the test:

```
In[81]:=  MeanTest[ndata, 1, TwoSided -> True, FullReport -> True,
             SignificanceLevel -> 0.05]

Out[81]=  {FullReport ->    Mean          TestStat     DF,
                         -0.0178212     -9.88197      99
                                                                  -16
             StudentTDistribution, TwoSidedPValue -> 1.97921 10      ,
             Reject null hypothesis at significance level -> 0.05}
```

The various tests that are available parallel the confidence interval functions. Thus, we can test for the variance of the ndata population to be unity, for the two samples to come from populations with a given difference of means, and for the two samples to come from populations with a given ratio of variances. All the tests come with an appropriate set of options. We apply each of these tests to our two data sets, with suitable options:

```
In[82]:=  VarianceTest[ndata, 1, TwoSided -> True,
            FullReport -> True]
Out[82]=  {FullReport ->    Variance    TestStat     DF,
                            1.06085     106.085      99
              ChiSquare Distribution, TwoSidedPValue -> 0.589795}

In[83]:=  MeanDifferenceTest[ndata, mdata, 0,
            SignificanceLevel -> 0.05]
Out[83]=  {OneSidedPValue -> 0.278,
              Accept null hypothesis at significance level -> 0.05}

In[84]:=  VarianceRatioTest[ndata, mdata, 1,
            FullReport -> True]
Out[84]=  {FullReport ->    Ratio      TestStat   NumDF    DenDF,
                            1.11419    1.11419    99       99

            FRatio Distribution, OneSidedPValue -> 0.295829}
```

5.6.3 Probability Distributions

Mathematica contains a standardized description of most continuous and discrete distributions. The most notable omission is perhaps the log-uniform distribution, but in Chapter 18 we show how you can add this to the system in a way that is consistent with the definitions of the other distributions. For each distribution, *Mathematica* knows what its probability density function is; what its cumulative distribution is; how to compute quantiles; what the domains of the variables, mean, variance, standard deviation, skewness, kurtosis, and the characteristic function are; and how to create random samples.

There is little point in showing all the quantities for all the distributions; Chapter 18 illustrates several of the functions that are available when applied to continuous distributions. We complete the discussion by taking a quick look at the representation of the binomial distribution, for which most of the results may be well known to you. This distribution is reasonably representative of the discrete distributions, although some other distributions have infinite domains:

```
In[85]:=  Domain[BinomialDistribution[n, p]]

Out[85]=  {0, 1,  ..., n}

In[86]:=  Binomial[n, 3]
Out[86]=  (-2 + n) (-1 + n) n
          -------------------
                  6

In[87]:=  PDF[BinomialDistribution[n, p], m]
Out[87]=                                              m       n - m
          If[0 <= m <= n, If[IntegerQ[m], Binomial[n, m] p  (1 - p)     ,
            0], 0]

In[88]:=  Mean[BinomialDistribution[n, p]]
```

```
Out[88]=  n p

In[89]:=  Variance[BinomialDistribution[n, p]]

Out[89]=  n (1 - p) p

In[90]:=  StandardDeviation[BinomialDistribution[n, p]]

Out[90]=  Sqrt[n (1 - p) p]

In[91]:=  Skewness[BinomialDistribution[n, 1/2]]

Out[91]=  0

In[92]:=  CharacteristicFunction[BinomialDistribution[n, p], t]

Out[92]=           I t   n
          (1 - p + E    p)

In[93]:=  binodata = Table[Random[BinomialDistribution[10, 0.5]], {100}];

In[94]:=  BarChart[Frequencies[binodata]]
```

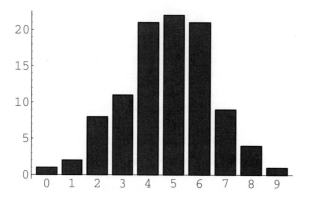

5.7 Solution of a PDE

In this section, we take a brief look at the solution of some simple partial differential equations. Your data may consist of a one-dimensional, two-dimensional, or three-dimensional list that constitutes the initial or boundary value data for a partial differential equation (or PDE). Here we illustrate some of the ideas that may be useful in constructing a solution.

5.7.1 The Diffusion Equation

We will look at two diffusion problems based on the equation

$$\frac{\partial C}{\partial t} = \kappa \frac{\partial^2 C}{\partial x^2} \ ,$$

with fixed and moving boundaries. Our interest is primarily in numerical schemes based on *Mathematica*'s list-processing abilities, and we shall focus on explicit schemes. If you wish to develop educational tools that illustrate various methods for solving PDEs, you should find this material useful because the method we shall develop, involving simultaneous solution and visualization, makes it clear what is happening, especially when you consider issues such as transitions to instability. In more serious applications, where implicit schemes are appropriate, *Mathematica* is also useful. For example, the Tridiagonal package contains many of the tools needed to treat implicit schemes. We begin by recalling the discrete form of the Laplace operator, as discussed in Chapter 3:

```
In[95]:=  Laplace[data_, step_:1] :=
          (RotateRight[data] - 2 data + RotateLeft[data])/step^2
```

```
In[96]:=  LaplaceInterior[data_List, step_:1] := Take[Laplace[data, step], {2, -2}]
```

Next, we consider a list-based form of the explicit updating scheme

$$C(x, t + \Delta t) = C(x, t) + \kappa \Delta t \, \frac{C(x - h, t) - 2C(x, t) + C(x + h, t)}{h^2} \, ,$$

which is appropriate for updating the interior points of a list and where we set $h = 1$:

```
In[97]:=  newconc[concentration_List, delta_, diffusivity_] :=
          Take[concentration, {2, -2}] +
          delta*diffusivity*LaplaceInterior[concentration];
```

If, at any stage, we have updated the interior values of the list concentration with newconc, we can then reimpose our boundary conditions. Here, for illustration, we will set $\frac{\partial C}{\partial x} = 0$ at $x = 0$ and set $C = 10$ at $x = 50$. These conditions require imposing boundary conditions according to the following schemes:

```
In[98]:=  concentration = Prepend[concentration, First[concentration]];
          concentration = Append[concentration, 10]
```

Once we have set up or imported our initial data, we can proceed. Here we will make up some rather trivial data and set the diffusivity to 5. This choice of diffusivity is consistent with the following stability condition:

$$\frac{\kappa \Delta t}{h^2} \leq 1/2 \, ,$$

provided that Δt, represented by the *Mathematica* variable delta, satisfies $\Delta t \leq 0.1$:

```
In[99]:=  inidata = Append[Table[0, {i, 0, 49}], 10];
          diffusivity = 5;
```

Having set up the problem, we can evolve the system. In the following, we first set the concentration variable C to the initial value and plot it. Then, we go into a loop, in which at each stage we update the concentration, according to the discrete form of Laplace's equation, and impose boundary conditions. Every twentieth update, we plot the results. To facilitate comparison of the plots with the exact solution, we have plotted concentration against a list {0, 1, 2, . . . ,50}, which we have generated by use of the Range function:

```
In[100]:= Clear[concentration];
          concentration = inidata;
          ListPlot[Transpose[{Range[0, 50], concentration}],
            PlotRange -> {0,  10}, AxesOrigin -> {0, 0},
            PlotJoined -> True];
          Do[
           Do[
            concentration = newconc[concentration, 0.1, diffusivity];
            concentration = Prepend[concentration, First[concentration]];
            concentration = Append[concentration, 10],
            {i, 1, 20}];
           ListPlot[Transpose[{Range[0, 50], concentration}],
           PlotRange -> {0, 10}, AxesOrigin -> {0, 0},
           PlotJoined -> True],
          {j, 1, 50}]
```

On a NoteBook interface, you can animate the resulting system directly. In this book, we just show the results at times $t = 0, 50, 100$. We have placed these results in an array mygraph[i], $i = 1, 2, 3$:

```
In[101]:= Show[GraphicsArray[{mygraph[1], mygraph[2], mygraph[3]}]]
```

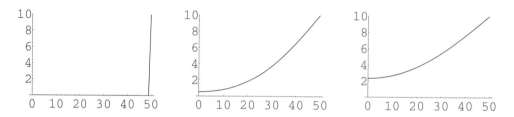

5.7.2 Comparison with the Exact Solution

The exact solution to the problem described in Section 5.7.1 may be found easily by the use of separation of variables and Fourier analysis. For a region of length L, with concentration C_0 at $x = L$, the exact solution is

$$C_0 - \frac{2C_0}{\pi} \sum_{n=0}^{\infty} \frac{(-1)^n}{(n+1/2)} \exp\left\{-\kappa(n+1/2)^2 \frac{\pi^2 t}{L^2}\right\} \cos\left\{(n+1/2)\frac{\pi x}{L}\right\} .$$

We define a *Mathematica* function by performing a finite summation, with n running from 0 to the value of a truncation point, and plot it for $t = 0, 50, 100$. The intermediate plots have been suppressed:

```
In[102]:= ExConc[x_, t_, L_, diff_, czero_, trunc_Integer] :=
          czero - (2*czero/Pi)*Sum[((-1)^n/(n + 1/2))*
          Exp[-diff*(n+1/2)^2*Pi^2*t/L^2]*
          Cos[(n+1/2)*Pi*x/L],
          {n, 0, trunc}]
```

```
In[103]:= plota = Plot[ExConc[x, 0, 50, 5, 10, 25], {x, 0, 50},
          PlotRange -> {-2, 10}, DisplayFunction -> Identity];
          plotb = Plot[ExConc[x, 50, 50, 5, 10, 25], {x, 0, 50},
          PlotRange -> {-2, 10}, DisplayFunction -> Identity];
          plotc = Plot[ExConc[x, 100, 50, 5, 10, 25], {x, 0, 50},
          PlotRange -> {-2, 10}, DisplayFunction -> Identity];
          Show[GraphicsArray[{plota, plotb, plotc}]]
```

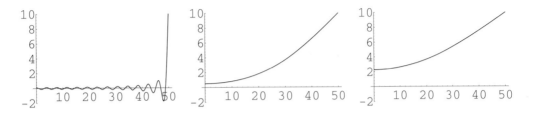

With the truncated series solution, we have demonstrated, at least visually, that our numerical scheme is reasonable. The "exact" plot for $t = 0$ is really illustrating the Gibbs effect, induced by the discontinuity in the initial condition at the endpoint and by our use of a truncated series.

The constructions that we have just outlined can be used as the basis for an extensive discussion of PDE solution techniques from both the analytical and the numerical point of view. A full discussion would easily take us outside the scope of this section and would basically be good material for another book! The solution of PDEs is, however, a subject of ongoing research within Wolfram Research, so an in-depth discussion could easily become out of date with the emergence of a new kernel or package facility for treating PDEs. As we wrote this book, we became aware of the package for solving certain types of first-order PDEs symbolically, and we included it in Chapter 1 as an illustration of the evolving capabilities of *Mathematica*. We will content ourselves with a second example, which is unlikely to be made out of date soon; its solution technique is less familiar, but it is open to treatment by our list-based processing technique.

5.7.3 Diffusion with a Moving Boundary

There are many types of diffusion processes in nature. The conduction of heat, under certain approximations, is reasonably well modeled by the diffusion equation, provided that we neglect such effects as convection and relativity. Many natural systems may have more than one state, with different diffusivities, and heat, chemicals, or energy may be required to transform from one state to the next. An obvious example is that of melting ice, where latent heat is required to convert the solid state to the liquid state. The diffusion of a chemical species into an environment where there exists a species with which it may react is another example. In both of these problems, a moving front is created. The front may be sharp (if the chemical reaction is sufficiently fast) or extended. For a sharp front, there exist well-tested, but perhaps not so widely known, numerical techniques. One forms the enthalpy function

$$H = q*C + Q*\theta(C - \tilde{C}) \ ,$$

where q is the specific heat capacity (or its chemical or geochemical equivalent, such as porosity), Q is the specific latent heat (or its chemical equivalent, such as concentration of ambient reactive species), and θ is a unit step function taking values 0 or 1 according to whether C is less than or greater than the critical value $\tilde{C}$. The equation to be solved is

$$\frac{\partial H}{\partial t} = D\frac{\partial^2 C}{\partial x^2} \ ,$$

and, for the updating of H, we proceed as before. Here D is the conductivity of the medium. We will work with $q = 1$, so there is no need to distinguish D from the diffusivity, and we can make a direct comparison with the free diffusion problem described earlier. The only new requirement is that once H has been updated, we need to update C from H. The updating of H is achieved by the following function, which represents the same operation as before:

```
In[104]:= newenthalpy[enthalpy_List, concentration_List, delta_, diffusivity_] :=
          enthalpy + delta*diffusivity*LaplaceInterior[concentration];
```

We set the values of two of the parameters:

```
In[105]:= q = 1;
          latentheat = 10;
```

The updating of the concentration is achieved by the following function, which is appropriate for a problem where there is no diffusion in the "solid" phase (in a more general problem, we would replace the last 0 by #/q):

```
In[106]:= conc[enthalpy_List, q_, latent_] :=
          Map[If[# >= latent, (# - latent)/q, 0]&, enthalpy]
```

We need to calculate only the initial value of the enthalpy. Once we have done so, we can proceed as before. We set the same boundary conditions and initial conditions, and we create the same movie. As before, just the frames for $t = 0, 50, 100$ are shown:

```
In[107]:= enthalpyzero =
          Take[Map[If[# > 0, q*# + latentheat, #*q]&, inidata], {2, -2}];
In[108]:= Array[myplot, 51]; Clear[enthalpy, concentration];
          enthalpy = enthalpyzero; concentration = inidata;
          myplot[1] = ListPlot[Transpose[{Range[0, 50], concentration}],
           PlotRange -> {0, 10}, AxesOrigin -> {0, 0}, PlotJoined -> True];
          Do[Do[enthalpy = newenthalpy[enthalpy, concentration, 0.1, diffusivity];
           concentration = conc[enthalpy, q, latentheat];
           concentration = Prepend[concentration, First[concentration]];
           concentration = Append[concentration, 10], {i, 1, 20}];
          myplot[j+1] = ListPlot[Transpose[{Range[0, 50], concentration}],
           PlotRange -> {0, 10}, AxesOrigin -> {0, 0}, PlotJoined -> True],
          {j, 1, 50}]
In[109]:= Show[GraphicsArray[{myplot[1], myplot[26], myplot[51]}]]
```

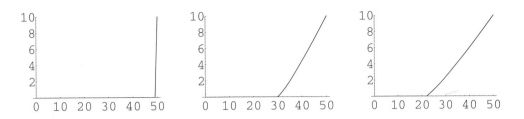

The front is clearly visible in the second and the third plot. You can use these simple routines to investigate a variety of features. You should consider, for both fixed and moving boundaries, the effect of increasing the diffusivity or time step beyond the stability limit. You should explore feeding in other initial conditions and boundary conditions. In the case of the moving-boundary-value problem, note that the concentration profile is nearly a straight line. Explore what happens as you increase the latent heat further, and also consider extremely small values of the latent heat. For further information, see J. Crank's book [5].

5.8 More Numerical Operations

A full discussion of *Mathematica*'s numerical capabilities could be the subject of another book. In the spirit of this chapter, we focus on matters appropriate to the treatment of imported data or list structures. There are, of course, various numerical functions built into the main kernel, and we shall touch on some of these shortly. For a systematic discussion of some of the fine details of the use of *Mathematica*'s N functions, such as NDSolve, we feel that we cannot improve significantly on J. Keiper's Wolfram Research report "The N Functions of *Mathematica*" [11], available from Wolfram Research. Here we shall point out some issues that have arisen in our own application of *Mathematica* to data structures, which are not, as far as we know, covered in standard texts or in Keiper's report.

5.8.1 Numerical Differentiation of Lists

We begin by constructing a standard time series. We intend this series to represent the position of an object at $t = 0, 0.1, 0.2, ...1, ...10$, in steps of interval 0.1 seconds:

$In[110]:=$ `xpos = Table[Sin[3 t], {t, 0, 10, 0.1}];`

In this case, we may construct the velocity analytically by constructing a table of values of the first derivative:

$In[111]:=$ `exactxvel = Table[3 Cos[3 t], {t, 0, 10, 0.1}];`

Suppose, instead, that all we have are our data in the form of our list xpos, with no knowledge of the function from which they came, and we wish to compute derivatives.

We have already seen one way of approaching this problem in our discussion of the Laplace operator. If we are content to estimate derivatives at the same time points, we can construct finite difference approximations to derivatives by the use of RotateLeft and RotateRight operations. We can achieve as much accuracy as we desire. We shall illustrate low-order schemes here, but there is no reason why higher-order schemes cannot be implemented. We consider the first derivative. The central difference approximation takes the form

$$\frac{\partial x}{\partial t} \sim \frac{(x[t + \Delta t] - x[t - \Delta t])}{(2\Delta t)} \quad .$$

Ignoring end-point complications, this approximation can be implemented with the following:

```
In[112]:= listd[data_,step_]:= (RotateLeft[data]-RotateRight[data])/(2*step);
```

```
In[113]:= approxxvel = listd[xpos, 0.1];
```

```
In[114]:= Short[%]
```

```
Out[114]= {6.41776, 2.82321, 2.43903, <<96>>, -0.427385, 4.94744}
```

If the data happened to be periodic, this scheme would be sufficient; as things stand, however, the endpoints are wrong. To treat the endpoints, we use appropriate one-sided three-point formulas.

```
In[115]:= listd[data_,step_]:=
          Module[{dleft, dright, len},
           len = Length[data];
           dleft = (4*data[[2]]-3*data[[1]]-data[[3]])/(2*step);
           dright = (3*data[[len]]-4*data[[len-1]]+data[[len-2]])/
           (2*step);
           Join[{dleft},
           Drop[Drop[(RotateLeft[data]-RotateRight[data])/
            (2*step), 1],-1],
           {dright}]]
```

```
In[116]:= approxxvel = listd[xpos, 0.1];
```

```
In[117]:= Short[approxxvel]
```

```
Out[117]= {3.08719, 2.82321, 2.43903, <<96>>, -0.427385, 0.456494}
```

```
In[118]:= Short[exactxvel]
```

```
Out[118]= {3, 2.86601, 2.47601, <<6>>3, <<95>>, -0.433864, 0.462754}
```

```
In[119]:= Plot[3 Cos[3 t], {t, 0, 10},
          Epilog -> Map[{PointSize[0.01], Point[#]}&,
          Transpose[{(Range[101] - 1)/10, approxxvel}]]]
```

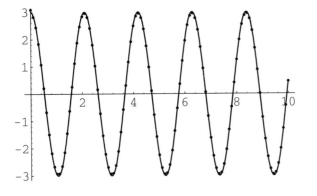

The maximum percentage error in our computation is

In[120]:= `Max[100*Abs[(approxxvel - exactxvel)/exactxvel]]`

Out[120]= `2.90639`

Higher-order schemes can be implemented easily — we can obtain five-point formulas for first derivatives, for example. For second derivatives, we can use the Laplace operator already discussed, together with suitable endpoint treatments. This discrete operator was based on a three-point formula; five-point formulas also can be used.

A completely different approach is to use the method of interpolation, followed by the numerical differentiation function ND in the package `NumericalMath`NLimit``.

5.8.2 Numerical Integration of Lists

The inverse operation of integration is a little more subtle than you might think, especially for periodic functions. We shall make two data sets to illustrate the process, and we shall calculate the exact integrals of the functions that we have used to generate them:

In[121]:= `nonperio = Table[x^5, {x, 0, 5, 0.1}];`
`perio = Table[N[Sin[2 x]^2 + Sin[4 x]^2],{x, 0, 2 Pi, Pi/20}];`

In[122]:= `N[Integrate[x^5, {x, 0, 5}], 10]`

Out[122]= `2604.166667`

In[123]:= `N[Integrate[Sin[2 x]^2 + Sin[4 x]^2, {x, 0, 2 Pi}], 10]`

Out[123]= `6.283185307`

Now we load the package for integrating lists directly:

In[124]:= `Needs["NumericalMath`ListIntegrate`"]`

We first apply it in default form. `ListIntegrate` just needs the data and the step size, or a list of {x, y} pairs, but here we just give the form for equally spaced values:

In[125]:= `N[ListIntegrate[nonperio, 0.1], 10]`

Out[125]= `2604.164625`

The default form almost gets it right. If we increase to 5 the default value of the order of the polynomials that ListIntegrate uses, we get it exactly right:

In[126]:= `N[ListIntegrate[nonperio, 0.1, 5], 10]`

Out[126]= `2604.166667`

Let's consider the same operation on our periodic data. This time, increasing the order of the polynomials underlying ListIntegrate does not help much in increasing the accuracy:

In[127]:= `N[ListIntegrate[perio, N[Pi/20]], 10]`

Out[127]= `6.278550123`

In[128]:= `N[ListIntegrate[perio, N[Pi/20], 10], 10]`

Out[128]= `6.285394975`

If, instead, we apply the trapezoidal rule directly to the list, we get a much more accurate result. Since the data are periodic, we can set up the application of the rule so as to add up all but the last element of the list and then multiply by the step size:

In[129]:= `N[(Pi/20)*Apply[Plus, Drop[perio, 1]], 10]`

Out[129]= `6.283185307`

On periodic data, this approach should be used in preference to ListIntegrate. It relies on special properties of error formulas for numerical integrals of (sufficiently differentiable) periodic functions. On nonperiodic data, the trapezoidal rule does not do nearly so well. We can carry out the calculation either manually or by forcing ListIntegrate to use linear methods:

In[130]:= `N[0.1*(Apply[Plus, Drop[Drop[nonperio, 1], -1]]+`
          `(First[nonperio] + Last[nonperio])/2), 10]`

Out[130]= `2606.770625`

In[131]:= `N[ListIntegrate[nonperio, 0.1, 1], 10]`

Out[131]= `2606.770625`

5.8.3 Solution of Equations Constructed from Lists

In some applications, the list that you have created or imported can be used to construct an equation whose solution is desired. Simple algebraic systems can often be treated by the Solve function. A detailed example of this technique is given in Chapter 15, where a collection of points is used to define a large set of hyperplanes whose equations are determined by the use of Solve. Often, we have to deal with a more complicated nonlinear system, and then FindRoot is the appropriate tool.

The following system called a *dividend discount model* arises in elementary financial applications. It associates a parameter R with a stock (the internal rate of return), based on the price of a stock and a stream of known and estimated dividends. As usual, we shall invent a stream of dividends, although it could just as easily have been imported as a list:

```
In[132]:= Price = 100;
```

```
In[133]:= Array[div, 50];
```

```
In[134]:= div[1] = 12;
          div[2] = 10;
          div[3] = 15;
          Do[div[k] = div[k-1]*(1 + 0.1 + (0.05 - 0.1)*(k-4)/10),
              {k, 4, 14}];
          Do[div[k] = div[14]*1.05^(k-14), {k, 15, 50}];
```

The function that we wish to equate to 0 is given by the following (this formula could be generalized to work with a general input dividend stream):

```
In[135]:= f[R_, price_] := price - Sum[div[k]/(1 + R)^k, {k, 1, 50}]
```

```
In[136]:= f[r, p] // Short
```

```
Out[136]=      192.257                 12
          p - --------- + <<48>> - -----
                  50                1 + r
             (1 + r)
```

We can use the system in two ways. First, we find the parameter R given the price. It is conventionally expressed as a percentage:

```
In[137]:= 100*R /. FindRoot[f[R, Price] == 0, {R, 0}]
```

```
Out[137]= 19.7997
```

In other applications, it may be useful to specify a value of R and to calculate the price that would be associated with it. We could use the explicit nature of f, as a function of R, to do this, but we can also use FindRoot:

```
In[138]:= p /. FindRoot[f[0.197997, p] == 0, {p, 10}]
```

```
Out[138]= 99.9997
```

5.8.4 Education Versus Application

In the previous example, we were not exposed to the workings of FindRoot. This concealment, together with related hidden machinations of NIntegrate and other numerical functions, raises the issue of whether we can sensibly use *Mathematica* to teach numerical methods. We hope that our examples with partial differential equations and our brief discussion about integration make it clear that the existence of clever built-in or package functions in no way undermines the ability of *Mathematica* to communicate the principles underlying numerical techniques. To make this point more vividly, we take a more detailed look at the operations of FindRoot. You should also look at J. Keiper's report on *Mathematica*'s N functions [11].

In its default form, FindRoot implements the Newton-Raphson algorithm, where we iterate

$$x_{n+1} = x_n - \frac{f[x_n]}{f'[x_n]}$$

with starting value x_0. We can use *Mathematica* intelligently to represent this process, at the same time as visualizing it. The following routine carries out a fixed number of iterations and gives the function, its derivative, the final value, and a plot showing the function and the iterative process:

```
In[139]:= NewtonRaphson[func_, x_, start_, iter_] :=
Module[{pts, xold = start, xnew, f, df, rangea, rangeb},
pts = {};
f = func[x]; Print[f];
df = D[f, x]; Print[df];
Do[
AppendTo[pts, {xold, 0}];
AppendTo[pts, {xold, (f /. x -> xold)}];
xnew = xold - (f /. x -> xold)/(df /. x -> xold);
xold = xnew,
{k, 1, 10}];
rangea = Floor[Min[pts]-1];
rangeb = Ceiling[Max[pts]+1];
Print[xnew];
Plot[f, {x, rangea, rangeb}, PlotRange -> All,
PlotStyle -> {{Thickness[0.001], Dashing[{0.02, 0.02}]}},
Epilog -> {Thickness[0.001], Line[pts]}]]
```

```
In[140]:= NewtonRaphson[Sin, x, 1.40428999, 10]
    Sin[x]
    Cos[x]
    -3.14159
```

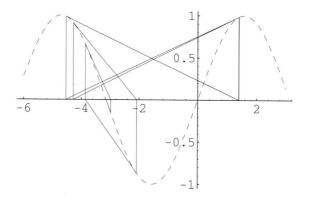

Our routine is quite capable of demonstrating the chaos that may result near interesting points! Once you have understood this process, you are allowed to just go ahead and use FindRoot:

In[141]:= `FindRoot[Sin[x], {x, 1.40428999}]`

Out[141]= `{x -> -3.14159}`

5.9 Summary

In this chapter we have considered a variety of techniques for processing information within *Mathematica*. You should now understand how to apply functions to lists by making use of the `Listable` attribute and how to fit functions to data by using the `Fit` command and the `LinearRegression` and `NonLinearFit` packages. You should also be able to carry out interpolation by using the `Interpolation` functions and to do Fourier analysis with the `Fourier` and `InverseFourier` functions. If you wish to carry out statistical analysis, a full set of tools may be loaded by inputting `Statistics`Master``. Further statistical tools are discussed in Chapters 3, 17, and 18. Lists may be used as the basis of several standard numerical techniques of applied mathematics — with them, we can solve a PDE, perform numerical differentiation and integration (with `NumericalMath`ListIntegrate``), and solve list-based and other equations with `FindRoot`.

In writing this chapter, we had to draw an arbitrary line dividing information-processing techniques into two groups. This chapter contains the first group — that is, the basic techniques that can be implemented by stringing together a few built-in functions and functions from standard packages, but without introducing any serious programming techniques. For more sophisticated information-analysis techniques and for an exposition of how to do your modeling and programming entirely within *Mathematica*, you should turn to Part Three.

Visualizing Data in Three or More Dimensions

In Chapter 4, we explored how to visualize information in just two dimensions. In this chapter, we consider graphical constructions for visualizing higher-dimensional structures, such as one or two functions of two variables, functions of three variables, three functions of a single variable, and so on.

6.1 Plots in Three Dimensions

Much about plotting in three dimensions can be inferred from what we have learned about plots in two dimensions. Also, we are not going to run through all the Plot3D variants and then all the ListPlot3D variants. Our focus here will be on the list versions. There are good reasons for this choice. S. Wolfram's *Mathematica* book [27] and the packages documentation give a detailed treatment of the plotting of explicit or implicit functions, but they offer less detailed information on the management of data. This subject will be our focus here. Furthermore, the parallelism between the various Plot3D and ListPlot3D operations is sufficient in that, if you learn how to handle one, then you can manage the other.

There are some places where the parallelism is not exact. We shall discuss an important one in a moment. If you are faced with a situation where, for example, you have some data and a package or function that handles only functions, note that you can treat this case by turning your data into a function by interpolation. The opposite situation can be treated by sampling. The three approximately parallel basic pairs of functions are:

1. Plot3D, ListPlot3D
2. DensityPlot, ListDensityPlot
3. ContourPlot, ListContourPlot

6.2 Plot3D for Functions

We can use much of what we learned about plotting in two dimensions when we construct three-dimensional plots. Let's begin by constructing an example with default options and then exploring the options:

In[1]:=   `Plot3D[Cos[x + Cos[y]], {x, 0, 4 Pi}, {y, 0, 4 Pi}]`

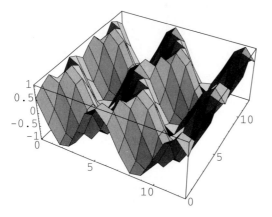

What is wrong with this plot? Clearly, too few points have been sampled. We can deal with this problem by using the `PlotPoints` option. `PlotPoints` is the number of points in each direction in which the function is sampled. The default value is 15, which we need to increase to obtain a smoother surface. As we increase the number of plot points, the influence of the mesh on our appreciation of the surface becomes inappropriate — the plot can become dominated by black lines, at least on the screen. On a high-resolution output device, this blackening of the plot is less of an issue. On a standard screen plot, we find that with meshes up to about 50×50, the mesh does not overwhelm the coloring. Above this number, it is usually better to remove the mesh or possibly to decouple the mesh from the number of plot points by using primitives to construct a mesh. We apply the options as follows:

In[2]:=   `Plot3D[Cos[x + Cos[y]], {x, 0, 4 Pi}, {y, 0, 4 Pi},`
`             PlotPoints -> 60, Mesh -> False, Axes -> False]`

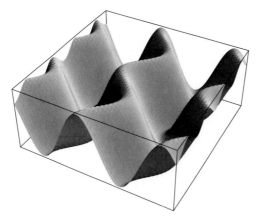

`PlotPoints` and `Mesh` are two of the many options that can be applied to `Plot3D`

(and to the list analogue ListPlot3D). Note that increasing PlotPoints increases the calculation time (generally quadratically). To explore the other options, let's consider a simple surface given by z = Exp[-x^2 - y^2]:

In[3]:=   `Plot3D[Exp[-x^2 - y^2], {x, -2, 2}, {y, -2, 2}, Axes -> False]`

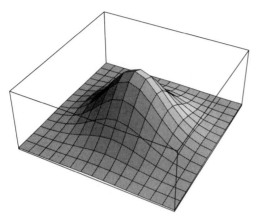

First, we note that it is possible to turn off the shading completely with Shading -> False. At the same time, it may be useful to turn off the default hidden-line removal:

In[4]:=   `Plot3D[Exp[-x^2 - y^2], {x, -2, 2}, {y, -2, 2}, Axes -> None,`
            `Shading -> False, HiddenSurface -> False, Boxed -> False]`

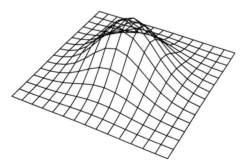

In[5]:=   `Plot3D[Exp[-x^2 - y^2], {x, -2, 2}, {y, -2, 2},`
            `PlotRange -> {0.1, 0.5}, PlotLabel -> "Exp[-r^2]",`
            `ViewPoint -> {0, -2, 1}, Boxed -> False, AspectRatio -> 0.5,`
            `Axes -> False, Lighting -> True, Mesh -> False]`

Exp[-r^2]

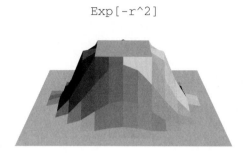

6.2.1 Coloring

Coloring is a topic in its own right. With the default settings in a function like Plot3D, *Mathematica* produces simulated illumination of surfaces (unless you are using an older Version 1.x of *Mathematica*).

The Lighting -> True option (the default in Version 2.x) causes simulated illumination to be activated. Frankly, for the purposes of producing scientific graphics, it is hard to see the point of this coloring. It does produce nice-looking pictures, but the color is not conveying any information if default light sources are used. You might, from time to time, want to simulate light sources — the difficulty is that there is no shadowing at present, so this option's use as a rendering tool is limited. For serious rendering applications, at least with current versions of *Mathematica*, you should consider exporting your plots to a rendering package. You can achieve this in various ways. Perhaps the most generically useful is to load the Utilities`DXF` package to export information about your plots to a DXF file. This format is supported by several commercial rendering packages.

Let's try a Plot3D with explicit simulated illumination and also with explicit clipping and some options:

```
In[6]:=    Plot3D[Exp[-x^2 - y^2], {x, -2, 2}, {y, -2, 2},
           PlotPoints -> 30,
           AmbientLight -> GrayLevel[0.],
           Axes -> None,
           Boxed -> False,
           LightSources -> {{{4, 0, 1}, RGBColor[0, 1, 0]},
           {{-4, 0, 1}, RGBColor[1, 0, 0]}},
           PlotRange -> {0.2, 0.7},
           ClipFill -> {GrayLevel[1], GrayLevel[0]}]
```

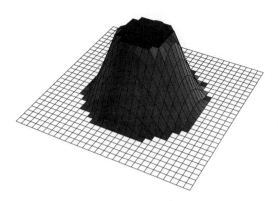

This sort of clipping is often genuinely useful — for example, if you were trying to illustrate some threshold behavior. A concrete example would be the concentration profile in a diffusion problem, where a fast chemical reaction was taking place at a moving front. The one-dimensional representation of this problem was treated in Section 5.7 — the corresponding problem in two space dimensions can be treated similarly, and plots like our clipped plot could be used to illustrate the results.

A more useful application of shading is to introduce extra variables. You can, for example, plot two functions of two variables by using the height to represent one function and the color to represent another. This technique is what is sometimes meant by *four-dimensional graphics*. By using simultaneous animation, you can get up to five dimensions.

If you turn off the simulated illumination with Lighting -> False (this setting was the default in Version 1.x), the pictures you obtain depend on the kernel that you are using. With Version 1.x and Version 2.0, you obtain a plot with the surface shaded gray according to the value of the function. In some versions of Version 2.1, the results of this command were rather unpredictable, generating purple or red and purple plots. This bug appears to have been fixed in Version 2.2.

The following code is appropriate for Version 2.x:

In[7]:=
```
Plot3D[Cos[x + Cos[y]], {x, 0, 4 Pi}, {y, 0, 4 Pi},
Lighting -> False]
```

If you are using Version 2.1 or later, you can achieve the same result by using the following, which overrides the Version 2.1 bug that exists on some systems (we will explain the ColorFunction specification in Section 6.3.5; for now, regard it as an incantation):

In[8]:=
```
Plot3D[Cos[x + Cos[y]], {x, 0, 4 Pi}, {y, 0, 4 Pi},
ColorFunction -> (GrayLevel[#]&)]
```

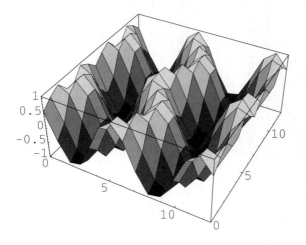

There is a natural area of application of coloring, and that is to complex variables. We can consider a complex function of x + I y, and we can plot its real and imaginary parts or perhaps its modulus and phase. This area is one where the Version 2.x Hue function is useful — it is periodic. (It is in the package Colors.m under HSBColor, for those of you still using Version 1.x.) The syntax is Plot3D[{function, colorfunction}, ranges, options]:

In[9]:=

```
Plot3D[ {Abs[Exp[-(x + I y)^2]],
Hue[N[(Pi + Arg[Exp[-(x + I y)^2]])/(2 Pi)] ]},
{x, -2, 2}, {y, -2, 2}, PlotPoints -> 30,
Mesh -> False,
FaceGrids -> All]
```

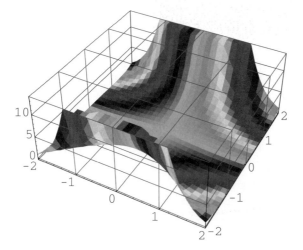

6.3 Lists in Three-Dimensional Plotting: A Case Study

The text file `newfrac.txt` contains a large column of 2500 numbers. It has been generated by an algorithm for generating fractal landscapes. This column of numbers is really a 50×50 array defining the height of a fractal landscape. Our goals are to import these data into *Mathematica* and to explore various ways of visualizing a subset of these data. It will help us to divide this project into more manageable tasks, as follows:

1. Read in the file `newfrac.txt`. Import the data into *Mathematica* without displaying them at all. Arrange them as a 50×50 array.
2. Extract a square subset consisting of the first 45×45 block, again without displaying the numbers. Find the maximum and minimum of this data subset.
3. Produce a default surface plot of these data represented as a height on a regular grid.
4. Produce a more interesting surface plot with all the following properties:
   a) There is no bounding box.
   b) The data are clipped at 0, and a level surface is placed at 0 and colored blue.
   c) The resulting surface is viewed from a raised point in the x-direction.
5. Repeat step 4, but simulate typical landscape colors.
6. Produce a density map of the same data set, showing only the above-sea-level region.
7. Produce a contour map of the same data set, showing only the above-sea-level contours.

Synthesis of a data set

If you wish to create a data set to use in experimenting with this exercise, here is one suggestion. Feel free to make up your own! Our plots have been based on yet another data set:

```
In[10]:=  newtest = Flatten[N[Table[1000*(2.5 - x + y/3 +
          0.5*Sin[5 x + 3 y] + 0.2*BesselJ[0, 8 x] + 0.2*Random[ ]),
          {x, 0.06, 3.0, 0.06}, {y, 0.06, 3.0, 0.06}], 6]];

In[11]:=  stuff = OpenWrite["newfrac.txt"];
          Do[Write[stuff, newtest[[i]]], {i, 1, 2500}];
          Close[stuff]

Out[11]=  newfrac.txt
```

6.3.1 Sample Code for Step 1

```
In[12]:=  t = ReadList["newfrac.txt", Number];

In[13]:=  Dimensions[t]

Out[13]=  {2500}

In[14]:=  t = Partition[t, 50]; Dimensions[t]

Out[14]=  {50, 50}
```

6.3.2 Sample Code for Step 2

```
In[15]:=   subt = t[[ Range[1, 45], Range[1, 45] ]];
           {Min[subt], Max[subt]}

Out[15]=   {-1030, 2410}
```

6.3.3 Sample Code for Step 3

```
In[16]:=   ListPlot3D[subt]
```

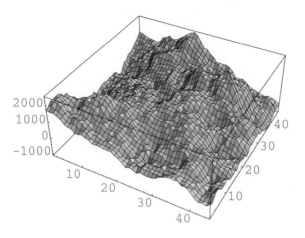

6.3.4 Sample Code for Step 4

```
In[17]:=   thePlot = ListPlot3D[subt,
           PlotRange -> {0, 3000},
           Boxed -> False,  Axes -> None,
           Lighting -> True, ClipFill -> {RGBColor[0, 0, 1], GrayLevel[1]},
           ViewPoint -> {2, 0, 1}] ;
```

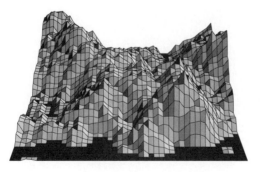

6.3.5 Sample Code for Step 5

For step 5, we need to understand the coloring of data sets. Coloring is accomplished by the use of the option `ColorFunction -> (f[#]&)`, where `(f[#]&)` is a pure function generating a color directive. If, for example, we use `(Hue[#]&)`, the argument `#` of the pure function should be understood to represent the data scaled linearly to lie between 0 and 1 so that lowest values are given `Hue[0]` and the highest values are given `Hue[1]`. Unless the function is periodic (as in Section 6.2.1 for the functional case), this is not very useful. A simple form suitable for false coloring of landscapes follows:

```
In[18]:=   thePlot = ListPlot3D[subt, PlotRange -> {0, 3000},
           Boxed -> False, Axes -> None, Lighting -> False,
           ClipFill -> {RGBColor[0, 0, 1], GrayLevel[1]},ViewPoint -> {2, 0, 1},
           ColorFunction -> (Hue[0.4 - #/2.5, 1, 1 - #/2]&)];
```

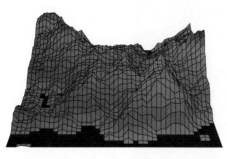

6.3.6 Sample Code for Step 6

```
In[19]:=   ListDensityPlot[subt, PlotRange -> {0, 3000},
           ColorFunction -> (If[# <= 0,RGBColor[0, 0, 1],
           Hue[0.4 - #/2.5, 1, 1 - #/2]]&), Mesh -> False]
```

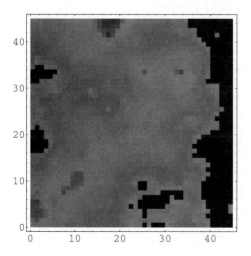

6.3.7 Sample Code for Step 7

```
In[20]:=  ListContourPlot[subt,
          PlotRange -> {0, 3000},
          Contours -> {0, 300, 600, 900, 1200, 1500, 1800,
          2100, 2400, 2700, 3000},
          ColorFunction ->
          (If[# <= 0,RGBColor[0, 0, 1], Hue[0.4 - #/2.5, 1, 1 - #/2]]&)]
```

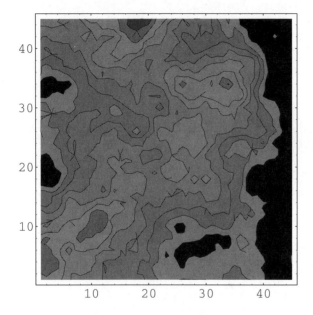

Let's add a simple legend to complete this plot:

```
In[21]:=  Needs["Graphics`Legend`"]

In[22]:=  ShowLegend[ListContourPlot[subt,
          Contours -> {0, 300, 600, 900, 1200, 1500, 1800,
          2100, 2400, 2700, 3000},
          ColorFunction ->
          (If[# < 0.01, RGBColor[0, 0, 1],
          Hue[0.4 - #/2.5, 1, 1 - #/2]]&),
          PlotRange -> {0, 3000},
          DisplayFunction -> Identity],
          {{{RGBColor[0, 0, 1], "Sea"},
            {Hue[0.4, 1, 1], "Lowland"},
            {Hue[0, 1, 0.5],"Highland"}},
          LegendPosition -> {1.1, -0.4},
          LegendSize -> {1.0, 1.0}}]
```

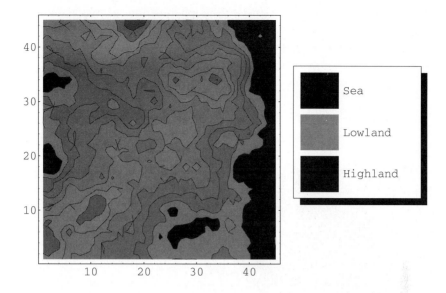

6.4 Parametric Plots in Three Dimensions

The idea is that {x, y, z} are given as a function of one or two parameters. In the first case, you generate a curve; in the second case, you generate a parametric surface. The second case is useful partly because some surfaces just cannot nicely be written in the form z = f(x, y), especially if f is to be single-valued, so it is a really necessary adjunct to Plot3D. To define a space curve, we simply give three functions of a single parameter, as in the following example:

```
In[23]:= ParametricPlot3D[{Cos[t/2] Cos[t], Sin[t/2] Sin[t], - t}, {t, 0, 20 Pi},
         PlotPoints -> 400, BoxRatios -> {1, 1, 1}, Axes -> False]
```

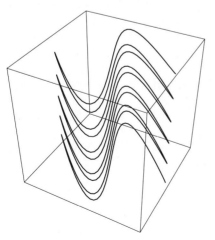

To define a surface plot, we need to supply functions of two variables. The following code will take a few moments to execute (note that we are constructing two surfaces together; you can plot a whole list of space curves in a similar fashion):

In[24]:= `ParametricPlot3D[{{Sin[v] Cos[u], Sin[v] Sin[u], Cos[v]},`
`{Sin[v] Cos[4 u/3]/2, Sin[v] Sin[4 u/3]/2, Cos[v]/2} },`
`{u, 0, 3Pi/2}, {v, 0, Pi}]`

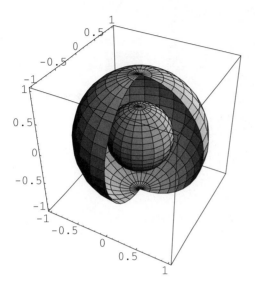

6.4.1 Minimal Surfaces

The function `ParametricPlot3D` can be used to visualize surfaces of extremal area by using some historic formulas that express such surfaces in terms of functions of a complex variable. This topic was discussed in some detail in at least two issues of the *Mathematica Journal* [14], [13]. Unfortunately, if you read these articles, you may have been left with the impression that more functions and integrals are needed to generate minimal surfaces than is actually the case. The cited articles relied on carrying out three integrals of two functions of a complex variable. In fact, armed with two such functions and only their derivatives, you can calculate generic minimal surfaces in four dimensions [18], a fact that was known by L. Eisenhart [6]in 1912! By making the specialization then to three dimensions, you can define minimal surfaces in dimension 3 by using just one function `H[w]` and its derivatives. A modern treatment of the derivation of this result, in an intrinsically three-dimensional argument, is given by N. Hitchin [9]. The parametric form is given by the following formula, where we try a cubic function of w:

In[25]:= `H[w_] = w^3;`
`x[w_] = (w^2 - 1) H''[w] - 2 w H'[w] + 2 H[w];`
`y[w_] = I ((w^2 + 1) H''[w] - 2 w H'[w] + 2 H[w]);`
`z[w_] = 2 w H''[w] - 2 H'[w];`

```
In[26]:= Expand[Evaluate[ComplexExpand[{Re[x[u + I v]],
          Re[y[u + I v]], Re[z[u + I v]]}]]]
```

```
Out[26]=         3    2            2       3    2      2
          {-6 u + 2 u  - 6 u v , -6 v - 6 u  v + 2 v , 6 u  - 6 v }
```

With this choice of function, we obtain Enneper's surface:

```
In[27]:= ParametricPlot3D[Evaluate[%],
          {u, -4, 4}, {v, -4, 4}, PlotPoints -> 30,
          Axes -> False]
```

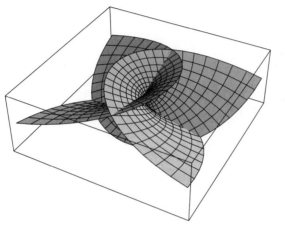

The catenoid is obtained by considering the function w Log[w]. In this case we adopt a polar representation of the parametrization, and we do some initial simplification, again using ComplexExpand to force the extraction of the real parts of our complex curve:

```
In[28]:= H[w_] = w*Log[w];
          x[w_] = (w^2 - 1) H''[w] - 2 w H'[w] + 2 H[w];
          y[w_] = I ((w^2 + 1) H''[w] - 2 w H'[w] + 2 H[w]);
          z[w_] = 2 w H''[w] - 2 H'[w];
          Simplify[Evaluate[ComplexExpand[{Re[x[u Exp[I v]]],
          Re[y[u Exp[I v]]], Re[z[u Exp[I v]]]}]]]
```

```
Out[28]=        2                   2
          (1 + u ) Cos[v]     (1 + u ) Sin[v]          2
          {-(---------------), ----------------, -Log[u ]}
                 u                   u
```

This surface can be plotted directly, but we have found that one further change of variable yields a smoother surface:

```
In[29]:= ParametricPlot3D[Evaluate[% /. u -> Exp[q]],
          {q, -2, 2}, {v, 0, 2 Pi}, PlotPoints -> 20,
          Axes -> False]
```

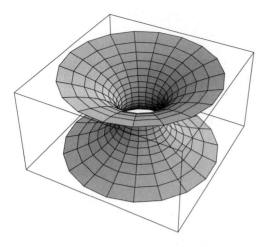

As noted in the *Mathematica Journal* article [13], you may need to be careful when using these formulas in conjunction with a function with branch points.

6.5 Interpolation and Irregular Grids

The plot operations that we have considered so far assume that our data are based on a regular grid. This assumption is not always the case, however, and we have to be more careful about constructing plots of our data. We shall motivate our treatment of this issue by considering various views of a simple function. Suppose first that we wish to visualize a function of two variables given by the following formula:

```
In[30]:=  z = Sin[x y]
```

To plot this function on the region $0 \le x, y \le 2.8$, you can apply the following:

```
In[31]:=  Plot3D[Sin[x y], {x, 0, 2.8}, {y, 0, 2.8}]
```

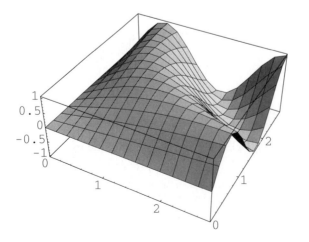

It happens that the default grid for Plot3D is a regular 15×15 matrix. If we do not specify any further options for Plot3D other than the range of x,y values to be plotted, it splits up these ranges into 14 (15 less 1) equal-sized intervals and plots a surface based on the values of the function at the endpoints of these intervals. Assuming that these assertions are correct, we should be able to reproduce the same surface given a knowledge of only the values of the function at a discrete set of points. Let's make a table of such values:

In[32]:=   zed = Table[Sin[i j], {i,0,2.8,0.2}, {j,0,2.8,0.2}];

Now we can display this table graphically by using the list-plotting analogue of Plot3D:

In[33]:=   ListPlot3D[zed]

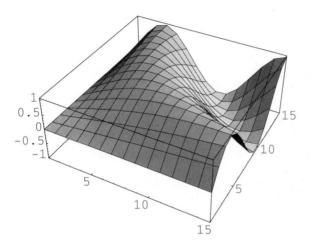

Apart from the labeling of the axes, this surface is identical to our previous surface.

6.5.1 Irregular Grids

We now make our data more interesting. Suppose that instead of sampling our function at a regular series of points, equally spaced by steps of 0.2, we sample it irregularly. We introduce x and y sampling points as follows:

In[34]:=   xgrid = {0,0.1,0.2,0.3,0.4,0.5,0.6,0.7,0.8,1.0,1.2,1.8,2.0,2.4,2.8};
            Length[xgrid]

Out[34]=   15

In[35]:=   ygrid = xgrid;

For simplicity, we have kept the x and y grids the same and have 15 points in each. Let's make a table of values of our function evaluated at these points:

In[36]:=   newzed = Table[Sin[xgrid[[i]] ygrid[[j]]], {i,1,15}, {j,1,15}];

As before, we can do a surface plot:

In[37]:= `ListPlot3D[newzed]`

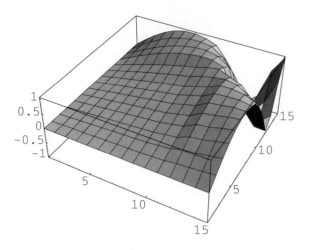

Our surface is now horribly distorted. The difficulty is that the built-in function `List-Plot3D` knows nothing about the grid. It just plots the values assuming that there is a regular grid. This assumption results in a sensible plot if and only if the underlying grid is regular.

You may never need to plot a function on an irregular grid, but people who solve partial differential equations have to do so as a matter of course. The point is that we can easily circumvent the problem by devoting a little thought to how *Mathematica* works. In fact, there are three ways to solve the problem, as shall be described next. The method of choice for this particular example is method 1, but we shall describe two alternatives as an illustration of technique. Users of older versions of *Mathematica* — that is, people who used Version 1.x — may well have used method 2 or 3 to handle the absence of the corresponding package in older versions of *Mathematica*.

Method 1: Check the packages!

Many plot routines for three dimensions that you might consider to be missing from the kernel are available in the `Graphics`Graphics3D`` package. We now load this package:

In[38]:= `Needs["Graphics`Graphics3D`"]`

The function that we require here is `ListSurfacePlot3D`. This function takes an array of the form $\{\{\{x_{11}, y_{11}, f_{11}\}, \ldots \{x_{1m}, y_{1m}, f_{1m}\}\}, \ldots, \{x_{nm}, y_{nm}, f_{nm}\}\}\}$. Therefore, our first step is to reorganize our data into this form:

In[39]:= `plotdata = Table[{xgrid[[i]], ygrid[[j]], newzed[[i, j]]},`
`{i,1,15}, {j,1,15}];`

In[40]:= `ListSurfacePlot3D[plotdata, BoxRatios -> {3, 3, 1}]`

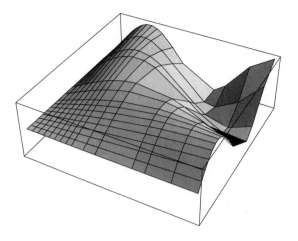

Method 2: Interpolation

A second method of treating the data for plotting is first to convert them to a function by interpolation and then to use Plot3D. The data must take the form

$$\{\{x_1, y_1, f_1\}, \{x_2, y_2, f_2\}, \ldots, \{x_n, y_n, f_n\}\} \ ,$$

so we carry out this reorganization first and follow it with a plot:

```
In[41]:=  interdata = Flatten[Table[{xgrid[[i]], ygrid[[j]], newzed[[i, j]]},
          {i, 1, 15}, {j, 1, 15}], 1];

In[42]:=  interfunc = Interpolation[interdata]

Out[42]=  InterpolatingFunction[{{0, 2.8}, {0, 2.8}}, <>]

In[43]:=  Plot3D[interfunc[x, y], {x, 0, 2.8}, {y, 0, 2.8}]
```

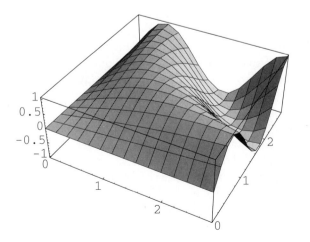

Method 3: Program with primitives

To solve our problem with primitives, we construct — manually and very carefully — a list of Polygons with vertices at the appropriate points and Show them in the Graphics3D environment:

```
In[44]:=  Show[Graphics3D[Table[Polygon[{
          {xgrid[[i]], ygrid[[j]], newzed[[i, j]]},
          {xgrid[[i]], ygrid[[j+1]], newzed[[i, j+1]]},
          {xgrid[[i+1]], ygrid[[j+1]], newzed[[i+1, j+1]]},
          {xgrid[[i+1]], ygrid[[j]], newzed[[i+1, j]]}}],
          {i, 1, 14}, {j, 1, 14}], BoxRatios -> {1, 1, 0.4}]]
```

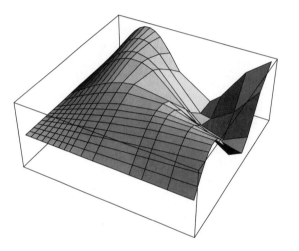

Our surface now has the correct overall shape. Any remaining distortions are due only to any inadequacy of how frequently we have sampled the function, and not to the way in which we have plotted it.

We emphasize once more that if you are given data based on an irregular but organized grid, you should use the package function ListSurfacePlot3D. The example of interpolation is meant to show you how you can force data to behave as a function by using interpolation. This technique is valid generally, as is our third method, which, once again, illustrates the fact that you can do anything with primitives if you need to!

Highly irregular grids

In the example of plotting the data for newzed, our data were highly organized. In general, we may not be so lucky, and the points at which a function is given may be much more irregular. To illustrate how to proceed, we shall load a package that allows us to shuffle our data into a random order. We have 15 times $15 = 225$ points, and we define a data set messydata, which is our original data randomly shuffled:

```
In[45]:=  Needs["DiscreteMath`Combinatorica`"]
```

In[46]:=   `ranind = RandomPermutation[225];`

In[47]:=   `messydata = interdata[[ranind]];`

The package for treating such a data set is in a slightly odd place, the `Computational-Geometry` section of the `DiscreteMath` packages directory. Note that the examples on highly irregular grids may take several minutes to execute on a workstation-class machine: If you have a 386 or regular Macintosh II, it is time to execute the commands and to take a coffee break!

In[48]:=   `Needs["DiscreteMath`ComputationalGeometry`"]`

There is a function `TriangularSurfacePlot`, but we have found that with versions of *Mathematica* numbered 2.1 or earlier, this function gives rather unpredictable results unless the data are rather trivial! (In the final stages of writing this book we had just received Version 2.2, and it should be pointed out that the following surface, or ones like it, are *not* obtained with data sets similar to this one in Version 2.2. However, this section also explains some of the mechanics of the `ComputationalGeometry` package — an understanding of which will help you in solving other visualization problems.) If you have not already done so, a good reason to upgrade to 2.2 is to avoid problems such as the following.

In[49]:=   `TriangularSurfacePlot[messydata, BoxRatios -> {3, 3, 1}]`

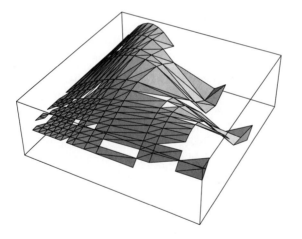

What should be happening, at least for our purposes, is that the surface is being triangulated according to a projection on the x, y plane. We can compute this triangulation manually, and we shall need the result shortly:

In[50]:=   `dtr = DelaunayTriangulation[Map[Drop[#, -1]&, messydata]];`

We can visualize the triangulation by a straightforward application of the `PlanarGraph-Plot` function applied to the (x, y) coordinates of our messy data:

In[51]:=   `PlanarGraphPlot[Map[Drop[#, -1]&, messydata],`
                   `LabelPoints -> False]`

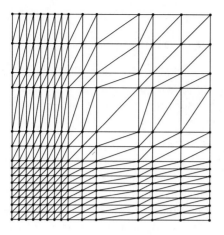

We see that the underlying way in which the points have been joined up is perfectly sound. We can produce a complete plot by combining our data with the triangulation manually. First, however, we need to understand the structure of the triangulation. This structure is as follows:

In[52]:= `Dimensions[dtr]`

Out[52]= `{225, 2}`

In[53]:= `dtr // Short`

Out[53]= `{{1, {175, 156, 150, 93}}, {2, <<1>>}, <<222>>, {225, <<1>>}}`

Thus, according to the result `dtr`, the first point in our shuffled list should be joined to six other points. We can construct a list of suitable primitives by joining up point 1 to points 175 and 156 with a triangle, and so on. There is some redundancy in the following code, which we have found to give reliable results at the price of most triangles being drawn twice. The simplicity of this method relies on the existence of a suitable ordering of the nearest neighbors in the results returned by `DelaunayTriangulation`:

In[54]:=
```
testtsp[data_, triang_] :=
Module[{lena, lenb, primlist, k, l},
primlist = {};
lena = Length[triang];
Do[lenb = Length[triang[[l,2]]];
Do[primlist =
Append[primlist,
Polygon[{data[[triang[[l,1]]]],
data[[triang[[l,2,k]]]], data[[triang[[l,2,k+1]]]]}]],
{k, 1, lenb - 1}],
{l, 1, lena}];
primlist]
```

In[55]:= `testoutput = testtsp[messydata, dtr];`

In[56]:= `Show[Graphics3D[testoutput, BoxRatios -> {3, 3, 1}]]`

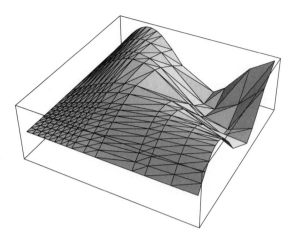

6.6 Other Constructions with Primitives

Now we shall discuss the visualization of data that comes from the numerical solution of some famous nonlinear equations — the Lorenz equations. The data here were generated long ago by FORTRAN code. Of course, you can solve the equations within *Mathematica*, and you may wish to read the following instructions on creating your own data set. The results of the internal solution can be fed directly into a ParametricPlot — here we are using NDSolve just so that you can create data, on disk, in a form similar to ours. Following this exercise, we import the data into *Mathematica*. It is structured as a list of (x, y, z) coordinates, so we read it in as triples.

To create your own data set, we suggest that you execute the following commands:

```
In[57]:=  NDSolve[{x'[t] == -3 (x[t] - y[t]),
            y'[t] == -x[t] z[t] + 26.5 x[t] - y[t],
            z'[t] ==  x[t] y[t] - z[t],
            x[0] == 0.53755,  y[0] ==-0.0071619, z[0] == 0.025124},
            {x, y, z}, {t, 0, 10}, MaxSteps -> 1500]

Out[57]=  {{x -> InterpolatingFunction[{0., 10.}, <>],
            y -> InterpolatingFunction[{0., 10.}, <>],
            z -> InterpolatingFunction[{0., 10.}, <>]}}

In[58]:=  chaosdata = Table[Evaluate[{x[(j-1)/100], y[(j-1)/100],
          z[(j-1)/100]} /. %1], {j, 1, 1001}];

In[59]:=  chaosdata[[1]]

Out[59]=  {{0.53755, -0.0071619, 0.025124}}
```

In the following commands, you should choose a convenient file name and directory to replace our Macintosh path and file Data:Book:chaos.dat:

```
In[60]:=  chaosstream = OpenWrite["Data:Book:chaos.dat"];
          Do[Do[Write[chaosstream, chaosdata[[j,1,k]]],
          {k, 1, 3}], {j, 1, 1001}]; Close[chaosstream]
```

Out[60]=   Data:Book:chaos.dat

We now have our data on disk. The following commands can be applied not only to our particular data, but also to any data that can be viewed as coordinates in three-dimensional space. We begin by reading in our data, organizing it into triples as we import it:

In[61]:=   Data = ReadList["Data:Book:chaos.dat", Table[Number, {3}]];

In[62]:=   Data[[1]]

Out[62]=   {0.53755, -0.0071619, 0.025124}

In[63]:=   Dimensions[Data]

Out[63]=   {1001, 3}

Our goal is to view this list as a swarm of points in two and three dimensions. First, let's consider a list of points in two dimensions, taking just the (x, y) coordinates:

In[64]:=   Pts2D = Table[Point[{Data[[i,1]],Data[[i,2]]}], {i,1,1001}];

Now we consider the following. Any one of the primitives may have certain attributes, such as PointSize, Color, and GrayLevel. To display a swarm of points in two dimensions, all we need to control the size is to prefix the primitive set by a qualifier:

In[65]:=   Show[Graphics[{PointSize[0.005], Pts2D}]]

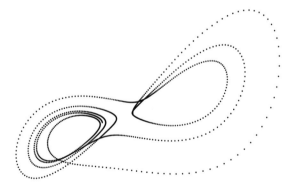

Next, let's construct the analogous three-dimensional example. We want red dots and identical x, y, z scales. We can do this in two ways. The first is

In[66]:=   Pts3D = Table[Point[{Data[[i,1]],Data[[i,2]],Data[[i,3]]}],
              {i, 1, 1001}];

The alternative, which is more elegant, is

In[67]:=   Pts3D = Map[Point, Data];

In[68]:=   Show[Graphics3D[{PointSize[0.005], RGBColor[1, 0, 0], Pts3D},
              BoxRatios -> {1, 1, 1}]]

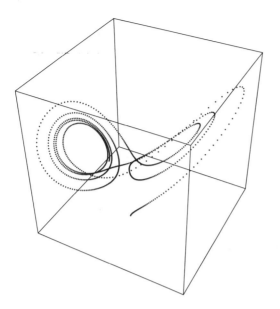

You may prefer a joined-up plot. You can create one rather more simply than you can the swarm plot since Line can digest a whole list of coordinate triples:

```
In[69]:= Show[Graphics3D[{Thickness[0.005], RGBColor[0, 1, 0],
         Line[Data]}, BoxRatios ->{1, 1, 1}]]
```

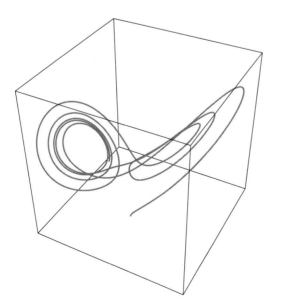

Devotees of the `Graphics3D` package may remark that all this can be done with the `ScatterPlot3D` function. This assertion is true, and this package uses constructions similar to those that we have just discussed. However, getting a grip on primitives is generally a valuable exercise, especially if you want to go beyond the capabilities of kernel or package functions. For example, once you know how to apply attributes with primitives, it is a simple matter to use color to show where in the dynamic you are, as in the next example:

```
In[70]:=  coldata2D = Table[{Hue[i/1001],Point[{Data[[i,1]],Data[[i,2]]}]},
          {i, 1, 1001}];
```

```
In[71]:=  Show[Graphics[coldata2D]]
```

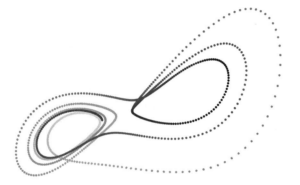

6.7 Animations

Animation is a popular favorite; however, in serious applications it should be used only when necessary. There are two important applications. First, there is parameter animation. This parameter may be time or some other variable to which we wish to assign a dynamic quality. Let's load the required package:

```
In[72]:=  Needs["Graphics`Animation`"]
```

The syntax for a two-dimensional animation is very easy:

```
In[73]:=  MoviePlot[Sin[t x], {x, 0, 4 Pi}, {t, 1, 2, 0.1}]
```

The implementation of animation is unfortunately front-end dependent, which is why we have not talked about it a great deal. On a NoteBook-based system, you just use a Do statement (either `MoviePlot` or `Do` works fine here). We have displayed only one frame, but you should construct the movie, provided you have sufficient memory:

```
In[74]:=  Do[Plot[Sin[t x], {x, 0, 4 Pi}], {t, 1, 2, 0.1}]
```

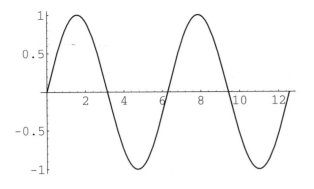

The resulting graphics can be grouped and animated. Parameter animation can also be used in three dimensions, but we also have the opportunity to use ViewPoint animation. It is critical to set the SphericalRegion -> True option. Here we just show the last frame:

```
In[75]:= Do[Plot3D[Sin[x] Cos[y], {x, -Pi, Pi}, {y, -Pi, Pi},
    SphericalRegion -> True, Axes -> False,
    ViewPoint -> {3 Cos[t], 3 Sin[t], 1}],
    {t, 0, 2 Pi - Pi/5, Pi/5}]
```

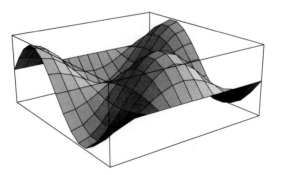

You should appreciate that the Do loop animation can be used on a NoteBook system in conjunction with any of the graphics operations that we have discussed.

6.8 Summary

Data may be visualized within *Mathematica* in many ways. There are three levels at which you can solve a problem in visualization. The first level involves using standard built-in functions such as ListPlot3D, ListContourPlot, and ListDensityPlot. Each of these functions has many options that can be used to control the appearance of the resulting graphic. These functions are approximately parallel to the functional plot commands `Plot3D`, `ContourPlot`, and `DensityPlot`. You can always turn your data into a function by using interpolation. Coloring should be used to communicate useful information, and not to add gratuitous special effects (unless that is what you are paid for). With data, this is best achieved by using the `ColorFunction` option with a pure function. Curves and surfaces can also be created using the `ParametricPlot3D` function. This command can take functions directly, and it can also take evaluated interpolation functions that have been applied to data.

The second level of problem solving is to use the packages. There are several useful graphics packages that add capabilities to the *Mathematica* kernel. We have found the most useful to be `Graphics`Graphics3D``, `Graphics`Animation``, and `DiscreteMath` `ComputationalGeometry``. Several other packages are available in the `Graphics` packages directory.

If there are no built-in or package functions that meet your needs, you can program *Mathematica* to produce almost any graphic by using primitives such as `Line`, `Point`, and `Polygon` in a `Show[Graphics3D[ ]]` operation. These can be applied most effectively to data by using the `Map` function to generate primitives directly from the data.

Exporting Results from *Mathematica*

This chapter addresses the problem of how to get your results out of *Mathematica*. The results may take the form of an entire formatted NoteBook — with graphics and equations — or may consist of only a few lines of text. We anticipate that the extent to which people desire to export material will diminish with time. We are aware, for example, that a version of *Mathematica* will soon be released that will have substantial capabilities for creating formatted mathematical material.

In writing this chapter, we were also aware that the capabilities for postprocessing and editing of *Mathematica* material are, to some extent, dependent on the computer system that you are using and the applications that you have. We have tried to give a balanced discussion, but inevitably there will be some material here that you will not be able to exploit immediately.

7.1 Converting and Exporting Entire NoteBooks

We begin by discussing techniques for exporting the bulk of a NoteBook. Techniques for exporting smaller components will be discussed in Section 7.2.

7.1.1 About This Book and TeX

Perhaps the topic about which we can talk most authoritatively is the process that was used to create this book. We worked on a Macintosh Quadra 700 and a Windows 486. NoteBooks were created on both systems and were assembled on the Quadra. It is worth pointing out first that NoteBooks are interchangeable between such systems, the NeXT platform, and other systems that will soon support NoteBooks under X-Windows.

A NoteBook usually has two components: There is a pure text component, which is visible under Windows, for example, as a file with an .ma extension; then there is a resource component, which under Windows, is given an .mb extension. On a Macintosh, you cannot see the separate identity of the files since the files are bundled in data and resource forks of an extended file type. The resource component is almost redundant in that it just contains screen images of the graphics that are contained in your NoteBook. The text part contains all the information needed to recreate the graphics, but at the price of some rendering time when you open the NoteBook.

The text parts of NoteBooks may be converted from one computer system to another by any reliable text-to-text translator. The entire NoteBook, complete with rendered graphics, is recreated when you next open it. In our experience, the only remaining complication is typeface mismatches, but you can sort them out easily by setting styles appropriately.

We needed, for many equations, to have formatted mathematical material included in our text. To do this, we just wrote in standard TeX, bearing in mind that our next step was to run each NoteBook through a system for converting NoteBooks to TeX.

Our process for converting NoteBooks to TeX made use of the public domain utility **nb2tex**, available as a compiled program, for a variety of platforms, through the Math-Source library. This program is free, and it is under continual development. It produces a plain TeX file, but with a large amount of sectioning information and a knowledge of many of the style changes that you may have made in the NoteBook. Some manual editing of the resulting file is needed, and you will certainly need to configure the typefaces to suit those supported by your TeX system. After a few test attempts, we found it possible to run **nb2tex** on a NoteBook, make a few standard changes, and then to process the resulting file without errors (that is, other than those in the TeX we had added to the NoteBook — this system does not stop those!). The graphics are stripped out of the NoteBook, and each one is converted properly to an *eps* file (see the discussion on graphics in Section 7.2.1 to understand why file creation is an issue). Being a generic system, it cannot convert specific resources for screen display of graphics, so, unless you happen to be working with a TeX preview system capable of displaying pure PostScript graphics, you will not be able to preview the full result. This drawback was a minor inconvenience compared to the overall benefits of this system.

7.1.2 Word and Other RTF-Supporting Programs

With Word, and indeed any word processor or page-makeup program providing full support for RTF (rich text or interchange format), the situation is reasonably straightforward. If your version of *Mathematica* allows you to save your NoteBook in RTF, then do so and simply open the resulting file in your copy of Word. The ability to save in RTF is a facility that is diffusing from the Macintosh to other versions as time goes by. We have also used it to import formatted NoteBooks directly into PageMaker. Note that although this format is reliable for formatted text in NoteBooks, the graphical elements should be treated separately, as discussed in Section 7.2.1.

7.2 Exporting Smaller Elements

You may need to export graphics, text, or data from *Mathematica* to another part of your computer system. In this section, we discuss techniques specific to the export of such elements.

7.2.1 Graphics

The fundamental description of *Mathematica* graphics is as (a form of) PostScript. This description of graphics has many benefits and one occasional drawback. The drawback is that on those occasions when you want to do a "quick and dirty" job of creating a screen image, possibly in an animation sequence, there is an overhead involved in creating a file of PostScript for each screen image. However, the resulting images can be rescaled and rendered on a variety of output devices in extraordinarily high quality and clarity. If you are serious about *Mathematica* graphics, we strongly recommend that you invest in an output device with a PostScript or PostScript-compatible interpreter. This investment does not have to be absurdly expensive. Although we use a PostScript laser printer for our own work in monochrome, for color test prints we use a software interpreter and an inexpensive inkjet color printer. *Mathematica* can often do a good job of talking to other output devices, but the quality can suffer in the translation. Macintosh users with QuickDraw printers for example, may be disappointed with the results of color printing. You can improve results considerably by working with such printers through a software PostScript interpreter. Let's take a closer look at the details of graphics storage within *Mathematica*.

How *Mathematica* stores graphics

The kernel creates graphics in a highly abbreviated form of PostScript. It is vital to appreciate that this abbreviated structure is not of a form that may be understood by a generic PostScript output device. It is abbreviated to speed up rendering, and, in fact, the extent of the abbreviation was increased considerably in moving from Version 2.0 to Version 2.1, resulting in much decreased rendering times (and in Version 2.0 front ends crashing when presented with a Version 2.1-sourced NoteBook!). Your computer display system can work directly off this abbreviated PostScript.

How you can extract graphics

When you want to print or export such graphics, it is important to come to terms with the implications of the abbreviated form of PostScript. There are essentially two ways to treat the problem: You can either translate the abbreviated code to ordinary PostScript or a variant thereof, or you can sandwich the code between a dictionary header and a simple trailer.

Let's consider the various ways in which you can handle PostScript export. The approach is, to some extent, system dependent. However, on any system, the `Display` command writes the abbreviated PostScript out to a file:

```
In[1]:=    Display["file.ps", graphic]
```

On most systems, except Macintosh and Windows, this use of `Display` is the first step in printing a graphic. The second step is to run a fixer program, such as `msdosps` or `rasterps`, that sandwiches the abbreviated code in a new file between a header and a footer. This new file can be sent to a printer. On a Macintosh or Windows system, the printing methodology is to choose `Print` from the appropriate menu. If you have selected normal printing, this selection will create a temporary file (in the case of the Macintosh, a sandwich and in the case of Windows, a file with Windows PostScript) that goes straight to the printer. If you set up your system to keep the file, the results can be printed later.

For Windows, printing to a file is, in our view, the best way to export graphics to other programs — set up Windows to save the print job in an *eps* file, and import this file to your word processor or other graphics package. A Macintosh offers a host of options. The two methods that we have found to be most reliable are these:

1. Copy the graphic and use the menu `Convert Clipboard` option to save the graphic in a complete eps file. This file may be imported and rescaled or overlaid in most good word processors and graphics packages, but it cannot be edited.
2. Copy the graphic and use the menu `Convert Clipboard` option to save the graphic in an *Illustrator* file. This file can be edited in programs such as *Illustrator* or *Freehand*. This approach is a flexible one — the only drawback that we have found is that sometimes color balance may be upset by the conversion.

How you can automate printing

One area where there is nonuniformity between systems is automatic printing from a *Mathematica* program. If you have a Windows system or a Macintosh, you will find automatic printing difficult since the print command is a menu operation. On other systems, the use of `Display` may be followed by some form of external shell command (under the UNIX operating system or MS-DOS) to fix the file with `rasterps` or `msdosps` and then be followed by a similar such command to send the file to a printer. It is intended that future versions of *Mathematica* allow the kernel to control the front end, so this problem is hopefully a temporary one. If you have Windows, and you know someone with a Macintosh, MS-DOS, or UNIX version of *Mathematica*, then there is a trick that you can do. Ask them to respectively `Print` to a file, run `msdosps` or run `rasterps` on some graphic, and extract from this file the header and footer information. Call this `header.ps` and `footer.ps`. In Windows *Mathematica*, commands of the form

```
In[2]:=   Display["myfile.ps", mygraphic];
          !sortit
```

where `sortit.bat` is a text file containing

```
copy header.ps + myfile.ps + footer.ps temp.ps
copy temp.ps lpt1
del temp.ps
```

will fix up and print the file to a port `lpt1`, on which should reside a connection to a PostScript printer. This trick relies on Windows' ability to fire up DOS shells and consequently does not work on a Macintosh under Finder.

7.2.2 Text

On non-NoteBook systems, there is never really a sense in which text is stored in *Mathematica*. A good working practice is to create your *Mathematica* commands in files and to keep one or more editor sessions active while you work on the system. The key point is to adopt a mode of working that allows outputs and inputs to be saved in a text file. If you subsequently import the results into a word processor or page-makeup program, then you should use a nonproportionately spaced typeface, such as Courier or a similar typewriter typeface, to display the results. *Mathematica*'s display of standard output relies on having such a typeface.

The same remarks apply to NoteBook systems, except that you probably have access to mouse-based copy-and-paste functions to export simple text information. Remember to use Courier or a similar typeface in your other program and, if you are copying more than one or two cells, to exploit the RTF export facility if you have it.

7.2.3 Data

There are many ways to export data. If you wish to export data dynamically to another program, then MathLink is your best choice, as discussed in detail in Chapter 14. If you wish to write data to a file, then you may find the following simple procedures useful. More general routines for exporting data in a FORTRAN-like format are given in Section 7.3.

I/O, I/O, it's off to disk we go

If you have created one or more *Mathematica* objects and wish to save them independently of any NoteBook, there are various techniques that you can use. We shall illustrate these techniques by considering the various ways in which you can save data in the form of a matrix, or list of lists. Let's define a *Mathematica* object:

In[3]:=   `mymatrix = {{1, 2, 3, 4}, {9, 8, 7, 6}, {4, 4, 4, 4}, {5, 6, 5, 6}};`

We can save our definition of `mymatrix` in a file called `mydef`:

In[4]:=   `Save["mydef", mymatrix]`

We clear the definition of `mymatrix`:

In[5]:=   `mymatrix =.`

We now ask about `mymatrix` in order to check that it has gone:

In[6]:=   `mymatrix`

Out[6]=   `mymatrix`

Now we get back the form of `mymatrix` (the following assumes a fresh session):

In[1]:=   `<<mydef;`

We can ask questions about `mymatrix` as before and we can find out what new variables have been added:

In[2]:=   `?Global`*`*`

`Exit      mymatrix Quit`

In[3]:=   `mymatrix`

Out[3]=   `{{1, 2, 3, 4}, {9, 8, 7, 6}, {4, 4, 4, 4}, {5, 6, 5, 6}}`

How else might we wish to output `mymatrix`? We can format our output in a variety of ways. We might want any of the following:

1. a long vertical list
2. a text file in *Mathematica* format
3. a comma-separated variable file
4. a tab-separated variable file
5. a file containing a specified number of characters per entry

The *Mathematica* object `Tab` is quite helpful for creating a tab-separated file. Note that spreadsheets and graphics programs may use *tab* or *csv* format, so the following example may be handy if you need to export data to such a package — not that we can imagine why!

`Write` is a simple command that automatically puts a new line at the end. `WriteString` is more low level, but it is adaptable. The following examples illustrate all five cases. Try each one in turn (note that the numbers associated with each output stream will vary, depending on the state of your *Mathematica* session).

```
In[4]:=  mymatrix

Out[4]=  {{1, 2, 3, 4}, {9, 8, 7, 6}, {4, 4, 4, 4}, {5, 6, 5, 6}}

In[5]:=  matout = OpenWrite["matrix.dat"]

Out[5]=  OutputStream[matrix.dat, 19]

In[6]:=  Do[Do[
            Write[matout, mymatrix[[i, j]]],
            {j, 1, 4}], {i, 1, 4}];
         Close[matout];

In[7]:=  !!matrix.dat
            1
            2
            3
            4
            9
            8
            7
            6
            4
            4
            4
            4
            5
            6
            5
            6

In[8]:=  matoutb = OpenWrite["matrixb.dat"]

Out[8]=  OutputStream[matrixb.dat, 13]

In[9]:=  Write[matoutb, mymatrix];
         Close[matoutb];
```

```
In[10]:=   !!matrixb.dat

           {{1, 2, 3, 4}, {9, 8, 7, 6}, {4, 4, 4, 4}, {5, 6, 5, 6}}

In[11]:=   matoutc = OpenWrite["matrixc.dat"]

Out[11]=   OutputStream[matrixc.dat, 32]

In[12]:=   Do[
           WriteString[matoutc,
           ToString[mymatrix[[i, 1]]],",",
           ToString[mymatrix[[i, 2]]],",",
           ToString[mymatrix[[i, 3]]],",",
           ToString[mymatrix[[i, 4]]],"\n"],
           {i, 1, 4}];
           Close[matoutc];

In[13]:=   !!matrixc.dat

           1,2,3,4
           9,8,7,6
           4,4,4,4
           5,6,5,6

In[14]:=   matoutd = OpenWrite["matrixd.dat"]

Out[14]=   OutputStream[matrixd.dat, 31]

In[15]:=   Do[
           WriteString[matoutd,
           ToString[mymatrix[[i, 1]]],Tab,
           ToString[mymatrix[[i, 2]]],Tab,
           ToString[mymatrix[[i, 3]]],Tab,
           ToString[mymatrix[[i, 4]]],"\n"],
           {i, 1, 4}];
           Close[matoutd];

In[16]:=   !!matrixd.dat
           1    2    3    4
           9    8    7    6
           4    4    4    4
           5    6    5    6
```

Finally, if you need to create formatted output where each entry has a fixed character width, you can do so. This format is useful if you want to read in the data to a system such as FORTRAN, where format statements such as F7.3 are used to indicate a number with a total of seven characters, three of which are after the decimal place. In the following example, we create a file where each number is preceded by two spaces, 2X in FORTRAN (you should consult Section 7.3 if you wish to go to town on this type of output because it contains a large number of routines for emulating standard FORTRAN-type output):

```
In[17]:=   data = {{-1.2,6.9999,6.888},{1, 21, 321}}

Out[17]=   {{-1.2, 6.9999, 6.888}, {1, 21, 321}}

In[18]:=   myformat[dat_] := PaddedForm[dat, {7, 3}]
```

```
In[19]:=   oute = OpenWrite["oute.dat"]

Out[19]=   OutputStream[oute.dat, 6]

In[20]:=   Do[WriteString[oute,
           ToString[myformat[data[[i, 1]]]],
           ToString[myformat[data[[i, 2]]]],
           ToString[myformat[data[[i, 3]]]],
           "\n"],{i, 1, 2}];
           Close[oute]; oute.dat;

In[21]:=   !!oute.dat
             -1.200    7.000    6.888
              1.000   21.000  321.000
```

7.2.4 Data Tables for Direct Output to a Printer

Suppose that you have completed all the analysis on a set of data and you want to package them all up in a table to send to a printer. What options are available? One possibility is to present the data in graphical form to create an output file (eps) containing the data in a format that can be read by another graphics package and printed. If you use the results of Section 7.2.3, you can write a tab-separated text file that can be read by most good spreadsheets, then possibly tidied up, and printed. You may even be able to send the ASCII file directly to your printer, although the output quality will be poor. Many printers can accept files written in PostScript, which is the language that *Mathematica* uses for its graphics. In this section, we show how it is possible to take a *Mathematica* list and to create a PostScript file containing these data in a presentable table form. Then, we give you tips on how to send this file to your printer.

Throughout the section, we shall make use of a particular example to illustrate our objective. The example is deliberately simple, but the techniques that we develop are of general applicability. Our aim will be to create a function that takes the fictional list data

```
In[22]:=   data = {{15,15,15},{"Name","Age","Salary"},
           {"John Smith","24","$40,000"}, {"Peter Long","63","$60,000"}};
```

(where the values in the first list refer to the widths of the respective fields) and creates a PostScript file containing the following table:

Name	Age	Salary
John Smith	24	$40,000
Peter Long	63	$60,000

Our overall plan will be as follows: First, we take the data file and make a string for each row in the table. This construction will involve careful consideration of the format, so that the various columns line up. Next, we open an output file, and, using the dimensions of the data file, we write PostScript instructions to draw lines enclosing the table and separating the title line from the data. Finally, we write the PostScript code to include the data within the table.

Formatting your data

The first task that we tackle is to ensure that the various columns and labels line up even when the entries in a particular column are of different length. We must create a function that takes a string or number and, by prepending spaces, converts the latter into a string with a given number of characters (this conversion will make our data line up on the right):

```
In[23]:=  rightalign[text_,paddedlength_Integer] :=
          Module[{textstring,textlength},
             textstring = ToString[text];
             textlength = StringLength[textstring];
             StringJoin[
                Apply[StringJoin,Table[" ",{paddedlength-textlength}]],
                textstring]
          ]

In[24]:=  FullForm[   rightalign["jason",10]   ]

Out[24]=  "     jason"
```

In this example, the string "jason" has been converted into a string of length 10. We forced the output through FullForm to make the leading spaces visible. When we apply rightalign to a list, *Mathematica* converts the list into a string and pads this string out:

```
In[25]:=  FullForm[rightalign[{1,2,3},10]]

Out[25]=  "   {1, 2, 3}"
```

It would be much more useful if, instead, rightalign forced its way inside the list and padded out every entry. We can achieve this action by telling *Mathematica* that the function has the attribute Listable:

```
In[26]:=  Attributes[rightalign] := {Listable}

In[27]:=  FullForm[rightalign[{1,2,3},10]]

Out[27]=  List["         1", "         2", "         3"]

In[28]:=  tabletostring[data_List] :=
          Module[{flip,widths},
          widths = data[[1]];
          flip = Transpose[Rest[data]];
          flip = Table[Map[rightalign[#,widths[[i]]]&, flip[[i]]],
          {i,1,Length[widths]}];
          Map[StringJoin,flip]];
```

```
In[29]:=  makefile[tablelist_List,filename_String]:=
          Module[{outline,tlx,tly,width,height},
             tlx = 50; tly = -125;
             width = 7*StringLength[tablelist[[1]]];
             height = 12*Length[tablelist]+10;
             outline = OpenWrite[filename];
             WriteString[outline,"%!PS-Adobe-3.0 \n"];
             WriteString[outline,"%%BoundingBox: ", ToString[tlx-10]," ",
                         ToString[tly-height-10]," ",ToString[tlx+width+10],
                         " ",ToString[tly+10],"\n\n"];
             WriteString[outline,"90 rotate\n"];
             WriteString[outline,ToString[tlx]," ",ToString[tly]," moveto "];
             WriteString[outline,ToString[width]," 0 rlineto "];
             WriteString[outline," 0 ",ToString[-height]," rlineto\n"];
             WriteString[outline,ToString[-width]," 0 rlineto "];
             WriteString[outline," 0 ",ToString[height]," rlineto \n"];
             WriteString[outline,ToString[tlx]," " ToString[tly-14]," moveto "];
             WriteString[outline,ToString[width]," 0 rlineto \n"];
             WriteString[outline,"\n stroke \n\n"];
             WriteString[outline,"/Courier-Bold findfont 10 scalefont setfont \n"];
             WriteString[outline,"60 -135 moveto (",tablelist[[1]],") show \n\n"];
             WriteString[outline,"/Courier findfont 10 scalefont setfont \n"];
             Do[
                WriteString[outline,
                  StringJoin["60 ",ToString[-130-10*i]," moveto (",
                  tablelist[[i]],") show \n"]]
                ,{i,2,Length[tablelist]}];
             WriteString[outline,"\nshowpage \n%%EOF \n"];
             Close[outline]
             ]
In[30]:=  output = tabletostring[data];
          makefile[output,"jas.ps"];
          !!jas.ps

          %!PS-Adobe-3.0


          %%BoundingBox: 40 -181 277 -115


          90 rotate

          50 -125 moveto 217 0 rlineto  0 -46 rlineto

          -217 0 rlineto  0 46 rlineto

          50   -139 moveto 217 0 rlineto


           stroke


          /Courier-Bold findfont 10 scalefont setfont
```

```
60 -135 moveto (      Name      Age       Salary) show


/Courier findfont 10 scalefont

setfont

60 -150 moveto (  John Smith    24        $20,000) show

60 -160 moveto (  Peter Long    66        $15,000) show



showpage


%%EOF
```

7.3 FORTRAN Output

The FORTRAN format statement allows programmers to exercise a great deal of control over the style of the output of their programs. Similar control is afforded in *Mathematica* by use of the PaddedForm and other commands. However, the job of determining the relevant argument to PaddedForm for a particular FORTRAN format often is not clear. It seemed sensible to us to define a set of *Mathematica* functions that allow rapid conversion of a FORTRAN format statement into *Mathematica* instructions. We have included this coding in a package in an appendix at the end of this chapter. If you are likely to use a lot of FORTRAN formatting, we recommend that you copy this package into a text file and load it up whenever you need to use it. We recommend that you do the following:

1. Find the *Mathematica* packages folder/directory.
2. Create a new folder/directory within it called personal.
3. Create a new *Mathematica* NoteBook (or use a text editor if you are on a system without a NoteBook interface), and enter the program as a single input cell. Change the cell attribute to initialization, and store the NoteBook as fortform.m in the personal directory.

Once you have completed these steps, you can load up the file from a session by simply entering the command Needs["personal`fortform`"]. Be careful in typing in the quotation marks. We stress that it does not matter whether you understand the details of this code. As long as you can type, you can use the code as a magical tool to make your FORTRAN format statements work. Suppose that we load the package to see what it can do:

In[31]:=   Needs["personal`fortform`"]

In[32]:=   ?Fortran*

```
FortranForm  FortranPrint FortranRead  FortranWrite
```

In addition to the resident FortranForm instruction, there are three further FORTRAN-related commands, each with online help. We shall look at them next.

7.3.1 FortranPrint

The online help gives us the following description of FortranPrint:

In[33]:= ?FortranPrint

```
FortranPrint[format,{data}]  prints the data list to the
screen using the format specified by FormatNo[format]
```

We can also pull up information on the syntax of FormatNo:

In[34]:= ?FormatNo

```
FormatNo[format] is a FORTRAN type format  specifier. For
example the FORTRAN format statement

  10 FORMAT(4A10,5X)

is implemented by

  FormatNo[10] = {"4A10", "5X"}

Supported specifiers are  A,X,I,E,F and /
```

This example should all be transparent to FORTRAN users. For the benefit of everyone else, another example is probably in order:

In[35]:= FormatNo[10] = {"A10","I7","5X","I4","A4","/","F5.2","E10.3"};

```
FortranPrint[10,{"Jason",-342,123456,"Alison",2.7818,2^200}]
    Jason   -342     ****Alis

  2.78  1.607E60
```

The first command specifies a layout containing the way in which we want our data to be printed. The second command uses this format to print a list of data. Notice that the format list is longer than is the data list. The command 5X represents an instruction to leave five spaces and does not correspond to any element in the first list. Similarly, the string "/" is a newline instruction and also has no partner in the data list. The remaining commands break down as follows:

1. Jason and A10: Print the string "Jason" right-justified in a field the width of 10 characters (FortranPrint makes up the extra space by prepending spaces).
2. -342 and I7: Print the integer -342 in a field of width 7, again right-justified.
3. 5X: Leave five spaces.
4. 123456 and I4: Print the integer 123456 in a field of width 4. This field is not wide enough to hold the number, so four asterisks are printed.
5. Alison and A4: Print the string "Alison" in a field of width 4. The leading four characters of the string are used.
6. "/": Make a new line.

7. `2.7818` and `F5.2`: Print the number 2.7818 in a field of width 5, with two digits after the decimal point.
8. `2^200` and `E10.3`: Print the number 2^200 in exponential format, using a field of width 10 and three decimal places.

It is also possible to define the same format for several fields:

```
In[36]:=  FormatNo[20] = {"I3","2X","4I3"};
          FortranPrint[20,{12,31121,2,3,4}]

          12  ***  2  3  4
```

In this case, *Mathematica* prints the first integer in a field of width 3, leaves two spaces, and then attempts to place the remaining four integers in fields of width 3, using asterisks when there is not enough room. The coding in FORTRAN would be

```
    PRINT 20,12,31121,2,3,4
10 FORMAT (I3,2X,4I3)
```

The only real difference is that, in *Mathematica*, the definition of the format must precede the format's use.

7.3.2 File Input/Output

In addition to using format statements to write to the screen, the package described in the appendix to this chapter allows formatted data to be read from and written to a file. This facility is extremely important to have if you want to make your *Mathematica* code compatible with other FORTRAN code.

FortranWrite

Suppose that we have a FORTRAN program that is generating data and we wish to store these data in a file. First, we open and assign a label to this file, so that we can write to it. Then, we send our data to the file, probably using a `Write` statement in conjunction with a format specifier. Finally, we close the file. The following chunk of code which writes the values of some useful physical constants to a file, illustrates this procedure:

```
    OPEN (UNIT = 2, FILE = 'PHYSCONS', STATUS ='NEW')
    WRITE (UNIT = 2, FMT = 10) 'Speed of Light m/s',3E8
    WRITE (UNIT = 2, FMT = 10) 'Speed of Sound m/s',330
    ENDFILE (UNIT = 2)
    CLOSE (UNIT = 2)
10 FORMAT (A20,E10.2)
```

The sequence of commands required in *Mathematica* is virtually identical to our sequence of FORTRAN commands. Once again, we open a new file and assign a label to it. Then, we write our data to the file, using the format specifiers developed in the previous section. Finally, we close the file:

```
In[37]:=    FormatNo[10] = {"A20","E10.2"};
            outline = OpenWrite["PHYSCONS"];
            FortranWrite[outline,10,{"Speed of Light m/s",300000000}];
            FortranWrite[outline,10,{"Speed of Sound m/s",330.0}];
            Close[outline];

            !!PHYSCONS
                Speed of Light m/s     3.00E8
                Speed of Sound m/s     3.30E2
```

FortranRead

Suppose that we have a data file that we have created using a FORTRAN program (or a *Mathematica* program using the format commands introduced in the previous section). From the format statement in the FORTRAN code, it should be clear how the data have been stored. The FortranRead command makes it possible to use this information to read the data back into *Mathematica*. For example, in the previous section, we sent some formatted data on the values of certain physical constants to the file PHYSCONS. In outputting the data, we used the format specifier {"A20","E10.2"}, and we can use the same specifier to read them back in:

```
In[38]:=    FormatNo[10] = {"A20","E10.2"};
            inline = OpenRead["PHYSCONS"];
            FortranRead[inline,10]

Out[38]=                                        8
            {  Speed of Light m/s, 3.  10 }

In[39]:=    FortranRead[inline,10]

Out[39]=    {  Speed of Sound m/s, 330.}

In[40]:=    Close[inline]

Out[40]=    PHYSCONS
```

7.4 Summary

In this chapter, we have presented a potpourri of techniques that have proved useful for exporting information from *Mathematica*. For exporting entire NoteBooks, users of TeX will have found the section on the utility nb2tex invaluable. On the other hand, if your word-processing package is Word, the information on exporting NoteBooks in *Rich Text Format* would have been more relevant.

Mathematica is capable of generating breathtaking graphics, and we have explored several ways that these objects may be exported. By necessity, the details of this process are system dependent, and we have considered three platforms: PC, Macintosh, and UNIX. The techniques used to export data are the same on all platforms. To be able to communicate with other applications, it is extremely important to have full control over output formats. We have seen that the built-in functions, such as Write, can deal with the simple cases. Complete control is possible through the use of FORTRAN specifiers, and we have presented a comprehensive package to deal with the most important of these specifiers.

7.5 Appendix: FORTRAN Formatting Code

```
BeginPackage["FortForm`"];

FortranPrint::usage = "FortranPrint[format,{data}]
prints the data list to the \nscreen using the format
specified by FormatNo[format]";

FortranWrite::usage = "FortranWrite[stream,format,{data}]
writes the data list to \nthe Output Stream specified by
stream using the format \nspecified by FormatNo[format]";

FormatNo::usage = "FormatNo[format] is a FORTRAN type format
specifier. For \nexample the FORTRAN format statement\n\n
10 FORMAT(4A10,5X)\n\nis implemented by\n\n
FormatNo[10] = {"4A10","5X"}\n\nSupported specifiers are
A,X,I,E,F and /";

FortranRead::usage = "FortranRead[stream,format] reads in a
list of data \nfrom the stream assuming a format
FormatNo[format]";

Begin["`Private`"];

        (* CODE TO WRITE FORMATTED DATA *)

  (* Define functions to create strings of spaces and
     stars *)
spaces[n_Integer]:= Apply[StringJoin,Table[" ",{n}]];
stars[n_Integer] := Apply[StringJoin,Table["*",{n}]];

  (* Define a function which converts the decimal part
     of a number into an integer *)
dec[x_String]:= ToExpression[ StringDrop[x,
              StringPosition[x,"."][[1,1]]]];

  (* Define a function which converts a format statement
     to a sensible form *)
Fconv[x_String] := Module[{},
    fieldpos = StringPosition[x,{"E","F","X","I","A","/"}][[1,1]];
    If[StringTake[x,{fieldpos}] == "X",
       return = {{"X",ToExpression[StringDrop[x,{fieldpos}]]}}],
    reps = If[fieldpos == 1, 1,
             ToExpression[StringTake[x,fieldpos-1]]];
    return = {StringTake[x,{fieldpos}]};
    rest = StringDrop[x,fieldpos];
    If[StringLength[rest] == 0,,
       return = Append[return,
                     Floor[ToExpression[rest]]];
     If[StringPosition[rest,"."] == {},,
      return = Append[return,dec[rest]]
        ]
      ];
```

```
        return = Table[return,{reps}];
      ];
      return
  ];
Fconv[x_List] := Apply[Join,Map[Fconv,x]];



  (* Define a function which formats a list of
     data according to a list of formats *)
Fformat[{},{}] = "";
Fformat[{a___},{{"/"},b___}]:=
      StringJoin["\n",Fformat[{a},{b}]];



  (* Define write and print statements which work like the
     FORTRAN version *)
FortranPrint[x_Integer,b_List] :=
        Print[Fformat[b,Fconv[FormatNo[x]]]];
FortranWrite[line_OutputStream,x_Integer,b_List] :=
        WriteString[line,Fformat[b,
        Fconv[Append[FormatNo[x],"/"]]]];



  (* Implementation of X capability *)
Fformat[{a___},{{"X",b_Integer},c___}] :=
    StringJoin[spaces[b],Fformat[{a},{c}]];

Implementation of A capability *)
Fformat[{a_String,b___},{{"A",c_Integer},d___}] :=
      StringJoin[asty[a,c],Fformat[{b},{d}]];
asty[text_String,field_Integer] :=
Module[{len = StringLength[text]},
      If[len < field,
        StringJoin[spaces[field-len],text],
       StringTake[text,field]
      ]
      ];

  (* Implementation of E capability *)
esty[x_,{field_Integer,pl_Integer}] :=
Module[{me = MantissaExponent[N[x]],temp},
     temp = StringJoin[fsty[me[[1]],
             {pl+5/2-Sign[me[[1]]]/2,pl}],"E",
             ToString[PaddedForm[me[[2]],2, NumberPadding -> "0",
             NumberSigns -> {"-","+"},SignPadding -> True]]
             ];
      If[StringLength[temp] > field, stars[field]
                       , asty[temp,field]]]
Fformat[{a_,b___},{{"E",c_Integer,d_Integer},f___}] :=
StringJoin[esty[a,{c,d}], Fformat[{b},{f}]];

  (* Implementation of F capability *)
fsty[r_Real,{a_Integer,b_Integer}] :=
Module[{len = StringLength[ToString[r]]},
     temp = ToString[PaddedForm[r,{len+5,b},
                  NumberPadding -> {"","0"}]];
      If[StringLength[temp]>a,stars[a],asty[temp,a]]];
Fformat[{a_Real,b___} ,{{"F",c_Integer,d_Integer},e___}] :=
StringJoin[fsty[a,{c,d}], Fformat[{b},{e}]];
```

```
(* Implementation of I capability *)
isty[a_Integer,b_Integer] :=
Module[{temp = ToString[a]},
       If[StringLength[temp] > b, stars[b], asty[temp,b]]];
Fformat[{a_Integer,b___},{{"I",c_Integer},d___}] :=
StringJoin[isty[a,c],Fformat[{b},{d}]];



            (* CODE TO READ IN FORMATTED DATA *)

First we define a function to read in a number
   of characters *)
cread[line_InputStream,n_Integer] :=
     Apply[StringJoin,Read[line,Table[Character,{n}]]]];

Implementation of A facility *)
fread[line_InputStream,{"A",x_Integer}] := cread[line,x];

Implementation of I facility *)
fread[line_InputStream, {"I",x_Integer}] :=
    ToExpression[cread[line, x]];

Implementation of E facility *)
fread[line_InputStream, {"E",x_Integer,y_Integer}] :=
     ToExpression[StringReplace[cread[line,x],
     {"e" -> " 10^","E" -> " 10^"}]];

Implementation of X facility *)
fread[line_InputStream,{"X",x_Integer}] :=
     Block[{},cread[line,x];];

Implementation of newline facility *)
fread[line_InputStream,{"/"}] := Block[{},cread[line,1];];

Implementation of F facility *)
fread[line_InputStream, {"F",x_Integer,y_Integer}] :=
    ToExpression[cread[line,x]];

Code to read in a multiple format statement *)
fread[line_InputStream,{b__List}] :=
    Select[Map[fread[line,#]&,{b}],!SameQ[#,Null]&];

Code to simulate FORTRAN read statement *)
FortranRead[line_InputStream,a_Integer] :=
    fread[line,Fconv[Append[FormatNo[a],"/"]]];

End[];

Protect[FortranRead,FortranPrint,FortranWrite];

EndPackage[];
```

Modeling with *Mathematica*

Different Programming Styles

When users are asked what programming style *Mathematica* uses, they frequently reply that it uses many — that the choice is up to the user. Such a statement probably seems vague and of dubious validity. In fact, it is not. It is true that there are invariably several ways to solve a problem, each with its own particular advantages and disadvantages. If speed is a particular problem, then the choice of the correct technique may require some careful thought (for instance, see Chapters 11 and 14); in most cases, however, you should feel free to use the method that feels most comfortable to you. We think that the best way to make our point is through an example. Do not worry if you fail to follow the exact details of how we have implemented the various possibilities. This chapter is meant to give you just a taste of what is to come in the rest of Part Three.

8.1 Binned Data

The following instruction creates a list of 100 random integers lying in the range 1 to 10. We have cloaked the instruction with Short to prevent unnecessary screen display:

```
In[1]:=   Short[ data = Table[ Random[Integer,{1,10}],{100}] ]
```

```
Out[1]=   {10, 6, 7, 8, 4, 5, 3, 8, 2, 2, 3, 9, <<82>>, 10, 2, 7, 6, 6, 5}
```

Our objective is to make a list from these data that contains the frequencies of the various integers. There are many ways to achieve this objective. Try them out and see which is the most efficient method and which you like the most.

8.1.1 Procedural Methods

By a *procedural method*, we basically mean a Do loop. The definition here is comprised of a set of instructions and uses a local variable called bins which holds the current frequencies. As we progress through the list in a stepwise fashion, we increment the relevant element of the list using ++, a well-known C instruction. On exit from the loop, the list of frequencies is returned. This method is an efficient way to implement the function:

```
In[2]:=   proc[x_List] := Module[{bins = {0,0,0,0,0,0,0,0,0,0}},
              Do[ bins[[ x[[i]] ]]++, {i,1,Length[x]}]; bins]
```

```
In[3]:=    proc[data]
```

```
Out[3]=    {8, 9, 12, 6, 11, 7, 14, 12, 8, 13}
```

This style is probably familiar to users of FORTRAN. Further details on procedural methods are presented in Chapter 11. Users of the C programming language, however, may feel more at home with a functional approach.

8.1.2 Functional Methods

The *functional approach* attempts to solve the problem by applying a series of rules (or functions) to the data. We have chosen to name our first attempt to solve the current problem func1. We shall need to use three definitions for this function, depending on the state of completion of the problem.

For the first definition, we supply the function with the list of data. The original data should be a one-dimensional array, and we can test for this condition using the Boolean test VectorQ. Our function takes each element in the list and pairs it with the number 1 (this value is a frequency counter for that element):

```
In[4]:=    func1[x_?VectorQ] := func1[Map[{#,1}&,x]]
```

```
In[5]:=    func1[{1,2,3,2}]
```

```
Out[5]=    func1[{{1, 1}, {2, 1}, {3, 1}, {2, 1}}]
```

For the second definition, we use an example in pattern matching. It requires a bit of explanation. Basically, we want to teach *Mathematica* to look for, as well as to merge, pairs with the same first element. For instance, suppose that *Mathematica* finds the pair {3, 2}, indicating two occurrences of the number 3, and also the pair {3, 5}, indicating five occurrences of the number 3. We would like to replace these two pairs by the single pair {3, 7}. The following instruction achieves this goal:

```
In[6]:=    func1[{a___,{b_,n_},c___,{b_,m_},d___}] := func1[{a,{b,n+m},c,d}]
```

```
In[7]:=    func1[{1,2,3,2,3}]
```

```
Out[7]=    func1[{{1, 1}, {2, 2}, {3, 2}}]
```

The triple underscore stands for a sequence of any number of elements. If you are confused, be patient. Chapters 10 and 12 give more details on pattern matching.

For the third definition, we drop the first member of each pair and return the list of frequencies:

```
In[8]:=    func1[a_List] := Map[Last,a];
           func1[Sort[data]]
```

```
Out[8]=    {8, 9, 12, 6, 11, 7, 14, 12, 8, 13}
```

How did *Mathematica* know in which order to apply the function definitions? See Chapter 10 for an explanation.

There are many other ways to solve the problem using a functional approach. Here is another possibility. The pattern on the left-hand side searches for a string of repeated numbers and pulls them outside the list. Is there a question here about how the patterns x and y are matched? See Chapter 12 for a discussion of this point.

```
In[9]:=    func2[{x___,y__}] := {func2[{x}], Length[{y}]} /; SameQ[y]
           func2[{}] := Null
```

To bin the data, we must sort them, then send them into func2, flatten the nested lists, and drop the first Null entry:

```
In[10]:=   Rest[ Flatten[ func2[Sort[data]] ] ]
```

```
Out[10]=   {8, 9, 12, 6, 11, 7, 14, 12, 8, 13}
```

If you do not understand how this method worked, try entering the instructions one at a time:

```
In[11]:=   func2[Sort[data]]
```

```
Out[11]=   {{{{{{{{{{Null, 8}, 9}, 12}, 6}, 11}, 7}, 14}, 12}, 8}, 13}
```

```
In[12]:=   Flatten[%]
```

```
Out[12]=   {Null, 8, 9, 12, 6, 11, 7, 14, 12, 8, 13}
```

8.1.3 *Mathematica* Style

You should always check to see whether *Mathematica* possesses the command that you need before you code one yourself. In fact, there is a function called Count that serves exactly our purpose:

```
In[13]:=   Table[ Count[data,i] ,{i,1,10}]
```

```
Out[13]=   {8, 9, 12, 6, 11, 7, 14, 12, 8, 13}
```

This method is probably the quickest way to implement the function.

8.1.4 Replacement Rules

We can make use of *Mathematica*'s replacement rules to select particular entries in a list. For instance, the following example drops all integers other than 3, which is spared from the massacre by disguising itself as the letter "a":

```
In[14]:=   {1,2,3,2,3,1,2,4} /. 3 -> "a" /. x_Integer -> 0
```

```
Out[14]=   {0, 0, a, 0, a, 0, 0, 0}
```

We can determine the quantity of occurrences of a particular number by culling all other numbers, replacing the interesting number by 1, and then summing the remaining list:

```
In[15]:=   rulemeth[data_List,n_] :=
           Apply[Plus, data /. n -> "a" /. x_Integer -> 0 /. "a" -> 1];
           Table[ rulemeth[data,n],{n,1,10}]
```

```
Out[15]=   {8, 9, 12, 6, 11, 7, 14, 12, 8, 13}
```

8.1.5 Packages

Do not forget the packages! In Statistics`DataManipulation`, we find several useful instructions to perform various binning activities:

In[16]:= Needs["Statistics`DataManipulation`"]

For our purposes, we set the bin size to 1 and choose ten bins starting at 0 and running up to 10:

In[17]:= BinCounts[data, {0,10,1}]

Out[17]= {8, 9, 12, 6, 11, 7, 14, 12, 8, 13}

Another package, Graphics`Graphics`, gives us the tools to view this information:

In[18]:= Needs["Graphics`Graphics`"]

In[19]:= BarChart[BinCounts[data, {0,10,1}]];

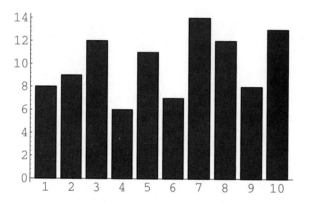

Yet another function, more useful for discrete data such as ours, is Frequencies:

In[20]:= Frequencies[data]

Out[20]= {{8, 1}, {9, 2}, {12, 3}, {6, 4}, {11, 5}, {7, 6}, {14, 7},

{12, 8}, {8, 9}, {13, 10}}

In[21]:= Map[First, Frequencies[data]]

Out[21]= {8, 9, 12, 6, 11, 7, 14, 12, 8, 13}

8.2 Summary

In this chapter, we have shown that there are many methods and different programming styles that can be used to tackle a problem in *Mathematica*. In the rest of Part Three, we shall look in more detail at the various possibilities, as well as their respective merits.

Important Built-In Structures

Much of what goes on inside *Mathematica* is hidden from the casual user. For beginners, this behavior is a good thing. They do not care that *Mathematica* has no division command, but makes do instead with a combination of `Times` and `Power`. However, much can be gained by a knowledge of what happens behind the scenes. For instance, when you realize that there is only a minimal difference between the way *Mathematica* stores the sum a + b + c and the list {a,b,c} and that there is a function to convert between the two, you have a powerful tool at your disposal for summing lists of data. The ideas developed in this chapter are fundamental, and they are prerequisite to the work in the remainder of Part Three. You should read the text here and then experiment with *Mathematica* before continuing. Let's first consider the most fundamental of *Mathematica*'s structures — the *list*.

9.1 List Structures

Mathematica stores data in lists. An example of a one-dimensional list is

```
In[1]:=    list1d = {a,b,7,Pi,44.2};
```

Note that we can mix different types of objects in a list. For example, `list1d` contains symbols, integers, and floating-point numbers. To implement a two-dimensional set of data, you must use a list of lists:

```
In[2]:=    list2d = {{1,2,a},{4,Pi},{1.5}};
```

An important feature that is demonstrated by `list2d` is that the individual records in a list can be of unequal length. This option is not easily available in conventional computer languages such as C or FORTRAN. We take this opportunity to make a pertinent point on the subject of aesthetics. *Mathematica* supplies two functions, `TableForm` and `MatrixForm`, that can greatly assist you in the visualization of a two-dimensional list:

```
In[3]:=    SetOptions[TableForm, TableSpacing -> {0,2}];
           TableForm[list2d]

Out[3]=    1    2    a
           4    Pi
           1.5
```

In Chapter 3, we presented a method for visualizing three-dimensional lists. The technique could be extended to lists of higher dimension.

9.1.1 Listable Operators

With a single command, it is possible to perform an operation on every element of a list — regardless of the dimension of that list. For instance, we can square each element in list1d:

```
In[4]:=    list1d^2
Out[4]=      2   2        2
           {a , b , 49, Pi , 1953.64}
```

Similarly, the command list2d^2 squares each element in the two-dimensional list. This operation is not what is conventionally meant by "squaring a matrix." If you want to perform conventional matrix algebra, then you use a period to denote multiplication and MatrixPower in place of ^.

All the built-in *Mathematica* functions that take only one argument operate on lists in the same way. That is, they apply themselves to the individual elements:

```
In[5]:=    Sin[list2d] // TableForm
Out[5]=    Sin[1]    Sin[2]  Sin[a]
           Sin[4]    0
           0.997495
```

Other functions, such as ListPlot, require a list on which to operate — it would be disastrous if these functions were allowed to operate on a list in the same way as Sin. *Mathematica* avoids the potential problem by associating a list of attributes with each function. Functions that can safely apply themselves to individual elements of a list possess the attribute Listable:

```
In[6]:=    Attributes[Sin]
Out[6]=    {Listable, Protected}

In[7]:=    Attributes[ListPlot]
Out[7]=    {Protected}
```

By default, when you define a function in *Mathematica*, it has no attributes. However, the function may still *behave* as though it is Listable if its definition relies solely on Listable operators:

```
In[8]:=    f[x_] := x^2 + Sin[x];
           f[list1d]
Out[8]=      2              2                        2
           {a  + Sin[a], b  + Sin[b], 49 + Sin[7], Pi , 1953.86}
```

The following function performs a logical NOT on a binary digit:

```
In[9]:=    not[x_] := If[x==1,0,1];
           not[0]
```

Out[9]=   1

The If command does not have the Listable attribute, so our function will not apply itself to every element of a list:

In[10]:=   not[{1,1,0,1,0,0,1}]

Out[10]=   If[{1, 1, 0, 1, 0, 0, 1} == 1, 0, 1]

There are two ways to resolve this problem; one is temporary, and the other more permanent. If we do not want our function to be Listable in general, we can map the function onto the elements of the list:

In[11]:=   Map[not, {1,1,0,1,0,0,1}]

Out[11]=   {0, 0, 1, 0, 1, 1, 0}

Alternatively, if we want to make not thread its way automatically through any list to which we apply it, we can set the attribute ourselves:

In[12]:=   Attributes[not] = {Listable};
              not[{1,1,0,1,0,0,1}]

Out[12]=   {0, 0, 1, 0, 1, 1, 0}

9.2 *Mathematica*'s Perspective on Structures

Consider the expression a + b c. If we were to describe this combination of symbols and operations in words, we might say "Add a to the product of b and c." Moreover, without the shorthand notation of a "+" to denote the addition function Plus and of a space to denote the multiplication function Times, this expression would have to be written as Plus[a, Times[b,c]]. To achieve consistent representation with functions that do not have a standardized shorthand symbol, *Mathematica* stores a + b c in this longer representation:

In[13]:=   FullForm[a + b c]

Out[13]=   Plus[a, Times[b, c]]

The conversion to the form that is more familiar to Homo sapiens is made only for the purpose of screen display.

The words Plus and Times are referred to as the Heads of their respective functions:

In[14]:=   Head[a+b]

Out[14]=   Plus

Every function is comprised of a head and a set of arguments, and *Mathematica* lists are no different:

In[15]:=   FullForm[list1d]

Out[15]=   List[a, b, 7, Pi, 44.2]

It is important that you appreciate that the only difference between the two expressions
a + b + c and {a,b,c} lies in their heads:

```
In[16]:=  FullForm[a+b+c]

Out[16]=  Plus[a, b, c]

In[17]:=  FullForm[{a,b,c}]

Out[17]=  List[a, b, c]
```

A knowledge of this internal representation is invaluable in understanding why *Mathematica* behaves the way it does. Operations that would seem strange in normal mathematics actually do have a logical meaning in *Mathematica*. For instance, consider raising the symbol x to the power of the list {1,2,3}. What will *Mathematica* do? Internally, this command will be stored as Power[x,List[1,2,3]]. Power possesses the Listable attribute, so it will thread its way through the list, creating the expression List[x, Power[x,2], Power[x,3]]. The evaluation is now complete, but the screen representation makes use of the standard tools for visualizing lists (curly brackets) and powers (superscript characters):

```
In[18]:=  x^{1,2,3}

Out[18]=       2   3
          {x, x , x }
```

9.2.1 Head Swaps

An appreciation of the manner in which *Mathematica* stores expressions internally opens the door to an entirely new style of programming. If you are used to procedural programming, you may need a little while to acclimatize, but the vista is worth it! The following example should demonstrate the advantage of the different style.

Suppose that we want to add up the numbers in a one-dimensional list. First, we present the procedural approach

```
In[19]:=  datalist = {1,2,3,4,5,6};

          sum = 0;
          Do[sum = sum + datalist[[i]],{i,1,Length[datalist]}];
          sum

Out[19]=  21
```

We can perform the calculation significantly more efficiently by changing the datalist head to a Plus using the Apply function:

```
In[20]:=  Apply[Plus,datalist]

Out[20]=  21
```

It is easy to see how we could extend this idea to define a function that computes the arithmetic mean of a list of numbers. Such a function is detailed in S. Wolfram's book

[27]. Slightly more ambitious is the creation of a harmonic mean function. The harmonic mean, H, of a set of numbers $a_1, \ldots, a_n$ is defined by the equation

$$\frac{1}{H} = \frac{1}{n} \sum_{i=1}^{n} \frac{1}{a_i}.$$

This function can be implemented rapidly:

```
In[21]:= harm[x_List] := 1/(1/Length[x] Apply[Plus,1/x]);
         harm[{1,2,3}]
```

```
Out[21]= 18
         --
         11
```

The function `harm` performs the following sequence of operations on its argument x. First, $1/x$ is computed. The reciprocal-taking operation threads it way through the list, creating a list whose elements are the reciprocals of the elements in x. By now, you might guess that such behavior implies that division has the `Listable` attribute. You would be almost correct! In fact, *Mathematica* does not need a division function because it possesses multiplication and power functions:

```
In[22]:= FullForm[2/a]
```

```
Out[22]= Times[2, Power[a, -1]]
```

We have already seen that both `Times` and `Power` are `Listable` functions. We sum the elements in the reciprocal list, $1/x$, by changing the head to `Plus`. Finally, we perform simple algebraic manipulation to get from this value to H.

9.2.2 Unusual Heads

Hopefully, you are now comfortable with the concept that what *Mathematica* prints to the screen may not be the same as what it stores internally. However, do you appreciate that every *Mathematica* expression has a head associated with it? Consider the following substitution rule:

```
In[23]:= rule1 = a -> b;
```

The symbol `->` is another shorthand notation for the following internal representation:

```
In[24]:= FullForm[rule1]
```

```
Out[24]= Rule[a, b]
```

Similarly, when you type x = 3 to assign a value to x, *Mathematica* first converts the = into the head `Set`. To demonstrate this conversion, we must exercise care:

```
In[25]:= FullForm[x = 3]
```

```
Out[25]= 3
```

Mathematica has assigned the value 3 to x, and has shown us the full form of this value. This response is not very useful! To stop the evaluation, we use the `Hold` head:

```
In[26]:=  FullForm[Hold[x = 3]]
```

```
Out[26]=  Hold[Set[x, 3]]
```

If we change the head of rule1 from Rule to Set, we can make the assignment permanent rather than temporary:

```
In[27]:=  Apply[Set, rule1];
          a
```

```
Out[27]=  b
```

The output indicates that a has been assigned the value b. Of course, it would have been more efficient to enter simply a = a /. rule1, but you get the point!

We are now in a position to appreciate a problem that once plagued a colleague of ours. He was working with an odd function, $f(-x) = -f(x)$, and he wanted to make *Mathematica* simplify expressions such as $f(a) + f(-a)$ (which is zero because of the oddness condition). We stress that there is a simple way to perform this simplification using conditional evaluation, which we shall discuss in Chapter 10. However, our friend's idea was to use a replacement rule:

```
In[28]:=  rule2 := f[-x_] -> -f[x];
```

He was slightly perplexed with the outcome:

```
In[29]:=  Clear[f,a,x];
          f[a] + f[-a] /. rule2
```

```
Out[29]=  0
```

Great! On the other hand, consider the following:

```
In[30]:=  f[2 a] + f[-2 a] /. rule2
```

```
Out[30]=  f[-2 a] + f[2 a]
```

When you have an understanding of the full form of expressions, this behavior does not seem so odd:

```
In[31]:=  FullForm[rule2]
```

```
Out[31]=  Rule[f[Times[-1, Pattern[x, Blank[]]]], Times[-1, f[x]]]
```

Although this output looks messy, the problem is now obvious. *Mathematica* will apply the rule only when it finds f[Times[-1, pattern]]. Comparing the full forms of f[-a] and f[-2a], we see that the latter does not have this form:

```
In[32]:=  {FullForm[f[-a]], FullForm[f[-2a]]}
```

```
Out[32]=  {f[Times[-1, a]], f[Times[-2, a]]}
```

When you enter the instruction ?name into *Mathematica*, you are using another shorthand. The internal form of this instruction uses the head Information:

```
In[33]:=  Information[Information]
```

```
Information[symbol] prints information about a symbol.

Attributes[Information] = {HoldAll, Protected}
```

We can use the longer form to see what is happening to the local variables inside a Module:

```
In[34]:=  f[x_] := Module[{a}, a = x^2 + 1;
                          Information[a];
                          Cos[a]]
```

```
f[4]
Global`a$5

Attributes[a$5] = {Temporary}

a$5 = 17
```

```
Out[34]=  Cos[17]
```

We shall discuss the Module construction in more detail in Chapter 10. For the time being, we note that since a is a variable local to the Module, it is assigned the attribute Temporary and is given a unique name to prevent collision with global variables. *Mathematica* knows to remove the symbol when it exits the module, so we must ask for information on the symbol from inside. We cannot do so with the ? shorthand, but we achieved the same effect with a knowledge of the relevant head.

9.3 Deeply Nested Structures

We have already seen that *Mathematica* expressions differ from lists only in their heads. Thus, all the usual list-manipulating commands can be applied to functions. For instance,

```
In[35]:=  Reverse[{a,b,c}]
```

```
Out[35]=  {c, b, a}
```

```
In[36]:=  Reverse[f[a,b,c]]
```

```
Out[36]=  f[c, b, a]
```

We can extract particular elements of an expression in the same way. Here we extract the second element of the expression a + b + c:

```
In[37]:=  (a + b + c)[[2]]
```

```
Out[37]=  b
```

Warning: If you use the C programming language you are aware that the first element of an array corresponds to position 0. For *Mathematica* expressions, however, the element at position 0 refers to the expression's head:

```
In[38]:=  (a+b+c)[[0]]
```

```
Out[38]=  Plus
```

Sometimes, when you attempt to extract an element from an expression, you may obtain a confusing result. For example,

In[39]:= `(c + a + z)[[2]]`

Out[39]= `c`

Why did *Mathematica* return the first element in the list that we typed in, and not the second? The clue lies in one of the attributes of the `Plus` command:

In[40]:= `Attributes[Plus]`

Out[40]= `{Flat, Listable, OneIdentity, Orderless, Protected}`

`Orderless` tells *Mathematica* that there is no difference between, for instance, `a + b` and `b + a` (the function is *commutative*, in mathematical jargon). Whenever a function with this attribute is encountered, the arguments of the function are immediately ordered alphabetically. So, when we asked for the second element of `Plus[c,a,z]`, *Mathematica* first reordered the expression as `Plus[a,c,z]` and then outputted the second element of this expression, which happens to be c.

When you define your own functions that have orderless behavior, it is a good idea to add `Orderless` to the attributes list. This attribute aids greatly in the simplification procedure:

In[41]:= `g[3,1,2] + g[1,3,2]`

Out[41]= `g[1, 3, 2] + g[3, 1, 2]`

In[42]:= `Attributes[g] = {Orderless};`
           `g[3,1,2] + g[1,3,2]`

Out[42]= `2 g[1, 2, 3]`

So far in this section, since we have considered only one-dimensional structures, we have needed to supply only a single integer in order to extract a particular element. With lists, it is rare to use structures with more than two dimensions, but it is certainly not rare to do so with other expressions. For instance, the seemingly innocuous expression a + 2 b^2 is a three-dimensional structure:

In[43]:= `FullForm[a+2 b^2]`

Out[43]= `Plus[a, Times[2, Power[b, 2]]]`

At level 1, we have the entries a and 2 b^2. The first entry has no further structure, but 2 b^2 divides at level 2 into 2 and b^2. At level 3, the subdivision ends with b^2 dissected into b and 2. Clearly, the depth of the structure is nonuniform (similar to the layout of a book where some chapters have sections only and others have both sections and subsections, and so on). Because the depth of nesting can be deep in *Mathematica* expressions, it is sometimes difficult to visualize the structure with `FullForm` alone. An alternative tool is `TreeForm` (trees have many levels of branching and nonuniform depth):

In[44]:= `TreeForm[a + 2 b^2]`

```
Out[44]= Plus[a, |                              ]
                 Times[2, |                ]
                         Power[b, 2]
```

We have already noted that because there is little difference between *Mathematica*'s internalization of lists and that of its other structures, we can use the same commands to access particular entries of the latter. This correspondence also holds for deeply nested structures. For instance, the zeroth element extracts the head of the top level of a structure:

```
In[45]:=  (a + b^(c-d))[[0]]
```

```
Out[45]= Plus
```

Since the top level of a + b^(c-d) is Plus[a, b^(c-d)], the expression's second element is b^(c-d):

```
In[46]:=  (a + b^(c-d))[[2]]
Out[46]=   c - d
          b
```

Of course, this expression still has a good deal of structure within it. We can resolve the structure by using more depth specifiers:

```
In[47]:=  (a + b^(c-d))[[2,2]]
```

```
Out[47]=  c - d
```

```
In[48]:=  (a + b^(c-d))[[2,2,0]]
```

```
Out[48]= Plus
```

The similarity does not end there. We can use all the standard list-searching functions, such as Position and Cases. Suppose that we generate a fairly complicated object and observe its tree structure:

```
In[49]:=  TreeForm[a + 4 b^(c-d^3)]
Out[49]= Plus[a, |                                                      ]
                 Times[4, |                                        ]
                         Power[b, |                          ]
                                 Plus[c, |                 ]
                                         Times[-1, |      ]
                                                  Power[d, 3]
```

The following instruction searches for all symbols, down to the fourth level, in this structure:

```
In[50]:=  Cases[a + 4 b^(c - d^3),_Symbol,4]
```

```
Out[50]= {a, b, c}
```

We can run through the structure one level at a time, printing out every integer that has been found at each step:

```
In[51]:=  TableForm[ Table[{"Level ",n,"Cases   ",
                  Apply[Sequence,Cases[a + 4 b^( -d^3),_Integer,n]]},
              {n,1,6}]]
```

```
Out[51]=    Level   1   Cases
            Level   2   Cases   4
            Level   3   Cases   4
            Level   4   Cases   4
            Level   5   Cases   4   -1
            Level   6   Cases   4   -1   3
```

Finally, we look for the position of the symbol b in the structure:

```
In[52]:=    Position[ a + 4 b^(c - d^3), b]
Out[52]=    {{2, 2, 1}}
```

9.4 Evaluation Order

Mathematica breaks up long instructions into pieces that it can handle. The question then arises, in what order should these pieces be performed and what evaluations should be allowed, if any? An example should make the problem clear.

Consider the instruction a = b. We know by now that the equals sign is merely a shorthand notation for the actual internal representation of a function with a head and various arguments. In this case, the head is Set and there are two arguments. What should *Mathematica* do first with the instruction? The default is to check to see whether b has been assigned a value and, if it has been, to make the necessary replacement (that is, evaluate b). This value is then assigned to the symbol a. Three other possible combinations of evaluation and nonevaluation are possible. Why has *Mathematica* chosen this one? If we try out the other possibilities, the reason soon becomes apparent. When a and b have no previous assignments, all four methods are equivalent. However, suppose that we make prior numerical assignments to a and b and then investigate the options. To override the default settings, we can force or prevent evaluation using Evaluate and HoldForm:

1. *Hold evaluation of both* a *and* b. This choice is not useful because we want a to end up with the value 5:

```
In[53]:=    Clear[a,b]; a = 4; b = 5;
            Evaluate[ Set[ a , HoldForm[b] ] ];
            {a,b}
Out[53]=    {b, 5}
```

2. *Hold evaluation of* a *but evaluate* b. This choice is the default. The correct result is obtained — a ends up set to the value of b:

```
In[54]:=    Clear[a,b]; a = 4; b = 5;
            Evaluate[ Set[ a , b ] ];
            {a,b}
Out[54]=    {5, 5}
```

3. *Evaluate* a *and set the result equal to* b. This choice fails completely because *Mathematica* ends up trying to set 4 = b, which it really does not want to do! The 4 is a raw object, and assignments to raw objects are not allowed:

In[55]:=
```
Clear[a,b]; a = 4; b = 5;
Set[ Evaluate[a] , HoldForm[b] ];
{a,b}
```


```
Set::setraw: Cannot assign to raw object 4.
```

Out[55]=
```
{4, 5}
```

    4. *Evaluate* a *and set the result equal to the evaluated value of* b. This choice fails for the same reason as option 3 did:

In[56]:=
```
Clear[a,b]; a = 4; b = 5;
Set[ Evaluate[a] , b ];
{a,b}
```


```
Set::setraw: Cannot assign to raw object 4.
```

Out[56]=
```
{4, 5}
```

    Mathematica knows to choose option 2 because Set has the attribute HoldFirst:

In[57]:=   `Attributes[Set]`

Out[57]= `{HoldFirst, Protected}`

HoldFirst means that all arguments of the function, except the first, are evaluated before the function definition is invoked.

    You may be wondering what happens when we type in an expression such as a = b = 3. We would like this instruction to assign the value 3 to both a and b. However, what happens if b already has an assignment — for instance, to the value 4? It is reasonable to assume that a = b = 3 is stored internally as Set[a,b,3]. Because Set has the attribute HoldFirst, *Mathematica* would initially evaluate all arguments other than the first, leading to the expression Set[a,4,3]. The result is clearly undesirable, and *Mathematica* avoids the problem by using nesting. The instruction a = b = 3 is actually internalized as Set[a, Set[b,3]]:

In[58]:=   `FullForm[Hold[a=b=3]]`

Out[58]= `Hold[Set[a, Set[b, 3]]]`

The outer Set instruction is encountered first, and its second argument is evaluated. In other words, Set[b,3] is evaluated, assigning a value 3 to b and returning the value 3 to the outer Set. *Mathematica* now makes the final assignment; Set[a,3]:

In[59]:=
```
b = 4; a = b = 3;
{a,b}
```

Out[59]= `{3, 3}`

    When we are teaching *Mathematica* function definitions, we do not want the second argument to be evaluated. As usual, we know that := is just a shorthand notation for an internal function. In this case, the function has the name SetDelayed and its attributes are slightly different from those of Set:

```
In[60]:=  Attributes[SetDelayed]
Out[60]=  {HoldAll, Protected}
```

All the arguments in the assignment are now stored in unevaluated form:

```
In[61]:=  b = 3; a := b;
          ?a
          Global`a

          a := b
```

9.4.1 Prevention of Evaluation

Sometimes, *Mathematica* needs help to determine those evaluations that should be carried out and those that should not be. Consider the following function, which determines whether a user should have access to a particular program:

```
In[62]:=  entry[a_] := If[ StringMatchQ[ToString[a],"Jason"],
                       Print["Entry verified"],
                       Print["Intruder Alert"]]
          entry[Jason]

          Entry verified
```

```
In[63]:=  entry[Fred]

          Intruder Alert
```

So far, so good.

The problem is that this method is not robust. Suppose that the word "Jason" has already been assigned a value. We have frequently come across the following assignment:

```
In[64]:=  Jason = ace;
          entry[Jason]

          Intruder Alert
```

Furthermore, what if Fred is a hacker and has come up with the following cunning plan to crack our system? First, let's clear Jason of any involvement in this scam (actually, we are just clearing the unlikely assignment made to him):

```
In[65]:=  Clear[Jason];
          Fred = Jason;
          entry[Fred]

          Entry verified
```

The problem is caused by *Mathematica*'s evaluating a in entry[a] before going to the function definition. In other words, *Mathematica* immediately converts entry[Jason] into entry[ace]. We can prevent this evaluation by including an attributes list. HoldAll and HoldFirst have the same effect here because there is only a single argument:

```
In[66]:=  Attributes[entry] = {HoldAll};
          Jason = joker;
          entry[Jason]
```

Intruder Alert

The function still does not work, although we have gone some way toward resolving the problem. The trouble now is that although the word "Jason" is making it through to the function definition, it is converted into joker when it gets into ToString, because ToString does not have any holding attributes:

In[67]:= `Attributes[ ToString]`

Out[67]= `{Protected}`

When we prevent this evaluation with HoldForm, our function works as we wanted — and Fred cannot gain entry:

In[68]:= `entry[a_] := If[ StringMatchQ[ToString[HoldForm[a]],"Jason"] ,`
`                Print["Entry verified"],`
`                Print["Intruder Alert"]]`

`entry[Jason]; entry[Fred]`

`Entry verified`
`Intruder Alert`

9.4.2 The Reverse Problem: Forcing of Evaluation

There are times when we have the opposite problem of that considered in the previous section — namely, *Mathematica* may not evaluate what we want it to evaluate. In the case study of Chapter 15, we need to make use of a function that constructs a table. In that case, the iteration function and the list of iterators for the associated Table command must be computed within the function definition. For simplicity, we consider a case here where such a construction is not necessary. The point of the example is to demonstrate the evaluation problem.

Suppose that we want to construct a matrix of $i^2 + j^2$, where i and j run over the ranges 1 to 5. Furthermore, we assume, for some reason, that both this function and the iteration list have to be computed first and then inserted into the table. What happens?

In[69]:= `itfn = {i^2 + j^2};`
`itlist = {{i,1,5},{j,1,5}};`

`Table[itfn,itlist]`

`Table::itform: Argument itlist at position 2`
`        does not have the correct form for an iterator.`

Out[69]= `Table[itfn, itlist]`

Mathematica has not produced the desired output, and the error comment is a good clue to what went wrong. Perhaps the problem is one of syntax. When we use multiple iterators inside a table, these iterators should form a sequence rather than a list:

In[70]:= `Table[i,{i,3},{j,3}]`

Out[70]= `{{1, 1, 1}, {2, 2, 2}, {3, 3, 3}}`

In[71]:= `Table[i,{{i,3},{j,3}}]`

    `Table::iterb: Iterator {{i, 3}, {j, 3}} does not have appropriate bounds.`

Out[71]= `Table[i, {{i, 3}, {j, 3}}]`

How can we create itlist without using an outer list to group the individual iterators? We cannot just type

In[72]:= `itlist = {i,1,5},{j,1,5}`

    `Syntax::sntxf: { "}itlist = {i,1,5}{ "} cannot be followed by { "},{j,1,5}{ "}.`

One way around the problem — in fact, the one used in the case study of Chapter 15 — is to remove the protection on Table and to add a new definition to allow Table to cope with this situation. Less drastically, we can make use of the head called Sequence, which is meant for this type of problem:

In[73]:= `Table[i, Sequence[{i,3},{j,3}]]`

Out[73]= `{{1, 1, 1}, {2, 2, 2}, {3, 3, 3}}`

Even with this modification, we still have a problem with our predefined structures:

In[74]:= `itlist = Sequence[{i,1,5},{j,1,5}];`
       `Table[itfn, itlist]`

    `Table::itform: Argument itlist at position 2`
          `does not have the correct form for an iterator.`

Out[74]= `Table[itfn, itlist]`

In fact, there is a separate issue that must be addressed. One of the attributes of Table is HoldAll. Neither itfn nor itlist is actually being replaced by its definition. When we force this evaluation, all is well with the world:

In[75]:= `Table[Evaluate[itfn], Evaluate[itlist]]`

Out[75]= `{{{2}, {5}, {10}, {17}, {26}}, {{5}, {8}, {13}, {20}, {29}},`

      `{{10}, {13}, {18}, {25}, {34}}, {{17}, {20}, {25}, {32}, {41}},`

      `{{26}, {29}, {34}, {41}, {50}}}`

9.5 Mapping and Similar Operations

In Section 9.1, we demonstrated two ways to make a function map its way onto every element of a one-dimensional list. The example function that we used was called not, and the first method that we applied was to set the attribute to Listable. This method has the advantage of working regardless of the depth of your list:

In[76]:= `not[x_] := If[ x== 1, 0, 1];`
      `Attributes[not] = {Listable};`
      `not[{{1,1,0,0},{1,0,0}}]`

Out[76]= `{{0, 0, 1, 1}, {0, 1, 1}}`

Our second method was to map the function onto the list. This approach works for the one-dimensional case, but it does not work for deeper structures:

```
In[77]:=   Attributes[not] = {};
           Map[ not, {{1,1,0,0},{1,0,0}}]

Out[77]=   {If[{1, 1, 0, 0} == 1, 0, 1], If[{1, 0, 0} == 1, 0, 1]}
```

By default, Map operates at the first level of its argument. We can override this value by specifying our own setting:

```
In[78]:=   Map[ not,{{1,1,0,0},{1,0,0}},{2}]

Out[78]=   {{0, 0, 1, 1}, {0, 1, 1}}
```

Being able to specify levels is useful. If we want to add up the entries in the rows of a two-dimensional matrix, we do not enter

```
In[79]:=   Apply[Plus,{{1,2},{3,4}}]

Out[79]=   {4, 6}
```

because this operation sums the different rows. Instead, we must map the Plus head onto the first level:

```
In[80]:=   Map[ Apply[Plus,#]&,{{1,2},{3,4}}]

Out[80]=   {3, 7}
```

To add up the entries in the rows of a three-dimensional matrix, we must map our head-changing function at level 2. Making use of the function Viewlolol developed in Section 3.2 to view such matrices, we have

```
In[81]:=   Clear[a,b,c];
           mat3 = {{{a,b,c},{d,e}},{{f,g,h},{i,j,k,l}}};
           Viewlolol[data_] := Map[MatrixForm[#, TableSpacing -> {0,1}]&,data]

In[82]:=   Viewlolol[mat3]
Out[82]=   {{a, b, c},   {f, g, h}      }
           {d, e}        {i, j, k, l}

In[83]:=   Viewlolol[ Map[Apply[Plus,#]&, mat3,{2}]]
Out[83]=   {a + b + c, f + g + h      }
           d + e      i + j + k + l
```

Even more control of where the function is mapped is afforded by MapAt. In the following example, we target the diagonal entries in a matrix:

```
In[84]:=   TableForm[
           MapAt[ not, Table[1,{3},{3}],{{1,1},{2,2},{3,3}}]]

Out[84]=   0  1  1
           1  0  1
           1  1  0
```

There is a similar extension of the mapping facility for functions that take more than one argument. For instance, the logical AND instruction may take one or more arguments (the definition is a prime candidate for the use of the double underscore):

In[85]:= `and[x__Integer] := Min[x];`
`{and[1,1,1], and[1,0,1]}`

Out[85]= `{1, 0}`

What happens when we apply the built-in `Listable` functions (for instance, `Plus`) of more than one variable to a `Sequence` of several equal-dimensional lists? The output is the list obtained by application of the function to corresponding elements of the lists in the sequence:

In[86]:= `Plus[{a,b,c},{e,f,g}]`

Out[86]= `{a + e, b + f, c + g}`

As it stands, our definition of the `and` function will not display the same kind of behavior. We saw, with `Map`, that there was a permanent and a temporary fix. The same is true here. For the permanent case, we can set the attribute again:

In[87]:= `and[{1,1,1},{0,1,0},{1,1,0}]`

Out[87]= `and[{1, 1, 1}, {0, 1, 0}, {1, 1, 0}]`

In[88]:= `Attributes[and] = {Listable};`
`and[{1,1,1},{0,1,0},{1,1,0}]`

Out[88]= `{0, 1, 0}`

This method works for even higher-dimensional structures. Consider the following three-dimensional list:

In[89]:= `threedim = Table[Random[Integer,{0,1}],{i,3},{j,3},{k,3}]`

Out[89]= `{{{0, 0, 0}, {0, 0, 0}, {0, 1, 0}}, {{0, 0, 0}, {1, 1, 1}, {0, 1, 1}},`

`{{1, 0, 1}, {0, 0, 0}, {1, 1, 1}}}`

We can visualize this output with `Viewlolol`:

In[90]:= `Viewlolol[threedim]`

Out[90]= `{0 0 0, 0 0 0, 1 0 1}`
`  0 0 0  1 1 1  0 0 0`
`  0 1 0  0 1 1  1 1 1`

Because `threedim` is a list of matrices, rather than a sequence, we need to change the head to demonstrate our point:

In[91]:= `TableForm[ and[ Apply[Sequence,threedim] ] ]`

Out[91]= `0  0  0`
`0  0  0`
`0  1  0`

You can check that the only 1s in this matrix are in positions occupied by 1s in all three matrices in `threedim`.

The temporary approach to threading the function uses a relative of `Map` called `MapThread`. As usual, we must specify the depth at which the threading should operate:

```
In[92]:=  Attributes[and] = {};
          TableForm[ MapThread[and,threedim,2] ]
Out[92]=  0   0   0
          0   0   0
          0   1   0
```

9.6 Summary

In this chapter, we have guided you through some areas of *Mathematica* that have traditionally been viewed as mysterious, and you should now have a better feel for the structure of *Mathematica*. Our underlying message is that every object in *Mathematica* has a structure that is the same as that of a list. Getting a handle on this concept opens the door to a whole new programming style. This knowledge also will be indispensable to your full understanding of *Mathematica*'s behavior. Of only marginally less importance is the issue of function evaluation. It is important to understand that the settings on many functions allow for selective evaluation or nonevaluation of the different arguments before the function definition is invoked. In the majority of cases, *Mathematica* gets the evaluation order correct. There are times, however, when you cannot expect *Mathematica* to understand what you mean; then you must understand the tools for forcing or holding evaluation.

Function Definitions

Shortly after you start using *Mathematica*, you will want to define your own functions. At first, you will probably need your function to have only a single definition that should be applied, regardless of the value of the function's argument. Soon, however, you will want to use different definitions, depending on some feature of the argument — for instance, whether it is positive or negative. Subsequently, you might want one rule when the function is supplied with one argument and a different one when it is supplied with two arguments. Your function definitions could become long and require more than one instruction. It would be convenient if you could include a block of code, rather than a single instruction, in the function definition. Perhaps you could even introduce variables that are local to the block of code. This chapter shows you how to achieve these objectives. We start with a full overview of simple function definitions, and a description of what goes on inside *Mathematica* when functions are stored and used.

10.1 Simple Function Definitions

In earlier chapters of the book, we assumed that users possess a basic appreciation of how to define their own functions. Furthermore, in Chapter 1, we touched on the importance of delayed assignment (using :=), where the function definition is stored verbatim and is evaluated only when required. Sometimes, it is possible — even desirable — to get away with using only = rather than := . To fully appreciate the difference between the two instructions, we need to explore what happens when you define a function.

Suppose that we want to implement the function $f(x) = x^2$. Entering the mathematical expression literally — except for the conventional change to square brackets — does not have the desired effect when we subsequently try to use the function:

```
In[1]:=    f[x] = x^2;
           f[10]
```

```
Out[1]=    f[10]
```

It does work for one particular case, however:

```
In[2]:=    f[x]
Out[2]=    2
           x
```

Unintentionally, we have told *Mathematica* what value to assign to f only when f has the exact argument x; *Mathematica* has not recognized our instruction as representing a general template. To generalize our rule, we include an underscore character after the x on the left-hand side of the definition, indicating that, by x, we mean any object. Let's clear our definition of f and start over:

In[3]:=   ```
Clear[f];
f[x_] = x^2;
```

The function now works as planned:

*In[4]:=*    ```
f[2]
```

Out[4]=   4

So, what is the point of delayed assignment? Well, when we entered our function definition, we were lucky that the symbol x had not been assigned a value earlier in the session. When *Mathematica* came across the command f[x_] = x^2, it said to itself, "I have been instructed to set f[x_] equal to x^2. What is the value of x^2? x is undefined, so x^2 is already in its simplest form; I shall store f[x_] as x^2." Once f[x_] is stored, we are safe, even if we subsequently assign a value to x. The attempted simplification procedure happens only when we assign a value to f:

In[5]:=   ```
x = 3;
f[a]
```

*Out[5]=*    2
         a

Now consider the following scenario. x has the value 4, and we enter the instruction f[x_] = x^2. In this case, we can imagine *Mathematica* saying to itself "I have been instructed to set f[x_] equal to x^2. What is the value of x^2? x has a value 4, so x^2 is equal to 16. I shall assign a value of 16 to f[x_]."

*In[6]:=*    ```
Clear[f];
x = 4;
f[x_] = x^2;
?f
```

         Global`f

         f[x_] = 16

Subsequently, whenever we use the function f, we will obtain the response 16, which is not what we want. We recommend that you use := instead. When *Mathematica* sees the instruction f[x_] := x^2, it says " Ah, := means delayed assignment. I am not meant to do any simplification of the right-hand side until the function is called and I know what the various blanks are. I shall store this instruction literally as it has been entered."

In[7]:=   ```
Clear[f];
x = 4;
f[x_] := x^2;
?f
```

         Global`f

         f[x_] := x^ 2
```

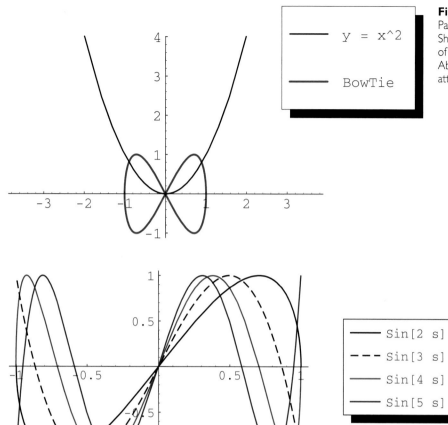

Figure 1
ParametricPlot used with ShowLegend, showing use of RGBColor and AbsoluteThickness attributes (Section 4.3.3)

Figure 2
ParametricPlot used with ShowLegend, showing use of RGBColor and AbsoluteDashing attributes (Section 4.3.3)

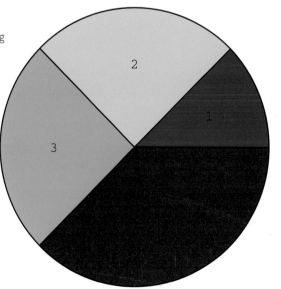

Figure 3
Simple pie chart (Section 4.4.2)

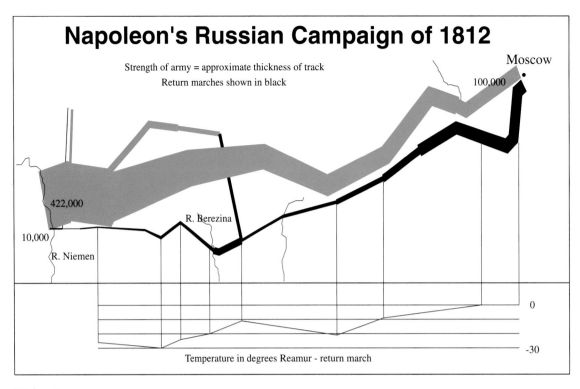

Napoleon's Russian Campaign of 1812

Strength of army = approximate thickness of track

Return marches shown in black

Moscow

100,000

422,000

R. Berezina

10,000

R. Niemen

0

-30

Temperature in degrees Reamur - return march

Figure 4
Thematic map in the style
of Minard illustrating the
use of graphics primitives
(Section 4.7.4)

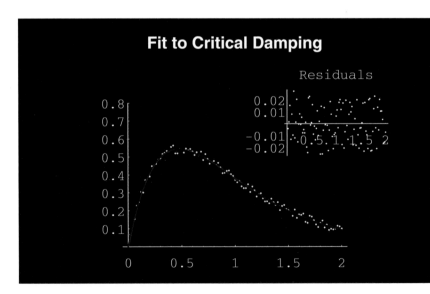

Figure 5
Fit to Critical Damping illustrating
graphical insert capability (Section 5.2.1)

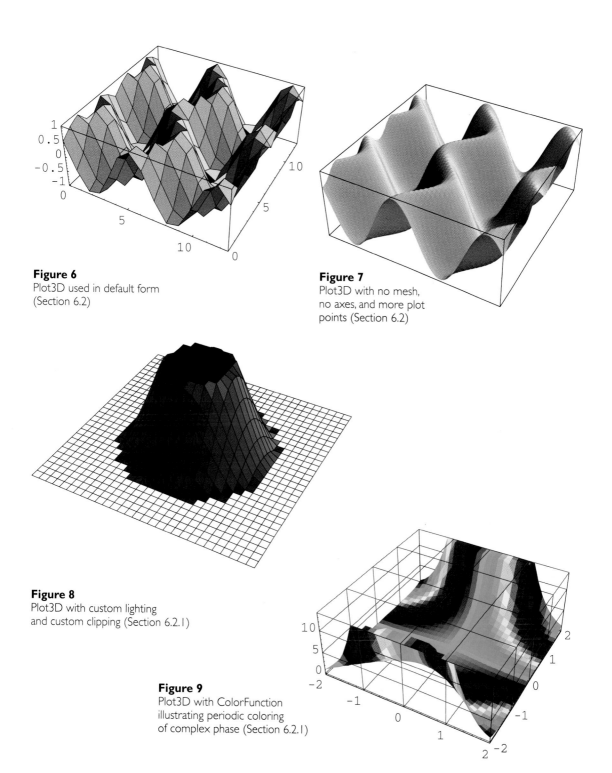

Figure 6
Plot3D used in default form
(Section 6.2)

Figure 7
Plot3D with no mesh,
no axes, and more plot
points (Section 6.2)

Figure 8
Plot3D with custom lighting
and custom clipping (Section 6.2.1)

Figure 9
Plot3D with ColorFunction
illustrating periodic coloring
of complex phase (Section 6.2.1)

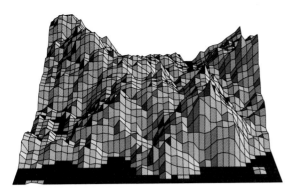

Figure 10
ListPlot3D with clipping
and default coloring
(Section 6.3.4)

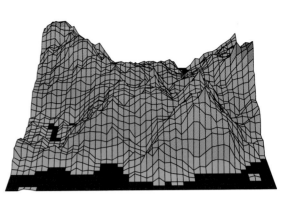

Figure 11
ListPlot3D with clipping and custom
ColorFunction (Section 6.3.5)

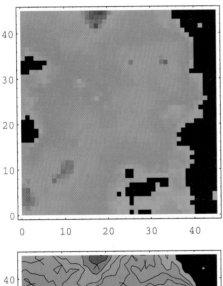

Figure 12
ListDensityPlot with custom
ColorFunction (Section 6.3.6)

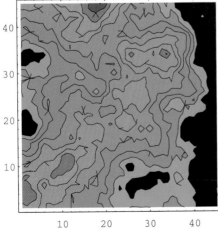

Figure 13
ListContourPlot with custom
ColorFunction and Legend
(Section 6.3.7)

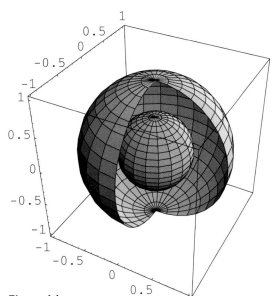

Figure 14
ParametricPlot3D illustrating
multiple functions and cut-out
(Section 6.4)

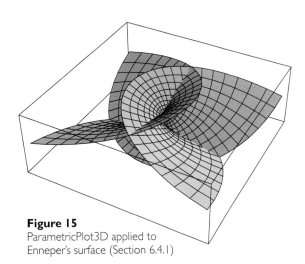

Figure 15
ParametricPlot3D applied to
Enneper's surface (Section 6.4.1)

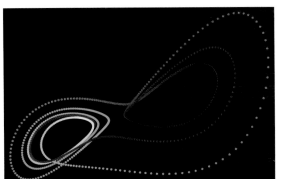

Figure 16
Custom coloring of graphics
primitives (Section 6.6)

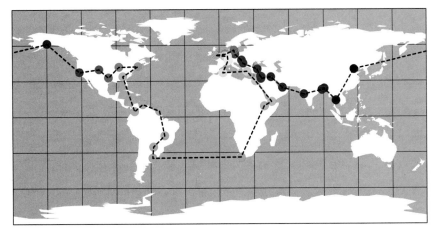

Figure 17
Jet-setting travelling
salesman (Section 14.3.5)

Figure 18
Illustration of computation of
lines joining all pairs of points,
for Robust Regression algorithm
(Section 15.3)

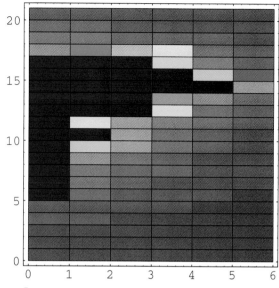

Figure 19
Transposed low-resolution fractal
with simple Hue ColorFunction
(Section 19.1)

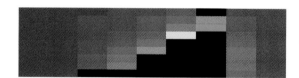

Figure 20
Oriented fractal with
sensible color scheme
(Section 19.1)

Figure 21
First high-resolution
fractal with MathLink
(Section 19.3)

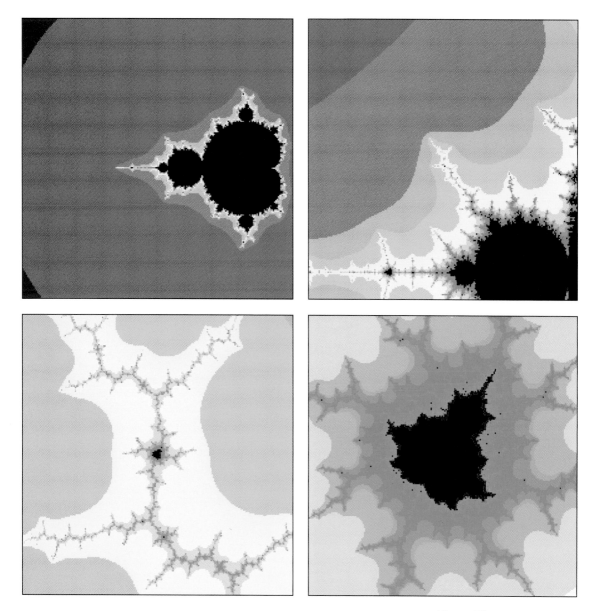

Figure 22
Diving into the Mandelbrot set:
Four frames of a movie made
with MathLink (Section 19.5)

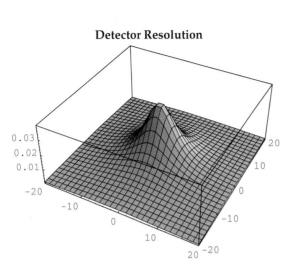

Figure 23
Detector Resolution Function
(Section 21.4.1)

Blurred d

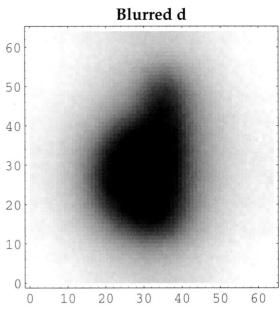

Figure 24
Letter "d" viewed by detector
in Figure 23 (Section 21.4.1)

Blurred d in color

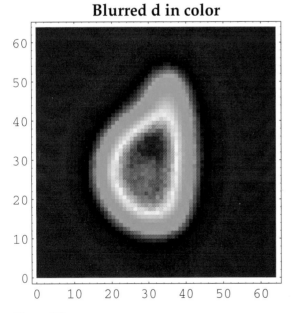

Figure 25
Letter "d" viewed by detector
in Figure 23, color map used to
enhance contrast (Section 21.4.1)

Reconstructed d

Figure 26
Reconstruction of original image
using Fourier-space filter
(Section 21.4.1)

You should now fully appreciate why it is generally best to use delayed assignment (:=) for your function definitions. However, as we shall discuss in Chapter 12, there are important cases where we need to use just =. If you have read and understood this section, you will be in a good position to appreciate the logic behind these decisions.

10.1.1 Hierarchy of Multiple Definitions

In the previous section, we defined a function f that had the effect of squaring its argument. Suppose that we want to override this definition for a few values of the argument. To do so, we simply enter the specific cases in addition to the general rule:

```
In[8]:=    f[x_] := x^2;
           f[1] = 2;
           f[2] = 8;
```

Notice that it makes no difference whether or not we delay the assignments for f[1] and f[2] since 2 will always be equal to 2 and 8 will always be equal to 8! That is why we used just = in these cases. When we subsequently use f, we take it for granted that *Mathematica* will know to apply the specific cases before resorting to the general rule:

```
In[9]:=    f[a]
Out[9]=    2
           a
```

```
In[10]:=   f[2]
Out[10]=   8
```

It is possible to look behind the scenes to see how *Mathematica* worked out not to use the rule f[x_] := x^2 in the evaluation of f[2]:

```
In[11]:=   ?f
           Global`f

           f[1] = 2

           f[2] = 8

           f[x_] := x^ 2
```

The important feature of this *rule table* is that f[1] and f[2] appear above f[x_]. When *Mathematica* comes across an occurrence of the function, it searches top-down through its rule table to see whether or not it knows an applicable rule. Suppose that the definitions of f had been stored in some other order — for instance, in the following random permutation:

```
f[1] = 2
f[x_] := x^ 2
f[2] = 8
```

If this permutation had been chosen and we had asked *Mathematica* for f[1], the progress through the rule table would have stopped at the first entry, and a value of 2 would have been returned — which is what we planned. However, had we asked for f[2], the progress would have stopped at the second entry (the first applicable rule), and a value of 4 would have been returned. The more specific rule that we have supplied for just this situation would be, for all intents and purposes, invisible.

In this situation, it was not difficult for *Mathematica* to determine the ordering. A function with an underscore in it should obviously go below one with no underscores. In the next section, we consider a more complicated example to see whether *Mathematica* is up to the task.

10.1.2 Implementation of the Delta Symbol

The Kronecker delta symbol, $\delta_{i,j}$, is an object that appears frequently in the mathematics and physics literature. The definition is

$$\delta_{i,j} = 1 \text{ if } i = j,$$
$$\delta_{i,j} = 0 \text{ otherwise.}$$

Despite its representation as a symbol, the Kronecker delta symbol is really a function of its two subscripts. In Section 10.3, we show how to implement this function using the If command; for the moment, we shall give *Mathematica* the two cases. First, the general rule is

```
In[12]:=  delta[x_,y_] = 0
```

```
Out[12]=  0
```

Then the more specific rule, corresponding to the case where the two arguments are the same, is

```
In[13]:=  delta[x_,x_] = 1
```

```
Out[13]=  1
```

Again, *Mathematica* must sort these two rules into a list in order of increasing generality before it stores them internally. Let's see what it does:

```
In[14]:=  ?delta
          Global`delta

          delta[x_, x_] = 1

          delta[x_, y_] = 0
```

The following is the correct ordering:

```
In[15]:=  Print[ delta[1,2] ];
          Print[ delta[1,1] ];
          0
          1
```

Clearly, storing the rules in the reverse order would render the rule for delta[x_, x_] invisible since that rule would be totally shadowed by the delta[x_, y_] definition. We can actually force *Mathematica* to store the definitions in this way. The definitions and order of precedence of the rules for a particular function can be accessed through the DownValues command:

```
In[16]:=  DownValues[delta]
```

```
Out[16]=  {Literal[delta[x_, x_]] :> 1, Literal[delta[x_, y_]] :> 0}
```

Do not worry about the exact manner in which the rules have been stored with Literal heads and the delayed substitution rules :>. We are interested purely in the order. Suppose that we reverse this order:

```
In[17]:=  DownValues[delta] = Reverse[ DownValues[delta] ];
          ?delta
          Global`delta

          delta[x_, y_] := 0

          delta[x_, x_] := 1
```

The second rule will never be used since any instance in which delta is called with a repeated argument will be caught by the more general first rule:

```
In[18]:=  { delta[1,0], delta[1,1] }
```

```
Out[18]=  {0, 0}
```

10.1.3 Overlapping Conditions

There are times when it is impossible for *Mathematica* to know in what order to store the rules that you give it. For instance, consider the following rules:

```
In[19]:=  shading[x_,y_] := GrayLevel[0.4] /; (x-1)^2 + y^2 <= 3;
          shading[x_,y_] := GrayLevel[0.7] /; (x+1)^2 + y^2 <= 3;
          shading[x_,y_] := GrayLevel[0.9];
```

Let's examine these rules. The expressions after the /; refer to the conditions under which the rules will be invoked. The first condition is true inside a circle with radius $\sqrt{3}$ and centered at $(1, 0)$; the second condition is true inside a circle with radius $\sqrt{3}$ and centered at $(-1, 0)$. Note that these two circles overlap. The last definition is applicable anywhere; this definition is obviously more general than are the first two definitions, so it will be stored at the bottom of the rule table. On the other hand, the first two rules are of equal complexity. *Mathematica* just stores these rules in the order in which they have been entered. We can demonstrate this result in a visual manner with a raster-graphics plot:

```
In[20]:=  regions = Table[ shading[x,y],
            {y,-3,3,0.1},{x,-3,3,0.1}];
          Show[Graphics[RasterArray[regions]],
            AspectRatio -> Automatic];
```

This picture shows one circle on top of another. Because *Mathematica* is not psychic, it cannot know which of the two possible shading functions that we want in the overlap region. If we wish, we can quickly swap the order that *Mathematica* has used:

```
In[21]:=  DownValues[shading] =
          Drop[ Prepend[ DownValues[shading], DownValues[shading][[2]]],{3}];

In[22]:=  regions = Table[ shading[x,y],{y,-3,3,0.1},{x,-3,3,0.1}];
          Show[Graphics[RasterArray[regions]], AspectRatio -> Automatic];
```

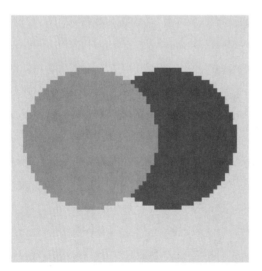

10.2 Pure Functions

Pure functions were discussed in Chapter 1. Their basic uses are to allow us to avoid defining a name for a function that we are going to use only once, and to facilitate list operations. For instance, suppose that we want to convert a list of complex numbers into a list of (x,y) pairs for plotting as an Argand diagram. First, let's generate some complex numbers:

```
In[23]:=  Clear[x];
          roots = x /. NSolve[x^4 + x^2 + x + 1 == 0, x]
Out[23]=  {-0.547424 - 0.585652 I, -0.547424 + 0.585652 I,

           0.547424 - 1.12087 I, 0.547424 + 1.12087 I}
```

We need to map a function onto the elements of this list so that we end up with (*real, imaginary*) pairs. One way to do so is to create a function:

```
In[24]:=  topairs[z_Complex] := {Re[z], Im[z]};
          Map[topairs, roots]
Out[24]=  {{-0.547424, -0.585652}, {-0.547424, 0.585652}, {0.547424, -1.12087},

           {0.547424, 1.12087}}
```

There is nothing fundamentally wrong with this approach — indeed, it is the correct one to use if you want to make repeated use of the operation. However, for a one-time calculation, it is double the length that it needs to be, and it clutters up the Global context with yet another name. If we think of our function definition in English, it might read, "Make a list comprising the real part of the argument and the imaginary part of the argument," which is exactly how we write the instruction as a pure function (denoted by an ampersand):

```
In[25]:=  Map[ ({Re[#], Im[#]}&), roots ]
Out[25]=  {{-0.547424, -0.585652}, {-0.547424, 0.585652}, {0.547424, -1.12087},

           {0.547424, 1.12087}}
```

Here are a couple of other examples of pure function use made in conjunction with Map and Apply. First, we sum the squared elements of a list:

```
In[26]:=  Map[#^2&, {1, 2, 3}]
Out[26]=  {1, 4, 9}
```

We could have achieved the same result by just squaring the list since Power is a Listable function (see Chapter 9). Second, we subtract the second row of a matrix from its first. There are two equally acceptable ways of doing this subtraction:

```
In[27]:=  ((#[[1]]-#[[2]])&) [{{a, b, c}, {d, e, f}}]
Out[27]=  {a - d, b - e, c - f}
In[28]:=  Apply[ ( (#1 - #2) &), {{a, b, c}, {d, e, f}} ]
```

Out[28]= {a - d, b - e, c - f}

When we define a pure function that takes more than one argument, we use #1 to denote the first argument, #2 to denote the second, and so on.

10.3 Conditional Evaluation

Mathematica contains several different tools for controlling whether and how the evaluation of a function takes place. Perhaps the simplest is conditional evaluation in the following form:

In[29]:= ```
r[x_] := x /; x > 0
r[x_] := -x /; x < 0

Plot[r[x], {x,-1,1}];
```

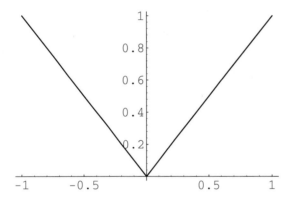

The expression /; means "use this rule when . . .". Another straightforward way of coding this function is with an *if, then, else* statement:

*In[30]:=*  ```
rr[x_] := If[x > 0, x, -x];
{rr[1], rr[-2]}
```

Out[30]= {1, 2}

We can also use an If instruction to implement the Kronecker delta symbol, introduced in Section 10.1.2:

In[31]:= ```
kroneck[x_,y_] := If[x == y, 1, 0];
{kroneck[1,1], kroneck[1,2]}
```

*Out[31]=*  {1, 0}

Note that we use a double equals sign to test equality because a single equals sign is used for assignment purposes.

Suppose that we want to define a function with the following properties:
```

$$f(x) = -1 \quad \text{for } x \le -1$$
$$f(x) = x \quad \text{for } -1 < x \le 1$$
$$f(x) = 2 - x \quad \text{for } 1 < x \le 2$$
$$f(x) = 0 \quad \text{for } x > 2$$

We cannot use an If statement because there are more than two possibilities. However, there is a generalization of this function, called Which:

```
In[32]:=  s[x_] := Which[ x <= -1,        -1,
                         -1 < x <= 1,     x,
                          1 < x <= 2,     2-x,
                          True,           0];

          Plot[s[x], {x, -3, 3}];
```

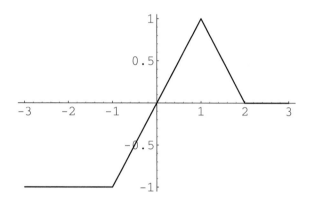

10.3.1 Boolean Tests

A *Boolean test* is a function that when applied to an object, gives a simple yes or no answer (which distinguishes it from a politician). The syntax is actually True for yes and False for no. Here is a simple Boolean test that checks to see whether a number is positive:

```
In[33]:=  {Positive[34], Positive[-100]}

Out[33]=  {True, False}
```

We can use Boolean tests in a function definition, again using /; after the instruction. For instance, the following function definition is equivalent to the one at the beginning of Section 10.3

```
In[34]:=  Clear[rr];
          rr[x_] := x /; Positive[x];
          rr[x_] := -x /; Negative[x];

In[35]:=  {rr[-2], rr[2]}

Out[35]=  {2, 2}
```

Alternatively, we could be really perverse and use a logical NOT operation "!" to write the definition as

```
In[36]:=  Clear[rr];
          rr[x_] := x /; !Negative[x];
          rr[x_] := -x /; !Positive[x];
          {rr[-2], rr[2]}
```

```
Out[36]=  {2, 2}
```

If a Boolean function exists for the condition that you want to test, then *Mathematica* supplies an alternative method for specifying this condition for an argument. Instead of using the /; construction, you can put the test after the underscore:

```
In[37]:=  Clear[rr];
          rr[x_?Positive] := x;
          rr[x_?Negative] := -x;
          {rr[-7], rr[42]}
```

```
Out[37]=  {7, 42}
```

Numerous Boolean tests are built into *Mathematica*. In some cases, the logical (excuse the pun) name for the function may already have been used. For instance, to test whether a number is prime, the command is PrimeQ, rather than Prime:

```
In[38]:=  {PrimeQ[43], Prime[43]}
```

```
Out[38]=  {True, 191}
```

As you can see, Prime[n] already has the job of generating the *n*th prime number. Boolean tests that check the head of an expression also have a letter Q appended in order to distinguish them from the head instruction itself. For instance, to determine whether {1,2,3} is a list, we do not enter

```
In[39]:=  List[{1,2,3}]
```

```
Out[39]=  {{1, 2, 3}}
```

but rather the following instruction:

```
In[40]:=  ListQ[{1,2,3}]
```

```
Out[40]=  True
```

Devising your own Boolean tests

You are not limited to the Boolean tests that *Mathematica* supplies. You can define your own tests, just as you would define any other function. For instance, the following function threediv determines whether or not a number is divisible by 3:

```
In[41]:=  threediv[x_] := If[Mod[x,3] == 0, True, False]
```

When we map this function onto a list of the first ten integers, we obtain a repeated pattern of False, False, True:

```
In[42]:=  Map[{#, threediv[#]}&, Range[10]]
Out[42]=  {{1, False}, {2, False}, {3, True}, {4, False}, {5, False},

          {6, True}, {7, False}, {8, False}, {9, True}, {10, False}}
```

You can use your own Boolean tests inside function definitions, just as you would the predefined ones:

```
In[43]:=  isit3divfolks[x_?threediv] := Print[x," is divisible by three, folks"];
          isit3divfolks[x_] := Print[x," divisible by three --- NOT!"];

          Do[ isit3divfolks[i];, {i,3}]
          1 divisible by three --- NOT!
          2 divisible by three --- NOT!
          3 is divisible by three, folks!
```

Stringing tests together

We can simultaneously test whether the argument of a function satisfies more than one Boolean condition. All we have to do is to string the tests together:

```
In[44]:=  fourposs[(x_?EvenQ)?Positive] := Print[x," is even and positive"];
          fourposs[(x_?OddQ)?Positive] := Print[x," is odd and positive"];
          fourposs[(x_?EvenQ)?Negative] := Print[x," is even and negative"];
          fourposs[(x_?OddQ)?Negative] := Print[x," is odd and negative"];
```

The parentheses breaking the tests are extremely important — in fact, without them, *Mathematica* will not even recognize the syntax of the expression because "?" has an extremely high priority as an operator. The results of our tests are as follows

```
In[45]:=  Map[fourposs, {-2,-1,1,2}];
          -2 is even and negative
          -1 is odd and negative
          1 is odd and positive
          2 is even and positive
```

10.3.2 Head Checks

Suppose that you wish to define a function that will operate on a structure only if that structure has a particular head. One way to achieve this objective is through a simple Boolean test, as described in Section 10.3.1. The following function is designed to normalize a vector to a unit vector pointing in the same direction:

```
In[46]:=  normalize[x_?ListQ] := x/Sqrt[Apply[Plus,x^2]]
```

```
In[47]:=  normalize[{1,2,3}]
Out[47]=      1             2         3
          {---------, Sqrt[-], ---------}
           Sqrt[14]           7   Sqrt[14]
```

The Boolean test ensures that the function will not work on any structure other than a list:

```
In[48]:=  normalize[54]
```

```
Out[48]=  normalize[54]
```

Because it is so common to want to specify function definitions for arguments with a certain head, there is a shorthand notation that omits the ? and the Q:

```
In[49]:=  newnorm[x_List] := x/Sqrt[ Apply[Plus,x^2] ];
          {newnorm[{1,2,3}], newnorm[54]}
```

```
Out[49]=         1            2        3
          {{--------- , Sqrt[-],  ---------}, newnorm[54]}
            Sqrt[14]        7    Sqrt[14]
```

The most general form of test that we can apply to an argument is
```
(((argHead?BooleanTest)?BooleanTest)?...)
```
For instance, the following pattern matches only positive integer arguments:

```
In[50]:=  posint[x_Integer?Positive] = True;
          posint[x_] = False;
          {posint[1], posint[-2], posint[2.4], posint[2.]}
```

```
Out[50]=  {True, False, False, False}
```

10.3.3 Error Messages

Frequently, a function makes no sense for certain values of its arguments. If it does not, you can either just throw the function back at the user or be more helpful and provide error information.

Suppose that we want to define a function that sums the elements in a one-dimensional list. The Boolean test for such a list is VectorQ:

```
In[51]:=  {VectorQ[{1,2,3}], VectorQ[{{1,2,3},{4,5}}]]}
```

```
Out[51]=  {True, False}
```

```
In[52]:=  sumalist[x_List?VectorQ] := Apply[Plus,x]
```

Everything works when we use the correct syntax:

```
In[53]:=  sumalist[{1,2,3}]
```

```
Out[53]=  6
```

However, inexperienced users often forget the curly brackets:

```
In[54]:=  sumalist[1,2,3]
```

```
Out[54]=  sumalist[1, 2, 3]
```

This response probably leaves them in complete confusion, and wondering what went wrong. We could be more accommodating, and extend the definition of sumalist such that it can cope with either a list or a sequence of numbers. At the least, we should inform users why we refuse to add up their numbers. There are, in fact, two reasons why such a refusal might happen.

The first is that the list that has been supplied is not a vector (that is, its depth is too large). So, we compose the error message and the rule for when this error should be invoked first:

```
In[55]:=  sumalist::matrix = "The list that you have supplied is not flat.
          sumalist operates on one-dimensional structures";

          sumalist[x_List] := Message[sumalist::matrix]
```

You may be concerned that this rule might overshadow the vector case. However, *Mathematica* can understand which of the two rules is more general:

```
In[56]:=  ?sumalist
          Global`sumalist

          sumalist[(x_List)?VectorQ] := Apply[Plus, x]

          sumalist[x_List] := Message[sumalist::matrix]
```

In the second instance, we are concerned with the easy mistake of leaving out the curly brackets. Again, although the new rule will be applicable to both vectors and matrices, it will be stacked below these rules in the rule table. We shall return to the subject of the double underscore that follows the x in the function definition in Chapter 12. Its purpose is to allow us to match for one or more entries (as opposed to a single underscore, which matches for only one):

```
In[57]:=  sumalist::sequence = "You have supplied a sequence of numbers
          when a List is required.";
```

```
In[58]:=  sumalist[x__] := Message[sumalist::sequence]
```

Suppose that we now try out the three possibilities:

```
In[59]:=  sumalist[{1,2,3}]
```

```
Out[59]=  6
```

```
In[60]:=  sumalist[1,2,3]
          sumalist::sequence:
             You have supplied a sequence of numbers  when a List is required.
```

```
In[61]:=  sumalist[{{1,2},{3}}]
          sumalist::matrix:
             The list that you have supplied is not flat.  sumalist operates on
                one-dimensional structures
```

The fact that the correct rules were found for each case is a credit to *Mathematica*'s ability to store rules in a sensible order.

In the case that we have just discussed, it would have been quicker to include separate definitions for the offending functions than to send back error messages:

```
In[62]:=  friendlysum[x_List] := Apply[Plus, Flatten[x]];
          friendlysum[x__] := Plus[x]

          {friendlysum[{1,2,3}],friendlysum[1,2,3],
           friendlysum[{{1,2,3},{4,3}}]}
```

Out[62]= {6, 6, 13}

There are situations when a function really makes no sense for certain arguments. For instance, the infinite sum

$$\sum_{n=1}^{\infty} \log(n)x^n$$

converges for only $-1 < x < 1$:

In[63]:= `infsum[x_] := NSum[Log[n] x^n,{n,1,Infinity}];`
`{infsum[-2], infsum[-0.5], infsum[0.5], infsum[2]}`

Out[63]= {ComplexInfinity, 0.0904117, 0.507834, ComplexInfinity}

It might be more useful to send back an error message explaining the problem, rather than just `ComplexInfinity`. We can even include the offending argument value in the message text:

In[64]:= `infsum::nonconv = "infsum[x] does not converge for x=`1`";`
`infsum[x_] := Message[infsum::nonconv,x] /; Abs[x] >= 1`

`infsum[3]`

`infsum::nonconv: infsum[x] does not converge for x=3`

10.4 Blocks of Code and Collision of Variables

Except for simple examples, you will want to use several commands in your function definitions. At first, you may be tempted to find an ugly way to do so. For instance, suppose that we want to define a function that generates a random permutation of the first n integers. The following method is included in the package `DiscreteMath`Combinatorica`. We take a list of the integers, group each number with a random number, sort the list according to these random numbers, and then drop them. Here is an ugly way to code this function:

In[65]:= `perm[n_] := Map[Last,Sort[Map[{Random[],#}&, Range[n]]]];`
`perm[6]`

Out[65]= {3, 4, 2, 5, 1, 6}

The definition comes from the school of thought, "Put as much code into one line as possible, making it completely unreadable." We should come clean and admit that this style is the one we often use. However, beginners may like to break up the code into bite-sized chunks, enhancing readability at the expense of more code. One way to simplify matters is to use two function definitions instead of the one that we have used. Here is another ugly method:

In[66]:= `innerperm[n_] := Map[{Random[],#}&, Range[n]];`
`perm2[n_] := Map[Last, Sort[innerperm[n]] ];`

`perm2[4]`

Out[66]= {3, 1, 2, 4}

Using two functions is really wasteful. Chances are that the function innerperm never will be used except by perm2, so the logical place for its definition is within that function.

What we need is a block of code. It would also be convenient if we could define a local variable in which to store any temporary work that we do. Both of these facilities are afforded by the use of the Module construction:

```
In[67]:=  neatperm[n_] := Module[{temp},
                        temp = Map[{Random[], #}&, Range[n]];
                        temp = Map[Last, Sort[temp]];
                        temp]
```

```
In[68]:=  neatperm[7]
```

```
Out[68]=  {7, 3, 5, 6, 2, 1, 4}
```

The variable temp is local to the module and is removed on exit:

```
In[69]:=  temp
```

```
Out[69]=  temp
```

What happens if temp already exists in the Global context before we go into the Module? Let's find out:

```
In[70]:=  temp = 6;
          neatperm[7];
```

```
In[71]:=  temp
```

```
Out[71]=  6
```

How does *Mathematica* avoid confusion? It is sneaky. When a variable is declared as local inside a module, the variable's name changes by appending a dollar sign, followed by a number. The chances of such a variable having been used by the user are remote. We can take a look at what is happening inside the Information instruction:

```
In[72]:=  Module[{temp}, Information[temp]]
```

```
Global`temp$22
```

```
Attributes[temp$22] = {Temporary}
```

On the whole, Temporary variables are removed when the Module is exited. You may be wondering where the 22 came from (do not expect to obtain the same number on your machine). So that *Mathematica* avoids using the same local variable name twice (for instance, a function may want to call itself), the number after the dollar sign is controlled by a variable called $ModuleNumber, which is incremented every time a module is defined:

```
In[73]:=  $ModuleNumber
```

```
Out[73]=  24
```

The reason that this number is now 24, rather than 23, is that Information also uses a module, as we can see by repeating the operation without the Information instruction:

```
In[74]:=  Module[{temp},];
          $ModuleNumber
```

Out[74]=   25

10.4.1 Collision of Variables

Sometimes, the built-in functions run into difficulties with variables colliding. Let's consider the Sum instruction; we use an iterator for which a value has already been defined:

In[75]:=   i = 5;
            Sum[i, {i,1,5}]

Out[75]=   15

No problem here. When Sum was entered, the value of i was stored temporarily and i was free to be used.

Now consider the following function and its behavior:

In[76]:=   Clear[i];
            sumthree[x_] := Sum[x^(1/i),{i,1,3}];

            sumthree[x]

Out[76]=   1/3
            x   + Sqrt[x] + x

In[77]:=   sumthree[i]

Out[77]=   1/3
            1 + Sqrt[2] + 3

You can see the problem. In the function definition, although any numerical assignments associated with x are ignored, symbolic assignments are not. Thus, x is evaluated to i, which subsequently collides with the iteration variable. We can circumvent this problem by putting the sum inside a module and declaring the iteration variable as local to that Module:

In[78]:=   newsumthree[x_] := Module[{i}, Sum[x^(1/i),{i,1,3}]];

            newsumthree[i]

Out[78]=   1/3
            i   + Sqrt[i] + i

In earlier versions of *Mathematica*, a function called Block existed that allowed the user to group together multiple instructions in a function definition. This function still exists in *Mathematica*, but it suffers from the same problems as do commands such as Sum:

In[79]:=   blocksumthree[x_] := Block[{i}, Sum[x^(1/i),{i,1,3}]];

            blocksumthree[i]

Out[79]=   1/3
            1 + Sqrt[2] + 3

We have never found a situation where Block was superior to Module, although such cases may exist.

10.5 Summary

In this chapter, we have looked at *Mathematica* functions. We started with functions that had a single definition and quickly moved on to functions that used different definitions depending on the nature of the function's arguments. We gave a comprehensive survey of the tools available to test the condition of the arguments, including Boolean tests (such as whether a number is positive or negative) and head checks (such as whether an argument is a `List`). When a function has more than one definition, *Mathematica* must decide an order in which to store the definitions. We showed that it is vital that this order be the correct one, and explained how to set the order manually on the rare occasions that *Mathematica* does not do what we want. It is useful to divide long function definitions into manageable chunks; we used the `Module` construction to assign a block of code to a function.

Procedural Methods

Without their DO and FOR loops, traditional languages such as FORTRAN would be impotent. *Mathematica* would not be, however, so we have deliberately discussed operations such as Map and Apply first because *Mathematica* programs written with them are generally shorter and more efficient.

Functional programming, which makes use of *Mathematica*'s range of pattern-matching facilities, provides another way to avoid procedural methods. However, you should appreciate that underlying every pattern-matching operation is a procedural method, even if this method is hidden from the user. This means that although your programs may be less elegant when you avoid pattern matching, it is often more efficient to do so. We shall see an example of such behavior later in this chapter. A good text for procedural methods in *Mathematica* is that of R. Crandall [4].

11.1 Procedural Commands

Mathematica supports the standard procedural instructions that are found in languages such as FORTRAN. For example, all the old favorites Do, For, and While are in *Mathematica*.

The operation of the Do command is similar to its implementation in any standard computer language, and the syntax is what you would expect. For instance, to print the first four cubes to the screen, you would enter

```
In[1]:=    Do[Print[n^3], {n,1,4}]

           1
           8
           27
           64
```

Alternatively, you could implement this operation using For. The syntax should be familiar to C users; it takes the form For[start, test, incr, body]. First, start is evaluated; then, body and incr are evaluated until test fails:

```
In[2]:=    For[n = 1, n < 5, n++, Print[n^3]]

           1
           8
           27
           64
```

Note the structure of the increment. It is one of several that are possible. The most important are illustrated in the following:

227

```
In[3]:=   For[i = 3, i >= -2, i--, Print[i^3]]
          27
          8
          1
          0
          -1
          -8

In[4]:=   For[i = 1, i < 1.3, i += 0.1, Print[i^3]]
          1
          1.331
          1.728
```

In the last example, we could have used $-$, $*$, and $/$ instead of the $+$ in the $+\,=$ construction. The test can be complicated and can involve a composition of smaller tests.

Yet another procedural possibility is offered by `While`:

```
In[5]:=   x = 1;
          While[x < 5, Print[x^3]; x++]
          1
          8
          27
          64
```

11.2 Disadvantages of the Procedural Approach

Mathematica supports specialized functions for several operations that customarily would be coded with a Do loop. We recommend that you use them because they are more efficient. An example is the computation of a sum of the terms in a general sequence. It can be achieved with `Do`:

```
In[6]:=   Timing[
            Module[{total = 0},
                Do[total = total + i^2,{i,1,2000}];
                total]]

Out[6]=   {3.46667 Second, 2668667000}
```

It is not only much more sensible, but also quicker, to use the existing `Sum` command:

```
In[7]:=   Timing[Sum[i^2, {i,1,2000}]]

Out[7]=   {2.08333 Second, 2668667000}
```

Similarly, if you want to find the root of the equation $\cos x = x$ by successively nesting `Cos` onto itself a large number of times from some start value, you should not enter

```
In[8]:=   Timing[ x = 0.5;
                  Do[x = Cos[x],{1000}];
                  x]

Out[8]=   {0.683333 Second, 0.739085}
```

but rather the following instruction:

In[9]:=   `Timing[ Nest[Cos, 0.5, 1000] ]`

Out[9]=   `{0.416667 Second, 0.739085}`

These timing differences are small. The method that you choose matters only when your loops are large, or when you have double or even triple loops. When either condition is satisfied, you should choose what is most efficient (see Chapter 14).

Another area where *Mathematica* has powerful built-in facilities is list manipulation. Here are two examples of list operations that are best not performed with `Do`. The first is to square the elements in a list. Procedurally, we have

In[10]:=
```
procsquare[x_List] :=
Module[{temp=x},
        Do[temp[[i]] = x[[i]]^2,{i,1,Length[x]}];
        temp]

procsquare[{2,3,4}]
```

Out[10]=   `{4, 9, 16}`

Do not be fooled — `Table` is only using a procedural method in disguise:

In[11]:=
```
procindisguise[x_List] := Table[x[[i]]^2,{i,1,Length[x]}];

procindisguise[{2,3,4}]
```

Out[11]=   `{4, 9, 16}`

All this coding is redundant when you learn about the `Listable` attribute and the fact that `Power` possesses it:

In[12]:=   `{2,3,4}^2`

Out[12]=   `{4, 9, 16}`

Bear in mind, however, that beneath this `Listable` facade lurks a procedural implementation, so we have not done anything philosophically different.

The second example is correlation between elements in a list. For instance, to go from a list x_i to a list where $y_i = x_i x_{i-1}$, you can use a procedural technique:

In[13]:=
```
correl[x_List] := Table[x[[i]] x[[i+1]],{i,1,Length[x]-1}];
correl[{1,2,3,4,5}]
```

Out[13]=   `{2, 6, 12, 20}`

Alternatively, you can make use of `RotateRight`:

In[14]:=
```
rotcorr[x_List] := Rest[x RotateRight[x]];
rotcorr[{1,2,3,4,5}]
```

Out[14]=   `{2, 6, 12, 20}`

Having expounded at length about those areas where it is probably better for you to avoid using a procedural approach, we now turn our attention to a case where procedural methods definitely have the upper hand.

11.3 Case Study: Printer Tables

During some recent work, we were having problems with the screen and printer display of several large tables. These tables were, in general, sparsely populated with a lot of 0s. We decided to use a shorthand notation where, for instance, a sequence of five 0s would be replaced by the string "<5>". We figured that this notation would reduce the width of our tables so that they could fit on a standard-sized sheet of paper. To us, this example seemed like a prime candidate for pattern matching. Our instincts were to use a set of patterns to reach our objective.

First, we defined a Boolean test to ascertain whether or not a number is effectively zero (we classed as zero any number smaller than 0.0001; all our numbers were positive):

In[15]:=
```
zero[x_] := If[x<0.0001,True,False]
notzero[x_] := !zero[x];

Map[{zero[#], notzero[#]}&, {0.3,0.000067,0.5}]
```

Out[15]=   {{False, True}, {True, False}, {False, True}}

Then, we defined a function that makes the necessary conversion into shorthand for a sequence of numbers:

In[16]:=
```
arrows[n__] := StringJoin["<",ToString[Length[{n}]],">"];

{arrows[2,3,4,2], Apply[arrows,Range[100]]}
```

Out[16]=   {<4>, <100>}

Next, we defined a rule that we expected would search for a sequence of one or more 0s and make the necessary replacement. In English, this definition reads, "Whenever you come across a (possibly empty) sequence of numbers followed by one or more 0s and then another sequence of (again possibly empty) numbers, replace the 0s by the shorthand notation."

In[17]:=   `funczero[a___,b__?zero,c___] := funczero[a,arrows[b],c]`

Unfortunately, there is a slight problem with this function:

In[18]:=   `funczero[1,2,3,0,0,2,3]`

Out[18]=   funczero[1, 2, 3, <2>, 2, 3]

We had not made any allowances for the order in which the pattern-matching operation takes place. There are, in fact, several ways in which the pattern that we had defined can be matched. The possibilities are

1.	$a = 1, 2, 3$	$b = 0, 0$	$c = 3, 3$
2.	$a = 1, 2, 3, 0$	$b = 0$	$c = 3, 3$
3.	$a = 1, 2, 3$	$b = 0$	$c = 0, 3, 3$

We would have liked the choice for which the length of b is greatest — that is, choice 1 — but, unfortunately, that is not what we get. By default, *Mathematica* opts for the possibility that makes a and b have the minimum length — which is choice 3. The first replacement then leads to the expression `funczero[1,2,3,<1>,0,3,3]`. There is no ambiguity in the simplification of this expression, and we then obtain the result quoted. We had to be slightly more subtle in our definition:

```
In[19]:=  Clear[funczero];
          funczero[a___,b__?zero] := funczero[a,arrows[b]];
          funczero[a___,b__?zero,c_?notzero,d___] := funczero[a,arrows[b],c,d]
```

```
In[20]:=  funczero[1,2,3,2,0,0,0,2,2,1,0,0]
```

```
Out[20]=  funczero[1, 2, 3, 2, <3>, 2, 2, 1, <2>]
```

At this point, we were feeling rather smug about our definition: Its complete formulation consisted of two Boolean tests and two patterns to be matched. However, pride frequently comes before a fall, as was to be the case here. The function as defined seemed to behave pathologically. Suppose that we generate a fairly large list of randomly distributed 0s and 1s and time how long the simplification takes:

```
In[21]:=  timinglist = Table[Random[Integer,{0,1}],{100}];
          Timing[Apply[funczero,timinglist]]
```

```
Out[21]=  {75.0667 Second, funczero[1, <2>, 1, <2>, 1, <1>, 1, <1>, 1, <3>, 1,

          1, 1, 1, <2>, 1, 1, 1, 1, <1>, 1, <3>, 1, 1, 1, 1, 1, 1, <2>, 1,

          <1>, 1, 1, <3>, 1, <1>, 1, <1>, 1, 1, <1>, 1, 1, <2>, 1, 1, 1, 1,

          <2>, 1, 1, <4>, 1, <2>, 1, <2>, 1, 1, <3>, 1, 1, 1, 1, 1, <1>, 1,

          1, 1, 1, 1, 1, <1>, 1, <1>, 1, 1, 1, <1>, 1, 1, <1>]}
```

What a ridiculous amount of time for such a trivial operation! There is clearly a great deal of redundancy. There are, in fact, two issues that must be addressed. We can address the first in a functional manner, but the second forces us to use a procedural approach. (As it turned out, it would have been better if we had pursued the latter line of attack all along.)

First, let's consider the problem that we can address functionally. What does *Mathematica* actually do when we apply `funczero` to a set of numbers? The answer is that it performs a search through the data set (effectively a loop) looking for a match to the patterns that it knows about. When a pattern is found, the replacement is made. If there is more than one correction to be made, the search starts again from the beginning of the sequence. This behavior is stupid — we can see that the procedure is really a once-through algorithm. Because of the way that we have programmed it, *Mathematica* makes as many passes through the data as there are groups of 0s. The way to get around this problem, while retaining the functional approach, is to remove any part of the list that has been corrected from inside the correcting function. If we used lists to achieve this objective, then we would end up with a deeply nested structure. Instead, we choose to use a Sequence structure because any nesting is flattened automatically:

```
In[22]:=  Sequence[Sequence[1,2,3],Sequence[5,6]]
```

```
Out[22]=  Sequence[1, 2, 3, 5, 6]
```

Apart from this modification, the function definition is virtually unchanged:

```
In[23]:=    newzero[a___,b__?zero] := Sequence[ newzero[a], arrows[b]];
            newzero[a___,b__?zero,c_?notzero,d___] :=
                Sequence[a, arrows[b], newzero[c,d]];
            newzero[a__] := a
```

There is a significant improvement in the timings:

```
In[24]:=    Timing[Apply[newzero, timinglist]]

Out[24]=    {5.8 Second, 1, <2>, 1, <2>, 1, <1>, 1, <1>, 1, <3>, 1, 1, 1, 1, <2>,

            1, 1, 1, 1, <1>, 1, <3>, 1, 1, 1, 1, 1, 1, <2>, 1, <1>, 1, 1, <3>,

            1, <1>, 1, <1>, 1, 1, <1>, 1, 1, <2>, 1, 1, 1, 1, <2>, 1, 1, <4>,

            1, <2>, 1, <2>, 1, 1, <3>, 1, 1, 1, 1, 1, <1>, 1, 1, 1, 1, 1, 1,

            <1>, 1, <1>, 1, 1, 1, <1>, 1, 1, <1>}
```

11.4 Advantages of the Procedural Approach

In the previous section, our third attempt to code the instruction using pattern matching was much quicker than the first, but it is still hard to believe that the operation is so difficult that it needs almost 6 seconds to run! What is *Mathematica* doing wrong now? This time, it is a matter of the overhead of the pattern matching, which just takes that amount of time, plain and simple. If we want better performance, we need to design our own algorithm. In other words, we need to adopt a procedural approach — the approach that we should have taken all along.

The following code takes a once-only sweep through the data. When a zero is encountered, the counter `numzero` is incremented. When a nonzero number is encountered and `numzero` is not zero, then a `newarrow` is inserted into the output and `numzero` is reset to zero. Regardless of the state of `numzero`, nonzero characters are also added to the list. A special case is included to deal with a string of zeros at the end of the list:

```
In[25]:=    newarrow[n_] := StringJoin["<",ToString[n],">"];

            squeeze[x_List] :=
            Module[{output = {}},
                    numzero = 0;
                    Do[If[ zero[x[[i]]], numzero++,
                            If[numzero > 0,
                                output = Append[output,newarrow[numzero]];
                                numzero = 0];
                            output = Append[output,x[[i]]]],{i,1,Length[x]}];
                    If[numzero > 0,output = Append[output,newarrow[numzero]]];
                    output]
```

This code is clearly the most efficient way to implement our algorithm — and it works!

In[26]:=   `squeeze[{0,0,0,0,1,1,0,0,0,1,0,0,0}]`

Out[26]=   `{<4>, 1, 1, <3>, 1, <3>}`

The timings for the long list are now believable for the complexity of the problem:

In[27]:=   `Timing[squeeze[timinglist];]`

Out[27]=   `{0.55 Second, Null}`

Finally, here is an example of the type of table that we wanted to generate. It is an example from neutron diffraction which is discussed in Chapter 14:

In[28]:=
```
rangeofphi[struc_] :=
TableForm[Table[{deg,"deg",Apply[Sequence,squeeze[
        N[10000 diffract[applyoffset[unitcell[struc],
          deg*0.25/15]],4]]]},{deg,0.,15.,1}]]
```

```
rangeofphi[{2}]
```

Out[28]=
```
0.    deg   <1>   9330.    <5>   669.9   <4>
1.    deg   <1>   9415.    <5>   585.3   <4>
2.    deg   <1>   9494.    <5>   506.    <4>
3.    deg   <1>   9568.    <5>   432.3   <4>
4.    deg   <1>   9636.    <5>   364.1   <4>
5.    deg   <1>   9698.    <5>   301.5   <4>
6.    deg   <1>   9755.    <5>   244.7   <4>
7.    deg   <1>   9806.    <5>   193.7   <4>
8.    deg   <1>   9851.    <5>   148.5   <4>
9.    deg   <1>   9891.    <5>   109.3   <4>
10.   deg   <1>   9924.    <5>   75.96   <4>
11.   deg   <1>   9951.    <5>   48.66   <4>
12.   deg   <1>   9973.    <5>   27.39   <4>
13.   deg   <1>   9988.    <5>   12.18   <4>
14.   deg   <1>   9997.    <5>   3.046   <4>
15.   deg   <1>   10000.   <10>
```

11.5 Summary

In this chapter, we have seen that *Mathematica* supports the standard procedural commands, such as DO and FOR. *Mathematica* also possesses several special commands to deal with procedural problems, and we have shown that using these, rather than Do and For, requires less code and is faster and more intuitive. Many problems that can be tackled procedurally can also be tackled with functions. We have also shown that the functional approach, although visually more elegant, can be less efficient than the procedural method. It is important to be familiar with both techniques.

Rule-Based Schemes and Iteration

So far, we have looked at the implementation of only simple functions. These functions were deliberately designed to be understood by inexperienced users of *Mathematica*. We have found that the initial demand of new *Mathematica* users is for simple functions.

This chapter unleashes the full power of functional programming. The discussion is in four sections. In the first section, we consider what happens to *Mathematica*'s results after they have been evaluated. An understanding of this issue is important to prevent *Mathematica* from repeating calculations unnecessarily. In the second section, we consider pattern matching and the tools that *Mathematica* supports in this area. The enormous power that pattern matching makes available is demonstrated through a selection of examples. In the third section we deal with iteration. Iteration allows us to find solutions to equations and to explore decision trees (we look at a well-known puzzle whose solution involves searching a tree of move sequences). Each of these applications has its own set of pattern-matching requirements. However, in each case, the patterns are one-dimensional. In the fourth section of this chapter, we consider the extension of pattern matching to two dimensions.

12.1 Storage of Results

Suppose that we define a simple function to square a number and that we subsequently apply the function to a few values:

```
In[1]:=    f[x_] := x^2;
           {f[5], f[8], f[1]}
```

```
Out[1]=    {25, 64, 1}
```

Following these calculations, has *Mathematica* remembered any of the results?

```
In[2]:=    ?f
           Global`f

           f[x_] := x^2
```

Although the values of f[1], f[5], and f[8] have been calculated, *Mathematica* has not remembered them. For instance, if we were to ask for the value of f[8] again, *Mathematica* would have to go back and evaluate it from the definition of f. In this case, the redundant work is no big deal; the function is hardly complicated, and its evaluation is not particularly time-consuming. In other cases, however, it is certainly important to be able to make *Mathematica* remember the results of calculations that it has already performed.

When you use := to define a function, the right-hand side of the definition will be evaluated whenever instances of that function arise in a calculation. This means that when we call our function f[x], x^2 is evaluated and outputted, but at no point is an *assignment* made or the result stored. However, if we make the right-hand side of the definition an assignment, then the values will be stored in addition to being calculated:

In[3]:=
```
f[x_] := f[x] = x^2;
{f[5], f[8], f[1]};
?f
```
```
Global`f

f[1] = 1

f[5] = 25

f[8] = 64

f[x_] := f[x] = x^2
```

We do not recommend that you make *Mathematica* store all its results, but you should store those that take a long time to calculate and that may be needed more than once. A simple example is the calculation of Fibonacci numbers. These numbers are defined for the positive integers through the recurrence relationship $f_n = f_{n-1} + f_{n-2}$, along with the initial conditions $f_0 = 1, f_1 = 1$. The obvious way to code this function in *Mathematica* suffers from a slight problem:

In[4]:=
```
fib[0] = fib[1] = 1;
fib[n_] := fib[n-1] + fib[n-2];

Do[ Print[Timing[fib[n]]], {n,1,20}]
```
```
{0. Second, 1}
{0. Second, 2}
{0. Second, 3}
{0. Second, 5}
{0.0166667 Second, 8}
{0.0333333 Second, 13}
{0.05 Second, 21}
{0.0833333 Second, 34}
{0.133333 Second, 55}
{0.25 Second, 89}
{0.4 Second, 144}
{0.633333 Second, 233}
{1.05 Second, 377}
{1.66667 Second, 610}
{2.75 Second, 987}
{4.48333 Second, 1597}
{7.16667 Second, 2584}
{11.5833 Second, 4181}
{18.7333 Second, 6765}
{30.35 Second, 10946}
```

The superficially simple calculation of f_{20} takes a staggering 30 seconds! When *Mathematica* comes across the instruction `fib[20]`, we can imagine it says, "My rule tells me that `fib[20]` = `fib[19]` + `fib[18]`. OK, I shall forget about `fib[18]` for the moment, and work out `fib[19]`." The calculation of `fib[19]` then proceeds, and when it is complete, *Mathematica* returns to `fib[18]` — which it already calculated in working out `fib[19]`. But because this value has not been stored, *Mathematica* has to work it out again. As the situation stands, the time taken to calculate a Fibonacci number is proportional to the number itself! (We can check that this claim is correct by inspecting the numbers: `Timing[fib[18]]` + `Timing[fib[19]]` = 30.3 seconds; `Timing[fib[20]]` = 30.4 seconds.) Since $f_{100} = 573147844013817084101$, we can estimate that as our function definition currently stands, it would take 5×10^{10} years to compute this value. If we store the values as we go along, there is a noticeable improvement!

```
In[5]:=    fastfib[0] = fastfib[1] = 0;
           fastfib[n_] := fastfib[n] = fastfib[n-1] + fastfib[n-2];
           Timing[fastfib[100]]

Out[5]=    {0.65 Second, 0}
```

12.2 Pattern Recognition

In Chapter 10 and in Section 11.3, we made frequent use of a single underscore character, sometimes qualified by one or more Boolean tests. For instance, when we give *Mathematica* the definition

```
In[6]:=    g[x_?Positive] := x^2
```

it will use this rule only when we call the function g with a single positive argument:

```
In[7]:=    {g[2], g[-3], g[5,2]}

Out[7]=    {4, g[-3], g[5, 2]}
```

That the negative number was ignored is fine because we specified that our rule should apply to only positive numbers.

Sometimes, we want to tell *Mathematica* to use the same rule, regardless of the number of arguments that are supplied to the function. A simple example is to sum up a sequence of numbers. We can implement this example by using the double underscore:

```
In[8]:=    sumsequence[x__] := Plus[x];
           {sumsequence[2], sumsequence[2,3,1], sumsequence[]}

Out[8]=    {2, 6, sumsequence[]}
```

Both the number 2 and the sequence 2,3,1 were matched by the double underscore, and the addition rule was invoked. The null sequence (with zero elements) was not matched because double underscore stands for *one or more* elements. Indeed, in this case it makes little sense to make the rule apply to the case where there are no arguments. In other cases, it does make sense. An example is the Union command. This command takes a list of elements, eliminates repeated entries, and then orders the result:

```
In[9]:=    Union[{1,3,a,b,2,4,2,a}]
```
```
Out[9]=    {1, 2, 3, 4, a, b}
```

Suppose that we want to write our own function that takes a list and, like Union, drops repeated elements, but, unlike Union, does not reorder the resulting list. In words, the instruction that we want to give our function is, "When you come across the sequence *anything, element, anything, same element, anything*, drop the second occurrence of the element." It does not matter whether an *anything* has a hundred entries or none; we still want the rule to apply. This problem is a job for the triple underscore, which stands for any sequence of *zero or more* elements:

```
In[10]:=   newunion[{a___,b_,c___,b_,d___}] :=
                 newunion[{a,b,c,d}];
           newunion[a_List] := a
```

The blanket second rule is reached only when no further matches for the first rule can be found. Then the operation is complete, and the list should be returned:

```
In[11]:=   {newunion[{1,1,a,b,a}], newunion[{1,3,a,b,2,4,2,a}]}
```
```
Out[11]=   {{1, a, b}, {1, 3, a, b, 2, 4}}
```

It is possible to achieve sophisticated rule-based systems with varieties of underscores and Boolean tests. We now present three examples that introduce the techniques. The first example describes how to search for patterns in written text; it is more amusing than practical, but it does illustrate several important points. The second example shows how to teach *Mathematica* about noncommutative algebra; it is of practical importance to physicists. The third example considers a class of integrals that give *Mathematica* trouble; we teach *Mathematica* how to do this type of integral properly and to remember the results.

12.2.1 Text Correction

We are concerned by the poor standard of English usage, so we have devised the following scheme to improve usage. All you have to do is to take your text and to enter it into the correct function. All occurrences of irrelevant words, split infinitives, and "a" and "an" misuse will be instantly cured. Moreover, the text will become politically correct, with equal probabilities of any character being referred to as "he" or "she." (Text processing is not one of *Mathematica*'s strengths — this example is instructive rather than serious.)

To assist in this conversion, we shall need to define certain Boolean conditions. We first make a function that tells us whether or not a word is irrelevant. irrellist contains a list of words that are deemed to be irrelevant:

```
In[12]:=   irrellist = {"damn","actually","very","really"};
```

We then define a Boolean test to check whether a word is a member of this list:

```
In[13]:=   irrelevant[x_] := MemberQ[irrellist, x];
           {irrelevant["very"], irrelevant["humidifier"]}
```
```
Out[13]=   {True, False}
```

So, "very" is an irrelevant word and should be chopped from the text, whereas "humidifier" seems to be important and should be allowed to stay.

To pick up on misuse of the words "a" or "an," we must make a function that tells us whether or not a word begins with a vowel. First, we create a list of vowels:

```
In[14]:=   vowellist = {"A","E","I","O","U","a","e","i","o","u"};
```

We then define a function to see whether a word begins with any of these characters:

```
In[15]:=   vowel[x_] := MemberQ[vowellist, First[Characters[x]]];
```

We can take the logical NOT (denoted by ! in *Mathematica*) of the vowel function to test whether a word begins with a consonant:

```
In[16]:=   conson[x_] := !vowel[x];

           {vowel["aardvark"], conson["aardvark"]}
```

```
Out[16]=   {True, False}
```

To consistently avoid split infinitives (the previous clause supplies an example of the error), we need to determine whether or not a word is an adverb. For this purpose, the following function, where probadverb stands for "probable adverb," is an adequate test:

```
In[17]:=   probadverb[x_] :=  If[Length[Characters[x]] < 2, False,
                              Take[Characters[x],-2] == {"l","y"}];
```

The logic behind this definition is that any adverb appearing in a split infinitive will probably end in "ly." (Of course, this is not an exhaustive rule. For example, "to first think" will not be corrected. Our purpose here is pedagogical.)

```
In[18]:=   {probadverb["consistently"], probadverb["humidifier"]}
```

```
Out[18]=   {True, False}
```

We are now in a position to use these Boolean tests together with pattern recognition to create a text-correction function. The first operation that we want this function to perform when we supply it with a string is to convert the string into a list of words:

```
In[19]:=   correct[x_String] := Module[{inline}, inline = StringToStream[x];
                              correct[ReadList[inline,Word]]];

           correct["to boldly go"]
```

```
Out[19]=   correct[{to, boldly, go}]
```

Next, we get rid of any irrelevant words:

```
In[20]:=   correct[{a___, b_?irrelevant, c___}] := correct[{a, c}];
```

The triple underscore following a and c means that these blanks will be matched by a list of zero or more elements:

```
In[21]:=   correct["It was very very good"]
```

```
Out[21]=   correct[{It, was, good}]
```

Next, we define a replacement rule that should be applied when the pattern consisting of the letter "a" followed by a word that has a vowel as its first letter is found (a similar rule is applied for misuse of the word "an"):

```
In[22]:=   correct[{a___, "a", b_?vowel, c___}] :=
               correct[{a, "an", b, c}];
           correct[{a___, "an", b_?conson, c___}] :=
               correct[{a, "a", b, c}];

In[23]:=   correct["an book and a very excellent book"]

Out[23]=   correct[{a, book, and, an, excellent, book}]
```

This example is pattern matched three times. First, the irrelevant "very" is removed. Then, the "an" in "an book" is changed to "a". Finally, the "a" before "excellent" (which was correct before the "very" was removed) is changed to "an."

Next, we remove split infinitives. We suggest that the program search for occurrences of the pattern "to <adverb> <verb>" and replace them with "to <verb> <adverb>" (we consider only the simplest example and not more complicated situations).

```
In[24]:=   correct[{a___,"to",b_?probadverb,c_,d___}] :=
               correct[{a,"to",c,b,d}];

           correct["to boldly go"]

Out[24]=   correct[{to, go, boldly}]
```

Finally, to avoid accusations of sexual bias in our writing, we arrange for "she" and "he" to be replaced with each other at equal probability. (We stress that we do not consider this function to be used at all seriously. Imagine the confusion that the following rule would create!)

```
In[25]:=   correct[{a___,"she",b___}] :=
               correct[{a,"he",b}] /; Random[] > 0.5;
           correct[{a___,"he",b___}] :=
               correct[{a,"she",b}] /; Random[] > 0.5;

           Table[ correct["did he say she did it ?"], {5}]

Out[25]=   {correct[{did, he, say, he, did, it, ?}],

             correct[{did, she, say, she, did, it, ?}],

             correct[{did, he, say, she, did, it, ?}],

             correct[{did, she, say, he, did, it, ?}],

             correct[{did, she, say, he, did, it, ?}]}
```

The last rule that we want to include in the rule table should be evaluated only when all corrections have been applied. That is, we should convert the list back into a string, reinstating the interword space that we have chopped:

```
In[26]:=   correct[a_] := StringJoin[ Map[StringJoin[#," "]&, a] ];
```

Now it is time to pause to reflect on what we have created!

```
In[27]:=  correct["he wanted to boldly go to an land where no
          very good man had been before --- a damn excellent land"]
```

```
Out[27]=  she wanted to go boldly to a land where no good man had
          been before --- an excellent land
```

Although this example has been rather light-hearted (and should in no way be thought of as a reflection upon our excellent copy editor), there is a serious message behind it. By providing a sufficient quantity of rules and cases, we can build a semi-intelligent package. The next example that we consider is a rule-based system with serious practical applications in physics.

12.2.2 Noncommutative Algebra

Warning: This section contains advanced material.

In everyday mathematics, the order in which multiplication or addition of two elements is performed does not matter. For instance, $a + b = b + a$ and $ab = ba$. Addition and multiplication are said to be *commutative* because they have this orderless property. In *Mathematica*, commutative operations are ascribed the attribute Orderless:

```
In[28]:=  Map[ MemberQ[Attributes[#], Orderless]&,
               {Times, Plus, Dot}]
```

```
Out[28]=  {True, True, False}
```

Dot is the full name for matrix multiplication, which is not orderless. In physics, non-commutative operators arise frequently. Usually, all that physicists know about these operators is comprised of a few facts concerning the degree of the deviation of the operators from orderless behavior. However, this knowledge is sufficient to allow them to perform certain simplification operations. To illustrate the procedure, we consider a rudimentary case here. The example should be accessible to nonphysicists, yet it gives sufficient insight into the technique so that physicists will be prepared to write their own code for more specific and complicated examples. A more detailed discussion is given by J. Tigg [23].

We have three operators a, b, and c that do not commute under multiplication. Since the built-in multiplication command is hardwired to be commutative, we shall define our own operator multiplication function opmult. The syntax that we shall use is that, for example, $abcbc = $ opmult[a,b,c,b,a]. What information do we have about the operators? In the first instance, suppose that the square of any operator gives the identity. That is, $aa = bb = cc = 1$. This simplification rule is an easy one to code:

```
In[29]:=  opmult[x___,y_,y_,z___] := opmult[x,z];
          opmult[] = 1;
```

The other information that we will usually have at our disposal is the values of the commutators of any two operators. The commutator of an operator A with an operator B is $AB - BA$; for orderless multiplication, it will be zero. Suppose that, for our operators, we are told that

$$ab - ba = c,$$

$$ac - ca = b,$$

$$bc - cb = a.$$

We can enter this information into *Mathematica* by defining a new function `commutator`:

```
In[30]:=   commutator[a,b] = c;
           commutator[b,c] = a;
           commutator[a,c] = b;
           commutator[x_,y_] := -commutator[y,x]
```

The final instruction here means that we do not have to include results for commutators such as $ba - ab$ when we have already stored the result for $ab - ba$.

Now for the $64,000 question: How do we use this information to simplify an arbitrary product of operators? The real question is, What do we mean by "simple"? For instance, we can manipulate the expression aba, using the result for the commutator of a with b, into the form $(c+ba)a = ca + baa = ca + b$, but is this form simpler than the original expression? For physicists, the answer is probably yes; they do not care that there are now two terms instead of one but are content that the longest operator product is comprised of only two parts rather than three. This statement is the clue to our simplification procedure. We look for repeated operators, and we then use the commutators to bring together these operators until they annihilate each other. Each time that we move the repeated operators together, we will obtain an extra term (because the commutators are not zero), but this extra term will be one unit shorter than the term that we are manipulating. When the operators meet, they annihilate each other, leading to a reduction of two units in the length of this object. We also need a rule to pull minus signs outside the multiplication (-1 does commute with any of the operators):

```
In[31]:=   opmult[u___,-v_,w___] := -opmult[u,v,w];

           opmult[u___,v_,w_,x___,v_,y___] :=
               opmult[u,commutator[v,w],x,v,y] + opmult[u,w,v,x,v,y];
```

Now for the acid test: Does the function do what we want it to do? The example that we gave earlier was that aba should simplify to $ca + b$. Let's see:

```
In[32]:=   opmult[a,b,a]
```

```
Out[32]=   opmult[b] + opmult[c, a]
```

So, the function appears to work. Before we give a more complicated example, we can tidy up the output. There is no reason why, for display purposes, we cannot use the conventional format for normal multiplication:

```
In[33]:=   Format[opmult[x_]]  := x;
           Format[opmult[x___]] := HoldForm[Times[x]]
```

```
In[34]:=   opmult[a,b,a]
```

```
Out[34]=   b + c a
```

Now for a more serious example:

In[35]:= `opmult[a,b,c,b,c,c,a,b,c,a,b]`

Out[35]= `2 a + c b`

12.2.3 An Integration Problem

Warning: This section contains advanced material.

In this section, we consider integrals of the form

$$I_{n,m}(p, k) = \int_0^\pi \frac{(\mathbf{p} \cdot \mathbf{k})^n}{(\mathbf{p} - \mathbf{k})^{2m}} \sin^2 \omega d\omega,$$

where ω is the angle between the vectors $\mathbf{p}$ and $\mathbf{k}$ and where n and m are integers with $n \geq 0$. When $m \leq 0$, the evaluation of the integral is simple. *Mathematica* has no problem with these cases. The following example shows the evaluation of $I_{2,-1}(p, k)$:

In[36]:= `Timing[Integrate[Sin[w]^2 (p k Cos[w])^2 (p^2 + k^2 - 2 p k Cos[w]),`
              `{w,0,Pi}]]`

Out[36]=
```
                       2   2    2     2
                      k   p   (k  + p ) Pi
          {7.51667 Second,  ------------------}
                             8
```

When m is positive, we run into problems with the built-in integration facility. Evaluation of these integrals is harder to achieve than it was for the previous example. Consider $m = 1, n = 0$. A manual evaluation using Chebyshev polynomials gives

$$\int_0^\pi \frac{\sin^2(\omega)}{(\mathbf{p} - \mathbf{k})^2} d\omega = \frac{\pi}{2 \operatorname{Max}(k^2, p^2)}.$$

The expression of results in terms of maximum and minimum functions is usually desirable. Unfortunately, *Mathematica* gives its results in a less useful format:

In[37]:= `Timing[Integrate[ Sin[w]^2/(p^2 + k^2 - 2 p k Cos[w]),{w,0,Pi}]]`

Out[37]=
```
                      4      2  2    4    2            2    2 2
          {26.4833 Second, ((-k  + 2 k  p  - p  + k  Sqrt[(k  - p ) ] +

               2        2    2 2                2  2         2    2 2
              p  Sqrt[(k  - p ) ]) Pi) / (4 k  p  Sqrt[(k  - p ) ])}
```

Taking positive square roots gives the result applicable for $k \geq p$, whereas taking negative square roots gives the result for $k \leq p$. Clearly, this answer is far from ideal — and it took 26 seconds on a fast computer.

In the rest of this section, we show how to implement a more satisfactory version of the integration function. This discussion is not intended as a criticism of *Mathematica*. Its purpose is to demonstrate how to extend the functionality in a seamless fashion, customizing the environment to your particular requirements.

So, our idea is to write our own integration function for $I_{n,m}$. This problem is complicated, and we shall preempt a number of problems before they arise. $I_{n,m}$ is defined most efficiently through two recurrence relationships. The first relationship allows us to express an integral that has a positive integer value of n in terms of integrals with $n = 0$:

$$I_{n,m}(x,y) = \frac{1}{2^n} \sum_{i=0}^{n} (-1)^i C_i^n (x^2 + y^2)^{n-i} I_{0,m-i}(x,y).$$

Do not worry about where this rule came from — unless, of course, you want to! The important issue is that we never want *Mathematica* to evaluate $I_{n,m}$ directly for $n > 0$; instead, it should use this rule to express the result in terms of $n = 0$ integrals, which are easier to compute.

We obtain the second recurrence relationship by taking the derivative of $I_{0,m}$ with respect to either of its arguments:

$$I_{0,m+1}(x,y) = \frac{1}{(m+1)(x^2 - y^2)} \left(x\frac{d}{dx} - 1 \right) I_{0,m}(x,y).$$

Again, do not worry about the derivation of this equation. We want *Mathematica* to use this equation to relate integrals with positive values of m to the $m = 1$ result, which we shall store. For negative m, we shall permit the use of the built-in integration routine because it works.

$I_{0,1}(x,y)$ involves a maximum function, so in the calculation of $I_{n,m}(x,y)$ for negative m using our recurrence relationship, the derivative of the maximum function will be encountered. This derivative is just the Heaviside step function $\Theta(x)$, referred to as Theta by *Mathematica*. The definition of the Heaviside step function is that $\Theta(x) = 0$ for $x < 0$, $\Theta(x) = 1$ for $x > 0$. We shall need to tell *Mathematica* about the properties of Theta.

First, we include definitions for derivatives. Although the function Max has the attribute Orderless, meaning that is a commutative function, we have to program separately the results for the derivatives with respect to the different arguments. To teach *Mathematica* these new rules, we Unprotect the derivative function and enter

```
In[38]:=  Unprotect[Derivative];
          Derivative[1,0][Max][x_,y_] := Theta[x-y]
          Derivative[0,1][Max][x_,y_] := Theta[y-x]
          Derivative[x__][Theta][y_] := 0
          Protect[Derivative];
```

Note that we are deliberately keeping the analysis simple here — strictly, the derivative of $\Theta(x)$ is $\delta(x)$.

There are a couple of other useful rules concerning Theta. $\Theta^n(x) \equiv \Theta(x)$, and $\mathrm{Max}(x,y)\Theta(x-y) \equiv x\Theta(x-y)$. We could tell *Mathematica* about the first of these rules by adding a definition to Power:

```
In[39]:=  Unprotect[Power];
          Power[Theta[x_],n_] := Theta[x];
          Protect[Power];
```

However, since we are teaching *Mathematica* a rule that is associated more with `Theta` than with `Power`, it is sensible to store the rule with the definitions of `Theta`:

In[40]:= `Theta/: Theta[x_]^n_ := Theta[x]`

Similarly, we do not associate the new rule for multiplication with `Times`, preferring instead the following instruction:

In[41]:= `Theta/: Theta[x_-y_] Max[x_,y_]^n_:1 := x^n Theta[x-y];`

The ":1" after `n` is used to force the rule when $n = 1$. We need to force this case because it is stored in a different internal format from other values that use `Power` (see Chapter 9). Here is a demonstration of the new functionality that we have added to *Mathematica*:

In[42]:= `D[1/Max[x,y],{x,2}]`

Out[42]= `2 Theta[x - y]`
`--------------`
`     3`
`    x`

The computation of this second derivative used several of the rules that we have just programmed. If we were to trace *Mathematica*'s progress, we would see that in the evaluation of the first derivative, one of the new differentiation rules was invoked and the following intermediate expression was generated:

$$\frac{-\Theta(x-y)}{\mathrm{Max}^2(x,y)}.$$

At this point, *Mathematica* would have realized that our new multiplication rule was applicable and would have replaced the expression by

$$\frac{-\Theta(x-y)}{x^2}.$$

Finding no further simplifying rules, *Mathematica* progressed with the second derivative, using the product rule to generate the following expression:

$$\frac{-\Theta'(x-y)}{x^2} + \frac{2\Theta(x-y)}{x^3}.$$

Finally, the second of our new differentiation rules would have been invoked to drop the first term. The remaining term could not be simplified further and was outputted.

We are now in a position to define our own integration function that will take over the job from `Integrate`. This function, which we shall call `newint`, should be assumed to have an implicit weighting factor of $\sin^2 \omega$. We shall also invent a new command `dot` to denote the scalar product of two vectors. For instance, $\mathtt{dot[p,k]} \equiv \mathbf{p} \cdot \mathbf{k}$. We tell *Mathematica* that `dot` is orderless and give the simplification rule for when the two arguments are the same:

In[43]:= `Attributes[dot] = {Orderless};`
`dot[x_?AtomQ, x_?AtomQ] := x^2;`

Why do we use the AtomQ Boolean test? We want *Mathematica* to apply the second rule to replace "atomic" expressions such as $\mathbf{k} \cdot \mathbf{k}$ by k^2, but not to replace expressions like $(\mathbf{p} - \mathbf{k}) \cdot (\mathbf{p} - \mathbf{k})$:

```
In[44]:=   {dot[p,p], dot[p-k,p-k]}
```

```
Out[44]=    2
           {p , dot[-k + p, -k + p]}
```

Now for the integration definitions. In order, we give

1. Two simple cases, $n = m = 0$ and $n = 1, m = 0$
2. The recurrence relation for $n > 0$ in terms of $n = 0$ integrals
3. The cases for which *Mathematica* can use its built-in integration function (that is, $n = 0, m \leq 0$)
4. The Chebyshev case, $n = 0, m = 1$
5. The recurrence relation for $n = 0, m \geq 0$

You should convince yourself that these rules cover all possible combinations of n and m.

```
In[45]:=   newint[1] = Pi/2;

           newint[ dot[x_,y_] ] = 0;

           newint[ dot[x_,y_]^n_:1 dot[x_-y_,x_-y_]^m_:1 ] :=
               newint[ dot[x_,y_]^n dot[x_-y_,x_-y_]^m] =
                   Factor[
                     Expand[1/2^n
                     Sum[ (-1)^i Binomial[n,i] (x^2+y^2)^(n-i)
                          newint[ dot[x-y,x-y]^(m+i)],{i,0,n}]] ];

           newint[ dot[x_-y_,x_-y_]^(m_?Positive)] :=
               newint[ dot[x_-y_,x_-y_]^m ] =
                   Integrate[(x^2 + y^2 - 2 x y Cos[w])^m Sin[w]^2,{w,0,Pi}];

           newint[ dot[x_-y_,x_-y_] ] := (x^2 + y^2) Pi/2;

           newint[ dot[x_-y_,x_-y_]^(-1) ] := Pi/(2 Max[x,y]^2);

           newint[ dot[x_-y_,x_-y_]^(m_?Negative)] :=
               newint[ dot[x_-y_,x_-y_]^m] =
               Factor[Together[
                 (x D[#,x]/(m+1) - #)/(x^2-y^2)& [newint[ dot[x-y,x-y]^(m+1)]]]]]
```

When we enter these instructions, *Mathematica* will issue a warning message to the effect that underscores appear on both the left-hand and right-hand sides of some of the definitions. Generally, *Mathematica* would be correct to warn us; in this case, however, we want the underscores. The reason is subtle but important. We have given a general set of rules for I[n_,m_,x_,y_], and when we get *Mathematica* to determine the integral for particular m and n, we want the result to be stored, not as a rule for I[n,m,x,y], but rather as one for I[n,m,x_,y_].

Not only does this new function give the result in the format that we desire, but also it stores the result for a given pair of n and m, which saves on subsequent computation. The following evaluation of $I_{2,4}(x,y)$ is a graphic demonstration of this point:

```
In[46]:=  Timing[ newint[ dot[x,y]^2 dot[x - y, x - y]^(-4)] ]
```
```
Out[46]=                        10       8  2        6  4      4  6
          {8.63333 Second, (Pi (-x    + 5 x   y  - 11 x   y   - x   y  +

                 10                   8  2
                x    Theta[x - y] - 4 x   y  Theta[x - y] +

                   6  4                    4  6
               22 x   y  Theta[x - y] - 4 x   y  Theta[x - y] +

                   2  8
                  x  y  Theta[x - y])) /

                   2       5       5           2
              (8 x   (x - y)  (x + y)  Max[x, y] )}
```

This result simplifies when we know which of x and y is the larger. For instance, when $x > y$, Theta[x-y] = 1 and Max[x,y] = x:

```
In[47]:=  Factor[ %[[2]] /. {Max[x,y] -> x, Theta[x-y] -> 1} ]
```
```
Out[47]=      2   6       4  2      2  4    6
          Pi y  (x  + 11 x   y  - 5 x   y  + y )
          ------------------------------------
                   2       5       5
              8 x   (x - y)  (x + y)
```

The way that we have coded the function determines that the result for $I_{2,4}$ is now stored and will be found even when we use symbols other than x and y:

```
In[48]:=  Timing[ Factor[
             newint[ dot[a,b]^2 dot[a - b, a - b]^(-4) ]
             /. {Max[a,b] -> a, Theta[a-b] -> 1} ]]
```
```
Out[48]=                     2   6       4  2      2  4    6
                         b  (a  + 11 a   b  - 5 a   b  + b ) Pi
          {0.333333 Second, ------------------------------------}
                                    2       5       5
                               8 a   (a - b)  (a + b)
```

A further discussion of these points is given by J. Tigg [23].

12.3 Iteration

What can you do when you want to solve the equation $x = f(x)$ and it is impossible to reduce the problem to a form for which an analytical result exists? A method that sometimes works is to operate repeatedly the function f on an initial guess value. Suppose that we consider the specific example $x = \cos\ x$. We can use *Mathematica*'s plotting abilities to determine the rough location of a solution:

In[49]:= Plot[{Cos[x],x},{x,0,3}];

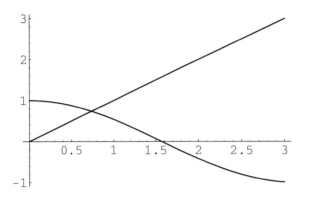

The crossover point on the graph tells us that there is a solution in the region of $x = 0.8$. Using this as our starting point and applying Cos successively, we can zoom in on the root:

In[50]:= {Cos[0.8], Cos[Cos[0.8]], Cos[Cos[Cos[0.8]]]}

Out[50]= {0.696707, 0.76696, 0.720024}

The function Nest allows us to iterate to any depth that we like:

In[51]:= Nest[Cos, x, 4]

Out[51]= Cos[Cos[Cos[Cos[x]]]]

Twenty iterations should give us a sufficiently accurate result:

In[52]:= Nest[Cos, 0.8, 20]

Out[52]= 0.739108

We can generate a list of the stages in this iteration with the NestList command:

In[53]:= iterstages = NestList[Cos, 0.8, 20]

Out[53]= {0.8, 0.696707, 0.76696, 0.720024, 0.75179, 0.730468, 0.744863,

 0.735181, 0.741709, 0.737315, 0.740276, 0.738282, 0.739626,

 0.738721, 0.73933, 0.73892, 0.739196, 0.73901, 0.739136,

 0.739051, 0.739108}

Using ListPlot, we see that this sequence corresponds to an oscillation about the solution. Because the amplitude of this oscillation is decreasing, so is our uncertainty in the solution:

```
In[54]:=  ListPlot[ iterstages,
            PlotJoined -> True, PlotRange -> All,
            AxesOrigin -> {0, 0.7}];
```

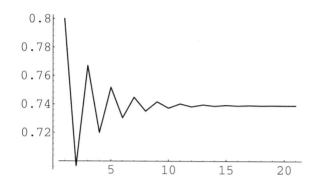

Mathematica possesses a function `FixedPoint`, which iterates a function on itself until the difference between consecutive iterations is extremely small:

```
In[55]:=  FixedPoint[Cos, 0.8]
```

```
Out[55]=  0.739085
```

Sometimes, this naive approach to root finding does not work. Consider the equation $x = 2 - \cos 2x$. A graphical estimate for the value of the single root of this equation is 2:

```
In[56]:=  Plot[{2 - Cos[2 x],x},{x,0,8}];
```

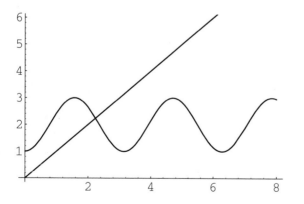

Iterating from this starting value, we obtain an oscillatory sequence with nondiminishing amplitude:

```
In[57]:=  ListPlot[ NestList[2 - Cos[2 #]&, 2, 50],
            PlotJoined -> True];
```

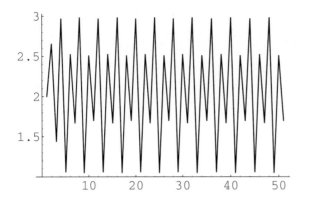

FixedPoint will similarly fail to find a solution, and you will have to interrupt the calculation manually.

Iterative techniques have widespread application in the solution of differential equations. Consider the following second-order differential equation:

$$\frac{d^2y}{dx^2} = -y.$$

A crude technique for solving this equation is to use the approximation $y(x+a) \approx y(x) + ay'(x) + a^2 y''(x)/2$, $y'(x+a) \approx y'(x) + ay''(x)$. If we know the values of $y(0)$ and $y'(0)$, we can choose a step size and iterate to obtain values for $y(x)$ away from the origin. The solution will be a list of triples $\{x, y, y'\}$:

In[58]:=
```
initialconditions = {0, 1, 0};
deiterate[triple_List, step_] :=
{triple[[1]]+step, (1-step^2/2) triple[[2]] + step triple[[3]],
 triple[[3]] - step triple[[2]]};
```

We have chosen to use a step size of 0.1 and 80 iterations. These values will provide coverage of the portion of the x-axis lying between $x = 0$ and $x = 8$. To view the function, we need to drop the third element of each triple, leaving a list of (x, y) pairs:

In[59]:=
```
desol = NestList[deiterate[#, 0.1] &, initialconditions, 80];
ListPlot[Map[ Take[#,2]&, desol] ];
```

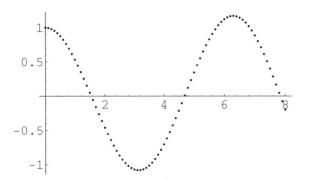

The plot demonstrates qualitative agreement with the analytic solution $y = \cos\ x$, but quantitative agreement is poor:

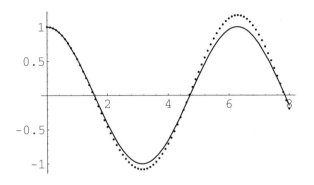

For serious applications, you must use an approximation of higher order than the one that we have used here. The standard method is a fourth-order Runge-Kutta as in W. Press et al. [15].

It is possible to continue applying a function on itself only when that function takes a single argument. If a function takes two arguments, then you must supply a list of values for the second argument to be *folded* in at each iteration. When the list is exhausted, the iteration must finish, so there is no need to specify an iteration depth:

```
In[60]:=   digits[x_,y_] := 10 x + y;
           Fold[digits,1,{4,2,6,1}]
```

```
Out[60]=   14261
```

Just as NestList allowed us to see the stages in a nested iteration, so FoldList allows us to see the stages in a folded iteration. For example, we can generate a random walk by first creating a list of random numbers between ± 0.5 and then using FoldList in conjunction with Plus to determine a cumulative sum that is then sent to ListPlot:

```
In[61]:=   ListPlot[ FoldList[ Plus, 0, Table[Random[] -0.5,{200}]],
                   PlotJoined -> True ];
```

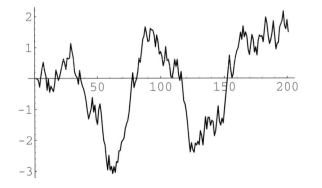

The examples that we have used in this section to introduce the iterative functions in *Mathematica* have been somewhat pedestrian. We now consider a couple of more interesting examples. In the first, we use iteration to investigate neutron scattering from an exotic crystal structure. In the second we use both pattern matching and `FoldList` to explore a decision tree in a well-known puzzle.

12.3.1 Neutron Diffraction

Holmium is a metal from the Rare Earth section of the Periodic Table. It possesses interesting magnetic properties that can be modeled easily with *Mathematica*. Holmium's crystal structure is planar hexagonal, which means that it consists of stacked layers that look like the next graphic:

```
In[62]:=  planehex[n_,m_] := {Thickness[0.001],
              Line[Table[
                {3 n/2 + Cos[i Pi/3], Sqrt[3] m/2 + Sin[i Pi/3]},{i,0,6}]]};


          Show[Graphics[Table[planehex[n,m+Mod[n,2]]
                  ,{n,0,5},{m,0,6,2}]], AspectRatio -> Automatic];
```

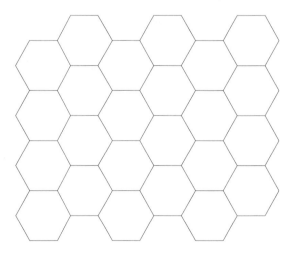

As you can see, `planehex[n,m]` generates a graphic for a hexagon of unit radius, centered at position (n,m) on a rectangular grid with x-spacing of $3/2$ and y-spacing of $\sqrt{3}$. The lowest six hexagons appearing in the graphic correspond to taking n from 0 to 5, with m simultaneously toggling between 0 and 1. In other words, the bottom right hexagon has (n,m) = (0,0), its neighbor (to the North-East) has (n,m) = (1,1) and its neighbor (center of the bottom row) has (n,m) = (2,0). The entire graphic is generated by displaying four rows. The instruction `AspectRatio -> Automatic` forces *Mathematica* to use the same scales in the x-direction and y-direction. If this option is not set, then the hexagons appear squashed.

Associated with each hexagon is a magnetic moment — in other words, a vector. Experimentally, researchers have found that, at low temperatures, these vectors tend to line up from the centers of the hexagons to the centers of the edges. To illustrate this phenomenon in *Mathematica*, we look down on a column of hexagons (actually, the column is staggered since successive layers are displaced):

```
In[63]:= stagger[n_] := If[EvenQ[n],0.43,0];

        hex[n_] := {Thickness[0.001], Dashing[{0.01,0.01}],
                Line[Table[{n, Cos[i Pi/3], Sin[i Pi/3]+stagger[n]}
                    ,{i,0,6}]]};
```

hex[n] creates the graphic for the hexagon in position n of our example column. We have chosen to align the column in the x-direction, which is why the x-component of the center of the hexagon is set equal to n. For odd n, the hexagons are centered at $(y, z) = (0, 0)$, whereas for n even, stagger is invoked to shift the center to $(y, z) = (0, 0.43)$.

In the following example, we look at seven hexagons in a column. We have defined a set of options, called holmsets, to be used in Show for the remainder of our three-dimensional graphics in this section:

```
In[64]:= hexplanes1 = Graphics3D[Table[hex[n],{n,0,6}]];
        holmsets = {ViewPoint -> {1.6, -3, 0.45}, Boxed -> False};
        Show[hexplanes1, holmsets];
```

Next, we generate the list of magnetic moment vectors. Each moment is defined by a position in space where the base of the vector arrow should be placed (that is, at the center of the appropriate hexagon — (n,0,stagger[n]) for hexagon n in our column), together with the direction vector of the moment itself (for our column, this will be a vector lying in the y-z plane, pointing to the center of an edge):

```
In[65]:= magneticmoments1 =
                Table[{{n,0,stagger[n]},
                    {0, Cos[n Pi/3+Pi/6], Sin[n Pi/3 + Pi/6]}}
                ,{n,0,6}];
```

We can use the ListPlotVectorField3D function to plot these vectors. Now is a good time to familiarize yourself with the command-completion facility if you have not done so already!

In[66]:=   `Needs["Graphics`PlotField3D`"];`

      `magplot1 = ListPlotVectorField3D[magneticmoments1, VectorHeads -> True,`
                                   `DisplayFunction -> Identity];`

      `Show[hexplanes1, magplot1, holmsets];`

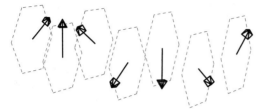

A physicist would describe the preceding sequence as 1111. . . because there is no grouping of the moments (that is, the group of hexagons for a particular moment direction has only one member). This structure is not observed in real life. The following structure, with moments paired together, however, is seen. The vector of the moment now returns to its initial orientation after 12 planes:

In[67]:=   `hexplanes2 = Graphics3D[Table[hex[n],{n,0,13}]];`

      `magneticmoments2 =`
          `Flatten[Table[{{2 n +m,0,stagger[2 n +m]},`
                    `{0,Cos[n Pi/3 + Pi/6], Sin[n Pi/3 + Pi/6]}},`
              `{m,0,1},{n,0,6}],1];`

      `magplot2 = ListPlotVectorField3D[magneticmoments2, VectorHeads -> True,`
                                     `DisplayFunction -> Identity];`

      `Show[hexplanes2, magplot2, holmsets];`

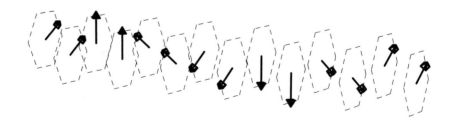

Note how this pattern has been generated by the two iterators of the Table command. When m is incremented, we step along one hexagon but the magnetic moment vector is not changed, generating a pair. When n is incremented, the magnetic moment rotates through one unit, moving us on to the next pair. For this example, the grouping is in pairs and the physicist's description would be 22222. ... More exotic groupings such as 221221... have been observed. This statement requires explanation — the observation is made by scattering neutrons off the crystal. Put simply, this scattering probes the Fourier transform of the moment structure.

If we want to predict the form of the scattering spectrum, we must take the physicist's description and create from it a list of the rotation angles of the magnetic moments. For example, take the sequence {2,1,2}. This corresponds to a pair of moments, followed by a single moment and then another pair — five moments in total. The angular separation of successive moments is 0 (start with a pair), 1 (jump to the single), 1 (jump to the next pair), and 0 (in a pair again), giving the sequence {0,1,1,0}. It is useful to tag on a final unit jump so that we may join repeated cells together. In other words, our first requirement is to define a function that will convert {2,1,2} into the list {0,1,1,0,1}:

```
In[68]:=  anglegenerate[{a___,2,b___}] := anglegenerate[{a,0,1,b}];
          anglegenerate[{2,1,2}]

Out[68]=  anglegenerate[{0, 1, 1, 0, 1}]
```

Note that the output from anglegenerate is not presented as a list because we are not done with it yet. We still have to convert this list of steps into a list of angle values (in units of $\pi/3$ — the numbers are like the numerals on a watch, the only difference being that we use only 1 to 6 instead of 1 to 12). Consider our simple example {2,1,2} once again. The first two moments are at an angle of 0, the third moment is at an angle of 1, and the fourth and fifth moments are at an angle of 2. For this case, we would like the list {0,0,1,2,2} to be outputted. One way to implement such a function is to take a cumulative sum of the elements in the step list:

```
In[69]:=  anglegenerate[a_List] := FoldList[Plus,0,a];

          anglegenerate[{2,1,2}]

Out[69]=  {0, 0, 1, 2, 2, 3}
```

Again, the last entry is useful because it tells us the clock position of the first moment in the next repeat unit. Note that we have given *Mathematica* two separate rules for anglegenerate. It should be clear that we want the rules to be invoked in the order that they have been presented in the text. In fact, *Mathematica* is sophisticated enough to work this out (see Chapter 10 for further details).

For now, let's consider a more interesting pattern:

```
In[70]:=  anglegenerate[{2,1,2,2,1}]

Out[70]=  {0, 0, 1, 2, 2, 3, 3, 4, 5}
```

A single case of the basic pattern has not succeeded in bringing us back to the original orientation 0 (or 6 or 12 — they are all equivalent in modulo 6 arithmetic). Hence, this result is of no use for the neutron scatterer who needs the basic unit cell to join up. We can solve this problem by stringing together several copies of anglegenerate's output until we get back to the start position. The number of extra copies that are needed depends on the modulo 6 value of the last entry. Thus, there are only six possibilities, which we have stored in the list howmany:

In[71]:=   `howmany = {0,5,2,1,2,5};`

When we concatenate a sequence with itself, we must include an offset on the second sequence so that the two sequences match up. First we give the code, with an example, and then we explain how it works:

In[72]:=   ```
clockitone[x_List] := clockittwo[Nest[Join[Drop[#,-1], Last[#]+x]&, x,
                                     howmany[[Mod[Last[x],6]+1]]]]
```

```
clockitone[{0,1,2,2}]
```

Out[72]=   `clockittwo[{0, 1, 2, 2, 3, 4, 4, 5, 6, 6}]`

The output of clockitone has been pipelined into a second function called clockittwo. We shall discuss the purpose of this function shortly. So, what exactly has *Mathematica* done? It took the list {0,1,2,2} and noted that the final entry was a 2, which remains 2 in modulo 6 arithmetic (the relevant code here is Mod[Last[x],6]). The appropriate entry in howmany is the third one, or 2, telling us that we must concatenate three sequences in order to return to the starting position (the initial sequence and two copies). The operation proceeds as follows:

1. Take the list and drop the last entry, giving {0,1,2}
2. Join this to an appropriately shifted version of the initial list {2,3,4,4}, resulting in {0,1,2,2,3,4,4}
3. Drop the last element of this list and join the result to another appropriately scaled version of the initial list; {0,1,2,2,3,4} + {4,5,6,6} = {0,1,2,2,3,4,4,5,6,6}

We have carried out the required number of concatenations as prescribed by the list how-many, so we should now be back to clock position 0 (modulo 6). If this layer corresponds to the same stagger (remember that successive planes are offset) as the initial layer, then we can drop the last entry of the list and return it to the user. If not, then we must go around again. This is the job of clockittwo:

In[73]:=   ```
clockittwo[x_List] :=
      Drop[x,-1] /; OddQ[Length[x]]
clockittwo[x_List] :=
      Drop[Join[Drop[x,-1],x+Last[x]],-1] /; EvenQ[Length[x]]
```

Finally, we can combine clockitone with anglegenerate so that we can go straight from the physicist's pattern to a unit cell of use to the neutron scatterer:

In[74]:=   ```
unitcell[pattern_List] := clockitone[anglegenerate[pattern]]
unitcell[{2,2,2,1}]
```
```

Out[74]=   {0, 0, 1, 1, 2, 2, 3, 4, 4, 5, 5, 6, 6, 7, 8, 8, 9, 9, 10,

                   10, 11, 12, 12, 13, 13, 14, 14, 15, 16, 16, 17, 17, 18, 18,

                   19, 20, 20, 21, 21, 22, 22, 23}

Note that the next number in this sequence would be 24, which is 0 in modulo 6 arithmetic, as planned. Also, since the list has length 42, the stagger condition is satisfied.

It is now a simple problem to deduce the diffraction pattern for a given physicist's description; we take the Fourier transform of the exponentiated phases of the unit cell sequence:

In[75]:=   `diffract[x_List] :=`
              `    Abs[Chop[Fourier[ N[Exp[-I Pi/3 x]]]]^2/Length[x]`

We have taken the squared absolute value of this list because we are interested in intensities, rather than in amplitudes. For the case with no pairing, we get only a single peak:

In[76]:=   `diffract[ unitcell[{1}] ]`

Out[76]=   {0, 1., 0, 0, 0, 0}

The paired structure has two Fourier components:

In[77]:=   `diffract[ unitcell[{2}] ]`

Out[77]=   {0, 0.933013, 0, 0, 0, 0, 0, 0.0669873, 0, 0, 0, 0}

The grouping that we have described is an idealization of the true situation. In the real world, the pairing is not exact — there is a slight splitting angle between the two members of a pair. We have designed a function `applyoffset` that operates on the unit cell and splits pairs by a fraction `phi` of a step:

In[78]:=   `applyoffset[{a___,b_,b_,c___}, phi_] :=`
              `    applyoffset[{a,b-phi,b+phi,c},phi];`

              `applyoffset[a_List, phi_] := a;`

              `applyoffset[unitcell[{2,1}],0.1]`
Out[78]=   {-0.1, 0.1, 1, 1.9, 2.1, 3, 3.9, 4.1, 5, 5.9, 6.1, 7, 7.9,

                   8.1, 9, 9.9, 10.1, 11}

We can then apply `diffract` to this list to investigate the spectrum. For instance, we can determine rapidly the effect of a splitting of 0.1 on the spectrum of the 21212121... structure:

In[79]:=   `TableForm[ {diffract[applyoffset[unitcell[{2,1}],0.1]],`
              `            diffract[unitcell[{2,1}]]} ]`

Out[79]=
| 0 | 0 | 0.96079 | 0 | 0 | 0 | 0 | 0.022373 | 0 | 0 | 0 | 0 | 0.016841 | 0 | 0 | 0 |
| 0 | 0 | 0.92121 | 0 | 0 | 0 | 0 | 0.047336 | 0 | 0 | 0 | 0 | 0.031458 | 0 | 0 | 0 |

We have deliberately kept the discussion in this section simplified for explanatory purposes. A more detailed exposition is given by D. Jehan [10] and references therein.

12.3.2 The 9 Puzzle

You have probably played with the 9 puzzle at one time or another. Its design is a 3 × 3 grid with eight tiles, on which are etched the digits 1 to 8, and an open position in the grid that is taken by a space. The aim of the puzzle is to shift the tiles around (from a random start position) until the following result is obtained:

The game plan

In this section, our goal is to write a suite of functions to solve the 9 puzzle for you, thus releasing hours of your time for more worthwhile activities. The ideas behind our approach are not new — a superb discussion is given by D. Levy [12]— but the implementation within *Mathematica* is probably more simple than it is in any other computer language. To achieve our goal, we shall need to fashion tools that

1. Give us all the available moves for a given state of the puzzle
2. Implement a particular move
3. Quantify, in some sense, how far we are from the solution
4. Explore promising move sequences, avoiding circular situations

Look again at this plan; it is more general than is the puzzle itself. The four steps can be applied to any scenario in which a set of decisions must be made, with the object of reaching a particular goal. Once you have read through the example, you should be able to follow a similar approach to solve a few of your own problems. You will find that steps 1, 2, and 4 are mechanical to implement. The black art lies in implementing step 3, and the performance of your program will depend entirely on how well you do that implementation — this point will become clear in our example.

We shall represent the state of the puzzle by a 3 × 3 list of lists. The final state that we want our puzzle to be in is as follows:

```
In[80]:=  SetOptions[TableForm, TableSpacing -> {1,1}];
          desired = Partition[ Evaluate[Range[9] /. 9 -> " ",3]];
          TableForm[desired]
Out[80]=  1 2 3
          4 5 6
          7 8
```

The move generator

Step 1 of our plan is to write the function that generates a list of the moves that are allowed from a given starting position. To avoid lack of generality, we design this function so that it will work on any rectangular grid. Furthermore, we describe moves in terms of the motion of the "blank" tile. That is, each move must be one of *right*, *left*, *up*, or *down*:

```
In[81]:=  moves[current_?MatrixQ]  :=
          Module[{ answer, xdim, ydim, place, xpos, ypos},
                  answer = {"Up","Down","Left","Right"};
                  ydim = Length[current];
                  xdim = Length[current[[1]]];
                  place = Position[current," "];
                  xpos = place[[1,2]]; ypos = place[[1,1]];
                  If[xpos == xdim, answer = Drop[answer,{4}],];
                  If[xpos == 1, answer = Drop[answer,{3}],];
                  If[ypos == ydim, answer = Drop[answer,{2}],];
                  If[ypos == 1, answer = Drop[answer,{1}],];
                  answer];
```

For instance, when the puzzle is in the desired position, the only allowed moves of the space are upward or to the left:

```
In[82]:=  moves[desired]
Out[82]=  {Up, Left}
```

Move implementation

Step 2 of our plan is to take a direction and to move the blank accordingly. We use pattern matching to achieve this result most effectively. First, we consider moves to the left or to the right (note carefully the quantity of underscores after each symbol, and try to appreciate why we use 1, 2, or 3 in each case):

```
In[83]:=  effectmove[{a___,{b___," ",c_,d___},e___}, "Right"] :=
                  {a,{b,c," ",d},e};
          effectmove[{a___,{b___,c_," ",d___},e___}, "Left"] :=
                  {a,{b," ",c,d},e};
```

Just to check that this function is working, let's apply Left to the space in the desired position:

```
In[84]:=  effectmove[desired,"Left"] // TableForm
Out[84]=  1 2 3
          4 5 6
          7   8
```

Next, we use a shortcut for moving the space up or down. We simply transpose the puzzle and move the space either left or right before transposing back again:

```
In[85]:=  effectmove[a_, "Up"] := Transpose[effectmove[Transpose[a], "Left"]];
          effectmove[a_, "Down"] := Transpose[effectmove[Transpose[a], "Right"]];
```

Let's take the whole set of functions for a spin to check that all motions work. From this point on, we use the function Viewlolol developed in Chapter 3 to display one or more puzzle positions:

```
In[86]:=  Viewlolol[a_List] := Map[MatrixForm[#, TableSpacing -> {1,1}]&,a];
          Viewlolol[FoldList[effectmove, desired, {"Left","Up","Right","Down"}]]
Out[86]=  {1 2 3,  1 2 3,  1 2 3,  1 2 3,  1 2 3}
           4 5 6   4 5 6   4   6   4 6     4 6 8
           7 8     7       8   7 5 8   7 5 8   7 5
```

The evaluation function: Manhattan distance

Our eventual goal is to get *Mathematica* to solve the puzzle for us. To allow it to do so, we must implement a function that will tell us how far we are from the solution (step 3 in our original plan). The game plan will then amount (in some way that we will specify later) to choosing the move at each stage that decreases the value of this function.

The evaluation function that we have chosen is known as the *Manhattan distance* or the *New York metric*. The streets in New York form a grid of east-west and north-south lines, so to determine the distance between two points, you sum their northerly and easterly separations. For the puzzle, our evaluation function amounts to summing up the Manhattan distances between each tile and that tile's intended position. Our implementation will be a function that takes as arguments two equal-sized matrices (an error message is returned if this condition is not satisfied) and

1. Takes the first matrix and replaces every element by the position of the corresponding element in the second matrix
2. Subtracts the coordinates of each element of this new matrix from the entry itself (this operation gives a matrix of *Manhattan vectors*)
3. Sums the absolute value of the elements in this matrix (we may have collected some negative values, but, as any pedestrian knows, the distance between two points is the same whether you walk forward or backward).

```
In[87]:=  manhattan::incompat = "Manhattan distance can only be computed for
          matrices with the same dimension";

          manhattandistance[x_, y_] :=
          Module[{temp},
                  If[Dimensions[x] != Dimensions[y], Message[manhattan::incompat],
```

```
        temp = Map[ Flatten[Position[y,#]]&, x ,{2}];
        temp = temp - Map[ Flatten[Position[x,#]] &, x, {2}];
        temp = Apply[Plus, Flatten[Abs[temp]]]
      ]
    ]
```

A more efficient implementation is presented in Chapter 14.

Let's take this function through a test run. Suppose that we supply two matrices for which it is impossible to compute the Manhattan distance:

In[88]:=   manhattandistance[{{1,2},{3,4}}, desired]

manhattan::incompat:
    Manhattan distance can only be computed for matrices with
       the same dimension

When we reach the desired position, the Manhattan distance should be zero:

In[89]:=   manhattandistance[desired, desired]

Out[89]=   0

As we move away from this setup, the distance function should increase:

In[90]:=   Map[manhattandistance[desired, #]&,
              FoldList[effectmove, desired, {"Left","Up","Left","Up"}]
            ]

Out[90]=   {0, 2, 4, 6, 8}

The tree generator

Now that we have both our move generator and evaluation function working, we can mesh them together into a function that operates on a configuration of the puzzle to create a list of the possible moves and the values of the resulting positions (step 4 in our original plan).

In[91]:=   listscores[x_] :=
            Module[{makemoves,ans},
                  makemoves = Map[{effectmove[x, #]}&, moves[x]];
                  ans = Flatten[Map[manhattandistance[#[[1]], desired]&,
                                    makemoves]];
                  Transpose[{ans,moves[x]}]]

For either possible move from the desired position, the resulting Manhattan distance will be 2:

In[92]:=   listscores[desired]

Out[92]=   {{2, Up}, {2, Left}}

What we want to do now is to enable *Mathematica* to keep building this tree, expanding the most promising node at each stage. A particular branch of the tree will correspond to a sequence of several moves. We must extend our effectmove function so that it can cope with multiple (and null) move sequences:

```
In[93]:=  effectmove[a_List, b_String, c__String] :=
              effectmove[ effectmove[a,b], c];

          Viewlolol[{desired, effectmove[desired,"Left","Left","Up","Up"]}]
Out[93]=  {1 2 3,    2 3}
           4 5 6  1 5 6
           7 8     4 7 8
```

We are almost ready to set our program chugging to find that winning move sequence! All that we need now is an iterate function that takes the current state of a tree and expands the most promising node (according to the definition of our evaluation function). We have chosen to sort the tree at each stage according to the Manhattan distance of the end nodes. When the built-in Sort function is applied to a list of equal-length lists, it orders them according to their first elements:

```
In[94]:=  Sort[{{18,"Right"},{14,"Left"},{16,"Up"}}]
Out[94]=  {{14, Left}, {16, Up}, {18, Right}}
```

This is just what we want except that when the lists have differing lengths (as ours will when we selectively grow the move tree), Sort first sorts according to list length and only then by first elements:

```
In[95]:=  Sort[{{10,"Right"},{8,"Left","Up"},{2,"Up"}}]
Out[95]=  {{2, Up}, {10, Right}, {8, Left, Up}}
```

We must devise our own Boolean test by which to sort:

```
In[96]:=  bestscore[x_List,y_List] := If[x[[1]] < y[[1]], True, False]
```

Sorting by this criterion works just fine:

```
In[97]:=  Sort[{{10,"Right"},{8,"Left","Up"},{2,"Up"}}, bestscore]
Out[97]=  {{2, Up}, {8, Left, Up}, {10, Right}}
```

When we sort by bestscore at each iteration, the most promising sequence will always be at the front of the tree list.

We call our first attempt to write our iteration function protoiter because it will require modification in the light of what we shall discover:

```
In[98]:=  protoiter[start_, {{x_,y__},z___}] :=
          Module[{},
                  endnode = effectmove[start,y];
                  newnodes = Map[Join[{First[#]},{y},Rest[#]]&,
                              listscores[endnode]];
                  Sort[ Join[newnodes,{z}], bestscore ]];
```

Let's generate a start position for our tree search and keep it simple — for the moment!

```
In[99]:=  start = effectmove[desired, "Left","Up","Left","Up"];
          {manhattandistance[start, desired],
          Viewlolol[{start}]}
```

Out[99]= {8, { 2 3}}
           1 4 6
           7 5 8

What are the first moves from this situation?

In[100]:= `firstmoves = listscores[start]`

Out[100]= {{6, Down}, {8, Right}}

When we operate on this tree, it should pick out the first element, expand this node, and sort the resulting positions according to their merit:

In[101]:= `protoiter[start, firstmoves]`

Out[101]= {{4, Down, Right}, {6, Down, Down}, {8, Right}, {8, Down, Up}}

Great! In theory, all we need to do is to carry on iterating on this list until we find the solution. There is a point that we should clear up, however — one that in general can be a big problem. Consider the final entry {8, Down, Up} in the previous output. This move sequence is clearly pointless and should be removed (it corresponds to shifting a tile back and forth mindlessly). We need to devise another Boolean test to see whether a branch is worthwhile:

In[102]:=
```
worthwhile[{x___,"Right","Left"}] := False;
worthwhile[{x___,"Left","Right"}] := False;
worthwhile[{x___,"Up","Down"}] := False;
worthwhile[{x___,"Down","Up"}] := False;
worthwhile[{x___}] := True
```

Remember that these rules are stored in increasing order of generality, so the blanket final rule will not shadow the earlier ones. We must incorporate this test into our iteration function, keeping only worthwhile nodes:

In[103]:=
```
iterate[start_, {{x_,y__},z___}] :=
Module[{},
        endnode = effectmove[start,y];
        newnodes = Map[Join[{First[#]},{y},Rest[#]]&,listscores[endnode]];
        Sort[ Join[Select[newnodes,worthwhile],{z}], bestscore ]];

        iterate[start, firstmoves]
```

Out[103]= {{4, Down, Right}, {6, Down, Down}, {8, Right}}

By an appropriate number of iterations, the solution can be found:

In[104]:= `Nest[iterate[start, #]&, firstmoves,3]`

Out[104]= {{0, Down, Right, Down, Right}, {4, Down, Right, Right},

{4, Down, Right, Down, Left}, {6, Down, Right, Up},

{6, Down, Down}, {8, Right}}

This output indicates that a correct sequence of moves that gives the solution is "down, right, down, right." We know that this sequence solves the puzzle because it is the reverse of the move sequence that we applied initially ("left, up, left, up").

To tidy up the implementation, we arrange for the iteration to stop when a solution is found and for the sequence of moves to be outputted. We include a parameter to allow us to set an upper bound on how many iterations should be performed:

```
In[105]:= try[start_,n_] :=
          Module[{temp, count},
                  count = 0;
                  temp = listscores[start];
                  While[temp[[1,1]] > 0 && count < n,
                      temp = iterate[start,temp];
                      count= count +1];
                If[count == n && temp[[1,1]] != 0,
                   Print["Solution not found, best sequence was"],
                   Print["The following solution was found"]];
                   temp[[1]]]

          try[start, 2]
```

          Solution not found, best sequence was

```
Out[105]= {2, Down, Right, Down}

In[106]:= try[start, 4]
```

          The following solution was found

```
Out[106]= {0, Down, Right, Down, Right}
```

So far, so good. However, this example hardly constitutes an accurate test of our package because the solution is so simple. Suppose that we generate a truly random starting position:

```
In[107]:= Needs["DiscreteMath`Combinatorica`"];

          realstart = Partition[RandomPermutation[9] /. 9 -> " ",3];
          Viewlolol[{realstart}]
Out[107]= {6 8 7}
           3   1
           4 5 2
```

This position represents a sterner test. What happens when we set off *Mathematica* from this position, imposing an upper bound of 200 iterations?

```
In[108]:= try[realstart, 200]
```

          Solution not found, best sequence was

```
Out[108]= {10, Up, Right, Down, Down, Left, Up, Up, Right, Down, Down,
          Left, Up, Left, Down, Right, Right, Up, Left, Up, Right, Down,
          Down, Left, Left, Up, Right, Right, Down, Left, Up, Right
          Down, Left, Up, Right, Down, Left, Up, Right, Down, Left, Up,
          Right, Down, Left, Up, Right, Down, Left, Up, Right, Down,
          Left, Up, Right, Down, Left, Up, Right, Down, Left, Up, Right,
          Down, Left, Up, Right, Down, Left, Up, Right, Down, Left, Up,
          Right, Down, Left, Up, Right, Down, Left, Up, Right, Down,
          Left, Up, Right, Down, Left, Up, Right, Down, Left, Up, Right,
          Down, Left, Up, Right, Down, Left, Up, Right, Down, Left, Up,
          Right, Down, Left, Up, Right, Down, Left, Up, Right, Down,
          Left, Up, Right, Down, Left, Up, Right, Down, Left, Up, Right,
          Down, Left, Up, Right, Down, Left, Up, Right, Down, Left}
```

What has gone wrong? A solution has not been found because of the evaluation function that we have used — a shortfall in the evaluation function is the most common source of problems in heuristic programs.

According to our philosophy, a 50-move sequence leading to a score of 10 is better than a 1-move sequence leading to a score of 12. Clearly, it makes more sense to expand the shorter move sequence in this situation, even though it has a larger Manhattan distance. The quickest way in which to implement a penalty on long move sequences is to alter our sorting function. We now redefine this function in terms of a free parameter delta that we can vary to alter the degree of penalization:

```
In[109]:= bestscore[x_List, y_List] := If[x[[1]] < y[[1]] + delta*
          (Length[Rest[y]]-Length[Rest[x]]), True, False]
```

With delta set to zero, our new implementation is just the same function as before. For very large values, the Manhattan distance becomes of only secondary importance to the length of the path:

```
In[110]:= delta = 20;
          Sort[{{2,"Left","Right","Left"},{10,"Left"}}, bestscore]

Out[110]= {{10, Left}, {2, Left, Right, Left}}
```

The previous example represents the other extreme! Clearly, the art is to choose just the right value of delta. If we use 0.2, then a 5-move sequence has the same penalty as an increase of 1 in the Manhattan distance. This penalty sounds reasonable. Let's see whether it works:

```
In[111]:= delta = 0.2;
          try[realstart, 200]
```

```
The following solution was found
```

```
Out[111]= {0, Up, Right, Down, Down, Left, Up, Up, Right, Down, Down, Left,
          Up, Left, Down, Right, Right, Up, Left, Left, Up, Right, Right,
          Down, Left, Left, Down, Right, Right, Up, Left, Down, Right,
          Up, Left, Down, Left, Up, Right, Right, Down}
```

We can use Viewlolol to get a clearer impression of what this move sequence looks like:

```
In[112]:= moveseq = Rest[%];
          puzseq = FoldList[effectmove[#1, #2]&, realstart, moveseq];
          Viewlolol[puzseq]
```

```
Out[112]= {6 8 7, 6   7, 6 7  , 6 7 1, 6 7 1, 6 7 1, 6 7 1, 6   1, 6 1   ,
           3   1   3 8 1   3 8 1   3 8     3 8 2   3 8 2   3     2   3 7 2   3 7 2
           4 5 2   4 5 2   4 5 2   4 5 2   4 5     4     5   4 8 5   4 8 5   4 8 5

           6 1 2, 6 1 2, 6 1 2, 6 1 2, 6 1 2, 6 1 2, 6 1 2, 6 1 2, 6 1 2,
           3 7     3 7 5   3 7 5   3     5     3 5   4 3 5   4 3 5   4 3 5   4 3
           4 8 5   4 8     4     8   4 7 8   4 7 8     7 8 7   8   7 8     7 8 5

           6 1 2, 6 1 2,   1 2, 1   2, 1 2  , 1 2 3, 1 2 3, 1 2 3, 1 2 3,
           4   3     4 3   6 4 3   6 4 3   6 4 3   6 4     6     4     6 4   7 6 4
           7 8 5   7 8 5   7 8 5   7 8 5   7 8 5   7 8 5   7 8 5   7 8 5     8 5

           1 2 3, 1 2 3, 1 2 3, 1 2 3, 1 2 3, 1 2 3, 1 2 3, 1 2 3, 1 2 3,
           7 6 4   7 6 4   7 6     7     6   7 5 6   7 5 6   7 5     7     5   7 4 5
           8     5   8 5     8 5 4   8 5 4   8     4   8 4     8 4 6   8 4 6   8     6

           1 2 3, 1 2 3, 1 2 3, 1 2 3, 1 2 3}
           7 4 5     4 5   4     5   4 5     4 5 6
           8 6   7 8 6   7 8 6   7 8 6   7 8
```

The final operation that we perform is to make this sequence into a movie so that you do not even have to move the tiles. *Mathematica* animation works by displaying a series of previously evaluated graphics objects on the screen. We have created a function that makes a graphics object out of a puzzle picture:

```
In[113]:= graphview[x_List] :=
          Module[{temp},
              temp = Flatten[{{Text[" ",{-1,-1}],Text[" ",{4,4}]},
                            Table[ Text[x[[j,i]],{i,4-j}],{i,3},{j,3}]}];
              Show[Graphics[temp]]]
```

The two blank text statements are used to force a full display of the grid. You may want to fiddle with the graphics output size because the default size is large. Now all we need to do is to create a sequence of graphics outputs for each puzzle position, to close up the cell output, and to select "Animate Selected Graphics" from the menu if you are using a NoteBook interface:

```
In[114]:= puzseq = FoldList[effectmove[#1, #2]&, realstart, moveseq];

          Do[graphview[puzseq[[i]]],{i,Length[puzseq]}]
```

12.4 Two-Dimensional Patterns

Despite the great scope for pattern matching afforded by underscores and Boolean tests, *Mathematica* is basically geared toward one-dimensional patterns. The upshot is that it is easier to search for horizontal patterns in two-dimensional cases, which reside in the

one-dimensional rows, than it is to search for vertical or diagonal patterns, which may
be spread across several rows and columns.

For simple line matching, we have found that the best way to solve this problem is
to perform a transformation that maps the desired pattern onto a horizontal row. The
function `rightalign` that we now describe takes a two-dimensional list together with
the direction vector in which we are interested and rotates this vector so that it ends up
aligned horizontally. The following set of rules has been coded:

1. If the direction vector is (1,0), then the pattern lies along the forward horizontal
   direction and no manipulation is necessary.
2. If the direction vector has a negative horizontal component, then when the rows
   are reversed, this vector is mapped onto one with a positive horizontal component.
   Similarly, if the vector has a negative vertical component, the columns are reversed.
3. If the direction vector is in the positive vertical direction, then when rows and
   columns are transposed, a reflection is performed that interchanges horizontal and
   vertical directions.
4. Any vector that has not been covered completely by rules 1, 2, and 3 will now have
   been mapped onto (1,1), which is a diagonal vector. If we rotate the first row of the
   array once, the second row twice, and so on, then we will map a diagonal line onto
   a vertical one that will be caught by rule 3.

```
In[115]:= rightalign[x_List,{1,0}] := x;
          rightalign[x_List,{-1,a_}] := rightalign[Map[Reverse,x],{1,a}];
          rightalign[x_List,{a_, b_?Negative}] := rightalign[Reverse[x],{a,-b}];
          rightalign[x_List,{0,1}] := rightalign[Transpose[x],{-1,0}];
          rightalign[x_List,{1,1}] :=
          rightalign[Table[RotateRight[x[[i]],i],{i,Length[x]}],{0,1}]
```

An example should make the purpose of this function clear. The array `diag` contains
the sequence of letters a,b, and c aligned along a diagonal:

```
In[116]:= diag = {{".",".",c},{".",b,"."},{a,".","."}};
          TableForm[diag, TableSpacing -> {0,1}]

Out[116]= .  .  c
          .  b  .
          a  .  .
```

The sequence in which we are interested is aligned along the vector (1,1). If we supply
this direction vector to `rightalign`, then we expect the sequence to be mapped onto a
horizontal line, reading left to right:

```
In[117]:= TableForm[rightalign[diag,{1,1}], TableSpacing -> {0,1}]

Out[117]= a  b  c
          .  .  .
          .  .  .
```

12.4.1 Othello

In Section 12.3.2, we discussed how *Mathematica* can be programmed to make decisions. An integral part of this process was the construction of a function that listed the possible options in a given situation — we used the example of a well-known puzzle. The move generator for the game of Othello provides an excellent example of two-dimensional pattern matching. The game is played on an 8 × 8 board, and the object is to sandwich your opponent's pieces between two of your own. The sandwiched pieces are then turned over (they are double-sided, black on one side and white on the other) and fall into the possession of the sandwiching side. The winner is the player with the greatest number of pieces at the end of the game.

Sandwiched lines in Othello may run horizontally, vertically, or diagonally. Consider the following position:

```
In[118]:= othello = Table[Table[".",{8}],{8}];
          othello[[5,3]] = othello[[4,4]] = othello[[4,5]] = othello[[5,4]] = "X";
          othello[[5,5]] = "O";
          TableForm[othello, TableSpacing -> {0,0}]
```

```
Out[118]= ........
          ........
          ........
          ...XX...
          ..XXO...
          ........
          ........
          ........
```

With "O" to play, there are several possibilities:

1. Row 5, column 2, creating a horizontal sandwich
2. Row 3, column 3, creating a diagonal sandwich
3. Row 3, column 5, creating a vertical sandwich

As we have already noted, the horizontal sandwich is easily found. First we construct a function that tests to see whether a square is occupied by an X, and then we search for any row containing the pattern *anything, ".", row of "X"s, "O", anything*. With the Cases command, we can perform operations on the matched blanks, such as outputting the length of the first *anything* in the pattern. The Hold instruction is important because, without it, *Mathematica* would evaluate the Length part of Length[{a}] before substituting the value of a, leading to the result 1 independent of a! The Release lets go of this hold, and the output is the position vector of a possible move for player "O":

```
In[119]:= xques[a_] := If[a == "X", True, False];
          Release[ Cases[{othello}, {a___,{b___,".",c__?xques,"O",d___},e___} ->
                Hold[Length[{a}]+1, Length[{b}]+1]]]
```

```
Out[119]= {5, 2}
```

To search for the diagonally allowed move, we align along the direction vector $(1,-1)$ and perform the same test:

```
In[120]:= Release[ Cases[{rightalign[othello,{1,-1}]},
               {a___,{b___,".",c__?xques,"0",d___},e___} ->
               Hold[Length[{a}]+1, Length[{b}]+1]]]

Out[120]= {1, 3}
```

Mathematica has found the move, but the position vector is associated with the rotated array rather than the original one. Must we perform an inverse operation on this vector to find the vector's position on the real board? The answer is no. A much quicker way is to perform the same alignment on an array of position vectors and to extract entry (1,3) from this matrix:

```
In[121]:= posvectors = Table[{i,j},{i,8},{j,8}];

           rightalign[posvectors,{1,-1}][[1,3]]

Out[121]= {3, 3}
```

The output tells us that row 3, column 3 is an allowed move, which is correct. You can use a simple extension of this code to create a move-generating function for Othello that you could use in conjunction with an evaluation function and a tree generator to create a powerful adversary!

12.5 Summary

In this chapter, we have considered two topics: Rule-based systems and iterative techniques. In the first half of the chapter, we have shown, through a series of examples, how to implement a knowledge-based system in *Mathematica* by using multiple function definitions. In the text-correction example, the rules referred to grammatical laws; in the noncommutative algebra example, they concerned properties under multiplication. The third example extended the built-in integration capability and allowed *Mathematica* to teach itself new rules. In all three problems, we needed to teach *Mathematica* to search for patterns. The various constructions with underscores made these searches possible. In the second half of the chapter, we have dealt with iteration, starting with simple problems, such as finding solutions to equations, and then considering two longer examples. The neutron-diffraction example demonstrated the power of *Mathematica*'s unique iterative constructions Nest and NestList in an unusual situation. The example of the 9 puzzle showed how we can use *Mathematica* to explore a decision tree. These two examples were long; the object was to see a problem through from start to finish, with all the steps included.

CHAPTER THIRTEEN

Contexts and Packages

This chapter deals with the subjects of contexts and packages. Frankly, you can do a lot of programming without worrying about either of these constructions. However, you should come to grips with these concepts if you want to do any of the following:

- Make your user-defined *Mathematica* functions behave like built-in ones
- Gather together into a file a group of functions with a common theme
- Provide documentation on your functions
- Hide from other users certain details of what you have done

In Chapter 10, we considered the `Module` construction; we noted that it isolates local variables by introducing a new symbol. Another, more generally useful, approach is to set variables in a new context. A simple way to understand contexts is to think of variables as having a full name that is composed of a context and a short name in the form *context short*. Clearly, setting variables in different contexts protects against collision of variables.

13.1 Contexts

The subject of *contexts* is particularly misunderstood by *Mathematica* users which is a shame because the underlying concept is probably familiar to them in (pardon the pun) a different context — namely, directory structure. When you arrange files on your computer, you do not want to put them all in the same place, so you create separate directories for files with a common feature. The situation is the same for functions and variables in *Mathematica* except that the name *directory* has been changed to *context*.

13.1.1 The Global Context

To determine what context you currently are in, enter the following command:

In[1]:= `$Context`

Out[1]= `Global`

`Global`` is the context in which most interactive use of *Mathematica* takes place. When you define a variable, it is stored here.

The specific details of the following discussion depend on the current state of your *Mathematica* session. To avoid confusion, we recommend that you start up a new session now. Suppose that we assign values to the three symbols a, b, and c and define a new function F:

In[2]:=   `a = 1; b = 9.2; c = 10.0;`
              `F[x_] := x^2`

The unwritten convention in *Mathematica* is that predefined functions should start with an uppercase character and user-defined functions should start with a lowercase character.

All these objects will be stored in the current context `Global``. We can display a list of the contents of this context using the wild-card character `*`:

In[3]:=   `?Global`*`

              `a  b  c  F  x`

The unwritten convention in *Mathematica* is that predefined functions should start with an uppercase character and user-defined functions should start with a lowercase character. If you make use of this convention (we have intentionally abused the convention with our function `F[x]` to demonstrate a point), then you can use the wild-card character `@` to display a list containing just user-defined characters (`@` matches any pattern of lowercase characters):

In[4]:=   `?Global`@`

              `a  b  c  x`

Incidentally, you can use the command `Remove["Global`@"]` to remove all user definitions from the `Global`` context. This instruction should be contrasted with the command `Clear["Global`@"]`, which just clears the values associated with these definitions but does not remove the symbols.

13.1.2 The System Context

In Section 13.1.1, we located our definitions successfully in the `Global`` context. *Mathematica*'s built-in functions are stored in a separate context, `System``. Try entering the following command:

In[5]:=   `?System`@`

              `Information::nomatch:: No symbol matching System`@ found.`

This response is what we expect. All the names in `System`` correspond to *Mathematica* functions and begin with uppercase letters, so they do not match the `@` pattern. To display all the names rather than just those beginning with a lowercase letter, you must enter `?System`*`. Because there are so many functions, we give here the result of a request for only those that begin with the letter "W":

In[6]:=   `?System`W*`

WeierstassP	While	WordSearch	Write
WeierstrassPPrime	With	WordSeparators	WriteString
Which	Word	WorkingPrecision	WynnDegree

13.1.3 User-Defined Contexts

You can make your own contexts to add to the two most important ones, `Global`` and `System``, which were discussed in the previous two sections. To create a new context and to move into it, set the $Context variable to the name that you want to use for the context. For instance, to create a context called user`, enter

In[7]:=   `$Context = "user`";`

If we now assign a value to a new symbol, that symbol will be stored in the current context, user` (the logic is the same as for file directories; if you create a new document, then it is stored in the current directory):

In[8]:=   `newvariable = 66;`
              `newfn[x_] := Sin[x];`

In[9]:=   `?user`@`

              `newfn            newvariable x`

While we remain in the context user`, we can access our new variable newvariable and our new function newfn by simply giving their names:

In[10]:=   `newfn[newvariable]`

Out[10]=   `Sin[66]`

We can also refer to symbols that were defined in Global`:

In[11]:=   `a`

Out[11]=   `1`

Suppose that we return to the Global` context. The objects that we defined inside user` are still there:

In[12]:=   `$Context = "Global`";`
              `?user`@`

              `user`newfn   user`newvariable user`x`

However, it is no longer possible to use short names to access any of these objects:

In[13]:=   `newfn[20]`

Out[13]=   `newfn[20]`

This result may seem illogical. When we were in user`, we could access objects in Global` or System`. So, why can we not access objects in user` when we are in Global`? Again, we can use the directory example to explain the behavior. When you try to run a program under MS-DOS, for instance, you must make sure that your computer can find that program. If it is present in the current directory, then there will be no problem. However, if the program is elsewhere, then the computer has to perform a search through other directories. It would be grossly inefficient — and undesirable — if this search was an exhaustive one. Instead, the computer checks only a few directories, usually those designated by some system variable, in MS-DOS this variable is called PATH and is usually given a value in the batch file AUTOEXEC.BAT, which is executed at start-up. *Mathematica* acts in exactly the same way. When you attempt to access an object, *Mathematica* first looks to see whether the object is present in the current context, and if the object is not present, it searches through only those contexts that are in the system variable $ContextPath. If we take a look at this variable, we will understand why newfn was not found in the previous command:

In[14]:= $ContextPath

Out[14]=   {Global`, System`}

After looking for an object in the current context, the search proceeds from left to right through the contexts in $ContextPath. newfn was not found because user` is not on the search path.

There are two ways to solve this problem. The first is to refer to an object explicitly by its context and name:

In[15]:=   user`newvariable

Out[15]=   66

The second is to add the context to $ContextPath. Be extremely careful how you make this addition — there is a definite right way and a definite wrong way. The accepted method is to use the PrependTo function:

In[16]:=   PrependTo[$ContextPath, "user`"]

Out[16]=   {user`, Global`, System`}

Note that we have chosen to prepend, rather than to append, the new context to the list. Clearly, it is preferable that System`, where all the built-in functions live, be the first place that is searched and that the search through $ContextPath proceed from right to left. Now newvariable is found easily:

In[17]:=   newvariable

Out[17]=   66

There is one last problem that we must resolve. If we try to use the function newfn, we are still blocked:

In[18]:=   newfn[20]

Out[18]=   newfn[20]

Why does *Mathematica* still fail to find the definition of this function? This type of problem is encountered often; it is caused by our earlier attempt to access the function before we had modified $ContextPath. Unable to find a prior definition of newfn, *Mathematica* automatically registered the name in the current context at the time — in this instance, Global`. The name newfn is now registered in both the Global` and user` contexts:

In[19]:=   ?*`newfn

newfn   user`newfn

Because we are now back in the Global`, we get the undefined version when we type newfn. If we remove this version, the search will be able to proceed through the contexts in $ContextPath, and the correct definition in user` will be found:

In[20]:= Remove[newfn];

In[21]:= newfn[20]

Out[21]= Sin[20]

We now return to the matter of adding the user`context to $ContextPath. You may be wondering what is wrong with issuing the following command:

In[22]:= $ContextPath = {"user`", "Global`", "System`"};

This instruction does what we want, but it uses a risky process. Suppose that you make a typing mistake and enter the following

In[23]:= $ContextPath = {"user`", "system`", "Global`"};

Because System` is no longer on the path — remember this context is where *Mathematica*'s built-in commands are stored — we are unable to issue any standard instructions!

System`In[24]:= Print[1]

System`Out[24]= Print[1]

Furthermore, the prompt has changed to a slightly confusing format. So, realizing our mistake, we set the path to its correct value:

*System`In[25]:=*  $ContextPath = {"user`", "Global`", "System`"};

You may be thinking that the panic is over and everything is as we had intended it. This assumption is far from true:

System`In[26]:= Integrate[x,x]

System`Out[26]= Integrate[x,x]

We are still unable to communicate with the standard instructions. Before you quit the session, you should know that all is not lost. The problem is that the relevant $ContextPath is itself stored in System`. Because this context is no longer on the search path, our last attempt to reset the path failed to change the relevant $ContextPath and, worse still, created a new one in our local context Global`:

*System`In[27]:=*  Global`$ContextPath

*System`Out[27]=*  {user`, Global`, System`};

*System`In[28]:=*  System`$ContextPath

*System`Out[28]=*  {user`, Global`, system`};

To change the value of the correct $ContextPath, we must use the latter's full description in terms of its context and its name:

*System`In[29]:=*  System`$ContextPath = {"user`", "System`", "Global`" };

Furthermore, we have registered the names Print and Integrate in Global`, so we should remove them:

In[30]:= `Remove[Print,Integrate];`
            `Remove[$ContextPath];`

Now everything is as we wanted it and the prompt is also back to normal:

In[31]:= `Print[newvariable]`

Out[31]= `66`

13.2 Packages

The idea of a *package* is to store a set of functions with a common theme, along with information on their use. Furthermore, the package allows the internal details of how the function operates to be hidden from the casual user. If you want to change the coding behind a function, you are free to do so, as long as what the user sees is unchanged. (This freedom is useful, for instance, if you discover a more efficient algorithm.)

Mathematica is designed so that only the most commonly used functions are loaded at start-up. A great number of other functions can be found in the `Packages` directory or obtained from third-party sources. Increasingly, packages can also be obtained over electronic mail by anonymous FTP to *mathsource.wri.com*.

A function that is not loaded automatically at start-up is `Mean`. This function computes the arithmetic mean of a list of numbers. If you try to use `Mean` without loading the package, your command cannot be processed:

In[32]:= `Mean[{1,2,3}]`

Out[32]= `Mean[{1,2,3}]`

A selection of descriptive-statistics functions (including `Mean`) is collected in the `Statistics`DescriptiveStatistics`` package. Suppose that we load this package:

In[33]:= `Needs["Statistics`DescriptiveStatistics`"]`

```
Mean::shdw: Warning: Symbol Mean appears in multiple contexts
   {Statistics`DescriptiveStatistics,` Global`};
   definitions in context Statistics`DescriptiveStatistics`
   may shadow or be shadowed by other definitions.
```

This warning is important, as we shall see shortly. The functions that we have loaded all reside in their own context:

In[34]:= `?Statistics`DescriptiveStatistics`*`

```
CentralMoment                              Quantile
DispersionReport                           QuartileDeviation
GeometricMean                              Quartiles
HarmonicMean                               QuartileSkewness
InterpolatedQuantile                       RootMeanSquare
InterquartileRange                         SampleRange
Kurtosis                                   ShapeReport
KurtosisExcess                             Skewness
LocationReport                             StandardDeviation
Statistics`DescriptiveStatistics`Mean      StandardDeviationMLE
MeanDeviation                              StandardErrorOfSampleMean
Median                                     TrimmedMean
```

MedianDeviation   Variance
PearsonSkewness1   VarianceMLE
PearsonSkewness2   VarianceOfSampleMean

When we load the package, the context is prepended to the context path, so all these functions are now available to us:

In[35]:=   `$ContextPath`

Out[35]=   {Statistics`DescriptiveStatistics`, Global`, System`}

In[36]:=   `Variance[{1,2,3}]`

Out[36]=   1

As we discussed in Section 13.1.3, if you try to use a function that does not yet exist, a copy of that function's name will appear in your current context (generally Global`). When the function is subsequently defined and its context added to $ContextPath, we must take care to remove the useless copy. Otherwise, the copy will overshadow the correct version, which explains the warning that we obtained when we loaded the statistics package:

In[37]:=   `Mean[{1,2,3}]`

Out[37]=   Mean[{1, 2, 3}]

In[38]:=   `Remove[Mean];`
              `Mean[{1,2,3}]`

Out[38]=   2

13.2.1 Creating a Package

Suppose that we have our own suite of functions and we wish to group them together as a package in a context. First, we set the context to the name of the package. Then, we define our functions. Finally, we reset the context to Global` and prepend the new context to $ContextPath. To assist us in this process, *Mathematica* supplies the two functions BeginPackage and EndPackage. We recommend that you use these functions, instead of risking direct manipulations of $Context and $ContextPath.

In Chapter 2, we described several functions for reading in data from a file. Suppose that we want to collect these functions together in a package called datainput`. Let's do so for the dropread command defined in Chapter 2 (note that we have started a new session):

In[1]:=   `BeginPackage["datainput`"];`

```
dropread[dropno_Integer,filename_String,opts___]:=
Module[{inline,result}, inline = OpenRead[filename];
    Read[inline,Table[String,{dropno}]];
    result = ReadList[inline,opts];
    Close[inline];
    result]
```

```
                EndPackage[];
```

The `datainput`` context has now been added to the context path:

In[2]:=   `$ContextPath`

Out[2]=   `{datainput`, Global`, System`}`

If we inquire about what user-defined objects *Mathematica* knows, we see that `dropread` is among them:

In[3]:=   `?@`

```
                dropread x
```

13.2.2 Providing Usage Information

If you type a question mark followed by the name of a built-in *Mathematica* function, you are supplied with information on how to use that function:

In[4]:=   `?Print`

```
                Print[expr1, expr2, ...] prints the expri, followed by a newline (line feed).
```

What happens when we ask for information on the command `dropread`, which we placed in the `datainput`` context in the previous section?

In[5]:=   `?dropread`

```
                datainput`dropread

                dropread[dropno_Integer,filename_String,opts__]:=
                Module[{inline,result},
                    inline = OpenRead[filename];
                    Read[inline,Table[String,{dropno}]];
                    result = ReadList[inline,opts];
                    Close[inline];
                    result]
```

Presumably, if you want to make this function available to other users, it would be more useful if typing `?dropread` gave a description of what `dropread` does and what syntax it uses, as was given in the `?Print` example. To include this usage information, we go back to the line defining the package, and we add the following code between the `BeginPackage["datainput`"]` instruction and the definition of `dropread`:

In[6]:=   `dropread::usage = "dropread[<dropno>,<filename>,<opts>] drops the first <dropno> lines of the file <filename>, and sends the rest to ReadList.";`

The response to the query `?dropread` is now slightly more revealing to users who did not write the function:

In[7]:=   `?dropread`

```
                dropread[<dropno>,<filename>,<opt>] drops the first <dropnno> lines
                of the file <filename>, and sends the rest to ReadList.
```

13.2.3 Tidying Up

Our dropread command is already looking more professional. However, we are not done yet — there are still a couple of points that need tidying up.

First, for the built-in functions, typing ?? followed by a function name gives both the usage information on the function and a list of the function's attributes:

In[8]:= ??Print

```
Print[expr1, expr2, ...] prints the expri, followed by a newline (line feed).

Attribute[Print] = {Protected}
```

For dropread as it stands, ?? brings up all the defining code once again:

In[9]:= ??dropread

```
dropread[<dropno>,<filename>,<opt>] drops the first <dropnno> lines
of the file <filename>, and sends the rest to ReadList.

dropread[dropno_Integer,filename_String,opts__]:=
Module[{inline,result},
   inline = OpenRead[filename];
   Read[inline,Table[String,{dropno}]];
   result = ReadList[inline,opts];
   Close[inline];
   result]
```

For more complicated functions, the ?? instruction could deluge the unsuspecting user with literally pages of unintelligible code. To prevent this undesirable phenomenon, you should ReadProtect your functions before the EndPackage[] instruction. That is, enter the following instruction just prior to EndPackage[]:

In[10]:= Attributes[dropread] = {ReadProtected}

The response to the ?? request is now correct:

In[11]:= ??dropread

```
dropread[<dropno>,<filename>,<opt>] drops the first <dropnno> lines
of the file <filename>, and sends the rest to ReadList.

Attributes[dropread] = {ReadProtected}
```

The second tidying up procedure is not strictly necessary for dropread, so we shall consider a slightly more relevant example. A term describing the problem is *function leakage*, by which we mean that functions that should stay hidden within the package become accessible to the outside world. Suppose that we want to write a function that reverses the words in a string. Our idea for implementing this function is as follows:

1. Convert the string into an input stream
2. Read a list of Words in from this stream
3. Prepend a space to each word
4. Reverse the list
5. Apply StringJoin

The code, packaged according to the rules in this chapter, is as follows:

```
In[12]:=  BeginPackage["stringfun`"]

          wordreverse::usage =  "wordreverse[<string>] reverses the order
          of the words in the string"

          wordreverse[x_String] := Module[{words,inline},
                                     inline = StringToStream[x];
                                     words = ReadList[inline,Word];
                                     convert[Reverse[words]]]

          addspace[x_String] := StringJoin[" ",x]

          convert[x_List] := StringJoin[Map[addspace,x]]

          Attributes[wordreverse] = {ReadProtected}

          EndPackage[]
```

Notice that our definition of wordreverse relies on two other functions, which we also define within the package. The function that we want to supply to the user behaves in the correct manner:

```
In[13]:=  ??wordreverse
          wordreverse[<string>] reverses the order of the words in the string

          Attributes[wordreverse] = {ReadProtected}

In[14]:=  wordreverse["Ground Control to Major Tom"]
Out[14]=  Tom Major to Control Ground
```

The only problem is that the functions addspace and convert have leaked out of the package:

```
In[15]:=  ?addspace
          stringfun`addspace

          addspace[x_String] := StringJoin["  ",x]
```

Such leakage may be undesirable. Users will be presented with undocumented functions, and if they make use of them, they may find that the functions are not supported in subsequent versions (the etiquette is that programmers guarantee only upward compatibility of documented functions). Altogether, leakage is best avoided.

For our example, the problem comes about because all three functions — wordreverse, convert, and addspace — were defined in the same context stringfun`, which is now on the search path. To avoid the leakage problem, we need to register wordreverse alone in this context and to register the other two functions in contexts that are not added to the context path.

First, to avoid confusion, we clear up the stringfun` context:

In[16]:=   Remove["stringfun`@"];

Then, we start our package all over again:

In[17]:=   BeginPackage["stringfun`"];

    wordreverse::usage = "wordreverse[<string>] reverses the order of the
    words in the string";

The usage message serves a dual purpose here. Not only does it supply information, but also it registers the appropriate function name in the current context. That is, stringfun`wordreverse now exists. According to our plan, we should now move into another context, which will not be added to the context path, so that all new functions that are encountered — that is, addspace and convert — will be invisible outside the package. The accepted way to make this change of context is to create a subcontext of the current context called Private (this process is analogous to creating a subdirectory inside another directory). We must not use the BeginPackage[] and EndPackage[] commands to move in and out of this new context because the latter will then be added to the context path — which rather defeats the object! Instead, we use plain Begin and End:

In[18]:=   Begin["`Private`"];

We are now in the context stringfun`Private`, as we can verify using $Context:

In[19]:= $Context

In[20]:=   stringfun`Private`

The stringfun`Private` context is where we put all the meat of the function definition:

In[21]:=   wordreverse[x_String] := Module[{words,inline},
                          inline = StringToStream[x];
                          words = ReadList[inline,Word];
                          convert[Reverse[words]]];

    addspace[x_String] := StringJoin[" ",x];

    convert[x_List] := StringJoin[Map[addspace,x]];

All that remains is to move back from stringfun`Private` into stringfun`, to read-protect wordreverse, and then to return to Global`:

In[22]:=   End[];

    Attributes[wordreverse] = {ReadProtected};

    EndPackage[];

Since stringfun`Private` is not on the context path, our leakage problem is solved:

In[23]:=   ?convert

    Information::notfound: Symbol convert not found.

Of course, we can still use the function by using its long name because we know where it is located:

```
In[24]:=    stringfun`Private`convert[{"hello","there"]
Out[24]=    hello there
```

You may be wondering how wordreverse can see convert and addspace directly when we cannot do so. The answer is that when the definition of wordreverse was stored, long names were used. We can see the full definition by switching off the ReadProtected attribute:

```
In[25]:=    Attributes[wordreverse] = {};
            ??wordreverse

            wordreverse[<string>] reverses the order of the words in the <string>

            wordreverse[stringfun`Private`x_String] :=
              Module[{stringfun`Private`words, stringfun`Private`inline},
                stringfun`Private`inline = StringToStream[stringfun`Private`x];
                stringfun`Private`words = ReadList[stringfun`Private`inline, Word];
                stringfun`Private`convert[Reverse[stringfun`Private`word]]]]
```

Although we have prototyped the code for our stringfun` package in interactive mode, it is destined to be stored in a file. Once we are sure that all the code and usage functions are working and that there is no leakage, the whole set of commands between the BeginPackage and EndPackage instructions should be placed into a file. (It is entirely up to you whether you give to this file the same name that you gave to the context.) Subsequently, another user can load the package by using either << or the Needs command that is considered in the next section.

13.2.4 Dealing with Interacting Packages

Suppose that you have written a package that needs to access packages itself. You have a choice about how to treat this requirement, depending on whether you wish the contents of these other packages to be on the search path after your package has been read in. If you do, just add their names to the BeginPackage arguments:

```
In[1]:=     BeginPackage["mypackage`","Statistics`DescriptiveStatistics`"];
            EndPackage[];

            $ContextPath
Out[1]=     {mypackage`, Statistics`DescriptiveStatistics`, Global`, System`}
```

If you do not, you can do a hidden import by using the Needs command:

```
In[1]:=     BeginPackage["mypackage`"];
            Needs["Statistics`DescriptiveStatistics`"];
            EndPackage[];

            $ContextPath
Out[1]=     {mypackage`, Global`, System`}
```

In the second case, the DescriptiveStatistics package is loaded, but it is not added to the search path. The functions that you define in mypackage` will be able to access the statistics functions, because long names will be stored in the definitions.

13.3 Summary

In this chapter, we have considered two topics; contexts and packages. In the first half of the chapter, we have discussed the mechanism by which *Mathematica* groups together into different contexts functions with similar properties. The examples given showed that context structure is similar to directory structure, which is familiar to most computer users. They also showed that the similarity can be extended to the concept of search paths — where *Mathematica* looks for the symbols and functions that we type in.

In the second half of the chapter, we have dealt with packages — how to load them into *Mathematica* and how to package your own functions in a professional manner. The discussion showed how to provide information on a function's operation to the user and also how to hide the specific code. Although we could have presented the rules for this procedure in an ad hoc fashion, we chose to explain exactly what was happening with the contexts and search paths at every stage. Although ad hoc rules are fine in theory, mistakes can be made in practice, and if you are to rectify the situation, you must have a proper grasp of contexts.

CHAPTER FOURTEEN

Increased Efficiency

There comes a time in your life when *Mathematica* just cannot keep pace with the calculation that you want to do. Before you heave a sigh of resignation and return to the dark ages of programming in FORTRAN, there are several things that you can do with *Mathematica* to increase the speed. The plan of attack comes in three stages, but you can stop at any stage when you have achieved the desired performance. The three stages involve the following:

1. Checking that your *Mathematica* code is written in the most efficient manner
2. Performing internal compilation of the most time-consuming processes
3. Performing external compilation of the most time-consuming processes

Stage 1 requires that you think carefully when you write your functions and check that the most efficient algorithms are used. *Mathematica* supports an internal compiler that, although limited, gives power when you need it most — namely, when you perform simple numerical calculations that may be repeated many times. The idea behind stage 2 is to isolate those parts of the code that would benefit from compilation. Sometimes, even the increase in speed afforded by stage 2 may be insufficient — for instance, in fractal calculations (Chapter 19). It is then time to write the slow code in the C programming language and to link the program into *Mathematica* using MathLink. Such external compilation is the basis of stage 3. If your program is still too slow, chances are that you are performing a task that is a real number cruncher, such as a Monte Carlo simulation or a virtual-reality calculation. In this case, you should write your own program in C or FORTRAN. However, for the majority of users, the plan that we describe here should provide sufficient speed-up.

14.1 Sources of Inefficiency

Before you try to compile your *Mathematica* code, you should check that it has been written in an optimum manner. Frequently, this task involves checking that you have chosen the correct algorithm, as well as implemented this algorithm in the most sensible way.

Several sources of useful algorithms have withstood the sands of time — which means that they are good! Before you try to reinvent the wheel, you should check as many sources as possible. Most likely, unless you are a genius, you will not discover the subtle technique that doubles the speed of a program. An invaluable book, possibly the bible of computer mathematics, is *Numerical Recipes, The Art of Scientific Computing* [15],

285

available with code in several computer languages. Later, in Section 14.3.5, we show how it is possible to link the C version into *Mathematica* using MathLink. There are many other excellent books; for instance *Numerical Analysis* [3] is a readable volume with good explanations.

If your problem is not a standard one, then, with a bit of thought, you should be able to improve its efficiency yourself. Take care to examine your motives for this investment of time before you embark on a solution. There is little point in making a function run in 1 second instead of 10 seconds if it is going to be used only once! On the other hand, if the function appears in the middle of a double loop, the investment could save you hours, if not days. Perhaps you could then solve a problem that you had discarded previously because of lack of CPU time.

14.1.1 The Most Efficient Algorithm

In Section 12.3.2, we described the function `manhattandistance` which acted upon two rectangular arrays containing the same set of numbers and computed the sum of the distances (in Manhattan distances — that is, the sum of east–west and north–south separations) between identical elements. We now explain the algorithm through an example. Consider the following two arrays

```
In[1]:=   list1 = {{1,2},{3,4}};
          list2 = {{3,4},{2,1}};

          SetOptions[MatrixForm, TableSpacing -> {0,2}];
          Map[MatrixForm,{list1,list2}]
Out[1]=   {1  2,  3  4}
           3  4   2  1
```

The first stage of the algorithm replaces each entry in the first array by the position vector of the corresponding entry in the second array:

```
In[2]:=   temp1 = Map[Flatten[Position[list2,#]]&,list1,{2}]
Out[2]=   {{{2, 2}, {2, 1}}, {{1, 1}, {1, 2}}}
```

The first entry in `list1` is 1, which appears at the bottom right-hand corner of `list2` so this entry has been replaced by the vector {2,2}. This is not the Manhattan vector separating the two instances of the number 1, because its first instance was located at {1,1}. The separation vector is the difference between these two values, or {2,2} - {1,1} = {1,1}. To obtain a matrix of Manhattan separation vectors, we subtract off the following matrix:

```
In[3]:=   temp2 = Map[Flatten[Position[list1,#]]&,list1,{2}]
Out[3]=   {{{1, 1}, {1, 2}}, {{2, 1}, {2, 2}}}
```

Finally, the total Manhattan distance between the two arrays is computed by summing up the absolute values of all the values in this array:

```
In[4]:=   Apply[Plus,Flatten[Abs[temp1 - temp2]]]
```

Out[4]= 6

We can check this result. The number 1 contributes 2 to the distance (the two instances are separated by 1 horizontal unit and 1 vertical unit). The contributions of the numbers 2, 3, and 4 are 2, 1, and 1 respectively, which totals to 6. The function manhattandistance performs all operations in a single sweep:

In[5]:=
```
manhattandistance[x_List,y_List] :=
    Module[{temp},
        temp = Map[Flatten[Position[y,#]]&, x, {2}];
        temp = temp - Map[Flatten[Position[x,#]]&,x,{2}];
        temp = Apply[Plus,Flatten[Abs[temp]]]]


manhattandistance[list1, list2]
```

Out[5]= 6

A little thought should convince you that our implementation of the algorithm is far from ideal. For every member of the first array, we have performed a search through the second array. On average, this search will get halfway through the array before a match is found. If the matrices under comparison are 100×100 this process will involve approximately 50×100 comparisons.

The algorithm that we have used is pathological in that the number of comparisons goes as n^2, where n is the size of each array. In fact, the number of necessary comparisons is proportional to n, as we now demonstrate. In this second case, we run through both arrays only once. For each element in the first list, we add its position vector, in a dummy list, at the spot where the element would be in an ordered array. Similarly for the second list, we subtract the position vector. Finally, we add up the Manhattan distances:

In[6]:=
```
betterman[x_List,y_List] :=
    Module[{xdim = Length[x], ydim = Length[x[[1]]], temp},
        temp = Table[{0,0},{xdim*ydim}];
        Do[ temp[[ x[[i,j]] ]] = temp[[ x[[i,j]] ]] + {i,j};
            temp[[ y[[i,j]] ]] = temp[[ y[[i,j]] ]] - {i,j},
            {i,xdim},{j,ydim}];
        Apply[Plus,Flatten[Abs[temp]]]]
```

For reasonably sized arrays there is a large improvement in speed:

In[7]:=
```
Needs["DiscreteMath`Combinatorica`"]


pos1 = Partition[RandomPermutation[625],25];
pos2 = Partition[RandomPermutation[625],25];
```

In[8]:=
```
{Timing[ manhattandistance[pos1,pos2] ],
 Timing[ betterman[pos1,pos2] ]}
```

Out[8]= {{60. Second, 10272}, {23.8667 Second, 10272}}

We did not bother to make the change in Chapter 12 because speed was not a great problem there. Besides, as it stood there, evaluation of the Manhattan distance was not the limiting operation as far as speed was concerned. However, if you are exploring large decision trees and you need to use a sophisticated evaluation function, you should ensure that the function runs as fast as possible. This extra bit of speed might allow your chess program to look an extra move or two ahead of its opponent and could make all the difference between victory and failure.

14.1.2 List Manipulation

Even when you have hit on the optimum algorithm, you should take care how you implement it. Consider the problem of generating a random subset from a given set of numbers, with no repetition. If repetition is allowed, then the problem is trivial because we can keep taking a random element from the set:

```
In[9]:=    repallowed[x_List,n_Integer] :=
               x[[Table[Random[Integer,{1,Length[x]}],{n}]]];

           Do[Print[repallowed[{1,2,3,4},3]],{4}]
           {2, 2, 1}
           {3, 3, 3}
           {1, 2, 1}
           {2, 3, 1}
```

To prevent repetition, we must remove a number from the list once it has been chosen. We use two lists. The first contains those numbers not yet chosen, and the second contains the chosen numbers. The user enters an instruction such as randomset[{1,2,3,4},2]. *Mathematica*'s first task is to create a second list to contain the chosen numbers. To generate the random subset, we keep moving randomly chosen entries from the first set to the second until we have the required quantity. The second list is then sorted and returned:

```
In[10]:=   randomset[x_List,n_Integer] := randomset[x,{},n];

           randomset[x_List,y_List,0] := Sort[y];

           randomset[x_List,y_List,n_Integer] :=
               Module[{pick = Random[Integer,{1,Length[x]}]},
                   randomset[Drop[x,{pick}], Append[y,x[[pick]]],n-1]]
```

You can see that this function generates subsets with no repetition:

```
In[11]:=   Do[Print[randomset[{1,2,3,4,5},3]],{4}]
           {2, 3, 4}
           {1, 3, 4}
           {1, 3, 5}
           {1, 2, 5}
```

What could possibly be a more efficient method? The timings are good:

```
In[12]:=   Timing[ Do[randomset[Range[100],50];,{10}]]

Out[12]=   {6.03333 Second, Null}
```

At least they were good until we came across the function we wanted already available in one of the packages (there is a moral there!). We wondered how our functions would compare:

```
In[13]:=  Needs["DiscreteMath`Combinatorica`"]

          Timing[ Do[RandomKSubset[Range[100],50];,{10}]]
```

```
Out[13]=  {2.73333 Second, Null}
```

OK, so we lost! What was perplexing was that the package code appeared to have used the same algorithm as ours. However, instead of two lists, the package code had only one, which turned out to be the key to the extra speed. If you look at `randomset` as defined, you will notice that the sum of the length of the list `x` and the length of list `y` is constant. With a bit of clever coding (see the packages!), it is possible to make do with just one list. This method is faster because the underlying C code does not have to fiddle around with memory allocation for arrays (which is basically what lists are) whose lengths are changing.

14.2 Internal Compilation

So stage 1 of our increased efficiency plan was not enough for you! Your algorithm is running efficiently, but it is still too slow. It could well be time to start compiling parts of your code. Suppose we take the function $f(x) = x/(1 + x^2)$ and program it in the usual manner:

```
In[14]:=  f[x_] := N[x/(1+x^2)];
```

When we apply this function to a single number, it takes hardly any time at all:

```
In[15]:=  Timing[ f[1] ]
```

```
Out[15]=  {0. Second, 0.5}
```

However, when we map the function onto every element of a long list, the time taken to perform the operation becomes noticeable:

```
In[16]:=  datavals = Table[1,{100}];
          Timing[ Map[f,datavals]; ]
```

```
Out[16]=  {0.35 Second, Null}
```

On its own, 0.35 second is not an appreciable amount of time, but suppose that this operation was inside a loop that iterated 100 times. The entire loop would then take 35 seconds. If the data list had 1000 entries and our loop ran 1000 times, we would wait for 3500 seconds — about an hour. Instances of double loops such as this one arise frequently. Because the time taken to perform such calculations increases as the square of the number of entries in each loop, it is essential to make the operation in the core of the inner loop run as fast as possible.

The reason why the code runs slowly is that *Mathematica* is a high-level language, and every calculation has to be translated into machine-level code, which takes extra time. Versions 2 and later of *Mathematica* have introduced compiler capabilities where it matters most — that is, in the treatment of simple numerical operations that may be repeated many times with high accuracy. This facility effectively allows the user access to a set of machine-level instructions for an idealized computer. These instructions can be translated typically five times faster than can the usual *Mathematica* instructions. Consider our function f[x_]. In machine language, this instruction might be converted to the following sequence:

1. Load argument 1 (in other words, x) into real register 1
2. Multiply register 1 by register 1 and store the result in real register 2; x^2
3. Load the real number 1.0 into real register 3; 1 + x^2
4. Add register 3 to register 2 and store the result in real register 4
5. Take the reciprocal of register 4 and store it in register 5 (just as we discovered in Chapter 9, there is no division command)
6. Multiply register 1 by register 5 and store the result in register 6;1/(1+x^2)
7. Output register 6

The *Mathematica* compilation facility allows us to write code just like that appearing in the previous list. The instruction set is included in "The *Mathematica* Compiler," a Wolfram Research technical report [26]. The machine-code instructions are, in order, as follows:

0. {1,17} — specify which instruction set we are going to use (at the moment the only option is 17)
1. {4,1,1} — {4,n,realreg} means load argument n into real register realreg
2. {36,1,1,2}
3. {13,1.0,3}
4. {33,2,3,4}
5. {41,4,5}
6. {36,1,5,6}
7. {8,6}

Before you start complaining that you do not have a list of the machine-code instructions, we should explain that although we are performing this calculation by hand, *Mathematica* is capable of doing the translation itself. We have chosen to give the explanation backward in the belief that an appreciation of how compilation works is indispensable if you want to know which problems it can tackle and which it cannot.

We store the machine-code program in a list that is ready for compilation:

In[17]:=
```
code = {{1,17},{4,1,1},{36,1,1,2},{13,1.0,3},{33,2,3,4},{41,4,5},
       {36,1,5,6},{8,6}};
```

In addition to the machine code, the CompiledFunction function takes three other arguments. The first is a list of the argument types, the second tells *Mathematica* how many registers are needed by the code, and the third is a standard *Mathematica* function to be used if the compilation breaks down for any reason:

In[18]:=
```
fasterf = CompiledFunction[{_Real},{0, 0, 6, 0}, code,
          Function[{},Print["Didn't work"]]]
```

Out[18]= ` CompiledFunction[{}, Print[Didn't work], -CompiledCode-]`

The machine code works fine as long as we apply the function to only real numbers:

In[19]:= ` Map[ fasterf, {1,2,3} ]`

Out[19]= ` {0.5, 0.4, 0.3}`

On the other hand, when `fasterf` is applied to an object other than a real number, the compilation fails, and the default *Mathematica* function is applied. In general, the default function will be the same as the compiled code. We have used a `Print` statement here for explanatory purposes:

In[20]:= ` fasterf[a]`

```
CompiledFunction::cfr:
    Argument a at position 1 should be a machine-size real number.
```

```
Didn't work
```

In real life, we simply send the function to be compiled to *Mathematica*:

In[21]:= ` realworldf = Compile[{x},x/(1+x^2)]`

Out[21]=
$$\text{CompiledFunction}[\{x\}, \frac{x}{1 + x^2}, \text{-CompiledCode-}]$$

The machine-code list is there, but it has been suppressed in the screen display to make the output form more compact. It is lurking behind the `-CompiledCode-` mask:

In[22]:= ` realworldf[[3]]`

Out[22]= ` {{1, 17}, {4, 1, 0}, {12, 1, 0}, {36, 0, 0, 1}, {20, 0, 2},`

` {33, 2, 1, 3}, {41, 3, 4}, {36, 0, 4, 5}, {8, 5}}`

Except that there has been a slight reordering of the instructions and the registers have been numbered from 0 instead of 1, this list contains exactly the same code as we used in `fasterf`. In general, it is best to allow *Mathematica* to perform the translation. As anyone who has experience with machine code knows, it is not difficult to cause the computer to crash!

If we apply `realworldf` to a nonreal object, the backup *Mathematica* version of the function gives us a result more useful than the one we obtained intentionally from `fasterf`:

In[23]:= ` realworldf[a]`

```
CompiledFunction::cfr:
    Argument a at position 1 should be a machine-size real number.
```

Out[23]=
$$\frac{a}{1 + a^2}$$

How do the compiled and uncompiled functions compare for speed? When we map the compiled function onto the length-100 list, the operation only takes one-seventh of the time:

```
In[24]:=  Timing[ Map[realworldf, datavals]; ]

Out[24]=  {0.05 Second, Null}
```

In Chapter 19, we shall use *Mathematica* to generate some fractal plots. The creation of a two-dimensional graphic is achieved by a double loop, running over the x and y pixel ranges. Inside this double loop is simple but repetitive code that determines the color that the pixel should take. This code is a prime subject for compilation and forms the basis of an in-depth case study in that chapter. Another area where compilation yields significant benefits in performance terms is in the solution of integral equations. We now turn our attention to this subject.

14.2.1 Integral Equations

If we wish to describe an integral equation, it is easiest to give an example. Consider the following equation, similar to one that arises in elementary particle physics:

$$\Sigma(x) = \int_a^b \frac{2y}{x^2 + y^2} \frac{\Sigma(y)}{1 + \Sigma^2(y)} dy$$

This equation defines a function $\Sigma(x)$ in the region $a \leq x \leq b$. In other words, there is a unique function in this range that satisfies the previous equation. We want to find that function.

We can use special techniques to solve certain simple integral equations. For instance, we can sometimes convert an integral equation into a differential equation that we can tackle with conventional numerical methods, such as a Runge-Kutta. In general, however, such a conversion is not possible. Therefore, we must resort to choosing a discrete set of values for x in the appropriate region and then using the integral equation to iterate from an initial guess to a solution. What is the depth of iteration in this process? For each value of x, we need to perform a numerical integral — effectively, a loop. Repeating this operation for the set of values of x makes a second loop. Finally, iterating until convergence makes a third loop. Unless the operation at the center of these loops runs exceedingly quickly, we could be waiting for a long time! Suppose that we try to solve this problem with *Mathematica* for a particular set of x values. Furthermore, let's adopt a procedural approach in the first instance, just to show how bad a technique that would be!

Procedural approach

First, we must select values for the parameters a and b (which we shall call lowlim and uplim) and the step size between neighboring points in the discretized set — this last value will determine the number of points that we have in our set. We have chosen the following values to start:

In[25]:=   `lowlim = 10; uplim = 110; stepsize = 10;`
              `pointno = (uplim - lowlim)/stepsize + 1;`

Using these values, we can generate a list of the discrete set of x values:

In[26]:=   `discretevals = Range[lowlim,uplim,stepsize]`

Out[26]=   `{10, 20, 30, 40, 50, 60, 70, 80, 90, 100, 110}`

Next, we must decide on the method used to perform the numerical integration. Suppose that we choose Simpson's rule. That is, for a constant step width h, we approximate

$$\int_a^{a+nh} f(x)dx = \frac{h}{3}(f(a)+4f(a+h)+2f(a+2h)+4f(a+3h)+\ldots+4f(a+(n-1)h)+f(a+nh))$$

(which forces us to use an odd number of data points — a criterion satisfied by our set, which has 11). For a general discussion of numerical integration of discrete data sets, refer to Chapter 5. To implement Simpson's rule, we make a list of weighting factors $\{1, 4, 2, 4, \ldots .4, 1\}$ and multiply this list by one-third of the step width:

In[27]:=   `simpvals = N[Join[{1},`
              `            Drop[Flatten[Table[{4,2},{(pointno-1)/2}]],-1],`
              `            {1}]*stepsize/3]`

Out[27]=   `{3.33333, 13.3333, 6.66667, 13.3333, 6.66667, 13.3333, 6.66667, 13.3333,`

              `6.66667, 13.3333, 3.33333}`

We are almost ready to implement our iteration. We shall need two arrays to store the value of Σ during the iteration — one for the old values and the other for the new values. At the end of each iteration, the old array is replaced by the new value. Our initial guess for Σ is that it is uniformly equal to 1:

In[28]:=   `sigold = Table[1.0,{i,lowlim,uplim,stepsize}];`
              `signew = sigold;`

Our iteration formula, which we obtain by discretizing the integral equation, is

$$\Sigma_i = \sum_{j=1}^{n} \text{simp}_j \frac{2x_j}{x_i^2 + x_j^2} \frac{\Sigma_j}{1 + \Sigma_j^2}$$
$$= \sum_{j=1}^{n} \text{kernel}_{i,j}$$

In *Mathematica*, we code the kernel function as follows:

In[29]:=   `kernel[i_,j_] :=`
              `Module[{x = discretevals[[i]], y = discretevals[[j]], sig = sigold[[j]]},`
              `       2.0 sig/(1+sig*sig) y/(x^2+y^2) simpvals[[j]]]`

It is then a simple matter to implement our iteration scheme. The following instruction performs five iterations, printing out timing values and the discrete set of $\Sigma(x)$ values at each stage:

```
In[30]:=  Do[
            Print[Timing[
              Do[signew[[i]] = Sum[kernel[i,j], {j,1,pointno}], {i,1,pointno}];
              sigold = signew;
              N[signew,4]]],{5}]
```

{2.6 Second, {2.051, 1.608, 1.282, 1.043, 0.8628, 0.7227, 0.6119, 0.523, 0.4508, 0.3915, 0.3425}}

{2.63333 Second, {1.83, 1.436, 1.139, 0.9199, 0.7549, 0.6278, 0.5282, 0.449, 0.3851, 0.3331, 0.2904}}

{2.7 Second, {1.814, 1.408, 1.106, 0.8874, 0.7243, 0.5998, 0.5029, 0.4263, 0.3649, 0.315, 0.2742}}

{2.66667 Second, {1.799, 1.392, 1.092, 0.8737, 0.7119, 0.5887, 0.4931, 0.4176, 0.3572, 0.3082, 0.2681}}

{2.7 Second, {1.794, 1.386, 1.086, 0.8683, 0.7069, 0.5843, 0.4892, 0.4141, 0.3541, 0.3055, 0.2657}}

These timings are restrictively slow. If we were to use a worthwhile number of x values — say, 101 — then each iteration would take about 4 minutes. Estimating that convergence will take about 20 iterations, the entire calculation would take 80 minutes. There are a number of tricks that we can use to speed up this timing. In the first instance, we can implement our iteration more efficiently (this type of improvement was discussed in the previous section). Then, we can speed up our implementation even more by compiling certain functions that we need to use frequently. As we move through these various steps, we shall use the timings for 101 values and 20 iterations as a benchmark to quantify the timing improvement that we can expect.

Matrix formulation

The method that we applied in Section 14.2.1 was remarkably inefficient because, at every stage in the calculation, the entire kernel matrix was reevaluated. Some parts of kernel[i,j] do not change and should be calculated only once. Specifically,

$$\text{simp}_j \frac{2x_j}{x_i^2 + x_j^2}$$

is iteration independent, whereas

$$\frac{\Sigma_j}{1 + \Sigma_j^2}$$

is iteration dependent. A more efficient method for solving the problem is to compute an initial matrix for the iteration-independent component and to compute only the second term at each iteration:

```
In[31]:=  Timing[ kernelmat = Table[
              2 discretevals[[j]]/(discretevals[[j]]^2+
              discretevals[[i]]^2) * simpvals[[j]],
              {i,1,pointno},{j,1,pointno}];]
```

Out[31]= {0.883333 Second, Null}

We can take a look at this 11×11 matrix:

```
In[32]:=  TableForm[ N[kernelmat,2], TableSpacing -> {0,1}]
Out[32]=  0.33    1.1    0.4    0.63   0.26  0.43 0.19  0.33 0.15  0.26 0.06
          0.13    0.67   0.31   0.53   0.23  0.4  0.18  0.31 0.14  0.26 0.059
          0.067   0.41   0.22   0.43   0.2   0.36 0.16  0.29 0.13  0.24 0.056
          0.039   0.27   0.16   0.33   0.16  0.31 0.14  0.27 0.12  0.23 0.054
          0.026   0.18   0.12   0.26   0.13  0.26 0.13  0.24 0.11  0.21 0.05
          0.018   0.13   0.089  0.21   0.11  0.22 0.11  0.21 0.1   0.2  0.047
          0.013   0.1    0.069  0.16   0.09  0.19 0.095 0.19 0.092 0.18 0.043
          0.01    0.078  0.055  0.13   0.075 0.16 0.083 0.17 0.083 0.16 0.04
          0.0081  0.063  0.044  0.11   0.063 0.14 0.072 0.15 0.074 0.15 0.036
          0.0066  0.051  0.037  0.092  0.053 0.12 0.063 0.13 0.066 0.13 0.033
          0.0055  0.043  0.031  0.078  0.046 0.1  0.055 0.12 0.059 0.12 0.03
```

We can now perform the iterations using the built-in matrix capabilities that *Mathematica* possesses. Because we can write down the iteration in one line, we do not need an intermediate store for the partially modified function list. In other words, we need only a single list singlesig, as opposed to the earlier case when we needed both sigold and signew. What is the effect of our modification on the timings?

```
In[33]:=  singlesig = Table[1.0, {pointno}];

          Do[
             Print[Timing[
               N[singlesig = kernelmat.(singlesig/(1.0+singlesig^2)),4]]],
             {5}]

          {0.1 Second, {2.051, 1.608, 1.282, 1.043, 0.8628, 0.7227, 0.6119, 0.523,
              0.4508, 0.3915, 0.3425}}

          {0.05 Second, {1.83, 1.436, 1.139, 0.9199, 0.7549, 0.6278, 0.5282,
              0.449, 0.3851, 0.3331, 0.2904}}

          {0.05 Second, {1.814, 1.408, 1.106, 0.8874, 0.7243, 0.5998, 0.5029,
              0.4263, 0.3649, 0.315, 0.2742}}

          {0.05 Second, {1.799, 1.392, 1.092, 0.8737, 0.7119, 0.5887, 0.4931,
              0.4176, 0.3572, 0.3082, 0.2681}}

          {0.05 Second, {1.794, 1.386, 1.086, 0.8683, 0.7069, 0.5843, 0.4892,
              0.4141, 0.3541, 0.3055, 0.2657}}
```

This improvement is significant; each iteration now takes only one-sixtieth of the time taken previously. Even allowing for the overhead of the initial kernel computation, we are still much better off overall. When we repeated the operation with 101 points instead of 11 (101 is our benchmark calculation), the timings were 60.55 seconds for the kernel computation and 1.75 seconds per iteration. Total computation time for 20 iterations amounted to $60 + 20 \times 1.75 = 95$ seconds. Clearly, the weakest link in the chain is the kernel computation, which is where we now channel our attention.

The first step is to replace the instruction in the middle of the loop by a predefined function. This replacement will cut down the time slightly because we will no longer be making the second (unnecessary) access to the discretevals list to determine x_j:

```
In[34]:=   kernelfunc[x_,y_] := 2 x/(x^2+y^2);

           lowlim = 1.0; uplim = 101.0; stepsize = 1.0;
           pointno = (uplim - lowlim)/stepsize + 1;
           discretevals = Range[lowlim,uplim,stepsize];
           simpvals = N[Join[{1}, Drop[Flatten[
             Table[{4,2},{(pointno-1)/2}]],-1], {1}]*stepsize/3];

           Timing[ kernelmat = Table[
             kernelfunc[discretevals[[j]],discretevals[[i]]]*simpvals[[j]],
               {i,1,pointno},{j,1,pointno}];]
```

```
Out[34]=   {69.4333 Second, Null}
```

Now, and only now, is it time to make use of compilation:

```
In[35]:=   kernelfunc1 = Compile[{x,y},2 x/(x^2 + y^2)]
```

```
Out[35]=
                                 2 x
           CompiledFunction[{x, y}, -------, -CompiledCode-]
                                   2   2
                                  x + y
```

```
In[36]:=   Timing[ Table[
             kernelfunc1[discretevals[[j]],discretevals[[i]]]*simpvals[[j]],
             {i,1,pointno},{j,1,pointno}];]
```

```
Out[36]=   {26.1167 Second, Null}
```

We can realize a further small saving by noting that because our discretized set of points is uniformly distributed, there is no need to access the discretevals array at all:

```
In[37]:=   Timing[kernelmat1 = Table[kernelfunc1[y,x],
           {x,lowlim,uplim,stepsize}, {y,lowlim,uplim,stepsize}];
           kernelmat1 = Map[Times[simpvals,#]&, kernelmat1];]
```

```
Out[37]=   {20.3167 Second, Null}
```

We can check that kernelmat and kernelmat1 are identical:

```
In[38]:=   {Min[#], Max[#]}&[ Flatten[kernelmat1/kernelmat] ]
```

```
Out[38]=   {1., 1.}
```

You may be wondering just how well the iteration scheme that we have devised converges. The following code runs through 20 iterations, adding the state of Σ to a list at each stage. Assuming that the function has converged by iteration 20, we can plot the deviation from this solution for the first few iterations (notice the different scales on the axes):

```
In[39]:=   singlesig = Table[1.0,{i,lowlim,uplim,stepsize}];
           store = {};
           Do[singlesig = kernelmat.(singlesig/(1+singlesig^2));
             AppendTo[store,singlesig];,{20}]
```

```
fig[n_] := ListPlot[store[[n]]-store[[20]],
            PlotLabel -> StringJoin["Iteration ",ToString[n]],
            DisplayFunction -> Identity]

Show[GraphicsArray[{{fig[1], fig[2]}, {fig[3], fig[4]},
                    {fig[5], fig[6]}}]];
```

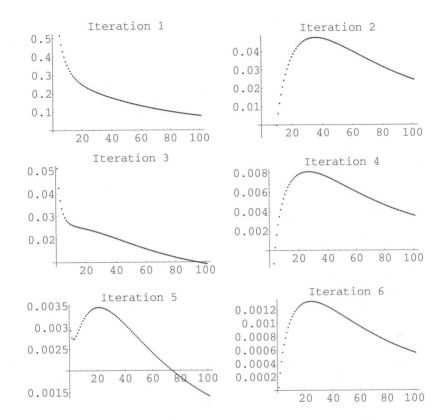

14.2.2 To Compile or Not To Compile

So far, we have compiled only simple functions. All the standard trigonometric formulas, such as Cos and Sin, also can be compiled. Other constructions that can be handled include simple Boolean tests in conjunction with operations such as If and Switch:

```
In[40]:=   iff = Compile[{x}, If[x > 2, x^2, x + Cos[x]]];
           {iff[3.0], iff[0.0]}
```

Out[40]=   {9., 1.}

Similarly, groups of instructions inside `Block` and `Module` can be compiled, as long as their insides contain only compilable instructions.

Many of the built-in numerical instructions such as `NIntegrate` and `NSum` compile their arguments by default. To obtain precision higher than that offered by the processor resident in the machine, you must turn off the compilation. It is perhaps surprising to find that `NIntegrate` sometimes works faster without compilation:

In[41]:=   ```
littlefn[x_] := Cos[x]/(1+x^2);

{Timing[NIntegrate[littlefn[x],{x,0,10}, Compiled -> True]],
  Timing[NIntegrate[littlefn[x],{x,0,10}, Compiled -> False]]}
```

*Out[41]=*    {{0.85 Second, 0.574239}, {0.733333 Second, 0.574239}}

There is a simple explanation for this behavior. `NIntegrate` does not have to sample the function at many points to obtain an accurate value for the integral. There is insufficient time for the overhead of compiling the function to be recovered. We can verify this statement by compiling the function before the integration:

*In[42]:=*    ```
littlecm = Compile[{x}, Cos[x]/(1+x^2)];

Timing[NIntegrate[littlecm[x],{x,0,10}]]
```

Out[42]=   {0.6 Second, 0.574239}

Sometimes — with highly oscillatory integrands for instance — `NIntegrate` will perform better with the compilation on. In these circumstances, the integrand must be sampled at many points. Situations of this kind are the reason why the default setting is `Compiled -> True`; the uncompiled version is faster only when the problem is quick anyway, whereas the compiled version wins out on the trickier calculations.

14.3 External Compilation: MathLink

When internal compilation is not sufficient, there is another option that is becoming increasingly popular. The idea is to write your function in a C program and to link that C code into *Mathematica* with a facility known as *MathLink*. To demonstrate the procedure, suppose that we compile the function that we used extensively in Section 14.2.1:

In[43]:=   ```
kernelfunc[x_,y_] := 2 x/(x^2 + y^2);
```

We want to send the two real numbers $x$ and $y$ to the C program, and we want that program to return a single real number equal to the value of the function. This process has two stages. First, we write a file containing a template of what data structures will be sent between *Mathematica* and the C program. Second, we write the C code. The two files are merged into a composite C file by an application program supplied with MathLink, and the merged file is then compiled. The executable code can be installed into *Mathematica* and will then be indistinguishable from any other function. The user may be unaware that an external program is involved in the calculation.
```

14.3.1 Template File

The template file for our function is

```
:Begin:
:Function: kernel
:Pattern: kernel[x_Real, y_Real]
:Arguments: {x, y}
:ArgumentTypes: {Real, Real}
:ReturnType: Real
:End:
```

The whole template is demarcated by :Begin: and :End: instructions. The name given to the function in the C code follows the :Function: entry. This name may be different from the name by which the function will be accessed in *Mathematica* once it has been installed. The :Pattern: entry in the template tells *Mathematica* the syntax of kernel — in this case, that kernel takes two real arguments. This information is duplicated in the next two entries. Because our function will return a single real number, the return type has been set to Real. There are other possibilities. If we want to return a list of integers, this entry would be set to IntegerList. If we want our C program to send back more complicated structures (actually, they do not need to be that complicated — even a list of real numbers qualifies), then we should set the return type to Manual. We can then send back any expression we like from the C code using *Mathematica*'s FullForm notation.

14.3.2 The C Code

The template file described in Section 14.3.1 sets up a structured communication link between *Mathematica* and a C program. We must now write the C code and merge it with the template. The following code is a realization of our kernel function:

```
#include "mathlink.h"

double kernel(x,y)
double x,y;
{
  double res;
  res = 2*x/(x*x+y*y);
  return res;
}

int main(argc,argv)
int argc; char* argv[];
{
  return MLMain(argc, argv);
}
```

Most of this code is independent of the function that we are writing. The real meat lies in the function definition from the line double kernel(x,y) to the end of the return res instruction. The function definition is self-explanatory. An important point to notice is that all real numbers sent by *Mathematica* to the program arrive in double precision. We have subsequently worked in double precision throughout the function. However, you may want to explicitly convert the arguments into floating-point types and then work in single precision (this is useful when you have a suite of libraries that take float arguments).

14.3.3 Function Installation

When we have merged our template file with the C code and have compiled it (the details of this process are both machine-dependent and time-dependent!), the time has come to install the function into *Mathematica*. Suppose that our executable code also has the name kernel. To install the function, we simply enter

```
In[44]:=  Clear[kernel];
          Install["kernel"]
```

```
Out[44]=  LinkObject[kernel, 2, 2]
```

When we ask for information on the function to which this program gives us access, we are informed that the function will make an external call to LinkObject:

```
In[45]:=  ?kernel
          Global`kernel

          kernel[x_Real, y_Real] :=
            ExternalCall[LinkObject["kernel", 2, 2], CallPacket[0, {x, y}]]
```

However, users are unaware that this function is doing anything particularly odd when they use it:

```
In[46]:=  kernel[1.0, 2.0]
```

```
Out[46]=  0.4
```

There is a slight difference from the compiled function. In that case, integer arguments were converted to reals. In this case, no conversion is made, and the evaluation does not happen:

```
In[47]:=  kernel[1, 2]
```

```
Out[47]=  kernel[1, 2]
```

How does the external compilation compare with the uncompiled version for speed? If you are expecting another amazing improvement, you may be shocked to find the reverse:

```
In[48]:=  {Timing[Do[kernelfunc[1.0,2.0],{100}];],
           Timing[Do[kernel[1.0,2.0],{100}];]}
```

```
Out[48]=  {{0.45 Second, Null}, {11.9667 Second, Null}}
```

Since the entire motivation for using MathLink was to increase speed, why has it not worked? It is stupid to set up a link for a function as simple as we have here. When kernel is called, *Mathematica* has to find the program and to communicate the two real numbers to that program. kernelfunc does not have this overhead. It is important to use MathLink only when the complexity of the calculation process exceeds the complexity of the communication between *Mathematica* and the external program. Although slightly vague, this rule of thumb works. In the next section, we shall consider an example where MathLink wins hands down. In this example, typically 1000 numbers are sent from

Mathematica to the C code, and 40 are returned. In between, about 40,000 computations are performed. Such a scenario fits our criterion, and, as we shall see, the subsequent increase in speed is staggering. Before we move on, we should `Uninstall` the function that we no longer need:

```
In[49]:=   Uninstall["kernel"]

Out[49]=   kernel
```

14.3.4 Improved Spectral Analysis

In the spectral analysis case study of Chapter 17, we shall be considering long data sets from which we shall need to define a correlation matrix whose (i, j)th entry is given by

$$M_{i,j} = \sum_n a(n + i)a(n + j)$$

where $a(n)$ denotes the nth entry in the data set. A typical size for the spectral matrix might be 6×6 (this number is referred to as the *window size*). n typically runs over a much larger range, frequently the length of the data set. Our objective is to make a function that takes a data set, window size, and range and computes the spectral matrix. The naive *Mathematica* code is

```
In[50]:=   spectralmatrix[dat_, windowsize_, range_] :=
           Table[ Sum[ dat[[n+k-1]]dat[[n+m-1]],
                  {n,1,range-windowsize+1}],
                  {k,1,windowsize},{m,1,windowsize}];
```

Unfortunately, this code is slow — principally because the algorithm has not been implemented efficiently. However, we may obtain a significant improvement in performance if we code the inefficient algorithm in C and link it to *Mathematica* using MathLink. (Alternatively, we can write a more efficient algorithm in *Mathematica*, which is the course of action taken in Chapter 17.)

The information that we want to send from *Mathematica* to the C program is comprised of a list of real numbers (corresponding to the data values) and an integer (corresponding to the window size). We shall assume that the summations will run over the whole range of the sent data set. In return from the C program, we want the matrix defined previously — in other words, a list of lists. A matrix is a sufficiently involved structure that we shall have to use `Manual` return operations.

The pattern for the *Mathematica* function that we wish to install is `spectral[x_List, window_Integer]`, which is the last clue we need to construct the template file for communication:

```
:Begin:
:Function: spectral
:Pattern: spectral[ x:{___Real}, window_Integer ]
:Arguments: { x, window }
:ArgumentTypes: {RealList, Integer}
:ReturnType: Manual
:End:
```

Although we are sending only two objects to the C code — a list and an integer — the program actually receives another integer that tells it the length of the list. The resulting program demonstrates one way in which it is possible to write the function definition. For those of you who are not familiar with C, the real list is stored in an array in the memory location pointed to by p.

The function type is defined to be Void because all the return operations will be performed manually. Outside the first loop (corresponding to running through the columns of the square matrix), we first send back to *Mathematica* the head of a list expression, with an integer value that tells *Mathematica* how many entries this list will contain. These entries may be any other type of *Mathematica* expression, in our case, the entries are themselves lists corresponding to the individual rows. The real values are sent back from the core of the loop by an MLPutReal instruction. stdlink means "standard link," which will be the link between your *Mathematica* session and the program:

```
#include "mathlink.h"

void spectral(list, len, winlength)
double* list;
int len, winlength;
{
 int dataloop, loopout, loopin;
 double current;

 MLPutFunction(stdlink,"List",winlength);
 for(loopin = 0; loopin < winlength; loopin++){
 MLPutFunction(stdlink, "List", winlength);
 for(loopout = 0; loopout < winlength; loopout++){
     current = 0.0;
     for( dataloop = 0 ; dataloop < len-winlength+1; dataloop++){
         current += list[dataloop+loopin]*list[dataloop+loopout];}
     MLPutReal(stdlink, current);
     }};
}


int main(argc, argv)
int argc; char* argv[];
{
  return MLMain(argc, argv);
}
```

As before, we install the executable code using whatever name we have given to it:

In[51]:= Install["spectral"];

Just to check that all is well, we now try a simple example:

In[52]:= TableForm[N[spectral[{1.0,6.0,3.0,4.0},4],2], TableSpacing -> {1,2}]

Out[52]=
1. 6. 3. 4.

6. 36. 18. 24.

3. 18. 9. 12.

4. 24. 12. 16.

We are definitely receiving a list of lists back from the program, but are these correct values?

In[53]:= `spectralmatrix[{1.0,6.0,3.0,4.0},4,4] - spectral[{1.0,6.0,3.0,4.0},4]`
Out[53]= `{{0., 0., 0., 0.}, {0., 0., 0., 0.}, {0., 0., 0., 0.},`

    `{0., 0., 0., 0.}}`

Suppose that we give *Mathematica* a real problem so that we can see what improvements in speed we have achieved:

In[54]:= `morevals = Table[Random[],{1000}];`
      `{Timing[spectralmatrix[morevals,4,1000];],Timing[spectral[morevals,4];]}`

Out[54]= `{{54.1333 Second, Null}, {1.63333 Second, Null}}`

This increase in speed is significant. Note that we can obtain similar improvements in this case, by using a more efficient algorithm. However, it actually took us longer to prototype that algorithm than implementing the inefficient algorithm with MathLink — for similar rewards. There is no hard and fast rule. Basically, you should try to reach the desired speed one way or another and, probably, as quickly as possible. After you make the initial investment of time in learning to compile the programs and link them in, MathLink provides an excellent tool for achieving this improvement.

14.3.5 Numerical Recipes

Earlier in this chapter, we mentioned the excellent work *Numerical Recipes: The Art of Scientific Computing* [15]. Not only does this book include a wealth of algorithms, but also it includes code for the functions that are defined there. We are lucky that a C version of the book is available and that all the programs can be obtained on disk. We can link these programs into *Mathematica* with minimal effort. In Chapter 13 of *Numerical Recipes,* the authors describe a function for computing the median of a set of data. Their code looks like this:

```
#include <math.h>

#define BIG 1.0e30
#define AFAC 1.5
#define AMP 1.5

void mdian2(x,n,xmed)
int n;
float x[],*xmed;
{
 int np,nm,j;
 float xx,xp,xm,sumx,sum,eps,stemp,dum,ap,am,aa,a;

 LOTS OF INTERESTING CODE --- BUY THE BOOK!

    *xmed = 0.5*(np == nm ? xp+xm : np > nm ? a+xp : xm+a);
  } else {
    *xmed = np == nm ? a : np > nm ? xp : xm;
  }
  return;
 }
 }
}
```

```
#undef BIG
#undef AFAC
#undef AMP
```

The function takes a list of data that is pointed to by x and has length n and returns the median in xmed, which makes the function type void. The calculations are performed with floats.

If we want to link this function using MathLink, one method is to make a set of changes to the mdian2 code to handle double-precision values (this is not the approach that we recommend):

```
#include <math.h>
#include mathlink.h

#define BIG 1.0e30
#define AFAC 1.5
#define AMP 1.5

double mdian2(x,n)
int n;
double x[];
{
  int np,nm,j;
  double xx,xp,xm,sumx,sum,eps,stemp,dum,ap,am,aa,a;

        LOTS OF INTERESTING CODE --- BUY THE BOOK!

    return 0.5*(np == nm ? xp+xm : np > nm ? a+xp : xm+a);
   } else {
    return np == nm ? a : np > nm ? xp : xm;
   }
  }
 }
}
```

The template file is similar to our spectral one:

```
:Begin:
:Function: mdian2
:Pattern: fastmedian[x:{___Real}]
:Arguments: {x}
:ArgumentTypes: {RealList}
:ReturnType: Real
:End:
```

Now, we can just install the code as usual:

In[55]:=   Install["nrmedian"]

Out[55]=   LinkObject[nrmedian, 4, 5]

We can check the result for a random data set against that from the Median function defined with *Mathematica*:

In[56]:=   data = Table[Random[],{100}];
            Timing[fastmedian[data]]

Out[56]=   {0.216667 Second, 0.549333725070130745}

```
In[57]:=   ?fastmedian
           Global`fastmedian

           fastmedian[x:{___Real}] :=
             ExternalCall[LinkObject["nrmedian", 4, 5], CallPacket[0, {x}]]

In[58]:=   Needs["Statistics`DescriptiveStatistics`"];
           Timing[ N[Median[data],18]]

Out[58]=   {0.0333333 Second, 0.549333725070130745}

In[59]:=   Uninstall["nrmedian"];
```

It is slightly surprising to discover that *Mathematica*'s version is faster. However, we are not doing justice to the *Numerical Recipes* version, since we have forced double precision, which is redundant and slows down the evaluation. There is, in fact, a much more efficient way to link in the code.

Traveling salesperson

The traveling salesperson problem is a well-known one: Given a set of cities, what is the shortest route that takes in all the cities? The problem is extremely difficult to solve. There is a function in the package `DiscreteMath`Combinatorica``, but the syntax is unclear and the results are produced slowly:

```
In[60]:=   Needs["DiscreteMath`Combinatorica`"]
```

First, we generate a set of randomly distributed cities:

```
In[61]:=   cities = Table[{Random[],Random[]},{7}];
```

Then, we compute a matrix containing their separations:

```
In[62]:=   edges = Table[Sqrt[(cities[[i,1]]-cities[[j,1]])^2
                         +(cities[[i,2]]-cities[[j,2]])^2],{i,7},{j,7}];
```

The two data sets are then merged into a graph!

```
In[63]:=   citygraph = Graph[edges,cities];
```

Next, the route is found:

```
In[64]:=   Timing[route = Line[cities[[TravelingSalesman[citygraph]]]];]

Out[64]=   {77.9833 Second, Null}
```

Look how long it took to get the answer. We ought to check that the result is plausible before we send out our publisher's salesperson to sell this book!

```
In[65]:=   citypoints = Graphics[{PointSize[0.03],Map[Point,cities]}];

In[66]:=   Show[Graphics[route], citypoints];
```

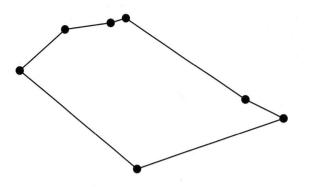

Numerical Recipes gives an extremely efficient algorithm for solving this problem that involves a process known as *simulated annealing*. We shall use MathLink to access this program. The first step is to generate the template file. The *Mathematica* function that we shall use will have the form salesperson[x-coords, y-coords], so we shall send to our C code two lists of reals. These will appear as lists of doubles and will be sent to the function salesperson:

```
:Begin:
:Function: salesperson
:Pattern: salesperson[x:{___Real},y:{___Real}]
:Arguments: {x,y}
:ArgumentTypes: {RealList, RealList}
:ReturnType: Manual
:End:
```

Rather than hacking the numerical recipe's C code, we make it the responsibility of the function salesperson to convert the information that it receives from *Mathematica* into a form that can be handled by anneal, which is the name of the function given in *Numerical Recipes*. anneal requests two float arrays, which correspond to the coordinates of the cities; an integer list in which to store the best route when it is found; and an integer telling it how many cities there are. We use the C command malloc to allocate two float arrays, and we then convert and store in there the arrays of doubles that we obtained from *Mathematica*. At the end of our calculation, we use free to surrender the memory that we were allocated so that it can be used again:

```
/* Include standard headers and numerical recipes routines */

#include "stdlib.h"
#include "mathlink.h"
#include "nrutil.c"
#include "anneal.c"
#include "irbit1.c"
#include "ran3.c"

/* This is the go-between function that converts MathLink data
   into a form that "anneal" can handle */

void salesperson(x,xl,y,yl)
double *x, *y;
long xl, yl;
```

```
{
int *result;
float *xf;
float *yf;
int i;
int xm, ym;

/* allocate space for the arrays */
xm = (int)x1;
xf = vector(1,xm);
yf = vector(1,xm);
result = ivector(1,xm);

/* copy double arrays into floating arrays */

for(i = 0; i < xm; i++){
                xf[i+1] = (float) x[i];
                yf[i+1] = (float) y[i];
                result[i+1] = i+1;}

/* call the function that does all the work */
anneal(xf,yf,result,xm);


/* Now all we have to do is to send back the route*/

MLPutFunction(stdlink,"List",x1);

for(i = 0; i < xm; i++) MLPutInteger(stdlink, result[i+1]);

/* and clear up our rubbish after us */

free_vector(xf,1,xm);
free_vector(yf,1,xm);
free_ivector(result,1,xm);
}



int main(argc, argv)
int argc; char* argv[];
{
return MLMain(argc, argv);
}
```

We think that you will agree that this method of linking to the recipes is much more civilized than that employed with mdian2. It also works magnificently (we named the application containing the C code after a famous salesperson). First, we try the easy case with only seven cities:

```
In[67]:=  Install["willyloman", LinkMode -> Connect];

In[68]:=  salesperson[Apply[Sequence,Transpose[cities]]]

Out[68]=  {5, 6, 7, 3, 2, 1, 4}

In[69]:=  route = Line[cities[[Append[%,First[%]]]]];
          Show[Graphics[route], citypoints];
```

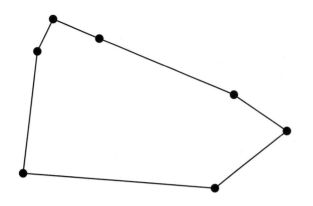

Now, for a tougher problem:

```
In[70]:=  data1 = Table[Random[],{40}];
          data2 = Table[Random[],{40}];
```

```
In[71]:=  route = salesperson[data1,data2]
```

```
Out[71]=  {29, 35, 21, 25, 27, 40, 9, 5, 17, 15, 11, 38, 39, 4, 16, 14, 30,

          22, 12, 33, 20, 2, 8, 24, 3, 34, 7, 19, 37, 36, 26, 31, 28, 1,

          18, 13, 23, 6, 32, 10}
```

```
In[72]:=  cities = Transpose[{data1,data2}];
          cities[[Append[route,First[route]]]];
          Show[Graphics[{Line[%],{PointSize[0.02],Map[Point,cities]}}]];
```

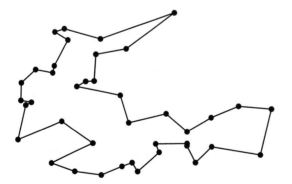

```
In[73]:=  Uninstall["willyloman"]
```

```
Out[73]=  willyloman
```

Jet-setting salesperson

As our final example, we consider the case where the salesperson is traveling world-wide. This example demonstrates the symbiotic relationship that can be forged between

Mathematica and C.

We begin by loading real data on cities and the world-plotting package:

In[74]:=
```
Needs["Miscellaneous`CityData`"];
Needs["Miscellaneous`WorldPlot`"];
```

We can use the graphics objects of countries to provide a background for the path of our salesperson:

In[75]:=
```
background = WorldPlot[World, WorldBorders -> None,
                WorldBackground -> GrayLevel[0.7]];
```

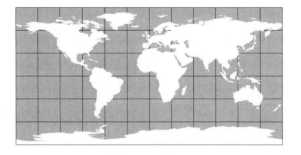

The city data give positions in terms of longitudes and latitudes. We need to write a function that computes the distance between two cities from this information. In the *Numerical Recipes* anneal program, there is a distance function called ALEN that achieves this aim. Its current definition is for a flat two-dimensional surface:

```
#define ALEN(a,b,c,d) sqrt((a-b)*(a-b)+(c-d)*(c-d))
```

This is just Pythagoras' theorem. For coordinates on a sphere, the formula is slightly trickier:

```
#define ALEN(a,b,c,d) acos(sin(a)*sin(b)+cos(a)*cos(b)*cos(fabs(d-c)))
```

This is the only change that we need to make to the source code, the rest is just manipulating the city data. First, we use a function to convert a degrees, minutes, and seconds angle into radians:

In[76]:=
```
rads[city_String] := N[Pi/180*Map[ToDegrees, CityData[city][[1,2]]]]
```

Next, we make a list of all the cities in the database (there are 120), and we group them with their longitude and latitude information:

In[77]:=
```
citylist = CityData[CityPosition];
```

To convert the data into a form to send via MathLink, we create a list of {*longitude, latitude*} pairs in units of radians:

In[78]:=
```
salespersondata = Map[rads,citylist];
```

We shall just send the first 40 cities — that is, first alphabetically — to the C code:

```
In[79]:=  temp = Transpose[Take[salespersondata,40]];
          tempx = temp[[1]];
          tempy = temp[[2]];
In[80]:=  Install["globalsales", LinkMode -> Connect];
          route = salesperson[tempx,tempy]
Out[80]=  {26, 18, 35, 6, 32, 25, 22, 19, 4, 10, 28, 3, 2, 30, 27, 9, 24, 33,

           31, 20, 11, 23, 34, 38, 40, 36, 7, 14, 13, 37, 29, 21, 1, 12, 5,

           39, 15, 8, 16, 17}
```

This list contains the order in which the cities should be visited. Now, we want to include this route on the world plot. We shall color the points cyclically using the Hue function, as in Section 6.6:

```
In[81]:=  pos[i_] := ToMinutes[ CityData[ citylist[[i]] ][[1,2]] ]

          dots = Map[ Point, Map[pos,route]];
          colors = Map[ Hue[(#-1)/40.0]&, Range[40] ];
          lights = Table[ {PointSize[0.02],colors[[i]],dots[[i]]},{i,40}];

          path = {Thickness[0.003],Dashing[{0.005,0.005}],
                  Line[Map[pos,Append[route,First[route]]]]};
In[82]:=  Show[
          {background,
           WorldGraphics[lights],
           WorldGraphics[path]}];
```

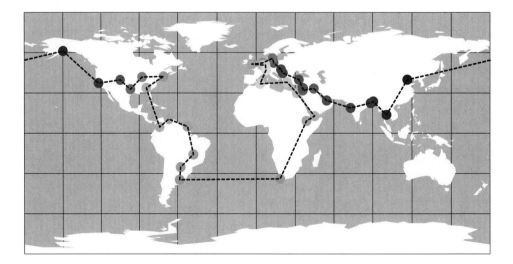

```
In[83]:=  Uninstall["globalsales"];
```

14.4 Summary

In this chapter, we have looked at a three-stage plan that can be taken to increase the efficiency of a *Mathematica* program. The first stage is to choose a sensible implementation for functions. Because of the wide range of high-level commands that are offered by *Mathematica*, it is easy to write code without considering the underlying actions that *Mathematica* must take to carry out these commands. This oversight frequently leads to redundant calculation. Even when you use sensible algorithms, *Mathematica* may be considerably slower than languages like C and FORTRAN. To alleviate this problem, you should use the internal compilation facility (stage 2) and/or farm out calculations to a C program using the MathLink communication language (stage 3). These facilities are particularly useful for simple repetitive tasks.

Case Studies

Robust Regression: An Application of *Mathematica* to Data Analysis

You may have used the Fit function. Chapter 4 gave a useful overview of Fit, the latter's extension in the LinearRegression package, and the generalization to models nonlinear in parameters in the NonlinearFit package. The principle behind these models is a common underlying mathematical principle: Given data and a list of variables, we use a standard least-squares algorithm to define a fitted model. Least-squares estimation is one of the most familiar, and one of the most abused, techniques. It is implemented by almost all statistics programs and is used with little regard for whether it is applicable. The method can give delightfully nonsensical results when misapplied. This chapter explores an alternative technique by the use of *Mathematica*.

15.1 Fit and Its Problems

Let's remind ourselves of how Fit works. In what follows, bear in mind that *Mathematica* can do regression on several independent variables. However, to keep the discussion simple, we shall consider only linear and polynomial regression in one variable.

First, we generate a set of linear and polynomial data with a bit of random noise:

```
In[1]:=    lindata = Table[{x, 2 + x + 0.1*Random[ ]}, {x, 0, 5, 0.5}]
Out[1]=    {{0, 2.07015}, {0.5, 2.5751}, {1., 3.03024}, {1.5, 3.59585},

           {2., 4.08751}, {2.5, 4.51491}, {3., 5.04377}, {3.5, 5.59416},

           {4., 6.02285}, {4.5, 6.55283}, {5., 7.0627}}
In[2]:=    quaddata = Table[{x, 2 + x + 0.2 x^2 + 0.1*Random[ ]},
           {x, 0, 5, 0.5}]
```

Out[2]=   {{0, 2.02707}, {0.5, 2.59193}, {1., 3.2178}, {1.5, 4.04814},

{2., 4.83606}, {2.5, 5.78329}, {3., 6.86172}, {3.5, 7.98935},

{4., 9.27872}, {4.5, 10.5569}, {5., 12.0443}}

Then, we determine the equations of the best least-squares fit to these data:

In[3]:=   linfit = Fit[lindata, {1, x}, x]

Out[3]=   2.06799 + 0.996444 x

In[4]:=   quadfit = Fit[quaddata, {1, x, x^2}, x]

Out[4]=
$$2.02896 + 1.01865 \ x + 0.196404 \ x^2$$

We have invented a standard command that allows us to overlay a plot of a function onto a plot of data:

In[5]:=
```
plotfit[fn_, data_] :=
Module[{minind, maxind, mindep, maxdep},
minind = Min[Transpose[data][[1]]];
maxind = Max[Transpose[data][[1]]];
mindep = Min[Transpose[data][[2]]];
maxdep = Max[Transpose[data][[2]]];
Plot[fn, {x, Floor[minind], Ceiling[maxind]},
AxesOrigin -> {0, 0},
PlotRange -> {Min[0, Floor[mindep]], Ceiling[maxdep] + 1},
Evaluate[Epilog -> {PointSize[0.03], Map[Point, data]}]]]

plotfit[linfit, lindata];
```

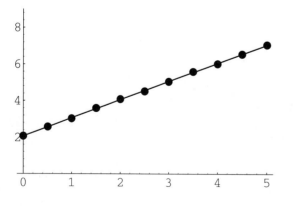

In[6]:=   plotfit[quadfit, quaddata];

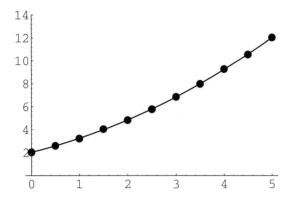

So far, so good, but consider what happens when the data contain an outlier or two. Let's perturb both data sets by moving two of the points off the main trend:

```
In[7]:=   badlindata = lindata;
          badlindata[[5]] = {2, 7};
          badlindata[[11]] = {5, 1};
          badquaddata = quaddata;
          badquaddata[[5]] = {2, 15};
          badquaddata[[11]] = {5, 1};

          badlinfit = Fit[badlindata, {1, x}, x]
```

Out[7]= $3.29188 + 0.392335\ x$

In[8]:=   `badquadfit = Fit[badquaddata, {1, x, x^2}, x]`

Out[8]= $0.425541 + 5.82375\ x - 1.00238\ x^2$

In[9]:=   `plotfit[badlinfit, badlindata];`

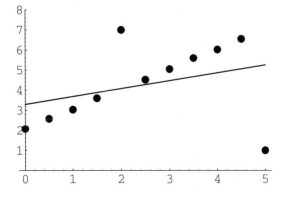

In[10]:= `plotfit[badquadfit, badquaddata];`

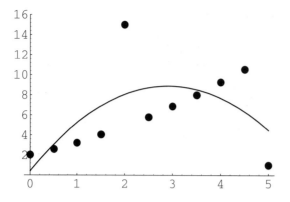

In both cases, we see that the fit has been considerably disturbed by the presence of errors or outliers. There are several ways to avoid this problem. If the data are two-dimensional, as in the previous examples, we can make scatter plots to isolate the difficult points and perhaps can remove the latter from the analysis. A study of the residuals can identify points off the main trend and can indicate points suitable for removal. However, in general, isolating rogue points may be difficult. If the data are multidimensional, we cannot do a simple scatter plot to spot bad points. If outliers do exist, they disturb the least-squares fit, so the residual of a good point may be larger than that of a bad point. This phenomenon can wreak havoc with automatic outlier-detection systems.

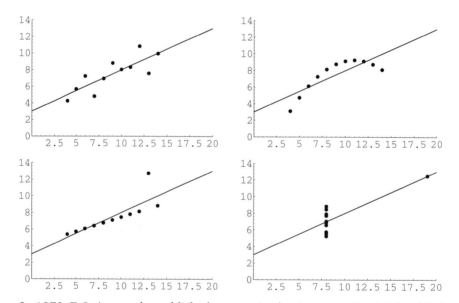

In 1973, F. J. Anscombe published a paper in the *American Statistician* [1] that highlighted the importance of graphs in statistical analysis. We have recreated his plots with *Mathematica*. The four data sets shown above have the same regression line ($y = 3 + x/2$) and several other identical statistical parameters (for instance, standard error of slope and correlation) — they are exactly the same apart from the residuals. These graphs have become well known; for example, they are featured in E. R. Tufte's book, *The Visual Display of Quantitative Information* [24]. The upper-left graph is the standard case, whereas the upper-right graph illustrates that a linear model does not describe polynomial data adequately. The two lower graphs are simple illustrations of the inadequacy of a standard least-squares fit in certain situations.

We should remember that the method of least squares is limited in applicability. In the standard implementation (the one that is programmed into most packages), the independent variables must be free of noise or errors, and, most important, the errors in the dependent variable must be independently and identically distributed. Under these circumstances, least squares gives the best estimate among all possible linear unbiased estimators; see *Applied Regression Analysis* [16]. For least squares to have the status of a maximum-likelihood estimator, the errors in the dependent variables must be independently and identically normally distributed.

The problem with the normal distribution is that the tails die off quickly. It is this property that causes an outlier to disturb the fit so significantly. Sometimes, people consider using a two-sided exponential distribution as the error distribution. If you follow the process of constructing the maximum-likelihood estimator, you obtain the method of *least absolute deviation*, in which you minimize the sums of the absolute deviations, rather than their squares.

When there are errors in the independent variables, standard least squares is plain wrong. The literature in medicine, finance, and most other applied disciplines is littered with regressions of noisy variables on other noisy variables without regard for the fact that such analysis leads to a biased estimate of the slope. If you have a feel for the relative variances of the errors in the independent and dependent variables, then you can construct an improved estimator [16]. In the absence of such information, it is difficult to proceed with confidence.

Another approach altogether is based on *robust regression*. A whole industry is devoted to this topic. A text that we have found useful is *Robust Regression and Outlier Detection* by P. J. Rousseeuw and A. N. Leroy [17]. Rousseeuw and Leroy note that the least-absolute-deviation method, which has been known since the late nineteenth century, is less sensitive than is the least-squares method to outliers in the y-direction. However, it too can be dragged off by just one outlier in the x-direction.

One of the most interesting alternative robust methods is called, instead of least squares, *least median of squares*. Suppose that you have a collection of n (x, y) points — say, (x_i, y_i) for $i = 1, ..., n$ — and you wish to choose a line $y = a + bx$ to fit the data. In standard least-squares regression, we minimize the sum

$$\sum_{i=1}^{n}(y_i - a - bx_i)^2$$

whereas, for example, in least-absolute-deviation regression, we minimize the following sum:

$$\sum_{i=1}^{n}|(y_i - a - bx_i)|$$

With least-median-of-squares regression, the idea is to choose a and b such that the median of the list

$$(y_1 - a - bx_1)^2, \ (y_2 - a - bx_2)^2, \ (y_3 - a - bx_3)^2, \ \ldots, \ (y_n - a - bx_n)^2$$

is minimized. This condition is easier to state geometrically than is the least-squares condition. In least-median-of-squares regression, we are trying to choose the narrowest vertical strip that contains one-half of the data.

15.2 Least Median of Squares

For some time, we have been interested in various types of data analysis, especially in financial and engineering applications. We have gone through several stages of prototyping *Mathematica* algorithms to deal with regression, and although the code we present here certainly could benefit from further development, we believe that both the results and the methods by which they are obtained are sufficiently interesting to form the basis for a discussion in this text.

Our initial objective is to implement the least-median-of-squares method for simple two-dimensional linear regression. First, we must establish a conceptual algorithm. In fact, the known method is crude, but it is easy to state.

We consider all the lines that join a pair of points in the data. For each line, we calculate a and b, and we pick the pair that overall yields the least median of squares. This procedure is computationally intensive, especially in high dimensions. However, we are defining our starting point as this algorithm, and our goal is to implement the latter. Some researchers claim this search method finds the solution in two dimensions; see the book by Rousseeuw and Leroy [17].

Our implementation will use the Median function, which we define now:

```
In[11]:=  Median[list_] := Sort[list][[(Length[list]+1)/2]] /;
              OddQ[Length[list]]

          Median[list_] :=
            Block[{s, n},
              s = Sort[list] ;
              n = Length[list] ;
              (s[[n/2]] + s[[n/2 + 1]]) / 2
            ] /; EvenQ[Length[list]]
```

The function that we aim to construct should take as its argument a list of (x, y) pairs and the name of the independent variable, usually x. Its output should be the equation of a straight line.

15.2.1 Conceptual Approach: Two Dimensions

We wish to define a module that accomplishes the following:

1. Works out the length of the data.
2. Defines all the lines between pairs of points by creating a list, each element of the form $\{\{x_m, y_m\}, \{x_n, y_n\}\}$. Note that $\{x_m, y_m\} = data_m$.

3. For each line in step 2, calculates the slope b and intercept a, a list of the squared deviations of all the points from the line, and the median of this list.
4. Creates and sorts a further list, where each element has the form { *Median, a, b* }.
5. Picks the first element of this sorted list and outputs $a + bx$.

Here is a simple attempt to effect these goals:

```
In[12]:=  lmsfita[data_, x_] := Module[{l, v, i, j, w, h, a, sl, dx},
          l = Length[data];
          v = Flatten[Table[{data[[i]], data[[j]]}, {i,1,l-1}, {j,i+1,l}], 1];
          w = Union[Map[
           Module[{dx},
           dx = #[[1, 1]] - #[[2, 1]];
           If[dx !=0,
           {(#[[1, 2]]-#[[2, 2]])/dx,
           (#[[1, 1]] #[[2, 2]] - #[[1, 2]] #[[2, 1]])/dx},
           {Infinity, #[[1, 1]]}]
           ]&, v]];
          h = Function[a,
          {Median[Map[
          (If[a[[1]] != Infinity,
          (#[[2]] - a[[1]] #[[1]] - a[[2]])^2,
          (a[[2]] - #[[1]])^2)&, data]],
           a[[1]], a[[2]]}];
          sl = Sort[Map[h, w]][[1]];
          If[sl[[2]] != Infinity, sl[[2]] x + sl[[3]],
          Print["x = ",sl[[3]]]]]]
```

Step 1 is taken care of in the calculation of l. Step 2 is treated by the definition of v. We shall explain this stage more carefully because its generalization to higher dimensions is interesting. Consider the following abbreviated module:

```
In[13]:=  DefineTheLines[data_] := Module[{l, v, i, j},
          l = Length[data];
          v = Flatten[Table[{data[[i]], data[[j]]},
              {i,1,l-1}, {j,i+1,l}], 1];  v]

          DefineTheLines[{{1, 2}, {2, 3}, {4, 5}}]
Out[13]=  {{{1, 2}, {2, 3}}, {{1, 2}, {4, 5}}, {{2, 3}, {4, 5}}}
```

Note that, by arranging that the iterators run from $i = 1$ to $l - 1$ and $j = i + 1$ to l, we have considered only distinct pairs of points. Given these lines, we calculate their slopes and intercepts by standard formulas. Suppose that we wish to define a line

$$y = \alpha + \beta x$$

through the points $(a_{11}, a_{12}), (a_{21}, a_{22})$. The difference in the x-coordinates of these points is $dx = a_{11} - a_{21}$, and the slope and intercept are

$$\beta = \frac{a_{12} - a_{22}}{dx}$$

$$\alpha = \frac{a_{11}a_{22} - a_{12}a_{21}}{dx}$$

The formulas are implemented in the calculation of w (step 3), where we turn the operation into a pure function and map it onto our list of lines (taking special care with lines of infinite slope). We take the union of the resulting list of (*slope, intercept*) pairs to remove any duplicates. We accomplish the rest of step 3 by applying the function h to each pair. The result is a triplet (*median residual, slope, intercept*) for each line. We perform step 4 by sorting the resulting list of these triples with respect to their first elements (a useful default property of Sort) and placing in s1 the triple with the smallest median. The slope and intercept components of s1 are used to define the output function, completing step 5. Throughout the analysis, we treat infinite slope in a special way, defining the residuals by squared horizontal distance.

Let's see how this module works:

```
In[14]:=  lmslinfit = lmsfita[badlindata, x]
```

```
Out[14]=  2.07015 + 0.988176 x
```

```
In[15]:=  plotfit[lmslinfit, badlindata];
```

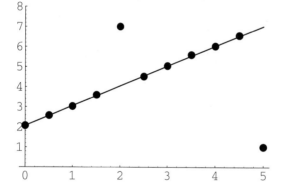

Just to check that we have forced the other Anscombe case (this check is not central to our discussion since it is a consequence of our special treatment of infinite slope, rather than of the least-median-of-squares algorithm), we evaluate:

```
In[16]:=  vertdata = {{1, 1}, {1, 2}, {1, 3}, {4, 5}};

         lmslinfit = lmsfita[vertdata, x]

         x = 1
```

15.3 Higher Dimensions

Now, how about multiple or polynomial regression using least median of squares? These cases are more subtle. For example, we do not know in advance how many dimensions we will need. Instead of considering all lines connecting two points in the plane, we must consider hyperplanes through various subsets of points. The construction of a suitable Table loop to define these hyperplanes is possible, provided that we understand the quirks in the way that Table operates. We shall discuss this construction shortly.

While considering the issue of higher dimensions, we happened to buy the book *Implementing Discrete Mathematics* by S. Skiena [20]. Although our interest in graph theory was limited to certain applied forms of combinatorial optimization, the graphic on the cover of this book suggested that the text could be useful. In fact, Skiena's methods removed two of the obstacles to using our more general regression package.

The aim, in the abstract, is to take a set (or a list, in *Mathematica* jargon) and to construct from it all distinct subsets of a given length. Why do we wish to do this? If we consider every line that joins a pair of points in a data set, we are effectively generating the length-2 subsets of this set. Similarly, when we perform quadratic regression, we need to determine all subsets of length 3.

We shall consider two different methods for determining subsets. One is a procedural approach that uses a Table construction; the other is iterative. This example is a good illustration of different *Mathematica* programming techniques, as well as the computational advantage of the procedural approach! (We will happily retract this comment on performance if you can provide a more cunning approach that improves the timings contained herein!) The first method that we implement is the iterative approach.

The following construction was developed by S. Skiena [20]. We are fortunate that (in Version 2.0 or later of *Mathematica*) the entire functional content is included in the package DiscreteMath`Combinatorica`:

```
In[17]:=  KSubsets[l_List,0] := { {} }
          KSubsets[l_List,1] := Partition[l,1]
          KSubsets[l_List,k_Integer?Positive] := {l} /; (k == Length[l])
          KSubsets[l_List,k_Integer?Positive] := {}  /; (k > Length[l])
          KSubsets[l_List,k_Integer?Positive] :=
              Join[Map[(Prepend[#,First[l]])&, KSubsets[Rest[l],k-1]],
                  KSubsets[Rest[l],k]]
```

KSubsets takes two arguments. The first is the set (or list) l, and the second is a non-negative integer that gives the length of the subsets that we require. If this length is 0, then *Mathematica* will return an empty list. If the length is 1, then we will obtain a list of subsets containing precisely one element each:

```
In[18]:=  KSubsets[{1, 2, 4, 3}, 1]
```

```
Out[18]=  {{1}, {2}, {4}, {3}}
```

Similar simple cases apply for subsets with lengths approaching or equal to that of the set. Now consider a general intermediate case, where we are generating all length-k subsets (k-subsets) of n elements. The operation is defined recursively. At the first step, we note that either the k-subset contains the first element of the supplied list or it does not. If it does, we can generate the subset by prepending this first element to each $(k-1)$-subset of the other $(n-1)$ elements. We perform this operation by mapping the Prepend function onto the $(k-1)$-subsets of the rest of the set. The other case is when the subset does not contain the first element. KSubsets considers both cases and joins the two lists of subsets that are generated. At each stage in this recursive calculation, either the size of the set or the size of the subset diminishes, and eventually one of the endpoint cases is encountered.

KSubsets is an elegant example of recursive programming. We can visualize its operation easily by constructing a set of points in the (x, y) plane:

```
In[19]:=  Vertices = Table[{Cos[2 Pi i/20], Sin[2 Pi i/20]}, {i, 1, 20}];
          Show[Graphics[{
          {Thickness[0.002], RGBColor[0, 0, 1], Map[Line, KSubsets[Vertices, 2]]},
          {PointSize[0.03], RGBColor[1, 0, 0], Map[Point, Vertices]}},
          AspectRatio -> 1]];
```

While we are discussing combinatorics, we shall define a function to generate random permutations. This function will be useful because it is computationally expensive to consider all lines through pairs of points in two dimensions — or, worse still, all hyperplanes through a cloud of points in several dimensions. We shall instead generate a random permutation of the lines or planes and shall consider a fraction of them that is large enough to allow us to obtain an accurate result.

In fact, Skiena has also defined a function that generates a random permutation of the first n integers. Here the idea is to create a set of pairs consisting of a random real number and an integer, to sort the set according to the random number, and then to pull out the integers again:

```
In[20]:=  RandomPermutation[n_Integer?Positive] :=
          Map[Last, Sort[Map[({Random[], #})&, Range[n]]]]

          myperm = RandomPermutation[5]
```
```
Out[20]=  {4, 3, 1, 2, 5}
```

```
In[21]:=  mylist = {a, b, c, d, e};
          mylist[[myperm]]
```

```
Out[21]=  {d, c, a, b, e}
```

Although this function is sufficient to solve the problem of coding the multiple regression, you may be interested to see how we eventually dealt with the problem by using a Module based on Table. We need to construct the iterator list on the fly because we do not know in advance how many independent variables will be used. Various attempts to do this construction and to feed the result through to Table persuaded us that we had to allow a slightly more flexible syntax in Table for the iterators:

```
In[22]:=  Unprotect[Table];
          Table[expr_, {l__List}] := Table[expr, l];
          Protect[Table];
```

Furthermore, we had to appreciate that Table has the attribute HoldAll, so if we construct an iterator list and simply substitute it into Table, it will not be recognized in its evaluated form. The solution to this confusion is to force the evaluation with Evaluate. The complete procedural analogue of KSubsets is given by the following Module, where we define a function PSubsets, making use of the redefined Table:

```
In[23]:=  PSubsets[l_List, n_Integer?Positive] :=
          Module[{itlist, expr, a},
          a[0] = 0;
          itlist =
              Table[{a[j], a[j-1] + 1, Length[l] + j - n}, {j, 1, n}];
          expr = Table[l[[Array[a, {n}]]], Evaluate[itlist]];
          expr = Flatten[expr, n-1]] /; (n <= Length[l])

          mylist = {a, b, c, d, e};
          PSubsets[mylist, 2]
```

```
Out[23]=  {{a, b}, {a, c}, {a, d}, {a, e}, {b, c}, {b, d}, {b, e}, {c, d}, {c, e},

          {d, e}}
```

How do the procedural and iterative methods compare for speed? Linear regression through to fourth-order polynomials requires subsets of dimension 2 through 5. The following comparisons are based on data sets of length 10 and 20. They indicate that the procedural approach is slightly more efficient. This finding is perhaps surprising because Table creates some redundant nesting of lists that we must subsequently flatten. Our experience is entirely consistent, however, with remarks made by S. Wolfram about the internal representation of lists; see [27], pp. 249–250.

```
In[24]:=  averes[data_] := Sum[Timing[KSubsets[data, n];][[1]], {n, 2, 5}]/
                           Sum[Timing[PSubsets[data, n];][[1]], {n, 2, 5}];

          {averes[Range[10]], averes[Range[20]]}
```

```
Out[24]=  {1.1, 1.10106}
```

At last, we present the code for our multiple-regression function. We happen to have used the iterative subset method. Basically, the first step is to transform the problem to that of multivariate linear regression. Then, we use KSubsets to generate the relevant hyperplanes. If the thoroughness parameter is less than 1, only a subset of the hyperplanes is considered. Solve is used to determine the equations of these hyperplanes, all the deviations are calculated, and the hyperplane corresponding to the least median is selected! (Note that there is no need to enter the comments as well as the code; these are intended to assist in your understanding only.)

```
In[25]:=  Fitlms[data_List, fns_List, vbls_List, thoroughness_:1] :=
          Module[{makelinear, lineardata, vlen, flen, calcmedian,
          aa, hyperplane, hyperplanes, numplanes, eqn, solver, solns,
          coeffs, sl},
          vlen = Length[vbls]; flen = Length[fns];

          (* makelinear takes a function list like {1,x,x y}, together with a
             variable list~--- in this instance {x,y}~--- to create the function
             {1,#1, #1 #2, #3}& *)

          makelinear = Evaluate[Join[
          fns /. Table[vbls[[i]] -> Slot[i], {i, 1, vlen}],
            {Slot[vlen + 1]}]]
              ]&;

          (* now we generate all hyperplanes, see how many there are and take a
             random subset if thoroughness < 1 *)

          lineardata = Apply[makelinear, data, 1];
          hyperplanes = KSubsets[lineardata, flen];
          numplanes = Length[hyperplanes];
          hyperplanes = If[thoroughness < 1,
          Take[hyperplanes[[RandomPermutation[numplanes]]],
          Ceiling[thoroughness*numplanes]],
           hyperplanes];

          (* eqn takes a hyperplane and constructs the relevant linear equations to
             determine the associated values of the parameters  *)

          coeffs = Array[aa, flen];
          eqn = Function[hyperplane,
          Dot[coeffs, Drop[hyperplane, -1]] ==
          Last[hyperplane]];

          (* now construct the parameters for all the hyperplanes chosen above *)

          solver = coeffs /. Solve[Map[eqn, #], coeffs]&;
          solns = Flatten[Map[solver, hyperplanes], 1];

          (* finally for each hyperplane, the median-square-deviation is computed,
```

and the hyperplane for which this is a minimum is returned *)

```
calcmedian = Function[coeffset,
{Median[Map[(Last[#] - Dot[coeffset, Drop[#, -1]])^2&,lineardata]],
coeffset}];
sl = Sort[Map[calcmedian, solns]][[1]];
Dot[sl[[2]], fns]]
```

In[26]:=   `lms = Fitlms[badquaddata, {1, x, x^2}, {x}, 0.2]`

Out[26]=
$$2.02707 + 1.0341\ x + 0.19126\ x^2$$

In[27]:=   `plotfit[lms, badquaddata];`

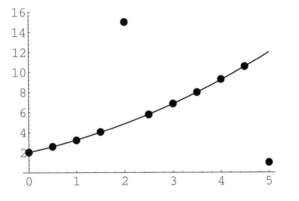

Work on this application is continuing. In the multidimensional case, we have not dealt with singular situations, and we have made no great attempt to optimize the procedures that we have used. However, one clear case where we can speed up the program is by not calculating a large number of redundant hyperplanes when we are using only a low thoroughness parameter. Thus far, we have first applied KSubsets and then taken a random subset of the resulting large set. This approach does have the advantage that we are sure about the meaning of the thoroughness parameter. However, we can consider just generating a fraction of random hyperplanes directly by gathering collections of points. The Combinatorica package contains the necessary function RandomKSubset, which is necessary to implement this modification:

In[28]:=   `RandomKSubset[n_Integer,k_Integer] := RandomKSubset[Range[n],k]`

```
RandomKSubset[set_List,k_Integer] :=
Module[{s=Range[Length[set]],i,n=Length[set],x},
set [[ Sort[ Table[
x=Random[Integer,{1,i}];
{s[[i]],s[[x]]} = {s[[x]],s[[i]]};
s[[i]],
{i,n,n-k+1,-1}
]]]]]
```

Given this capability, we add a method parameter to Fitlms. Method 1 (default) uses our original scheme, whereas method 2 makes use of the new approach:

```
In[29]:=  Fitlms[data_List, fns_List, vbls_List,
              thoroughness_:1, method_Integer:1] :=
          Module[{makelinear, lineardata, vlen, flen, calcmedian,
          aa, hyperplane, hyperplanes, numplanes, eqn, solver, solns,
          coeffs, sl},
          vlen = Length[vbls]; flen = Length[fns];
          makelinear =
          Evaluate[Join[ fns /. Table[vbls[[i]] -> Slot[i], {i, 1, vlen}],
              {Slot[vlen + 1]}]
              ]&;
          lineardata = Apply[makelinear, data, 1];
          datano = Length[lineardata];
          numplanes = datano!/(flen! (datano-flen)!);
          If[method == 1,
              hyperplanes = KSubsets[lineardata, flen];
              hyperplanes = If[thoroughness < 1,
              Take[hyperplanes[[RandomPermutation[numplanes]]],
              Ceiling[thoroughness*numplanes]],
                  hyperplanes],

              (* method 2 *)
              hyperplanes = Table[RandomKSubset[lineardata,flen],
                              {thoroughness*numplanes}]
              ];
          coeffs = Array[aa, flen];
          eqn = Function[hyperplane,
          Dot[coeffs, Drop[hyperplane, -1]] ==
          Last[hyperplane]];
          solver = coeffs /. Solve[Map[eqn, #], coeffs]&;
          solns = Flatten[Map[solver, hyperplanes], 1];
          calcmedian = Function[coeffset,
          {Median[Map[(Last[#] - Dot[coeffset, Drop[#, -1]])^2&,lineardata]],
          coeffset}];
          sl = Sort[Map[calcmedian, solns]][[1]];
          Dot[sl[[2]], fns]]
```

The following timing comparisons make the potential advantage of the new technique obvious. Note that there is no guarantee that method 2 searches exactly a fraction *thoroughness* of the possible hyperplanes because its choices may not be distinct. This shortfall is not an issue for small thoroughness; however, in principle, we would have to take infinitely many samples to get thoroughness 1 with method 2.

Let's compare the two techniques for various data sets and values of the thoroughness parameter:

```
In[30]:=  Timing[Fitlms[badquaddata, {1, x, x^2}, {x}, 0.2,2]]
Out[30]=
          {12.7833 Second, 2.02707 + 1.0112 x + 0.196517 x }
```

In[31]:= `Timing[FitlmS[badquaddata,{1, x, x^2},{x},0.2,1]]`

Out[31]=
$$\{12.5 \text{ Second}, 2.02707 + 0.985117 \text{ } x + 0.206949 \text{ } x^2 \}$$

Nothing in it! What about a larger data set?

In[32]:= `big = Table[{x, 2 + x + 0.2 x^2 + 0.1*Random[ ]},`
`{x, 0, 15, 0.5}];`

`Timing[FitlmS[big, {1, x, x^2}, {x}, 0.01,2]]`

Out[32]=
$$\{20.65 \text{ Second}, 1.99421 + 1.02354 \text{ } x + 0.198589 \text{ } x^2 \}$$

In[33]:= `Timing[FitlmS[big, {1, x, x^2}, {x}, 0.01,1]]`

Out[33]=
$$\{41.4333 \text{ Second}, 2.01987 + 1.01056 \text{ } x + 0.199412 \text{ } x^2 \}$$

So, working at low thoroughness and with large data sets, the advantage is beginning to show!

15.4 Summary

In this chapter, we have learned that it is easy to implement a new algorithm within *Mathematica*. The presence of powerful built-in functions such as Solve, the iterative capabilities of the system, and the extent to which graphics are integrated means that we can get answers from this approach and can test them quickly through visualization. The answers are both good and bad for the type of data analysis problems that we have been considering. In cases where the data are normal but where there may be odd errors, the approach yields valuable insight and prevents errors. In other applications — specifically, in time-dependent work — where we have not had data errors, but where we are looking for subtle changes in regression slope, the approach is so robust that a change in the most recent point does not alter the slope! It is not, therefore, a universally better method: It is a useful addition to the set of available tools.

Transform Calculus

This chapter takes an elementary look at applications of *Mathematica* to topics in transform calculus. We shall consider basic topics in transform theory and examine a few of the graphics commonly used in control applications.

16.1 The Calculus Packages

The version of *Mathematica* that we are considering is Version 2.1 or later. The advantage of this version (compared to 2.0 and older versions of *Mathematica*) is that it contains as standard new versions of a number of packages that are useful to control applications. We shall investigate the contents of these packages in turn.

16.1.1 Dirac Delta-Functions Package

We load the `Calculus`DiracDelta`` package in the usual way:

```
In[1]:=    Needs["Calculus`DiracDelta`"]

In[2]:=    $ContextPath

Out[2]=    {Calculus`DiracDelta`, FE`, Global`, System`}
```

We can find out what new functions have been added in the usual way:

```
In[3]:=    ?Calculus`DiracDelta`*
```

```
DiracDelta          SimplifyUnitStep   ZeroValue
SimplifyDiracDelta  UnitStep
```

The delta function and step function behave in the usual way:

```
In[4]:=    Integrate[DiracDelta[x - a] f[x], {x, -Infinity, Infinity}]

Out[4]=    f[a]

In[5]:=    D[UnitStep[x - a], x]

Out[5]=    DiracDelta[-a + x]
```

The `ZeroValue` option to `UnitStep` gives us a way to specify the precise value at zero:

```
In[6]:=    Table[UnitStep[x, ZeroValue -> 0.5], {x, -3, 3}]

Out[6]=    {0, 0, 0, 0.5, 1, 1, 1}
```

16.1.2 Fourier Transforms

The *Mathematica* core kernel can already do numerical Fourier transforms and their inverses by using the Fourier and InverseFourier functions. Here we load the package, which does an analytical treatment:

In[7]:=   Needs["Calculus`FourierTransform`"]

The function FourierTransform takes three arguments. The first argument is the function to be transformed, expressed as a function of the second argument. The third argument is the variable that is to be used for transform space. For example, to take the Fourier transform of the function of t given by e^{-t^2/s^2} and to express the result in terms of a *Mathematica* transform variable w, we apply:

In[8]:=   FourierTransform[Exp[-t^2/s^2], t, w]

Out[8]=
```
              2
        Sqrt[Pi s ]
        - - - - - - - - - - -
           2   2
          (s   w )/4
        E
```

In[9]:=   InverseFourierTransform[%, w, t]

Out[9]=
```
              Pi                2
        Sqrt[--] Sqrt[Pi s ]
               2
             s
        - - - - - - - - - - - - - - - - - - - -
                  2   2
                 t /s
               E          Pi
```

In[10]:=   PowerExpand[%]

Out[10]=
```
              2   2
         -(t /s )
        E
```

In[11]:=   FourierTransform[DiracDelta[x], x, w]

Out[11]=   1

16.1.3 Laplace Transforms

Mathematica also has a package for handling Laplace transforms. We can load this package and use it in the same way as we did with Calculus`FourierTransform`:

In[12]:=   Needs["Calculus`LaplaceTransform`"]

In[13]:=   LaplaceTransform[Sin[2 t] Exp[-t], t, s]

```
Out[13]=        2
         - - - - - - - - - - - -
                   2
         4 + (1 + s)
```

```
In[14]:=  InverseLaplaceTransform[%, s, t]
```

```
Out[14]=  Sin[2 t]
          - - - - - - - -
             t
            E
```

```
In[15]:=  LaplaceTransform[UnitStep[t], t, s]
```

```
Out[15]=  1
          -
          s
```

16.2 Approaches to Solving a Differential Equation

Let's now try the standard series of steps that might be involved in solving a differential equation by the standard Laplace transform method. The idea is to transform the equation, to solve for the transform, and then to invert the transform to obtain the solution:

```
In[16]:=  Clear[F]
```

```
In[17]:=  eqntfm = LaplaceTransform[f''[t] + 2 f'[t] + f[t], t, s]
```

```
Out[17]=  -(s f[0]) + LaplaceTransform[f[t], t, s] +

            2
           s  LaplaceTransform[f[t], t, s] +

           2 (-f[0] + s LaplaceTransform[f[t], t, s]) - f'[0]
```

```
In[18]:=  lhs = eqntfm /. LaplaceTransform[f[t], t, s] -> F[s]
```

```
Out[18]=                    2
          -(s f[0]) + F[s] + s  F[s] + 2 (-f[0] + s F[s]) - f'[0]
```

```
In[19]:=  F[s_] = (F[s] /. Solve[lhs == 1/s, F[s]])[[1]]
```

```
Out[19]=                       2
            -1 - 2 s f[0] - s  f[0] - s f'[0]
          -(---------------------------------)
                          2    3
                     s + 2 s  + s
```

```
In[20]:=  fsoln[t_] := InverseLaplaceTransform[F[s], s, t]
```

```
In[21]:=  fsoln[t]
```

```
Out[21]=     -1 + f[0]    t (-1 + f[0] + f'[0])
          1 + --------- + ----------------------
                  t                 t
                 E                 E
```

```
In[22]:=   ffsoln[t_] := fsoln[t] /. {f[0] -> 0, f'[0] -> 0}

In[23]:=   ffsoln[t]
Out[23]=          -t     t
            1 - E     - --
                        t
                       E
```

16.2.1 Back in the Space Domain

Do not forget that *Mathematica* is capable of solving linear differential equations directly without resorting to transforms:

```
In[24]:=   DSolve[{f''[t] + 2 f'[t] + f[t] == 1, f[0] == A, f'[0] == B}, f[t], t]
Out[24]=                       t
                    -1 + A + E  - t + A t + B t
            {{f[t] -> ---------------------------}}
                                 t
                                E

In[25]:=   f[t] /. %
Out[25]=                  t
              -1 + A + E  - t + A t + B t
            {---------------------------}
                        t
                       E

In[26]:=   soln[t_] =  %[[1]] /. {A -> 0, B -> 0}
Out[26]=            t
            -1 + E  - t
            -----------
                 t
                E

In[27]:=   Simplify[ffsoln[t]/soln[t]]

Out[27]=   1
```

16.2.2 Analogous Numerical Techniques

The problems to be considered may not lend themselves to a transform description. If the problems are nonlinear in the space or time domain, you can seek a numerical solution by using NDSolve, which carries out a purely numerical solution:

```
In[28]:=   Clear[x, y, t]

In[29]:=   NDSolve[{x'[t] == y[t], y'[t] == -4.0 x[t] - 0.1 y[t] - 0.3 y[t]^2,
               x[0] == 1, y[0] == 0}, {x, y}, {t, 0, 10}]

Out[29]=   {{x -> InterpolatingFunction[{0., 10.}, <>],
               y -> InterpolatingFunction[{0., 10.}, <>]}}
```

In[30]:= `{x[2], y[2]} /. %`

Out[30]= `{{-1.08165, 1.96271}}`

In[31]:= `ParametricPlot[Evaluate[{x[t], y[t]} /. %%], {t, 0, 10},`
`PlotRange -> All]`

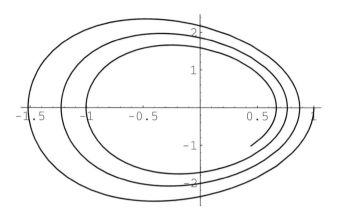

16.3 The Solution of Polynomial Equations

The transfer function of a linear system will contain various rational functions. Of particular interest is the denominator of the transfer function, whose zeros govern the stability of the solution in the time domain. Our example contained this polynomial:

In[32]:= `p[s_] := s + 2 s^2 + s^3`

Since this polynomial is only a cubic, and *Mathematica* can symbolically factorize polynomials of degree up to and including 4, we can use `Factor` to find its roots.

In[33]:= `Factor[p[s]]`

Out[33]=
$$s\,(1 + s)^2$$

The $s = 0$ root corresponds to the appearance of a constant in the solution, whereas the repeated root at $s = -1$ gives our exponential decay and t-times-decay behavior. More generally, we expect to generate some polynomial of higher degree for a more complex system. Consider the following:

In[34]:= `q = s^5 + 4 s^4 + 2 s^3 - 3 s^2 + s + a`

Out[34]=
$$a + s - 3 s^2 + 2 s^3 + 4 s^4 + s^5$$

Let's try to solve the associated quintic equation with a particular value of a:

In[35]:= `Solve[q == 0 /. a -> 1, s]`

Out[35]=
$$\{\text{ToRules}[\text{Roots}[s - 3 s^2 + 2 s^3 + 4 s^4 + s^5 == -1, s]]\}$$

This polynomial cannot be factorized explicitly. However, we can resort to a purely numerical approach:

```
In[36]:=  N[%]
Out[36]=  {{s -> -2.95302}, {s -> -1.69833}, {s -> -0.423943},

            {s -> 0.537649 - 0.425752 I}, {s -> 0.537649 + 0.425752 I}}
```

As usual, we extract the values by using the "given" qualifier:

```
In[37]:=  roots = s /. %
Out[37]=  {-2.95302, -1.69833, -0.423943, 0.537649 - 0.425752 I,

            0.537649 + 0.425752 I}
```

To visualize the roots, we convert this list of complex numbers into coordinates in the Argand plane:

```
In[38]:=  coords = Map[{Re[#], Im[#]}&, %]
Out[38]=  {{-2.95302, 0}, {-1.69833, 0}, {-0.423943, 0}, {0.537649, -0.425752},

            {0.537649, 0.425752}}
```

```
In[39]:=  ListPlot[coords, PlotStyle -> PointSize[0.02]]
```

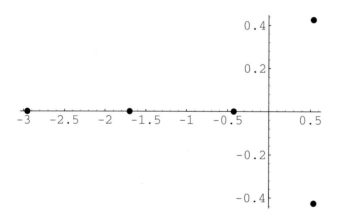

We can automate this process with a little programming:

```
In[40]:=  RootPlot[poly_] := Module[{roots, coords},
            roots = s /. NSolve[poly == 0]; coords = Map[{Re[#], Im[#]}&, roots];
            ListPlot[coords, PlotStyle -> PointSize[0.02],
            PlotRange -> {{-4, 1}, {-1, 1}}]]
```

```
In[41]:=  RootPlot[q /. a -> 1]
```

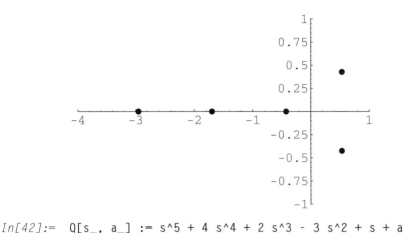

In[42]:= Q[s_, a_] := s^5 + 4 s^4 + 2 s^3 - 3 s^2 + s + a

To see how the roots depend on the parameter a, we can produce a movie by using the following:

In[43]:= Do[RootPlot[Q[s, a]], {a, -2, 10, 0.5}]

This elegant way of displaying the behavior of roots was first (as far as we know) given by Paul Abbott, formerly of Wolfram Research. We cannot, of course, show the film in this book, but we shall present another way of viewing the results in Section 16.4.1.

16.4 Control Theory Graphics

There are many simple graphics that are often associated with the transform description of linear systems. In this section, we present a few simple ideas that illustrate how *Mathematica* can be used to produce such graphics.

16.4.1 Root Loci Plots

The example that we considered in Section 16.3 gives a movie-style visualization of the roots of a polynomial. A core traditional approach in control theory is to plot trajectories. We can illustrate this approach with the same polynomial as the one we used before:

In[44]:= Q[s_, a_] := s^5 + 4 s^4 + 2 s^3 - 3 s^2 + s + a

First, we make a list of values of the roots for various values of the parameter a. Then, we reorganize this list into one that is suitable for plotting:

In[45]:= rootdata = Table[s /. NSolve[Q[s, a] == 0, s], {a, -2, 10, 0.1}];

In[46]:= trootdata = Transpose[rootdata];
coords = Flatten[Map[{Re[#], Im[#]}&, trootdata, {2}], 1];
Dimensions[coords]

Out[46]= {605, 2}

We show the results by an application of primitives:

```
In[47]:=  pts = Map[Point, coords];
          Show[Graphics[{PointSize[0.007], pts}], Axes -> True, Frame -> True]
```

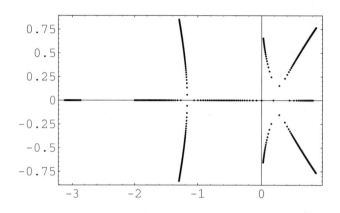

Traditionally, such loci are shown as continuous curves. In our plot, the dots are shown and the eye is left to join them up. We could consider asking the software to do this joining for us. However, in this case, we must appreciate that the solution of the polynomial equation is a list of (x, y) pairs and that the order of these pairs is not necessarily maintained as the parameter a varies. In other words, if we just join up the dots in the order that *Mathematica* generates them, then the wrong loci may be generated.

A more positive point, and one that we believe makes our plot superior, is that the separation of the dots communicates a sense of the dots' velocities and, hence, of the dots' sensitivities to the value of the parameter. This additional level of communication would be lost if we were to produce a simple set of curves for the root loci.

16.4.2 Complex Plane Graphics

Control theory often deals with functions of a complex variable. We can visualize such functions in several ways. Various types of contour drawing plots can be used to understand the structure of a complex function. We can consider the image, under a complex map f, of the lines $Re(z) =$ constant and $Im(z) =$ constant or of the lines $Mod(z) =$ constant and $Arg(z) =$ constant. We may also consider the opposite problem. Given f, we may seek to visualize the lines $Re(f) =$ constant and $Im(f) =$ constant, as well as the analogous polar forms. The first type of construction is handled by a package; the second type of construction is handled by the superposition of suitable contour plots.

Images of the coordinate grids

In this section, we consider how to construct the images of standard coordinate grids under a complex map. This case is handled by loading a package:

```
In[48]:=  Needs["Graphics`ComplexMap`"]
```

We shall arrange for all our plots to be drawn with a frame by default:

In[49]:= `SetOptions[Graphics, Frame -> True];`

In our first example, we consider the image of the polar coordinate grid. The function `PolarMap` takes three arguments. The first argument is the complex function that is to be applied. The second and third arguments are the ranges of the radial and angular coordinates, respectively. We can let *Mathematica* supply the step size, or we can supply it ourselves:

In[50]:= `PolarMap[Exp, {0, 1}, {0, 2 Pi, Pi/20}]`

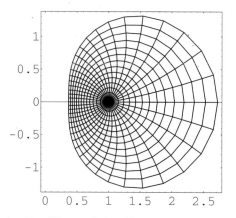

In[51]:= `CartesianMap[Exp, {-1, 1}, {-1, 1}]`

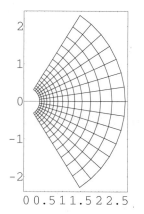

Contour plots and the Nichols chart

The opposite approach is straightforward to pursue. In this case, we wish to see the contours of some real function of a complex function, such as contours of the real and imaginary parts or contours of the modulus and phase. All we have to do is to draw a contour plot for each variable and to superimpose the results.

Here we illustrate one component of this construction for a function used in analysis of the complex error function, where we choose which values of the modulus should be shown in the plot (you may wish to experiment with the parameters of this plot):

```
In[52]:=  w[z_] := Exp[-z^2]*Erfc[-I*z]
```

```
In[53]:=  ContourPlot[Abs[w[x + I y]], {x, 0, 3.2}, {y, -2.2, 3},
          Contours -> {0.2, 0.3, 0.4, 0.5, 1, 2, 3, 4, 5, 10, 100},
          ContourShading -> False, PlotPoints -> 40]
```

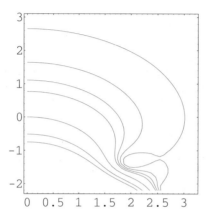

In Nichols charts, we wish to plot the contours of the magnitude and phase of a function of z against the magnitude and phase of z. Normally, logarithmic variables are used and are measured in dB. (In control theory, the dB value of a variable u is given by $20 \times \log_{10} u$.) The simplest type of function that we might consider for this construction, appropriate for a closed-loop frequency-response function of a unity-feedback system, is the following ratio:

```
In[54]:=  P[z_] := z/(1 + z)
```

We write z in polar form, apply P, and take the log magnitude and the argument of the result. We then take contour plots of each and superimpose the results. We can generate suitable contours manually or automatically as an alternative to using the defaults:

```
In[55]:=  contourlist = Table[k*10*Pi/180, {k, -18, +17}];
          contourlist = Join[contourlist, {-5 Pi/180, -2 Pi/180,
            2 Pi/180, 5 Pi/180}];
```

```
In[56]:=  absplot = ContourPlot[20*Log[10,
          Abs[P[10^(r/20) Exp[I v]]]],
          {v, -3*Pi/2, 0}, {r, -28, 32},
          ContourShading -> False,
          Contours -> {-24, -18, -12, -9, -6, -5, -4,
          -3, -2, -1, -0.5, 0, 0.25, 0.5, 1, 2, 3, 4, 6, 12},
          PlotPoints -> 60]
```

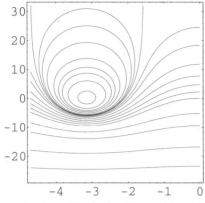

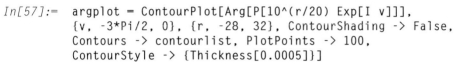

```
In[57]:=  argplot = ContourPlot[Arg[P[10^(r/20) Exp[I v]]],
          {v, -3*Pi/2, 0}, {r, -28, 32}, ContourShading -> False,
          Contours -> contourlist, PlotPoints -> 100,
          ContourStyle -> {Thickness[0.0005]}]
```

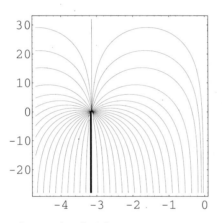

```
In[58]:=  Show[argplot, absplot]
```

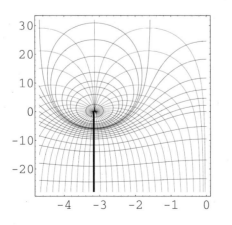

16.5 Summary

In this chapter, we have sampled several topics that arise in the treatment of linear differential equations. You can use transform methods analytically by loading the packages `Calculus`DiracDelta``, `Calculus`FourierTransform``, and `Calculus`LaplaceTransform``. These packages allow you to compute forward and inverse transforms and to construct solutions of differential equations by using transform techniques. Differential equations can also be solved by nontransform methods by using the `DSolve` and `NDSolve` functions. The transfer function of a linear system can be analyzed by using `Solve` to establish the locations of poles and zeros. You can visualize these points by constructing traditional root loci plots or by constructing *Mathematica* movies. Several other standard types of complex-plane graphics can also be constructed. In such applications, the `ContourPlot` function and the `Graphics`ComplexMap`` package are especially useful.

Time Series Analysis

This chapter takes a look at methods for investigating series of data, usually in the context of a time series. *Mathematica* contains a number of tools for traditional types of analysis, but, unlike many other off-the-shelf systems, its powerful programming environment allows the system to be extended rapidly to cope with novel techniques. This chapter is only an introduction to what is possible, and we shall focus mainly on reduction of series to other forms — for example, for the purpose of elimination of noise.

17.1 Working Data

In order to provide working data, we shall begin by creating three standard time series with different characteristics and saving the results to disk. You should create and save the data right away so that you can try out the various examples. The examples all assume that the data are in a file on disk, and they begin by retrieving the data with a ReadList statement. If you work through this chapter all in one session, you may skip saving the data to disk and then reading them in again; just use the lists that you have created within *Mathematica*.

17.1.1 A Random Walk

Our first series is a random walk generated as a cumulative sum of 2000 steps randomly distributed between −0.5 and 0.5:

```
In[1]:=    randata = NestList[(# + Random[] - 0.5)&, 0, 1999];
In[2]:=    rstream = OpenWrite["rseries.dat"];
           Do[
           Write[rstream, randata[[j]]],
           {j, 1, 2000}];
           Close[rstream]
Out[2]=    rseries.dat
In[3]:=    ListPlot[randata]
```

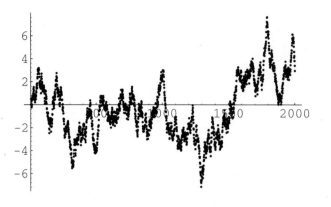

17.1.2 A Noisy Oscillatory Series

Our second series is generated by combining two sine waves with random noise:

```
In[4]:=   osccidata = Table[N[Sin[x] + Cos[Pi x] + 0.1*Random[]],
          {x, 0, 10, 0.01}];

In[5]:=   ostream = OpenWrite["oseries.dat"];
          Do[
          Write[ostream, osccidata[[j]]],
          {j, 1, 1001}];
          Close[ostream]

Out[5]=   oseries.dat

In[6]:=   ListPlot[osccidata]
```

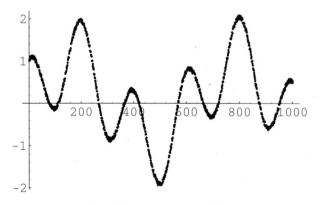

17.1.3 A Chaotic Series

Our third series arises from solving a well-known set of nonlinear differential equations — the Lorenz attractor — that have a chaotic solution:

```
In[7]:=    NDSolve[{x'[t] == -3 (x[t] - y[t]),
              y'[t] == -x[t] z[t] + 26.5 x[t] - y[t],
              z'[t] ==   x[t] y[t] - z[t],
              x[0] == 0.53755,
              y[0] ==-0.0071619,
              z[0] == 0.025124},
                 {x, y, z}, {t, 0, 10}, MaxSteps -> 1500]
```

The solution to these equations is a trajectory in three-dimensional space. We generate a single time series by discretizing the trajectory at 1000 points and projecting the result onto the vector $(1,1,-3)$:

```
In[8]:=    cdata = Table[Evaluate[x[(j-1)/100] + y[(j-1)/100] -
           3*z[(j-1)/100] /. %],
           {j, 1, 1001}];
```

```
In[9]:=    cdata[[1]]
```

```
Out[9]=    {0.455016}
```

```
In[10]:=   chaosstream = OpenWrite["cseries.dat"];
           Do[
           Write[chaosstream, cdata[[j,1]]],
           {j, 1, 1001}];
           Close[chaosstream]
```

```
Out[10]=   cseries.dat
```

```
In[11]:=   ListPlot[Flatten[cdata]]
```

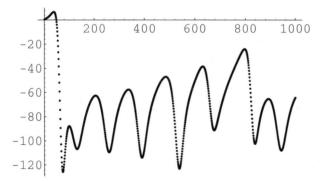

17.2 Moving Averages

The computation of a moving average is facilitated by a package whose function is simply to compute moving averages:

```
In[12]:=   Needs["Statistics`MovingAverage`"]
```

Let's analyze the random walk by using moving averages. We read in the data, and then we compute the average over 100 data points:

```
In[13]:=  madata = ReadList["rseries.dat", Number];

          MovingAverage

In[14]:=  averaged = MovingAverage[madata, 100];
```

We can do a ListPlot of the results and compare it with the original series. This analysis is often used in financial applications. However, the original data and our averaged list are now of two different sizes. The question arises, How should we fix the origin of the two lists? Usually, we want the last point of the time series to be plotted at the same time as the last point of the moving average. The ability to make this choice is not included in the package, but we can deal with it ourselves. We do so manually, making explicit use of the known lengths of the series:

```
In[15]:=  modmadata = Transpose[{Range[2000], madata}];
          modaveraged = Transpose[{Range[101, 2000], averaged}];

In[16]:=  ListPlot[modaveraged,
          PlotJoined -> True, PlotStyle -> {Thickness[0.002]},
          Epilog -> Map[{PointSize[0.001], Point[#]}&, modmadata]]
```

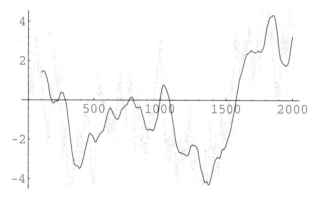

The following more automatic routine allows us to compute and display the data and a moving average all in one step. It assumes that the MovingAverage package has been loaded:

```
In[17]:=  CompareAverage[data_, n_] := Module[{moddata,
          modaveraged, inter},
          inter = MovingAverage[data, n];
          moddata = Transpose[{Range[Length[data]], data}];
          modaveraged = Transpose[{Range[n + 1, Length[data]],
          inter}];
          ListPlot[modaveraged,
          PlotJoined -> True, PlotStyle -> {Thickness[0.002]},
          Epilog -> Map[{PointSize[0.001], Point[#]}&, moddata]];
          modaveraged]

In[18]:=  mynewave = CompareAverage[madata, 200];
```

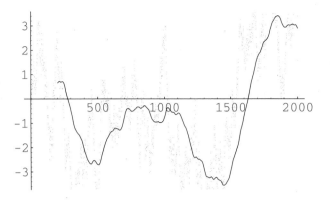

17.3 Fourier Analysis

As discussed in Chapter 5, Fourier techniques often can be used successfully to remove noise from periodic systems.

In[19]:=   `osccidata = ReadList["oseries.dat", Number];`

We now apply a Fourier transform and, to get an idea of the size of the noise, carry out a default list plot (the use of `PlotRange -> All` will show the peaks):

In[20]:=   `ListPlot[Abs[Fourier[osccidata]]]`

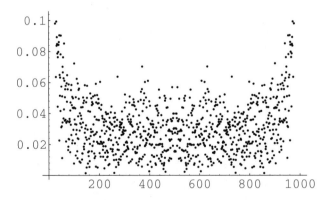

We then `Chop` the transform data at 0.1, transform them back, and `Chop` again to remove small imaginary numbers:

In[21]:=   `tran = Chop[Fourier[osccidata], 0.1];`

In[22]:=   `itran = Chop[InverseFourier[tran], 0.001];`

In[23]:=   `ListPlot[itran, PlotJoined -> True]`

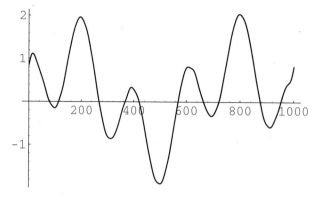

17.4 Spectral Analysis

As an example, we shall develop a package that does time series analysis by using modern ideas from dynamical system theory. This is an exciting subject, and the underlying mathematical ideas are involved. In brief, given a time series, we want to find out whether it comes from some low-dimensional dynamical system, such as some coupled ordinary differential equations, possibly with extraneous noise. We can answer this question by windowing the data and calculating the eigenvalues of a matrix constructed from these windowed data. Typically, there will be some eigenvalues that are much bigger than all the others, and the number of such eigenvalues is related to an estimate of the dimension of the system. For details and further references, see D. S. Broomhead and G. P. King [2] and the references contained therein.

Spectral analysis can be computationally expensive on real data sets. To save time, we will work with small data sets and small windows, bearing in mind that real applications require large data sets to provide reliable results.

The three files oseries.dat, rseries.dat, and cseries.dat contain saved data. If you have not already done so, read them in now:

```
In[24]:=  osccidata = ReadList["oseries.dat", Number];
          randata = ReadList["rseries.dat", Number];
          chaosdata = ReadList["cseries.dat", Number];

In[25]:=  osccidata[[1]]

Out[25]=  1.171450239516468341

In[26]:=  Length[osccidata]

Out[26]=  1001
```

Here is the typical result of basic *Mathematica* hacking to get the spectral analyis working. In the following discussion, we explain each command and show how it works on the oscillator data.

The first command defines the construction of a spectral matrix; it takes the name of the data, the size of the window, and a parameter governing how far into the data you wish to go. The ideas behind it are as follows. Let x_i denote a time series of data, with $i = 1, N$ and N large. We pick a window size n with $n \ll N$ and form the $N - n$ window vectors:

$$w_1 = (x_1, x_2, x_3, \ldots, x_n),$$

$$w_2 = (x_2, x_3, x_3, \ldots, x_{n+1}),$$

$$w_j = (x_j, x_{j+1}, x_{j+2}, \ldots, x_{j+n-1}).$$

We also build a matrix A composed of these window vectors as columns. Our spectral matrix is just $A^T A$. A crude attempt at a function to generate this matrix is given here:

```
In[27]:=  spectralmatrix[dat_, windowsize_, range_] :=
          Table[Sum[dat[[n + k - 1]] dat[[n + m - 1]],
          {n, 1, range - windowsize + 1}],
          {k, 1, windowsize}, {m, 1, windowsize}];
```

Let's compute an 8×8 matrix from the first 100 points:

```
In[28]:=  Timing[ mymatrix = spectralmatrix[osccidata, 8, 100]; ]
```

```
Out[28]=  {19.4333 Second, Null}
```

As you can see, the function as defined is slow — so slow, in fact, that if we were to use this function, we would be somewhat restricted in the length of data sets and the window size that we could realistically investigate.

There are two solutions to the timing problem. First, it is possible to code the function into C and to link the program in with MathLink; we did that in Chapter 14. To effect an improvement here, we note that many of the entries in `mymatrix` are similar:

```
In[29]:=  TableForm[ mymatrix, TableSpacing -> {1,1}]
```

```
Out[29]=  47.5039 46.914  46.3611 45.7787 45.0955 44.4519 43.7336 43.021
          46.914  46.5031 45.8767 45.3456 44.6811 44.051  43.3483 42.6565
          46.3611 45.8767 45.4315 44.829  44.2122 43.5982 42.9108 42.2341
          45.7787 45.3456 44.829  44.4078 43.7212 43.1519 42.4835 41.8209
          45.0955 44.6811 44.2122 43.7212 43.2092 42.5752 41.9461 41.3048
          44.4519 44.051  43.5982 43.1519 42.5752 42.119  41.4232 40.8218
          43.7336 43.3483 42.9108 42.4835 41.9461 41.4232 40.9059 40.2377
          43.021  42.6565 42.2341 41.8209 41.3048 40.8218 40.2377 39.7481
```

The first simplifying feature is that the matrix is symmetric. Making use of this fact will lead to a doubling in the speed. More important is a less obvious relation among the entries. The upper-left entry corresponds to the sum

$$M_{11} = \sum_{i=1}^{93} \text{oscill}_i^2,$$

whereas the second entry in the leading diagonal corresponds to the following sum:

$$M_{22} = \sum_{i=2}^{94} \text{oscill}_i^2.$$

Clearly, once M_{11} has been calculated, we can determine M_{22} using the result

$$M_{22} = M_{11} + \text{oscill}_{94}^2 - \text{oscill}_1^2.$$

There will be a great reduction in computation time if we eliminate all redundant calculations. We shall create a function specentry[i,j] that creates the (i,j)th entry of the spectral matrix. We now teach *Mathematica* about this function. First, the symmetry result:

```
In[30]:=   specentry[i_,j_,data_,range_,windowsize_,correls_] :=
              specentry[j,i,data,range,windowsize,correls] /; j > i
```

Next, we remove the redundant calculations by defining a recurrence relationship:

```
In[31]:=   specentry[i_,j_,data_,range_,windowsize_, correls_] :=
              specentry[i-1,j-1, data, range, windowsize, correls] +
              data[[range-windowsize+i]] data[[range-windowsize+j]]-
              data[[i-1]] data[[j-1]];
```

Eventually, we shall need to put an end to this recurrence before the recurrence depth is exceeded! We can end it by evaluating the values for the first column of the matrix. This first column is stored in the list correls:

```
In[32]:=   specentry[i_,1,data_,range_,windowsize_, correls_] :=
              correls[[i]];
```

Finally, we are in a position to define our new function that creates the one-dimensional correlation list and uses specentry to calculate the matrix. We can use RotateRight to perform the sum so long as we are careful with the end values (which we do not want to loop around to the front again):

```
In[33]:=   betterspec[data_,windowsize_,range_] := Module[{correls},
              data1 = Take[data,range];
              data2 = Join[Drop[data1,1-windowsize],
                           Table[0,{windowsize-1}]];
              correls = Table[ Apply[Plus, data1*RotateRight[data2,n-1]],
                           {n,1,windowsize}];
              Table[specentry[i,j,data1,range,windowsize,correls],
                    {i,1,windowsize},{j,1,windowsize}]]
```

This new function runs much faster:

```
In[34]:=   Timing[ mymatrix = betterspec[osccidata, 8, 100]; ]

Out[34]=   {2.55 Second, Null}
```

It also generates the same answer:

```
In[35]:=   TableForm[ mymatrix, TableSpacing -> {1,1}]
```

```
Out[35]=  47.5039 46.914  46.3611 45.7787 45.0955 44.4519 43.7336 43.021
          46.914  46.5031 45.8767 45.3456 44.6811 44.051  43.3483 42.6565
          46.3611 45.8767 45.4315 44.829  44.2122 43.5982 42.9108 42.2341
          45.7787 45.3456 44.829  44.4078 43.7212 43.1519 42.4835 41.8209
          45.0955 44.6811 44.2122 43.7212 43.2092 42.5752 41.9461 41.3048
          44.4519 44.051  43.5982 43.1519 42.5752 42.119  41.4232 40.8218
          43.7336 43.3483 42.9108 42.4835 41.9461 41.4232 40.9059 40.2377
          43.021  42.6565 42.2341 41.8209 41.3048 40.8218 40.2377 39.7481
```

Now we calculate the eigenvalues and eigenvectors — a normal system function:

```
In[36]:=  {vals, vecs} = Eigensystem[mymatrix]
Out[36]=  {{348.675, 0.706292, 0.0504754, 0.0944174, 0.0559154, 0.0895239,
           0.0766679, 0.0800658}, {{0.368127, 0.364584, 0.360596, 0.356614,
           0.351742, 0.347114, 0.341828, 0.336602},
          {-0.543087, -0.376198, -0.22866, -0.0540382, 0.104925, 0.264847,
           0.391265, 0.523531}, {-0.370986, 0.114259, 0.641295, 0.159095,
           -0.542566, -0.280914, 0.143343, 0.1375},
          {-0.330048, 0.49453, -0.471135, 0.55102, -0.23044, 0.206497,
           -0.11815, -0.105897}, {0.0873297, -0.398654, -0.0438817, 0.632778,
           0.225433, -0.474751, -0.292219, 0.263657},
          { 0.394105, -0.0623543, -0.117293, -0.109735, -0.548077, 0.265004,
           -0.370522, 0.554159}, {0.336421, -0.436421, -0.116459, 0.314074,
           -0.397897, 0.145267, 0.520497, -0.365802},
          {-0.216455, -0.338619, 0.393969, 0.172859, 0.090869, 0.609177,
           -0.449404, -0.26847}}}
```

With regard to our spectral analysis, the most important eigenvectors will be those that have the largest eigenvalues; we need to sort the eigenvectors in decreasing order of the size of the eigenvalues. To do this, we join each eigenvalue to its eigenvector, forming a list of entries (*eigenvalue, eigenvector*), sort these entries, and then untangle the eigenvalues from the eigenvectors:

```
In[37]:=  sorter[{evals_, evecs_}] :=
          Module[{bigset},
          bigset = MapThread[Join[{#1}, #2]&, {evals, evecs}];
          bigset = Reverse[Sort[bigset]];
          bigset = Transpose[Map[{First[#], Rest[#]}&, bigset]]]
```

```
In[38]:=  {svals, svecs} = sorter[{vals, vecs}]
```

```
Out[38]=  {{348.675, 0.706292, 0.0944174, 0.0895239, 0.0800658, 0.0766679,
           0.0559154, 0.0504754}, {{0.368127, 0.364584, 0.360596, 0.356614,
           0.351742, 0.347114, 0.341828, 0.336602},
          {-0.543087, -0.376198, -0.22866, -0.0540382, 0.104925, 0.264847,
```

```
        0.391265, 0.523531}, {-0.330048, 0.49453, -0.471135, 0.55102,
       -0.23044,  0.206497, -0.11815, -0.105897},
     { 0.394105, -0.0623543, -0.117293, -0.109735, -0.548077, 0.265004,
       -0.370522, 0.554159}, {-0.216455, -0.338619, 0.393969, 0.172859,
        0.090869, 0.609177, -0.449404, -0.26847},
     { 0.336421, -0.436421, -0.116459, 0.314074, -0.397897, 0.145267,
        0.520497, -0.365802}, {0.0873297, -0.398654, -0.0438817, 0.632778,
        0.225433, -0.474751, -0.292219, 0.263657},
     {-0.370986, 0.114259, 0.641295, 0.159095, -0.542566, -0.280914,
        0.143343, 0.1375}}}
```

We want a special plot to display the eigenvalues on a log scale (it is not necessary to use the package for plotting graphs with logarithmic tick marks):

```
In[39]:=  displayEval[u_List] :=
          ListPlot[Log[10, Reverse[Sort[u]]],
          AxesOrigin -> {0,0}, PlotStyle -> PointSize[0.02]]
```

```
In[40]:=  displayEval[svals]
```

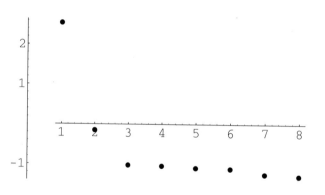

This plot reveals that there are two eigenvalues that are larger than the smaller ones in the background. We shall build a custom plot to see what the eigenvectors look like.

Note that the first eigenvector defines, in this case, what is almost the moving average, while the second looks at the rate of change:

```
In[41]:=  displayEvec[u_List] :=
          ListPlot[u, PlotRange -> {-1, 1},
          AxesOrigin -> {0, 0}, PlotStyle -> PointSize[0.02]]
```

In[42]:= displayEvec[svecs[[1]]]

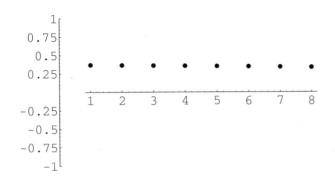

In[43]:= displayEvec[svecs[[2]]]

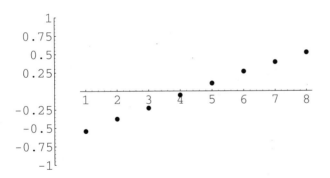

We can define a projection operator that projects the data onto the eigenvectors corresponding to the largest *n* eigenvalues:

In[44]:= dynamAve[vecs_, data_, range_, n_] :=
          Table[
            Sum[vecs[[k, 1]]*Sum[vecs[[k, u]] data[[i + u - 1]],
            {u, 1, Length[vecs]}],{k, 1, n}], {i, 1, range}]

In[45]:= projecttwo = ListPlot[dynamAve[svecs, osccidata, 900, 2],
          PlotJoined -> True]

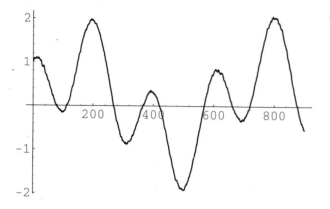

In[46]:=   `origplot = ListPlot[Take[osccidata, 900]]`

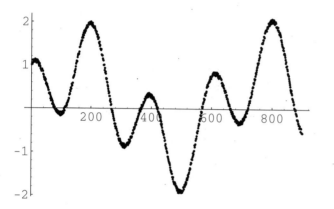

We can discuss these functions from several points of view. The projection has done a reasonable job of eliminating the noise from our data, but by using a different algorithm from the Fourier transform. At the same time, we have seen how to generalize the moving-average capability in a way that adapts itself to the data. These are the first steps in a powerful methodology for analyzing diverse types of time series, and it is possible to take the analysis much further by use of *Mathematica*. Our interest here is slightly different. Now that we have hacked up useful functions, the following question arises: How are we to package and tidy up this collection of functions?

We can consider creating a package and a context for all these functions. We have created this package in the usual way and have added a few wrinkles. Let's consider first how to import the package, which has the context called Spectral` (the functions in the package all begin with capital letters in order to avoid conflicts with the basic ones we have defined).

In[47]:=   `Needs["Spectral`"]`

We can check that the path now includes Spectral` and can inquire what functions are available within this context:

In[48]:= `$ContextPath`

Out[48]= `{Spectral`, Global`, System`}`

In[49]:= `?Spectral`*`

```
DisplayEval    Sorter
DisplayEvec    Spectral
DynamAve       Spectralmatrix
```

In[50]:= `?Spectralmatrix`

Spectralmatrix[data, windowsize, range] computes XT.X for X the matrix of
    windowed data

These functions work in the same way as the previous ones did. Let's try the random walk:

In[51]:= `newtest = Spectralmatrix[randata, 8, 1000];`

In[52]:= `Spectralmatrix[randata, 6, 5]`

Spectral::badrangeone: Range is smaller than Window Size!

In[53]:= `Spectralmatrix[randata, 6, 3000]`

Spectral::badrangetwo: Range is bigger than Length of data!

You may receive messages like the ones that we have just generated when you give a built-in function silly arguments. Messages can be given for your own functions quite easily, whether or not the latter are contained within a package.

Let's now use our package. We combine two of our new functions with the built-in eigensystem function in order to go straight to a plot of the eigenvalues. With this random walk, we see that there is really just one outstanding eigenvalue and that it corresponds to an approximate moving average (you should also try out these functions on the chaotic data series, as well as on your own real or synthesized data sets):

In[54]:= `esystem = Sorter[Eigensystem[newtest]];`

In[55]:= `DisplayEval[esystem[[1]]]`

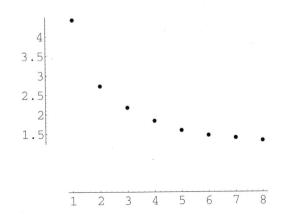

In[56]:= `DisplayEvec[esystem[[2, 1]]]`

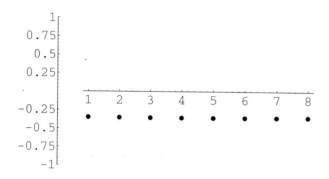

17.5 Summary

In the case study of this chapter, we looked at standard techniques for smoothing data in the time and frequency domains and then applied some recent ideas from time series analysis to large data sets. Our implementation of the ideas involved several important aspects of *Mathematica* programming. The issue of efficiency was addressed when we considered the construction of the spectral matrix; with an investment of thought concerning the coding of this function, we achieved considerable savings on time. When we were satisfied that our functions were operating sensibly, we grouped them together in a package (see the appendix to this chapter) and included error checks. Overall, we hope that the case study has demonstrated the progress from a conceptual idea through to a packaged and efficient implementation.

17.6 Appendix: Spectral Matrix Package

```
BeginPackage["Spectral`"]

Spectral::usage = "Spectral.m is a package for time series analysis."

Spectralmatrix::usage = "Spectralmatrix[data, windowsize,
range] computes XT.X for X the matrix of windowed data"

Sorter::usage = "Sorter[Eigensystem] sorts an
Eigensystem into decreasing order of eigenvalues"

DisplayEval::usage = "DisplayEval[uList] does a standard log
plot of eigenvalues in decreasing order"

DisplayEvec::usage = "DisplayEval[uList] does a standard plot to
show components of an eigenvector"

DynamAve::usage = "DynamAve[vecs, data, range, n] computes the
projection of the data onto the eigenvectors corresponding to
the n largest eigenvectors."
```

```
Begin["`Private`"]

(* Error messages for the exported objects *)

Spectral::badrangeone = "Range is smaller than Window Size!";
Spectral::badrangetwo = "Range is bigger than Length of data!";

(* Function Definitions *)

specentry[i,j,data,range,windowsize,correls] :=
  specentry[j,i,data,range,windowsize,correls] /; j > i

specentry[i,j,data,range,windowsize, correl] :=
    specentry[i-1,j-1, data, range, windowsize, correls] +
    data[[range-windowsize+i]] data[[range-windowsize+j]]-
    data[[i-1]] data[[j-1]];

specentry[i,1,data,range,windowsize, correls] :=
    correls[[i]];

Spectralmatrix[data,windowsize,range] := Module[{correls},
    data1 = Take[data,range];
    data2 = Join[Drop[data1,1-windowsize],
                 Table[0,{windowsize-1}]];
    correls = Table[ Apply[Plus, data1*RotateRight[data2,n-1]],
                 {n,1,windowsize}];
    Table[specentry[i,j,data1,range,windowsize,correls],
          {i,1,windowsize},{j,1,windowsize}]] /;
Length[dat] >= range && range >= windowsize;
Spectralmatrix[dat, windowsize, range]:=
Message[Spectral::badrangeone, range] /; range < windowsize;
Spectralmatrix[dat, windowsize, range]:=
Message[Spectral::badrangetwo, range] /; Length[dat] < range

Sorter[{evals, evecs}] := Module[{bigset},
bigset = MapThread[Join[{#1}, #2]&, {evals, evecs}];
bigset = Reverse[Sort[bigset]];
bigset = Transpose[Map[{First[#], Rest[#]}&, bigset]] ]

DisplayEval[uList] :=
ListPlot[Log[10, Reverse[Sort[u]]],
AxesOrigin -> {0,0}, PlotStyle -> PointSize[0.02]]

DisplayEvec[uList] :=
ListPlot[u, PlotRange -> {-1, 1},
AxesOrigin -> {0, 0}, PlotStyle -> PointSize[0.02]]

DynamAve[vecs, data, range, n] :=
Table[
  Sum[
    vecs[[k, 1]]*Sum[vecs[[k, u]] data[[i + u - 1]],
{u, 1, Length[vecs]}],
    {k, 1, n}],
{i, 1, range}]

End[]

EndPackage[]
```

Probabilistic System Assessment

This case study is designed to illustrate the utility of *Mathematica* as a tool for *probabilistic system assessment* (PSA). We shall examine one serious application of the *Mathematica* statistics packages and shall consider the construction of a package that makes use of other packages.

We wish to show how the statistical package supplied with *Mathematica* is already set up to provide most of the functionality of a PSA shell. By a *shell*, we mean a system for defining probabilistic inputs to a model, executing the model, and performing a statistical analysis of the output with appropriate numerical and visual tools. In this example, the models are all simple ones capable of rapid execution within *Mathematica* itself. It is possible to extend the processes described here to include execution of a model embodied in an external FORTRAN or C program by use of, for example, the MathLink communications standard.

Second, we wish to illustrate the usefulness of Wozniakowski's algorithm [28] for the efficient sampling of the points in a high-dimensional numerical integration in the context of a PSA. We demonstrate the value of *Mathematica* for prototyping such an algorithm and that algorithm's application to PSA. We shall make use of both the built-in functions and the powerful set of statistics packages supplied with *Mathematica*.

The utility of Wozniakowski's algorithm is not limited to PSA. There are many contexts in pure and applied mathematics where it is necessary to have an efficient algorithm for sampling points in a high-dimension integration region. Other potential applications are described by P. Yam [29].

Note that the algorithm under discussion uses an error concept different from the one that might be employed traditionally. Suppose that we wish to have an error for our numerical integration that is less than e. The question arises, How many integration sample points n are needed to guarantee such an error bound? The answer depends on how the question is posed or, as Wozniakowski phrases it, on the *setting*. We might consider the worst-case setting, with respect to a defined class of functions, or an average-case setting. In what follows, we are concerned with an average-case setting. For details, refer to H. Wozniakowski [28] and to the references contained therein.

18.1 Use of Statistics Packages

Consider a process that can be regarded as the application of a model to input data to produce output data. The input data may be uncertain, in which case one approach is to model them probabilistically. The input probability density functions can be sampled, and the model run for each sample. We then wish to generate information about the output — for example, its mean.

Most of the ingredients that we shall need are contained in the statistics packages in Version 2.1 of *Mathematica*. To load them, you could grab each of the packages individually, but do *not* do this:

In[1]:=
```
Needs["Statistics`ConfidenceIntervals`"]
Needs["Statistics`ContinuousDistributions`"]
Needs["Statistics`NormalDistribution`"]
Needs["Statistics`DataManipulation`"]
Needs["Statistics`DescriptiveStatistics`"]
Needs["Graphics`Graphics`"]
```

Instead, we can load them all at once:

In[2]:=
```
Needs["Statistics`Master`"]
Needs["Graphics`Graphics`"]
```

These two Needs statements import a significant portion of what we need. By way of illustration of the content of these packages, we add definitions for LogUniformDistribution, which happens to be absent. The following definitions will suffice for this discussion, although the analogous definitions in the ContinuousDistributions package contain more information for other distributions and present it in a more structured manner. The idea is to define the distribution as an abstract quantity, about which various questions may be asked. First, the definitions:

In[3]:=
```
LogUniformDistribution::usage =
"LogUniformDistribution[min, max] represents the
continuous loguniform distribution with endpoints
min and max with min < max. Log[10, x] of the random
variable x is uniformly distributed on
[Log[10, min], Log[10, max]]";

LogUniformDistribution/:
Domain[LogUniformDistribution[min_:1, max_:10]] :=
{min, max}

LogUniformDistribution/:
Random[LogUniformDistribution[min_:1, max_:10]] :=
10.0^Random[Real, {N[Log[10, min]], N[Log[10, max]]}]

LogUniformDistribution/:
PDF[LogUniformDistribution[min_:1, max_:10], x_] :=
With[{result = 1/(x*Log[max/min])},
If[NumberQ[N[result]],N[result],result]]
```

Now, let's ask a few questions and set up some obvious calculations:

In[4]:=   `?LogUniformDistribution`

LogUniformDistribution[min, max] represents the continuous
loguniform distribution with endpoints min and max with
min < max. Log[10, x] of the random variable x is uniformly
distributed on [Log[10, min], Log[10, max]]

In[5]:=   `q = LogUniformDistribution[3, 300]`

Out[5]=   `LogUniformDistribution[3, 300]`

In[6]:=   `PDF[q, x]`

Out[6]=

$$\frac{1}{x \ \text{Log}[100]}$$

In[7]:=   `Plot[PDF[q, x], {x, 3, 300}];`

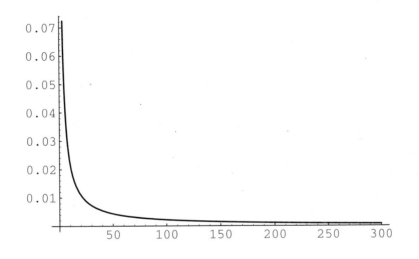

In[8]:=   `logunidata = Table[Random[q], {i, 1, 1000}];`

Using the `DataManipulation` package, we can bin the data:

In[9]:=   `binned = BinCounts[logunidata, {3, 300, 25}]`

Out[9]=   `{482, 139, 110, 50, 47, 49, 25, 23, 15, 26, 26, 8}`

With the `Graphics` package loaded, we can plot a histogram of the binned data:

In[10]:=   `plotted = BarChart[binned, PlotRange -> All];`

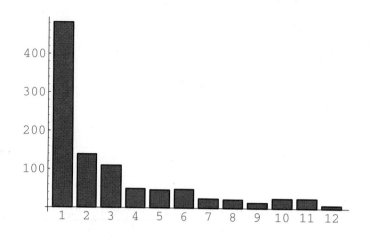

18.2 An Environmental Example: Migration

The utility of probabilistic assessment can be appreciated from a simple model. The one that we shall use models a simple arithmetical fluid-migration problem; it is borrowed from standard work in nuclear environmental safety. This problem was originally used to illustrate the SYVAC code for PSA [8], and we have considered it previously in a different context [19]. Here we consider a formula for the transit time T for groundwater flow in a sand medium (one-dimensional flow). We write down a simple arithmetical estimate for the transit time T (in years) in terms of the hydraulic gradient H, the hydraulic conductivity K (in meters per second), the porosity P, and the length L (in meters):

```
In[11]:=  T[L_, P_, H_, K_] := (3.1688*10^-8*L*P)/(H*K)
```

For a typical system in a sand medium, a hydrologist might recommend certain typical values for the variables, which we can substitute into our expression for T:

```
In[12]:=  T[100, 0.38, 0.01, 3*10^-5]
Out[12]=  4.01381
```

As a basis for the SYVAC calculations [8], it was assumed that an analysis of hydrology data led to a probabilistic technique, but with L fixed at 100 m. It was suggested that P was uniformly distributed between 0.35 and 0.4; that $\log(H)$ was uniformly distributed, with $0.003 < H < 0.03$; and that K was normally distributed, with appropriate truncation to ensure that it is positive, with mean 3×10^{-5}, and with standard deviation 10^{-5}. How can we implement this information in *Mathematica*? (Note that although our example is environmental — indeed, geological — the ideas developed here are applicable to many areas where uncertainty is present. Finance is one such application.)

18.2.1 *Mathematica* Implementation

We can proceed almost right away — all we need is a method to truncate the distributions. We consider resampling until a point within the desired range is obtained. If we are given a distribution and truncation points a, b, we set

```
In[13]:=   TruncateRandom[dist_, a_, b_] :=
           Module[{q},
           (Label[start];
           q = Random[dist];
           If[q < a || q > b, Goto[start], q])]
```

Next, we introduce substitution rules that encode all our knowledge and uncertainty about the input variables. These rules represent the programming meat of this example. For the particular problem at hand, we make use of *Mathematica* substitution rules to trivialize the question of how to replace deterministic variables by probabilistic ones:

```
In[14]:=   Randomizer :=
           {L -> 100,
            P -> Random[UniformDistribution[0.35, 0.40]],
            H -> Random[LogUniformDistribution[0.003, 0.03]],
            K -> TruncateRandom[NormalDistribution[3 10^-5, 10^-5],
            0.5 10^-5, 5.5 10^-5]}
```

To see how we use `Randomizer`, we first consider our formula in a deterministic context:

```
In[15]:=   T[L, P, H, K]
```
$$Out[15]= \frac{3.1688 \ 10^{-8} \ L \ P}{H \ K}$$

We then look at the formula in a probabilistic setting. Do not expect to get the same result here — in fact, enter this calculation three or four times:

```
In[16]:=   T[L, P, H, K] /. Randomizer
```
```
Out[16]=   9.39789
```

We have generated an answer based on random samples from the input distributions. To carry out a probabilistic analysis, we generate a `Table` of such values and feed it into the data analysis system provided. The following steps should be self-explanatory; they illustrate some of the commands from the statistics package:

```
In[17]:=   Tdata = Table[T[L, P, H, K] /. Randomizer, {i, 1, 1000}];

In[18]:=   LocationReport[Tdata]
```
```
Out[18]=   {Mean -> 5.93806, HarmonicMean -> 3.33312, Median -> 4.28237}
```
```
In[19]:=   DispersionReport[Tdata]
```
```
Out[19]=   {Variance -> 28.0627, StandardDeviation -> 5.29742,

           SampleRange -> 54.1939,  MeanDeviation -> 3.66984,

           MedianDeviation -> 2.30295,  QuartileDeviation -> 2.72483}
```
```
In[20]:=   Quartiles[Tdata]
```

```
Out[20]=  {2.40091, 4.28237, 7.85056}

In[21]:=  {Min[Tdata], Max[Tdata]}

Out[21]=  {0.848644, 55.0425}

In[22]:=  BinCounts[Log[10, Tdata], {-0.5, 2, 0.125}]

Out[22]=  {0, 0, 0, 9, 40, 83, 115, 116, 132, 111, 120,
           113, 87, 48, 13, 8, 2, 3, 0, 0}

In[23]:=  BarChart[%];
```

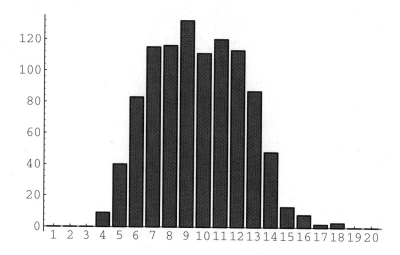

18.3 A Financial Example: Aggregation

Consider a trivial mythical sector of the equity market in the United Kingdom that contains two companies: Oxford System Solutions (OSS) and its arch rival, Cambridge System Solutions (CSS). OSS has exactly noss million shares and CSS has ncss million. (For simplicity, we assume that no changes in this number apply over the fiscal year 1993.) Between them, OSS and CSS dominate the mathematical-modeling sector of the equity market! We wish to compute the earnings per share of the mathematical-modeling sector for 1993. Both companies have December 1993 year ends, so no calendarization is needed.

Let's first pretend that there is a superb city analyst named Norma Lamarre who always makes her estimates of company earnings exactly right. The estimated earnings per share (eps) for the two companies for December 1993 are Eoss and Ecss. The aggregated earnings per share for the sector are then as follows:

```
In[24]:=  Emms[Eoss_, Ecss_, noss_, ncss_] :=
            (Eoss*noss + Ecss*ncss)/(noss + ncss)
```

The company accounts show that noss = 1,000,000 and ncss = 500,000. Norma claims that Eoss = 26.3 and Ecss = 21.1. The sector aggregate is therefore (in millions of shares):

```
In[25]:=  Emms[26.3, 21.1, 1, 0.5]

Out[25]=  24.5667
```

18.3.1 *Mathematica* Implementation

Norma resigns, and nobody can be found who can make such accurate predictions. However, as a result of careful analysis of consensus data of several analysts, as well as further inquiries, we decide that the earnings of the two companies might well be described by probability density functions. OSS is regarded as a highly stable company, with eps equally likely to be anywhere in the range 24 and 30, whereas CSS is less certain, with eps estimates between 5 and 50. We model these forecasts by uniform and loguniform distributions, respectively:

```
In[26]:=  Randomizer :=
          {noss -> 1,
           Eoss -> Random[UniformDistribution[24, 30]],
           Ecss -> Random[LogUniformDistribution[5, 50]],
           ncss -> 0.5}
```

To see how we apply `Randomizer` to our problem, consider our formula in a deterministic context:

```
In[27]:=  Emms[Eoss, Ecss, noss, ncss]

Out[27]=  Ecss ncss + Eoss noss
          ---------------------
                ncss + noss
```

Next, consider the probabilistic formula (reevaluate several times):

```
In[28]:=  Emms[Eoss, Ecss, noss, ncss] /. Randomizer

Out[28]=  21.9237
```

We aim to understand the behavior of Emms by sampling this formula many times:

```
In[29]:=  Edata = Table[Emms[Eoss, Ecss, noss, ncss] /. Randomizer,
          {i, 1, 1000}];

          LocationReport[Edata]

Out[29]=  {Mean -> 24.6591, HarmonicMean -> 23.9329, Median -> 23.6066}

In[30]:=  bindata = BinCounts[Edata, {15, 40, 2.5}]

Out[30]=  {0, 125, 285, 179, 148, 113, 86, 56, 8, 0}

In[31]:=  bins = Table[16.25 + 2.5 (n - 1), {n, 1, 10}]

Out[31]=  {16.25, 18.75, 21.25, 23.75, 26.25, 28.75, 31.25, 33.75, 36.25, 38.75}

In[32]:=  BarChart[bindata, PlotRange -> All, BarValues -> True,
          BarLabels -> Map[ToString, bins],
          DefaultFont -> {"Courier", 6}];
```

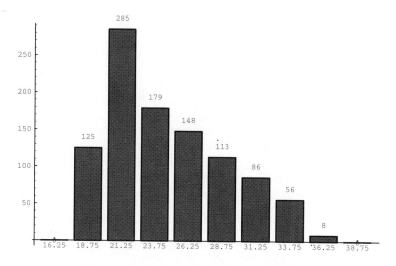

In this example, the whole problem could have been worked out analytically, but this numerical approach is valuable when applied to more realistic problems. As it turned out, Norma's estimate was close to the mean, but the standard deviation is now available as a measure of uncertainty, as are other details of the location report and a visualization of the distribution of results.

18.4 A More Structured Approach to PSA

How can we turn what we have developed into a more structured package? The package, which in our simple approach is called Prosysas, should be loadable in the usual way; the following assumes that a fresh session of *Mathematica* has been started, which we recommend you do. If you have the CleanSlate package, you can use that instead:

```
In[1]:=    CleanSlate[];
           Needs["Prosysas`"]
```

The ContextPath is now extended dramatically. You should check by evaluating the command:

```
In[2]:=    $ContextPath
```

```
Out[2]=    {Prosysas`, Graphics`Graphics`, Utilities`FilterOptions`,
             Statistics`NormalDistribution`, Statistics`NonlinearFit`,
             Statistics`MovingAverage`, Statistics`LinearRegression`,
             Statistics`InverseStatisticalFunctions`, Statistics`HypothesisTests`,
             Statistics`DiscreteDistributions`, Statistics`DescriptiveStatistics`,
             Statistics`DataManipulation`, Statistics`ContinuousDistributions`,
             Statistics`ConfidenceIntervals`, Statistics`Common`HypothesisCommon`,
             Statistics`Common`DistributionsCommon`, CleanSlate`, Global`,
             System`}
```

Information about what is in Prosysas can be obtained in the usual way, whether it came from the standard included packages or the new material:

```
In[3]:=    ?Prosysas`*

           LogUniformDistribution Prosysas          TruncateRandom
           MakeRandom

In[4]:=    T[L_, P_, H_, K_] := (3.1688*10^-8*L*P)/(H*K)

           ranset :=
           MakeRandom[T[L, P, H, K],
           {{L, 100}, {P, Random[UniformDistribution[0.35, 0.40]]},
           {H, Random[LogUniformDistribution[0.003,
            0.03]]}, {K, TruncateRandom[NormalDistribution[3 10^-5,
            10^-5], 0.5 10^-5, 5.5 10^-5]}}]

           ranset

Out[4]=    1.69653

In[5]:=    Tdata = Table[ranset, {i, 1, 1000}];
```

The prosysas package is included in the appendix at the end of this chapter.

18.5 Expectations and Volume Integration

A key output of a PSA is the expected result. This result and several quantities of interest are essentially expectations defined initially as volume integrals. In the sampling method in Sections 18.2–18.4, we have estimated these expectations by carrying out a random sample of integration points and summing the values of a function at those points.

To develop a simple working example to compare with the effects of sampling at Hammersley points, as is required by Wozniakowski's algorithm, we consider the function prod[x, y, z] = x y z, defined on the unit cube. We wish to know the expected value of this function if x, y, and z are all uniformly distributed on [0, 1]. The answer is 1/8, or 0.125.

Now consider how this problem would be treated in the context of PSA. We have three inputs, each of which is uniformly distributed on [0, 1], and we wish to calculate the expectation of

```
In[6]:=    prod[x_, y_, z_] := x y z
```

We produce the randomizing substitution rules as before:

```
In[7]:=    Randomizera :=
           {x -> Random[UniformDistribution[0.0, 1.0]],
            y -> Random[UniformDistribution[0.0, 1.0]],
            z -> Random[UniformDistribution[0.0, 1.0]]}
```

We generate a sample random value:

```
In[8]:=    prod[x, y, z] /. Randomizera

Out[8]=    0.181128
```

Next, we define a function that calculates the average for a given number of sample points, and we plot the result as a difference from the exact value 0.125:

```
In[9]:=    average[n_] := Mean[
             Table[prod[x, y, z] /. Randomizera, {i, 1, n}]];

           nvalues = {50, 50, 50, 250, 250, 250,
             500, 500, 500, 750, 750, 750};

           averages = Table[average[nvalues[[b]]], {b, 1, 12}];

           PsaIntegralData = ListPlot[Transpose[{nvalues, averages}],
           PlotStyle -> {PointSize[0.01]},
           PlotRange -> {0.09, 0.14},
           AxesOrigin -> {0, 0.125}];
```

18.6 Wozniakowski's Method and Hammersley Points

Wozniakowski's method [28] shows how to construct sample points for numerical integration. The proof that this new sampling method does not suffer from dimensional complexity is the theme of Wozniakowski's paper. Here we shall be concerned with using *Mathematica* to illuminate the method, to give a simple example, and to indicate how this type of sampling could enhance PSA.

Central to the construction of optimal sampling points is the construction of Hammersley points based on expansion of integers in powers of primes. Essentially, the location of the points is based on the expansion of an integer in base p_j, where p_j is the jth prime. We note first that the *Mathematica* built-in function IntegerDigits computes the digits of a number in a given base — for example, that of the jth prime — and that the Prime function generates the primes in an efficient fashion. We define a function a[k, j] that produces a list of the digits:

```
In[10]:=   a[k_Integer, j_Integer] := IntegerDigits[k, Prime[j]];
```

Thus, for example, if we write 38 in base 3, the second prime, we have

In[11]:= a[38, 2]

Out[11]= {1, 1, 0, 2}

since

$$38 = 1 \times 3^3 + 1 \times 3^2 + 0 \times 3^1 + 2 \times 3^0 .$$

We define the radical inverse function by replacing powers of p by inverse powers of p:

$$p^i \rightarrow \frac{1}{p^{i+1}}$$

Our code is as follows:

In[12]:=
```
phi[k_, j_] := Module[{b, len, pj},
    pj = Prime[j];
    b = IntegerDigits[k, pj];
    len = Length[b];
    Sum[b[[len - i]]/(pj^(i+1)), {i, 0, len-1}]]

phi[38, 2]
```

Out[12]=
58
--
81

This answer corresponds to the sum

In[13]:= 1/3^4 + 1/3^3 + 0/3^2 + 2/3

Out[13]=
58
--
81

In dimension d, we construct the Hammersley points as follows. Loosely, we define a sequence

$$u_k = \{\phi_{k,1}, \phi_{k,2}, \ldots, \phi_{k,d-1}\} , \quad k = 0, 1, \ldots, n$$

of $(d-1)$-dimensional points, with k running up to n, the number of sample points. In detail, we will let the u_k repeat with periodicity M (we shall define M soon; for now, and in some applications, we can ignore the periodicity issue since n is less than M). To this sequence, we adjoin a (nonperiodic) first coordinate k/n.

The sampling points defined by Wozniakowski are not quite the Hammersley points. The difference depends on precisely which form of the algorithm we adopt. Three forms are described by Wozniakowski. The first is most accurate, but it is not fully constructive. The second is more constructive, with slightly less (average) accuracy. The third algorithm is independent of the sample size and is even less accurate. In each of these cases, the number of sample points, n, needed to obtain an average error less than e is given by an incompletely defined formula. Wozniakowski conjectures that we should be able to write an approximate formula

$$n = A(d)\frac{1}{e}(\log \frac{1}{e})^{f(d)} ,$$

where $A(d)$ is independent of the error e and $f(d)$ is given by $(d-1)/2$, $(d-1)$, and d, respectively, for the three algorithms. The form of $A(d)$ is unknown. For now, we set the quantity $A(d)$ to 1 and work with the following basic numbers of sample points:

```
In[14]:=  Anzero[e_, d_] = Floor[(1/e)*(Log[1/e])^((d - 1)/2)];
          Bnzero[e_, d_] = Floor[(1/e)*(Log[1/e])^(d - 1)];
          Cnzero[e_, d_] = Floor[(1/e)*(Log[1/e])^d];
```

Next, we compute the periodicity of the sampling for $d = 3$:

```
In[15]:=  M[d_, n_] := (Product[Prime[i],
                {i, 1, d-1}])^Ceiling[N[Log[n]]]

          M[3, n]
```

```
Out[15]=  Ceiling[Log[n]]
          6
```

Since $\log 6 \approx 1.8$, we can write the previous result as $n^{1.8}$. In what follows, we will be working in dimension 3 initially, so we can ignore the cyclic aspects since $n << n^{1.8}$ for large enough n. For now, we consider the second algorithm. In this case, we obtain the integration sampling points by subtracting the coordinates of the Hammersley points from the vector with constant component unity: $(1, 1, 1, \ldots, 1)$. Thus, we define

```
In[16]:=  X[d_, n_] := Table[
            Which[m < 2, 1 - k/n,
            m > 1, 1 - phi[k, m-1]],
            {k, 1, n}, {m, 1, d}]
```

Let's see how many sample points are needed to get an average error of 0.1 with the second algorithm:

```
In[17]:=  n = Bnzero[0.1, 3]
```

```
Out[17]=  53
```

We can now generate the sampling points. An inspection of the resulting list provides insight into how the integration region is filled out:

```
In[18]:=  Short[S = X[3, 53], 4]
```

```
Out[18]=     52  1  2      51  3  1      50  1  8      49  7  5
          {{--, -, -}, {--, -, -}, {--, -, -}, {--, -, -},
             53  2  3      53  4  3      53  4  9      53  8  9

             48  3  2      47  5  7      46  1  4      45  15  1
           {--, -, -}, {--, -, -}, {--, -, -}, {--, --, -},
             53  8  9      53  8  9      53  8  9      53  16  9

             44  7  26                 3  45  11      2  13  56
           {--, --, --}, <<40>>, {--, --, --}, {--, --, --},
             53  16  27                53  64  81     53  64  81

              1  53  29           21  2
           {--, --, --}, {0, --, --}}
             53  64  81           64  81
```

Inspection of this table gives us a good idea of how the sampling proceeds to fill out the domain in a systematic and even fashion. Furthermore, we can visualize how these points fill out the unit cube:

In[19]:=   `Show[Graphics3D[Map[Point, S]]];`

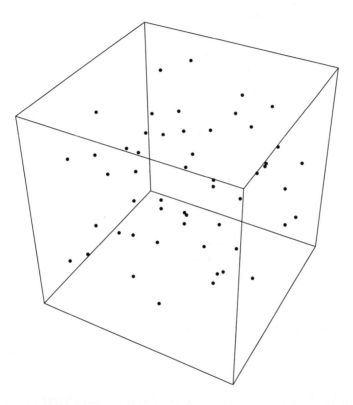

18.7 Efficient Integration

Suppose now that we have a function f that takes as its argument a list of d points in the unit hypercube. If we considered the function xyz in three dimensions, we would set

In[20]:=   `g[r_List] := r[[1]]*r[[2]]*r[[3]]`

We can define the Wozniakowski estimate (of the second kind) through the following formula

In[21]:=   `WozIntegral = N[Apply[Plus, Map[g, S]]/n]`

Out[21]=   `0.129815`

More generally, given a function f, with desired average error e, and an integration domain of the unit d-dimensional hypercube, we set

In[22]:=   `WozInt[f_, e_, d_] :=`

`Module[{n, S},`
`  n = Bnzero[e, d];`
`  S = X[d, n];`
`  {n, N[Apply[Plus, Map[f, S]]/n]}];`

WozInt returns a list of two numbers, consisting of the number of sample points and the estimate of the integral, computed by the second sampling method:

In[23]:=   `WozInt[g, 0.06, 3]`

Out[23]=   `{131, 0.127904}`

Let's make a table of values for different average errors:

In[24]:=   `wozdata = Table[WozInt[g, u, 3], {u, 0.02, 0.2, 0.02}]`

Out[24]=   `{{765, 0.125875}, {259, 0.126841}, {131, 0.127904},`

`{79, 0.128679}, {53, 0.129815}, {37, 0.129928},`

`{27, 0.131144}, {20, 0.131377}, {16, 0.13151},`

`{12, 0.128022}}`

We can compare these values with the sampled estimates established earlier:

In[25]:=   `ListPlot[wozdata, PlotJoined -> True,`
`PlotRange -> {0.09, 0.15},`
`AxesOrigin -> {0, 0.125},`
`PlotStyle -> {Thickness[0.001]},`
`Evaluate[Epilog -> {PointSize[0.01],`
`Map[Point, Transpose[{nvalues, averages}]]}]];`

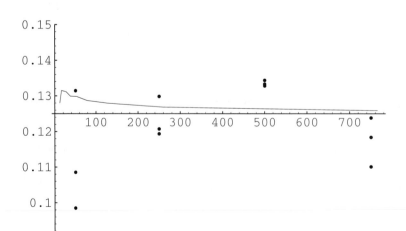

We could proceed to quantify the relative accuracy if it was important to do so. The lesson of this simple example is that the convergence of Wozniakowski's method is faster and less erratic than is that of the sampling method. Of course, we could write simpler and better deterministic algorithms based on standard methods like Simpson's rule, which would achieve better results for this particular example. The point is that Wozniakowski's algorithm suffers less from dimensionality as we increase the complexity — this feature, coupled with its reasonable convergence, is an indication of the algorithm's power.

18.8 Summary

In this chapter, we have demonstrated that *Mathematica* is a useful tool for PSA since it contains many of the necessary tools in its standard release; that *Mathematica* is a powerful method for prototyping new algorithms, such as Wozniakowski's sampling method; and that the construction of optimal sampling points through Wozniakowski's use of Hammersley points may make a valuable contribution not only to numerical methods, but also to PSA in particular.

This case study opens up two areas for further development. First, the basic use of *Mathematica* to investigate simple probabilistic models, as described here, could be expanded to a general, fast, and efficient workstation-based PSA system. Key requirements for further development include the ability to call external deterministic models (in C, for example) for the execution of complicated numerical models with probabilistic inputs, a complete list of distributions, and a good treatment of correlated sets of variables.

Wozniakowski's method is likely to be an active area of research in many fields of application. At the basic level, there are three forms of the algorithm, and the most accurate involves parameters that are not completely defined at present. These parameters are the extent to which Hammersley points are shifted and the quantity $A(d)$, which normalizes the relation between errors and numbers of sample points. Further work is needed on this subject to produce a more constructive method. Work on the relationship between the average error and that likely to be encountered in the integration of functions that typically arise in PSA is also needed. We are doing basic work on mapping PSA problems generally to the unit hypercube so that Hammersley point sampling is appropriate.

18.9 Appendix: Prosysas Package

Here is the text of the package `Prosysas` (note that the statistics packages are included in the `BeginPackage` statement to ensure that the contents of these included packages are available to the user):

```
BeginPackage["Prosysas` ","Statistics` Master` ",
            "Graphics` Graphics` "]

Prosysas::usage = "Prosysas.m is a prototype package for
probabilistic system assessment."

(* Usage Messages for exported  objects *)

LogUniformDistribution::usage =
 "LogUniformDistribution[min, max] represents the
```

```
            continuous loguniform distribution with endpoints
            min and max with min < max. Log[10, x] of the
            random variable x is uniformly
            distributed on [Log[10, min], Log[10, max]]"

TruncateRandom::usage = "TruncateRandom[dist, a, b]
produces a random sampling of dist truncated between a and b"

MakeRandom::usage = "MakeRandom[fn, {{x1, dist1}, {x2, dist2} ...}]
 produces a random sampling f with each variable xi replaced by
 a random sampling from disti"

Begin["`Private`"]

(* Function Definitions *)

LogUniformDistribution/:
Domain[LogUniformDistribution[min:1, max:10]] :=
       {min, max}

LogUniformDistribution/:
Random[LogUniformDistribution[min:1, max:10]] :=
10.0^ Random[Real, {N[Log[10, min]], N[Log[10, max]]}]

LogUniformDistribution/:
PDF[LogUniformDistribution[min:1, max:10], x] :=
With[{result = 1/(x*Log[max/min])},
If[NumberQ[N[result]],N[result],result]]

TruncateRandom[dist, a, b] :=
Module[{q},
(Label[start];
q = Random[dist];
If[q < a || q > b, Goto[start], q])]



MakeRandom[fn, vblesList] :=
fn /. Map[(((#[[1]] -> #[[2]])&), vbles]

End[]

EndPackage[]
```

Visualization of the Mandelbrot Set

The benefits of compilation are particularly dramatic when we consider operations of a similar type, such as simple numerical operations that must be performed many times. We can illustrate the improvements that can be achieved by considering the generation of fractals. You may have seen pictures of fractals, or possibly you have written code to generate them. To minimize the mathematics and to lower the likelihood of unfamiliarity, we shall work with the best-known fractal of all — the Mandelbrot set.

19.1 The Mandelbrot Set

We consider iteration of the map $z \rightarrow z^2 + c$ for complex numbers z, c. That is, we start with an initial value of z — say, z_0 — and c, and we apply this function over and over to z:

$$z_1 = z_0^2 + c$$

$$z_2 = z_1^2 + c$$

and so on. The pictures that you see on many book covers and, increasingly, on coffee mugs and the covers of investment magazines correspond to one or two common ways of visualizing this process. We obtain the Mandelbrot set by fixing a value of z_0 — say, zero — and considering, as c varies over the complex plane, how many iterations it takes before z_n is bigger than a certain threshold value. We shall look at the calculation of the Mandelbrot set and at its visualization in several ways. For simplicity, we will work with real variables so that z and c have real and imaginary components (for instance, cr and ci). The Mandelbrot set is discussed briefly in the Wolfram Research Technical Report on the *Mathematica* compiler [26], but the variables are treated as complex. In Section 19.3, we shall consider how to farm out some of the computation to C code by the use of MathLink. By restricting ourselves to real variables, it will be perfectly transparent that the algorithm we are using is the same, whether it is implemented in uncompiled *Mathematica* code, compiled *Mathematica* code, or externally compiled C.

First, we write a simple module to calculate, for given z_0 and c, how many iterations it takes for z to get beyond a disk of radius $\sqrt{10000}$. The number is capped at 100. (The threshold and cap value can be set at any number you like — these values have been chosen to create interesting pictures, with or without compilation, on machines with power from a 386/7 PC or 68030 Macintosh to a NeXTStation, 486 PC, or 68040 Macintosh.) Note the conversion to numerical types — without this, *Mathematica* may waste time doing symbolic exact calculations. This process is time-consuming as it is!

In[1]:=
```
IterationsToLeave[zr_, zi_, cr_, ci_] :=
Module[{cnt, nzr, temp, nzi, ncr, nci},
   nzr = N[zr]; nzi = N[zi]; ncr = N[cr]; nci = N[ci];
   For[cnt = 0,
      (nzr^2 + nzi^2 < 10000) && (cnt < 100), cnt++,
      temp = nzr^2  - nzi^2 + ncr;
      nzi = 2*nzr*nzi + nci; nzr = temp];
   cnt];
```

```
IterationsToLeave[0, 0, 1, 0.5]
```

Out[1]= 5

What we want to do is to show the number of iterations needed for various values of c. Roughly speaking, we want a table of the `IterationsToLeave` function and a `ListDensityPlot` with an appropriate coloring algorithm. Here is a first attempt:

In[2]:=
```
fractaldata = Table[IterationsToLeave[0, 0, x, y],
{x, -3.0, 1.0, 0.2}, {y, 0.0, 1.0, 0.2}];
ListDensityPlot[fractaldata, ColorFunction -> (Hue[#]&)];
```

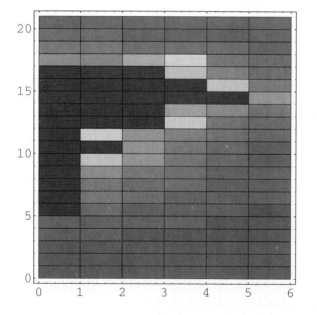

The result is disappointing — it took too long, has low resolution, and does not obviously look like anything that we have seen before. We use this illustration here to make the point that *Mathematica* does not get us past the problem of garbage in, garbage out. In fact, this plot is correct, but we need to work on it to get satisfactory results. We shall come back to the speed issue in a moment. The area to the left, approximately central vertically, is a crude representation of the interesting set, usually colored black. It is also up against the y-axis, rather than the x-axis, and the whole picture is distorted in scale. To fix the scales, we need to pass the real and imaginary c range to the plot routine in addition to the array. To fix the orientation, we need to swap the x and y lists in the Table command. To get the coloring right, we define a new coloring function. The following batch of commands does the job.

First, we calculate the iteration values for x and y. We obtain square pixels by using the same number of steps in the x-direction and y-direction:

```
In[3]:=  FractalM[zOr_, zOi_, {{ReMin_, ReMax_}, {ImMin_, ImMax_}}, steps_] :=
         {{{ReMin, ReMax}, {ImMin, ImMax}},
         Table[IterationsToLeave[zOr, zOi, x, y],
           {y, ImMin, ImMax, (ImMax - ImMin)/steps},
           {x, ReMin, ReMax, (ReMax - ReMin)/steps}]}
```

Next, we define a coloring function that assigns the color black to values of $c = 100$ and uses the Hue function otherwise:

```
In[4]:=  Colorit[x_] := If[x == 1, Hue[1, 1, 0], Hue[5*x/6]]
```

Finally, we define a plot routine that makes use of these new functions:

```
In[5]:=  fractalPlot[{{{ReMin_, ReMax_}, {ImMin_, ImMax_}}, matrix_}] :=
         ListDensityPlot[matrix,
         MeshRange -> {{ReMin, ReMax}, {ImMin, ImMax}},
         Mesh -> False, Frame -> False,
         PlotRange -> {1, 100}, AspectRatio -> Automatic,
         ColorFunction -> (Colorit[#]&)]
```

Let's recompute the same fractal using our new functions:

```
In[6]:=  fractaldata =
         FractalM[0.0, 0.0, {{-3.0, 1.0}, {0.0, 1.0}}, 8]
Out[6]=  {{{-3., 1.}, {0., 1.}}, {{4, 4, 100, 100, 100, 100, 100, 7, 5},

         {4, 4, 6, 9, 100, 100, 100, 8, 5}, {4, 4, 6, 8, 100, 100, 100, 8, 5},

         {4, 4, 5, 7, 11, 100, 100, 8, 5}, {4, 4, 5, 6, 8, 100, 100, 7, 5},

         {4, 4, 5, 6, 7, 23, 100, 7, 5}, {4, 4, 5, 5, 6, 9, 37, 6, 5},

         {4, 4, 5, 5, 6, 7, 11, 6, 5}, {4, 4, 4, 5, 5, 6, 100, 5, 5}}}}
```

```
In[7]:=  fractalPlot[fractaldata];
```

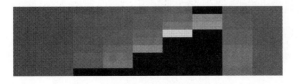

19.2 The *Mathematica* Compiler

So far, so good, but we need more speed to compute higher-resolution fractals that we can can be proud of. To accomplish the necessary speed, we use the compiler (see Chapter 14 for details about the compiler) on the calculation of the number of iterations to leave the disk. In the following code we have omitted the conversion to numerical types since the compile treats the inputs as numerical anyway:

In[8]:=
```
NITL = Compile[{zr, zi, cr, ci},
Module[{cnt, nzr, nzi, temp}, nzr = zr; nzi = zi;
  For[cnt = 0,
    (nzr^2 + nzi^2 < 10000) && (cnt < 100), cnt++,
    temp = nzr^2  - nzi^2 + cr;
    nzi = 2*nzr*nzi + ci; nzr = temp];
  cnt]]
```

Out[8]=
```
CompiledFunction[{zr, zi, cr, ci},

    Module[{cnt, nzr, nzi, temp}, nzr = zr; nzi = zi;

                      2      2
      For[cnt = 0, nzr  + nzi  < 10000 && cnt < 100, cnt++,

                  2      2
        temp = nzr  - nzi  + cr; nzi = 2 nzr nzi + ci; nzr = temp]; cnt],

      -CompiledCode-]
```

In[9]:=
```
FractalMC[z0r_, z0i_, {{ReMin_, ReMax_}, {ImMin_, ImMax_}}, steps_] :=
  {{{ReMin, ReMax}, {ImMin, ImMax}},
  Table[NITL[z0r, z0i, x, y],
  {y, ImMin, ImMax, (ImMax - ImMin)/steps},
  {x, ReMin, ReMax, (ReMax - ReMin)/steps}]}
```

The compilation yields a dramatic improvement. The following timings are first runs on a Macintosh Quadra at 25 MHz. First, here is the uncompiled function:

In[10]:=
```
Timing[fractalPlot[FractalM[0, 0, {{-3, 1}, {0, 2}}, 4]];]
```

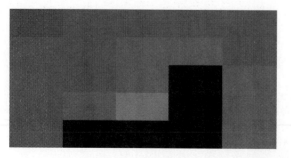

Out[10]=   `{5.56667 Second, Null}`

In[11]:= `Timing[fractalPlot[FractalM[0, 0, {{-3, 1}, {0, 2}}, 8]];]`

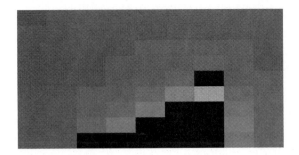

Out[11]= `{14.8 Second, Null}`

Now here is the compiled function:

In[12]:= `Timing[fractalPlot[FractalMC[0, 0, {{-3, 1}, {0, 2}}, 8]];]`

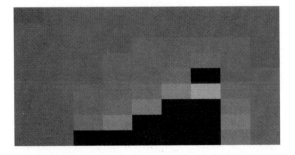

Out[12]= `{1.36667 Second, Null}`

The timings and the improvement will depend on your system, but this type of internal compilation can be used to great effect on any system with Version 2.0 or later of *Mathematica*.

19.3 Use of MathLink

If we want more speed, we can reap further benefit by linking *Mathematica* to other code. The details of this procedure take us into highly system-specific areas. First, in a UNIX environment, we can use the UNIX operating system to make calls from *Mathematica* to other programs and vice versa, and data can be passed between the two. This communication is achieved with low-level instructions.

Also on a UNIX system, on a Macintosh with System 7 and Version 2.1 of *Mathematica* or later, and under Windows 3.1, with Version 2.2.2 or later, high-level interprocess communication is possible by use of the MathLink communications standard. (See Chapter 14 for a detailed discussion of MathLink.)

In the MathLink system, we can write external C code, together with a MathLink template file. When this code is compiled, we can install the new functions. The following command does the job on a Macintosh if the external program dfractal has been started (if the program has not been started and *Mathematica* knows where to find it, you can omit the LinkMode -> Connect option):

In[13]:= Install["dfractal", LinkMode -> Connect]

Out[13]= LinkObject[dfractal, 1, 1]

In[14]:= ?FractalML

Global`FractalML

FractalML[a_Real, b_Real, {{c_Real, d_Real}, {e_Real, f_Real}}, g_Integer] := ExternalCall[LinkObject["dfractal", 1, 1], CallPacket[0, {a, b, c, d, e, f, g}]]

FractalML returns the table of iteration numbers, but without the preamble:

In[15]:= FractalML[0.0, 0.0, {{-3.0, 1.0}, {0.0, 2.0}}, 5]

Out[15]= {{4, 100, 100, 100, 5}, {4, 5, 8, 100, 5}, {4, 4, 5, 100, 5},

{4, 4, 5, 5, 4}, {3, 4, 4, 4, 4}}

In[16]:= FractalMLfull[zOr_, zOi_, {{ReMin_, ReMax_}, {ImMin_, ImMax_}}, steps_] := {{{ReMin, ReMax}, {ImMin, ImMax}}, FractalML[zOr, zOi, {{ReMin, ReMax}, {ImMin, ImMax}}, steps]}

In[17]:= FractalMLfull[0.0, 0.0, {{-3.0, 1.0}, {0.0, 2.0}}, 5]

Out[17]= {{{-3., 1.}, {0., 2.}}, {{4, 100, 100, 100, 5}, {4, 5, 8, 100, 5},

{4, 4, 5, 100, 5}, {4, 4, 5, 5, 4}, {3, 4, 4, 4, 4}}}}

In[18]:= Timing[fractalPlot[FractalMLfull[0.0,0.0,{{-3.0,1.0},{0.0,2.0}},8]]]

Out[18]= {0.8 Second, -DensityGraphics-}

Superficially, we have gained a factor of 2 over the internal compilation. However, note that the constant rendering time applies to both cases. Let's do a "meatier" example — with and without rendering:

In[19]:= Timing[FractalMC[0,0,{{-3,1},{0,2}},50];]

Out[19]= {14.3833 Second, Null}

In[20]:= `Timing[FractalMLfull[0.0,0.0,{{-3.0,1.0},{0.0,2.0}},50];]`

Out[20]= `{1.8 Second, Null}`

In[21]:= `Timing[fractalPlot[FractalMC[0.0,0.0,{{-3.0,1.0},{0.0,2.0}},50]]]`

Out[21]= `{33.4 Second, -DensityGraphics-}`

In[22]:= `Timing[fractalPlot[FractalMLfull[0.0,0.0,{{-3.0,1.0},{0.0, 2.0}},50]]]`

Out[22]= `{23.45 Second, -DensityGraphics-}`

So, now the production of the picture is dominated by rendering, rather than by computation. Let's produce our first "serious" picture!

In[23]:= `fractalPlot[FractalMLfull[0.0,0.0,{{-3.0,1.0},{0.0,2.0}},200]];`

19.4 Further Optimization with MathLink

How can we improve the speed even further? The rendering time now appears to be the dominant factor, and the question arises of how MathLink could be used to reduce this time. Our MathLink function is returning a list of iteration counts, and *Mathematica* is turning this list into an array of color directives and rendering the result. There is no reason why we cannot give the task of computing the color directives to our C code. The detailed code is given at the end of this chapter. Here we install a compiled C program rast, which contains a new definition of FractalML:

```
In[24]:=  Install["rast", LinkMode -> Connect]
```

```
Out[24]=  LinkObject[rast, 2, 2]
```

```
In[25]:=  ?FractalML
          Global`FractalML

          FractalML[a_Real, b_Real, {{c_Real, d_Real}, {e_Real, f_Real}}, g_Integer] :=
            ExternalCall[LinkObject["rast", 2, 2], CallPacket[0, {a, b, c, d, e, f, g}]]
```

```
In[26]:=  FractalML[0.0, 0.0,{{-2.0, 1.0},{-1.5, 1.5}}, 3]
```

```
Out[26]=  {{Hue[0.0333333333], Hue[0.0416666666667], Hue[0.033333333]},

          {RGBColor[0, 0, 0], RGBColor[0, 0, 0], Hue[0.0416666666666666667]},

          {Hue[0.0333333333], Hue[0.041666666667], Hue[0.0333333333]}}
```

We show these color directives as a RasterArray:

```
In[27]:=  Show[Graphics[RasterArray[%], AspectRatio -> 1]];
```

In short, we have carried out timing experiments and have found that on a Macintosh Quadra the overall time to compute a complex picture is reduced by a factor of 2 if we use this method of returning the color directives, rather than the number of iterations.

19.5 A Visit to MathMovies

With enough memory or a little patience, we can also use the capability developed in Section 19.4 to make movies. A key point of interest about the Mandelbrot set is its self-similarity. A highly stimulating way to demonstrate this feature is by literally to dive into the set. First, we define a scale factor that has the effect of zooming in to 80 percent of the image from one frame to the next:

```
In[28]:=  f[n_] := 0.8^n
```

Next, we define a function centered on a point of interest that produces a square box centered on the point, with a size determined by the current scale factor. We have found that the point $-1.40835915 + 0.13627737i$ is the center of a set of shape similar to that of the region found in a large-scale view of the Mandelbrot set, so zooming in on this point provides a good illustration of one feature of self-similarity:

```
In[29]:=  g[n_] := {{-1.40835915-f[n], -1.40835915+f[n]},
              {0.13627737-f[n], 0.13627737+f[n]}}
```

Thus, for example,

```
In[30]:=  g[0]
```

```
Out[30]=  {{-2.40836, -0.408359}, {-0.863723, 1.13628}}
```

Fixing attention on the point we have defined, we define a plot for the level-n zoom as follows (you may wish to experiment with more general functions that, for example, take as an argument the zoom point and a magnification factor — here we have fixed these values):

```
In[31]:=  plot[n_] := Show[Graphics[RasterArray[
              FractalML[0.0, 0.0, g[n], 216]],
              AspectRatio -> 1]]
```

All that is required to generate a series of frames, within a NoteBook interface, is execution of the command. *Warning: This animation takes a long time, even with MathLink!* Exact times depend on the system. Before executing, consider lowering the value of 216 to, say, 20, and run the loop from, say, 3 to 0. When you are sure that execution time is reasonable and that your system has enough memory, proceed. Remember also that you can create frames in batches and then group them for animation.

```
In[32]:=  Do[plot[n], {n, -3, 30}]
```

We cannot show the resulting movie in this book, so we have reproduced the start and end frames, as well as two intermediate frames:

In[33]:= `plot[-3];`

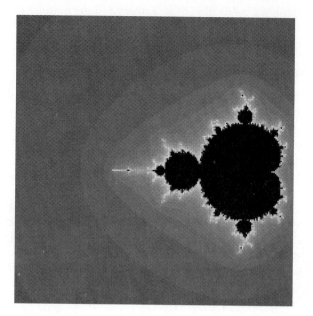

In[34]:= `plot[8];`

In[35]:= `plot[19];`

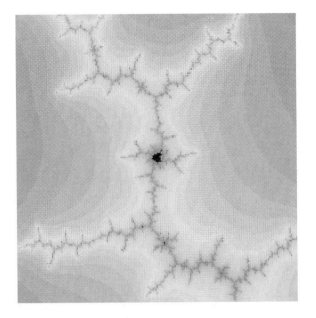

In[36]:= `plot[30];`

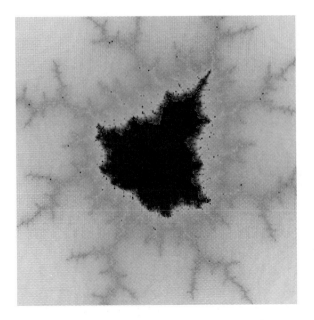

19.5.1 C Code and MathLink Template Files

If you have a version of *Mathematica* that supports MathLink, you have documentation for the system. (Macintosh users currently need to send for the MathLink Developer's Kit.) With an appropriate C compiler (the generic one for UNIX systems; MPW or Think C for a Mac), compilation of the following template file and C code will generate the functions used in Sections 19.3 and 19.4. Our own experiments were done using Think C 5.0.2 on a Macintosh running System 7.0.1. Take care to read any "Read Me" files that come with your software.

First, we give the template file for the code that returns the number of iterations. Here we define the C function name, followed by the *Mathematica* pattern to which it will be matched. We also define the names of the arguments and their types:

```
:Begin:
:Function:    fractalml
:Pattern: FractalML[a_Real,b_Real,{{c_Real,d_Real},{e_Real,f_Real}},g_Integer]
:Arguments:   { a,b,c,d,e,f,g }
:ArgumentTypes: { Real,Real,Real,Real,Real,Real,Integer}
:ReturnType:   Manual
:End:
```

Next, we give the C code (note that we do not include the header stdio.h; a MathLink header is included instead):

```
#include "mathlink.h"

void fractalml(a,b,c,d,e,f,g)
double a,b,c,d,e,f;
int g;
{
  double x0,y0,xmin,ymin,xmax,ymax;
  double x,y,dist, xadd, yadd, temp;
  int xco,yco, counts;
  int divs;

  x0 = (double) a;
  y0 = (double) b;
  xmin = (double) c;
  xmax = (double) d;
  ymin = (double) e;
  ymax = (double) f;
  divs = g;

  MLPutFunction(stdlink,"List",divs);

  for(yco = 0; yco <divs; yco++){
  yadd = ymin + (ymax-ymin)*yco/(divs-1.0);
  MLPutFunction(stdlink,"List",divs);

  for(xco = 0; xco <divs ; xco++){

  x = x0;
  y = y0;
  xadd = xmin + (xmax-xmin)*xco/(divs-1.0);

  dist = x0*x0+y0*y0;
  for(counts = 0; counts<100 && dist < 10000; counts++){
```

```
      temp = x*x-y*y+xadd;
      y = 2*x*y+yadd;
      x = temp;
      dist = x*x+y*y;
      }
      MLPutInteger(stdlink,counts);
      }
      }
}

int main(argc,argv)
int argc; char* argv[];
{
return MLMain(argc, argv);
}
```

The code for the MathLink program that returns color directives is similar. The template file is identical, and the C code is as follows:

```
#include "mathlink.h"

void fractalml(a,b,c,d,e,f,g)
double a,b,c,d,e,f;
int g;
{
   double x0,y0,xmin,ymin,xmax,ymax;
   double x,y,dist, xadd, yadd, temp;
   int counts;

   int xco,yco;
   int divs;

   x0 = (double) a;
   y0 = (double) b;
   xmin = (double) c;
   xmax = (double) d;
   ymin = (double) e;
   ymax = (double) f;
   divs = g;

   MLPutFunction(stdlink,"List",divs);

   for(yco = 0; yco <divs; yco++){
   yadd = ymin + (ymax-ymin)*yco/(divs-1.0);
   MLPutFunction(stdlink,"List",divs);

   for(xco = 0; xco <divs ; xco++){

   x = x0;
   y = y0;
   xadd = xmin + (xmax-xmin)*xco/(divs-1.0);

   dist = x0*x0+y0*y0;
   for(counts = 0; counts<100 && dist < 10000; counts++){
   temp = x*x-y*y+xadd;
   y = 2*x*y+yadd;
   x = temp;
   dist = x*x+y*y;
   }
   if(counts == 100){
```

```
        MLPutFunction(stdlink,"RGBColor",3);
        MLPutReal(stdlink,0.0);
        MLPutReal(stdlink,0.0);
        MLPutReal(stdlink,0.0);}
    else{
        MLPutFunction(stdlink,"Hue",1);
        MLPutReal(stdlink,counts/120.0);
        }
    }
  }
}

int main(argc,argv)
int argc; char* argv[];
{
return MLMain(argc, argv);
}
```

19.6 Summary

In this chapter, we have presented a case study in optimization. The computation of the Mandelbrot set provides a good example of a simple task that must be repeated a large number of times. Using internal compilation for this task, it is possible to achieve a significant increase in performance. Even further benefits can be obtained by using a C program linked to *Mathematica* via MathLink. In the first instance, we used this C program for simple numerical calculations only. Subsequently, we arranged for the graphics instructions to be returned also.

Maximum Entropy Reconstruction

In experimental sciences, much effort is devoted to reconstructing underlying data from the data that are obtained in an experiment. For instance, consider an astronomical photograph of a group of stars. The underlying data will be a set of point sources, but this will not be what the astronomers observe. The instrument they use has a finite resolution that will tend to blur the image. Usually, there will be the added complication of noise. We can write the generic operation from underlying data d to observed data o as follows:

$$o = R \cdot d + \sigma.$$

R is a linear transformation (in the astronomical example, convolution with the resolution of the detector), and σ is noise. If we assume that R is known, the goal is then to reconstruct d from o. We may have the added disadvantage that our data set is incomplete. In terms of the generic equation, loss of information implies that R is not square (and cannot be inverted).

This chapter looks at various techniques that are used to reconstruct underlying data. When the observed data are incomplete, there is a degree of freedom to this process. To isolate a unique solution, further assumptions have to be made concerning the underlying data. For instance, we may have reason to believe that the data set is smooth; Section 20.2 deals with this possibility. Astronomical images are obviously not smooth; rather they contain pronounced peaks (stars are point sources). For such images, we have the constraint that the underlying data are positive, but this is insufficient to fix a unique solution. Many researchers impose the further restriction that the reconstructed data set should have maximum entropy because it is believed that this suppresses any erroneous features in the output. Section 20.3 uses *Mathematica* to perform maximum entropy reconstruction. The algorithm is a trimmed-down version of that presented by J. Skilling and R. K. Bryan [21].

20.1 Singular Value Decomposition

Any square matrix with a nonzero determinant can be inverted. *Mathematica* can perform the inversion for us:

```
In[1]:=    MatrixForm[ squarematrix = N[{{1,2},{3,4}}] ];

In[2]:=    Inverse[squarematrix]
```

Out[2]=   {{-2., 1.}, {1.5, -0.5}}

Alternatively, and somewhat perversely in this instance, it is possible to use the `Sin-gularValues` command to generate the inverse matrix. We do not consider the theory behind this decomposition. If you are interested, refer to J. Stoer and R. Bulirsch [22].

In[3]:=   {u,w,v} = SingularValues[squarematrix];

In[4]:=   squareinverse = Transpose[v].DiagonalMatrix[1/w].u

Out[4]=   {{-2., 1.}, {1.5, -0.5}}

Consider our generic problem, $R \cdot d = o$. If R is square and invertible and there is no noise ($\sigma = 0$), then we can determine the underlying data from $d = R^{-1} \cdot o$. Now consider what happens when R has more columns than rows. In other words, R maps a vector onto a shorter vector, leading to a loss of information. In this instance, the equation $R \cdot d = o$ possesses an infinite set of solutions for d, and there is no way to reconstitute the original vector; in other words, the inverse matrix R^{-1} does not exist:

In[5]:=   MatrixForm[rectangularmatrix = N[{{1,2,3},{3,4,5}}]]
Out[5]=   1.   2.   3.
             3.   4.   5.

In[6]:=   Inverse[rectangularmatrix]
             Inverse::matsq:
                 Argument {{1., 2., 3.}, {3., 4., 5.}} at position 1
                 is not a square matrix.

Out[6]=   Inverse[{{1., 2., 3.}, {3., 4., 5.}}]

However, the `SingularValues` approach may still be used to generate a matrix :

In[7]:=   {u,w,v} = SingularValues[rectangularmatrix];

In[8]:=   singinverse = Transpose[v].DiagonalMatrix[1/w].u

Out[8]=   {{-1.16667, 0.666667}, {-0.166667, 0.166667}, {0.833333, -0.333333}}

We can use this matrix to obtain one solution to the equation $R \cdot d = o$. For instance, when $o = \{4,5\}$, a solution for u is as follows:

In[9]:=   onesolution = singinverse.{4,5}

Out[9]=   {-1.33333, 0.166667, 1.66667}

To test that this is indeed a solution, we multiply by `rectangularmatrix`:

In[10]:=   rectangularmatrix.onesolution

Out[10]=   {4., 5.}

We have taken care to stress that $R \cdot d = o$ possesses an infinite set of solutions. What is so special about `onesolution`? The general solution for d comprises this particular solution, added to any vector b for which $R \cdot b = 0$. The list u that we obtained from `SingularValues` contains the two vectors that span the nonnull space; we can determine a vector that lies in the null space — that is, b — by taking the vector product of these two vectors:

```
In[11]:=  Needs["LinearAlgebra`CrossProduct`"]
```

```
In[12]:=  freedirection = Cross[v[[2]],v[[1]]]
```

```
Out[12]=  {-0.408248, 0.816497, -0.408248}
```

Just to check that freedirection does lie in the null space, we can enter the following:

```
In[13]:=  rectangularmatrix.freedirection
```

$$Out[13]= \quad \{2.1684\ 10^{-19}, \ 4.33681\ 10^{-19}\}$$

The most general vector for which $R \cdot d = o$ is onesolution + lambda freedirection. Suppose that we consider the length of this vector d for the set of solutions:

```
In[14]:=  Plot[Apply[Plus,(onesolution + lambda freedirection)^2],
              {lambda,-2,2}]
```

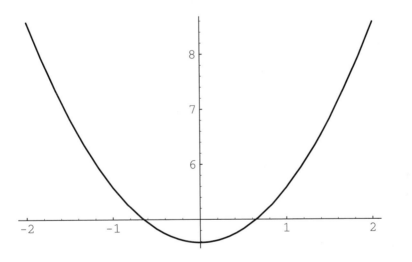

So, the shortest vector corresponds to lambda = 0; in other words, the singular value decomposition has chosen the solution with the minimum length.

20.2 Incomplete Data Sets with Smooth Underlying Image

The situation that we described in Section 20.1, where we must reconstruct the underlying data from incomplete data, occurs frequently in experimental sciences. Consider the situation where we have the following underlying one-dimensional data set containing 64 points:

```
In[15]:=  oneddata = Table[Sin[2 x] + Exp[-x^2],{x,-4.0,4.0,8/63.0}];
```

```
In[16]:=  origpic = ListPlot[oneddata, PlotJoined -> True];
```

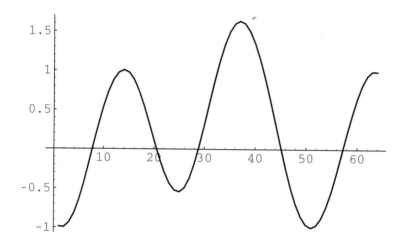

We shall assume that the experimentalist observes a linear function of these data (for the radio astronomer, it would be the Fourier transform). For simplicity, we use a random matrix to simulate this linear operation (subject to the constraint that the matrix has more columns than it has rows so that there is a loss of information):

In[17]:=   `convmatrix = Table[Random[],{i,30},{j,64}];`

The output of our experiment will consist of the data multiplied by this matrix, with random noise added:

In[18]:=   `output = convmatrix.oneddata + Table[0.1 (Random[] - 0.5),{30}];`

In[19]:=   `ListPlot[output, PlotJoined -> True]`

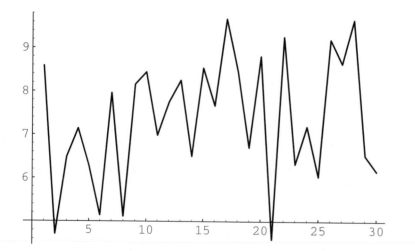

Note that the output — that is, the data that the experimentalist observes — has only 30 data points. Our aim is to reconstruct the original data from this output. Note, further, that we have introduced noise so that the relation between the underlying data and the observed data is the full equation $R \cdot d = o + \sigma$. Our criterion for inverting this equation is that the χ^2 of the solution d, defined by

$$\chi^2 = \sum_{i,j} |R_{ij}d_j - o_j|^2 / \sigma_i^2 \ ,$$

should be a minimum. Of course, this condition will be insufficient to reconstruct the underlying data; the singular values technique again extracts the shortest vector possessing the minimum χ^2:

```
In[20]:=  {u,w,v} = SingularValues[convmatrix];
```

```
In[21]:=  svdmat = Transpose[v].DiagonalMatrix[1/w].u;
```

```
In[22]:=  recondat = svdmat.output;
```

```
In[23]:=  reconpic = ListPlot[recondat, PlotJoined -> True]
```

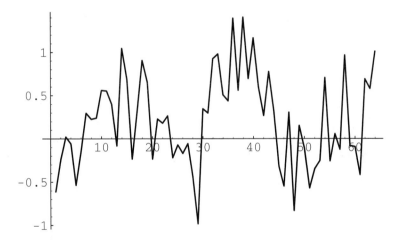

We can see that this solution has a very small χ^2 (from its definition, we see that χ^2 is necessarily positive):

```
In[24]:=  chisol[x_List] := Apply[Plus,(convmatrix.x-output)^2]*100;
          chisol[recondat]
```

$$Out[24]= \qquad 2.81931 \ 10^{-32}$$

Note that the factor of 100 equals the variance of the noise term that we added. Despite this low value of χ^2, the solution is not a good fit to the underlying data:

```
In[25]:=  Show[reconpic, origpic]
```

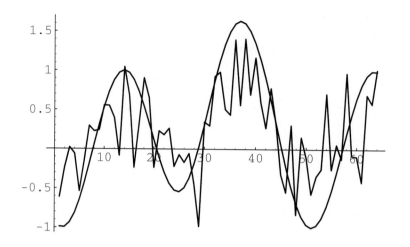

Is there a better way to reconstruct the underlying data? We really do not need such a small χ^2; in fact, a value less than the number of data points is unrealistic. A much better idea is to introduce a penalty on nonsmooth solutions and to minimize a suitable combination of this penalty term and χ^2, rather than χ^2 alone. The penalty operator should be a quadratic $d^T \cdot H \cdot d$ and, hence, positive for all nonsmooth solutions. We construct this operator as follows:

```
In[26]:=  firstdiff[x_Integer] :=
          IdentityMatrix[x-1] /. {a___,1,b___} -> {a,-1,1,b}
```

```
In[27]:=  firsth[n_] := Transpose[firstdiff[n]].firstdiff[n]
```

firsth[n] constructs the appropriate $n \times n$ matrix. We can check that we have constructed this matrix correctly by taking a flat list and a linear list, each with four entries, and looking at the value of the penalty term in the two cases:

```
In[28]:=  flatsol = {2,2,2,2};
          linearsol = {1,2,3,4};
```

```
In[29]:=  MatrixForm[ firsth[4] ]
```

```
Out[29]=  1    -1    0    0
          -1    2   -1    0
          0    -1    2   -1
          0     0   -1    1
```

```
In[30]:=  flatsol.firsth[4].flatsol
```

```
Out[30]=  0
```

So, the flat vector has zero penalty associated with it, whereas for the linear vector there is a penalty:

```
In[31]:=  linearsol.firsth[4].linearsol
```

```
Out[31]=  3
```

The inclusion of the penalty matrix actually simplifies the inversion process because the combined matrix R is now invertible:

In[32]:= `newmat= (Transpose[convmatrix].convmatrix + firsth[64]);`

In[33]:= `smoother = Inverse[newmat].Transpose[convmatrix].output;`

In[34]:= `flatpic = ListPlot[smoother, PlotJoined -> True]`

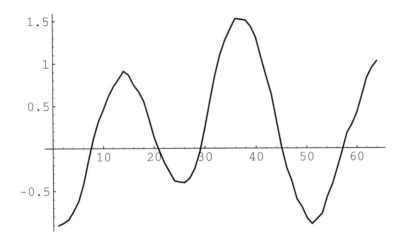

This reconstruction is considerably closer to the underlying data. The following plot shows the two data sets together with their residuals (points):

In[35]:= `Show[flatpic, origpic, ListPlot[smoother - oneddata,`
            `DisplayFunction -> Identity]]`

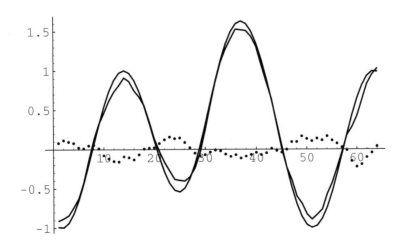

We check that we have used a reasonable value for χ^2 to obtain this solution:

In[36]:= chisol[smoother]

Out[36]= 9.29202

This is much less than our upper bound of 30, so we could increase the coefficient of the penalty term. We leave this as an exercise for you, preferring to turn our attention to a better approximation.

In this second instance, we construct a matrix that penalizes solutions that are not linear (as opposed to our first approximation, which penalized nonflat solutions):

In[37]:= seconddiff[x_Integer] :=
         IdentityMatrix[x-2] /. {a___,1,b___} -> {a,-1,2,-1,b}

In[38]:= secondh[n_] := Transpose[seconddiff[n]].seconddiff[n]

This matrix now gives no penalty to either the flat vector or the linear vector:

In[39]:= flatsol.secondh[4].flatsol

Out[39]= 0

In[40]:= linearsol.secondh[4].linearsol

Out[40]= 0

What does the reconstruction look like when we include this new penalty term?

In[41]:= newmat= (Transpose[convmatrix].convmatrix + secondh[64]);

In[42]:= linsol = Inverse[newmat].Transpose[convmatrix].output;

In[43]:= linpic = ListPlot[linsol, PlotJoined -> True]

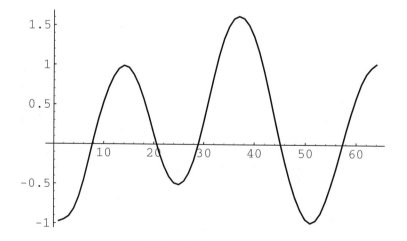

The agreement is staggering. The following plot shows the reconstruction and the underlying data together with the residuals:

```
In[44]:=  Show[linpic, origpic, ListPlot[linsol - oneddata,
              DisplayFunction -> Identity]]
```

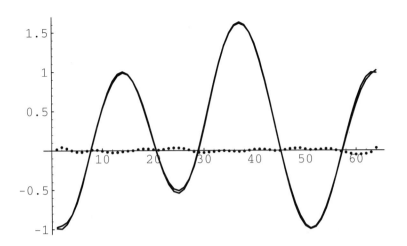

The message here is, with a priori information concerning the structure of the underlying data, we can do a good job of reconstructing that data from incomplete and noisy information.

20.3 Maximum Entropy Reconstruction

For large data sets, the analysis of the previous section may not be feasible. If our data set has a million values (not uncommon for images), we would be forced to invert a one million by one million matrix. Furthermore, our a priori information about the system may not be expressible as a quadratic matrix. How would you implement a penalty proportional to $\sum_i \log d_i$? In cases like this, we are forced to use an iterative technique.

The maximum entropy reconstruction technique falls into the category of problems described in the previous paragraph. The idea behind the reconstruction is as follows. Given a set of data, we choose a χ^2 for our reconstruction. Of the infinite set of solutions corresponding to this value of χ^2, we select the one with the highest entropy $-\sum_i d_i \log(d_i)$. In practical terms, the problem lies in implementing a robust algorithm to find this solution. J. Skilling [21] has produced an algorithm that has become widely accepted; we implement part of this algorithm in the rest of this chapter. The approach is suggested by an example.

First, we generate an image of two peaks sampled at 64 points:

```
In[45]:=  f[x_] := N[2/(1+2 x^2) + 2/(1+2 (x-3)^2)]+0.7;
          underlying = Table[f[x],{x,-5,10,15/63}];
```

These data are shown in the following plot, and the two peaks are clearly visible:

```
In[46]:=  ourhope = ListPlot[underlying, PlotJoined -> True, PlotRange -> {0,3}]
```

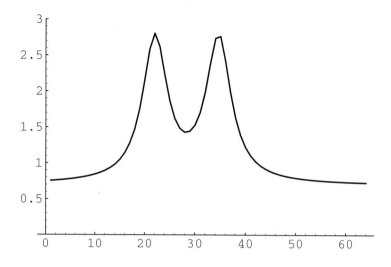

Suppose that our detector has a Gaussian resolution function; this means that the observed peaks will be blurred:

```
In[47]:=  resolution = Fourier[RotateRight[Table[N[Exp[-2 x^2]],{x,-4,4,8/63}],32]];

In[48]:=  observed = Chop[InverseFourier[resolution Fourier[underlying] ]];

In[49]:=  ListPlot[observed, PlotRange -> {0,4}]
```

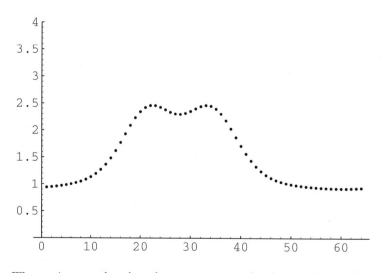

We can just resolve that there are two peaks there. If we add Gaussian noise to these data, then we lose even that information:

```
In[50]:=  Needs["Statistics`ContinuousDistributions`"]

In[51]:=  noise = Table[Random[NormalDistribution[0,0.2]],{64}];

In[52]:=  observed = observed + noise;
```

In[53]:= `ListPlot[observed, PlotJoined -> True, PlotRange -> {0,4}]`

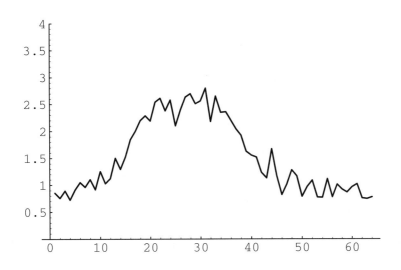

A first guess at reconstructing the image might be to take the Fourier transform, to divide by the convolution function, and then to apply the inverse Fourier transform. This approach fails (the reconstruction of the letter "d" in Chapter 21 fails for a similar reason):

In[54]:= `ListPlot[Chop[Fourier[InverseFourier[observed]/resolution]]];`

```
                              1
    Power::infy: Infinite expression --------- encountered.
                              0. + 0. I

    Fourier::fft1:
        Argument {9.8786 + 0. I, <<62>>, -2.62913 + 1.64964 I}
        is not a non-empty list of numbers.

    Fourier::fft1:
        Argument {9.8786, -2.62913 + <<1>>, <<61>>, -2.62913 + 1.64964 I}
        is not a non-empty list of numbers.

    ListPlot::list:
        List expected at position 1 in
        ListPlot[Fourier[{9.8786, <<62>>, -2.62913 + <<1>>}]].
```

The problem arises because the convolution function is very small (effectively zero) for the high-frequency components. A kludge solution to this problem is to divide by the convolution only when it takes a larger value than a minimum value (you should experiment with this cutoff value; for our example, 0.1 worked best):

In[55]:= `crudeinverse = Map[If[Abs[#] > 0.1,1/#,0]&,resolution];`

In[56]:= `recon = ListPlot[Chop[Fourier[InverseFourier[observed] crudeinverse]],`
`            PlotJoined -> True, PlotRange -> {0,3}]`

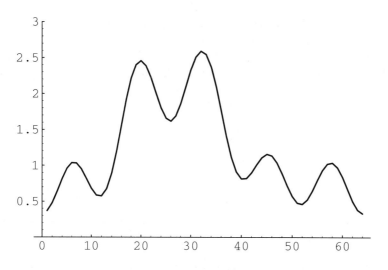

The two peaks are clearly visible, but other spurious peaks, not in the underlying data, have been introduced. This is a general feature of all methods used to selectively deconvolve in Fourier space. They all involve the a priori assumption that the underlying data set does not have high-frequency components. This assumption leads to spurious peaks in the data (which the high-frequency terms are needed to cancel).

Suppose that we apply the maximum entropy method instead, along with Skilling's algorithm [21]. As our first guess to the underlying data, we shall assume that it is uniform and takes the average value of the observed data:

```
In[57]:=   aveval = Apply[Plus,observed]/64;
           guess = Table[aveval,{64}];
```

Since the noise has variance 0.1, we impose the constraint that in our solution $\sigma^2\chi^2 = 64 \times 0.1^2$:

```
In[58]:=   Caim = 64 0.1^2;
```

We can inspect the χ^2 and the entropy of our first guess. We also define two operators R and R^T (which we describe in more detail in the next paragraph):

```
In[59]:=   R[x_List]  := Chop[InverseFourier[resolution Fourier[x] ]];
           Rt[x_List] := Chop[Fourier[resolution InverseFourier[x] ]];
In[60]:=   initchisq = Apply[Plus,(R[guess]-observed)^2];
           initent = -Apply[Plus,Log[guess] guess];
           {initchisq,initent}
Out[60]=   {37.0406, -41.045}
```

The next task is to choose a direction to search for an improved estimate for the solution. We are working in a 64-dimensional space here, but we shall restrict the search at each stage to a three-dimensional subspace. To generate the search vectors, we need to define the matrix R that maps our underlying data onto the observed data. This matrix is given by

$$R = F^{-1}CF,$$

where F stands for a Fourier transform and C stands for a convolution. The matrix R is never calculated explicitly (its size is the square of the length of the data set). We also need to define the transpose of R. A little thought should convince you that both F and C are symmetric matrices, so $R^T = FCF^{-1}$, as defined previously. We can use these operators to construct the three search directions. This construction is complicated; to understand the logic behind the choice, consult [21].

```
In[61]:=  grad[1] = -( Log[guess] + 1);
          grad[2] = 2 Rt[R[guess] - observed];
          len[1] = Sqrt[ grad[1].(grad[1]/guess) ];
          len[2] = Sqrt[ grad[2].(grad[2]/guess) ];
          vec[1] = guess grad[1]; vec[2] = guess grad[2];
          vec[3] = 2 guess Rt[R[(vec[1]/len[1]-vec[2]/len[2])]];
```

We can inspect these basis vectors after we have loaded the necessary package:

```
In[62]:=  Needs["Graphics`MultipleListPlot`"]
```

```
In[63]:=  MultipleListPlot[vec[1],vec[2],vec[3],PlotJoined -> False]
```

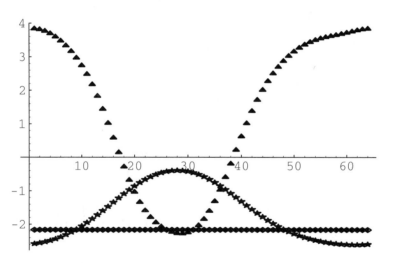

Unfortunately, these basis vectors are not orthogonal:

```
In[64]:=  vec[1].vec[2]
```

```
Out[64]=  -185.443
```

Our future analysis will be simplified considerably if we use an orthogonal set of basis vectors. It is a useful digression to write a function that achieves this, and we do so now.

20.3.1 Choosing Suitable Basis Vectors

Consider the case in which the underlying structure has 6 entries:

```
In[65]:=  d = N[{1, 3, 5, 2, 6, 4}]
```

Out[65]=   {1., 3., 5., 2., 6., 4.}

Our objective will be to change this vector in order to maximize the entropy, subject to a constraint on χ^2. Suppose that we are told to look for the next iterate in a subspace spanned by the following three vectors:

In[66]:=
```
e[1] = N[{5, 3, 1, 5, 3, 3}];
e[2] = N[{1, 4, 1, 4, 6, 2}];
e[3] = N[{6, 4, 3, 1, 5, 3}];
```

These vectors are probably not orthogonal — for instance,

In[67]:=   `e[1] . e[2]`

Out[67]=   62.

Actually, we shall need to define the scalar product slightly differently. The result that we have just written assumes that we are working in Euclidean space (don't panic!) in that the dot product of two vectors a and b is just $\sum_i a_i b_i = \sum_{ij} a_i \delta_{ij} b_j$. In *Mathematica* notation, a.b = a.IdentityMatrix[Length[a]].b. The space that we shall need to deal with here will not be Euclidean, and we shall have to replace the identity matrix by a diagonal matrix formed from the data set d (the object is to avoid negative values for the data at all stages in the reconstruction):

In[68]:=   `metric = DiagonalMatrix[1/d];`

The scalar product of e[1] with e[2] is now defined as

In[69]:=   `e[1].metric.e[2]`

Out[69]=   23.7

Alternatively — and crucially — for large data sets, since the metric matrix is diagonal, we can enter

In[70]:=   `e[1].(e[2]/d)`

Out[70]=   23.7

This is still not zero, but it is different from the Euclidean result. Our objective is to choose an orthogonal set of three vectors that are linear combinations of e[1], e[2], and e[3]. These vectors are obtained by diagonalizing the matrix $M_{ij} = e_i.e_j$:

In[71]:=   `Table[e[i].(e[j]/d),{i,3},{j,3}] // MatrixForm`

Out[71]=
44.45	23.7	41.85
23.7	21.5333	20.4333
41.85	20.4333	50.05

The standard method for diagonalizing matrices is to use the associated eigenvectors:

In[72]:=   `transfer = Eigensystem[%][[2]];`

In[73]:=   `({en[1],en[2],en[3]} = transfer.{e[1],e[2],e[3]})// TableForm`

Out[73]=
7.6209	6.0776	3.02397	5.35389	7.4765	4.6787
0.4247	-1.45456	-1.14105	1.50139	-2.82935	-0.0797601
-1.93429	1.39536	-0.744045	3.32892	2.46915	0.32158

These three vectors are orthogonal:

```
In[74]:=  (newmat = Chop[Table[en[i].(en[j]/d),{i,3},{j,3}]])//  MatrixForm
Out[74]=  101.34    0         0
          0         3.60889   0
          0         0         11.084
```

They are not yet normalized. This is the last step:

```
In[75]:=  Do[ en[i] = en[i]/Sqrt[newmat[[i,i]]],{i,3}]
In[76]:=  Chop[Table[en[i].(en[j]/d),{i,3},{j,3}]] // TableForm
Out[76]=  1.   0    0
          0    1.   0
          0    0    1.
```

Here are the three vectors that we have generated:

```
In[77]:=  TableForm[{en[1],en[2],en[3]}]
Out[77]=  0.757033    0.603727    0.300391    0.531836   0.742689   0.464765
          0.223561    -0.765673   -0.600642   0.790327   -1.48936   -0.0419855
          -0.580996   0.41912     -0.223486   0.999894   0.741648   0.0965916
```

The beauty of these vectors is that if we move a units in the direction of en[1], b units in the direction of en[2], and c units in the direction of en[3], there is a simple result for how far we have traveled:

```
In[78]:=  Chop[ Expand[ Apply[Plus,(a en[1] + b en[2] + c en[3])^2/d] ] ]
Out[78]=         2         2         2
          1. a  + 1. b  + 1. c
```

Automate it

The function basisvectors automates the construction of the basis vectors:

```
In[79]:=  basisvectors[origvectors_List,u_List] :=
          Module[{transfer, newmat, en, novecs = Length[origvectors]},
             transfer = Eigensystem[Table[origvectors[[i]].
                        (origvectors[[j]]/u),{i,novecs},{j,novecs}]][[2]];
             en = transfer.origvectors;
             newmat = Chop[Table[en[[i]].(en[[j]]/u),{i,novecs},{j,novecs}]];
             Do[ en[[i]] = en[[i]]/Sqrt[newmat[[i,i]]],{i,novecs}];
             en]

In[80]:=  basisvectors[{e[1],e[2]},d]
Out[80]=  {{0.61896, 0.605959, 0.178988, 0.825945, 0.74395, 0.467969},
           {-0.700897, 0.694945, 0.122287, 0.283353, 1.35111, 0.0387784}}

In[81]:=  basisvectors[{e[1],e[2],e[3]},d]
Out[81]=  {{0.757033, 0.603727, 0.300391, 0.531836, 0.742689, 0.464765},
           {0.223561, -0.765673, -0.600642, 0.790327, -1.48936, -0.0419855},
           {-0.580996, 0.41912,-0.223486, 0.999894, 0.741648, 0.0965916}}
```

20.3.2 Quadratic Expansion

We use the analysis of Section 20.3.1 to generate new basis vectors for our 64-dimensional data set:

```
In[82]:=  {newvec[1],newvec[2],newvec[3]} =
           basisvectors[{vec[1],vec[2],vec[3]},guess];
```

We must expand χ^2 in terms of distance traveled in the direction of these vectors. Since $\sigma^2\chi^2 = |R \cdot d - o|^2 = d^T \cdot R^T \cdot R \cdot d - o^T \cdot R \cdot d - d^T \cdot R^T \cdot o + o^T \cdot o$, its second derivative is just $2R^T \cdot R$. In our three-dimensional subspace, this amounts to

```
In[83]:=  M = 2 Map[Rt[R[#]]&,{newvec[1],newvec[2],newvec[3]}];
           M = Table[newvec[i].M[[j]],{i,3},{j,3}]

Out[83]=  {{4.41877, -0.329247, -0.159216},
           {-0.329247, 4.1414, -0.284632},
           {-0.159216, -0.284632, 2.35876}}
```

In other words, if we move a distance a[1] newvec[1] + a[2] newvec[2] + a[3] newvec[3], then χ^2 will change by

```
In[84]:=  linear terms + Expand[{a[1],a[2],a[3]}.M.{a[1],a[2],a[3]}]/2

Out[84]=                                   2
           linear terms + (4.41877 a[1]   - 0.658495 a[1] a[2] +


                      2
           4.1414 a[2]   - 0.318431 a[1] a[3] - 0.569264 a[2] a[3] +


                      2
           2.35876 a[3] ) / 2
```

Again, to simplify future analysis, it is advisable to get rid of cross terms like a[1] a[3]. We must make a second transformation of the basis vectors, while maintaining their orthogonality:

```
In[85]:=  vecmat = Eigensystem[M][[2]];
           Eigenvalues[M]

Out[85]=  {4.63764, 3.98771, 2.29359}

In[86]:=  {finvec[1],finvec[2],finvec[3]} =
           Table[Sum[vecmat[[j,i]] newvec[i],{i,1,3}],{j,3}];
```

At this point, let's pause to reflect. We should now have three vectors that are orthogonal and that diagonalize the quadratic terms in an expansion of χ^2. We can check both these conditions. First, are the vectors still orthogonal?

```
In[87]:=  Chop[Table[finvec[i].(finvec[j]/guess),{i,3},{j,3}]]

Out[87]=  {{1., 0, 0}, {0, 1., 0}, {0, 0, 1.}}
```

Second, the quadratic question:

```
In[88]:=  M = 2 Map[Rt[R[#]]&,{finvec[1],finvec[2],finvec[3]}];
           M = Chop[Table[finvec[i].M[[j]],{i,3},{j,3}]]
```

Out[88]= {{4.63764, 0, 0}, {0, 3.98771, 0}, {0, 0, 2.29359}}

What do our final vectors look like? We have plotted them together with the desired solution. You can assess for yourself whether a suitable combination of these basis vectors will move us closer to the solution.

In[89]:= `Do[pic[i] = ListPlot[finvec[i], PlotJoined -> True,`
`    DisplayFunction -> Identity],{i,3}];`
`Show[GraphicsArray[{{pic[1],pic[2]},{pic[3],ourhope}}],`
`    DisplayFunction -> $DisplayFunction]`

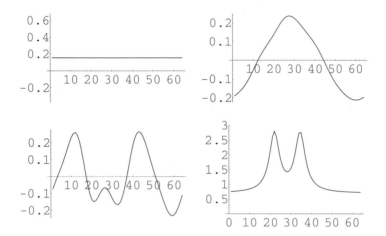

The simple form of the entropy function — a local operator with no correlation between different sites in the image — means that the quadratic terms in its expansion are automatically diagonal. We have now successfully chosen orthogonal basis vectors that simultaneously diagonalize χ^2 and the entropy function. All that remains is to determine the linear terms in the quadratic expansion in terms of these vectors:

In[90]:= `cderiv = Chop[ Table[finvec[i].grad[2],{i,3}] ]`

Out[90]= {8.67553, -14.273, 2.85291}

In[91]:= `sderiv = Chop[ Table[finvec[i].grad[1],{i,3}] ]`

Out[91]= {-14.031, 0, 0}

At last, we can proceed with minimizing the entropy, subject to the constraint that χ^2 takes a predetermined value. This minimization is most easily performed using a Lagrangian multiplier. That is, we minimize the combination $C + \alpha S$, with respect to α, and then choose the value of α that gives the requested χ^2:

In[92]:= `Do[x[i] = (alpha sderiv[[i]] - cderiv[[i]])/(M[[i,i]]+alpha),{i,1,3}]`

In the end, we want χ^2 to take the value Caim. This may not be possible to begin with, in the subspace that we have chosen, in which case a temporary aim is used instead. It is always possible to achieve this aim, and when we reach the solution, it tends toward the required value:

In[93]:= `Ctempaim = Max[Caim,initchisq-2/3 Sum[cderiv[[i]]^2/M[[i,i]]/2,{i,3}]];`

The following plot shows how χ^2 (in units of the desired value) and the distance traveled vary as we change α:

In[94]:= `dist = Sqrt[x[1]^2+x[2]^2+x[3]^2];`
`chisquare = initchisq +`
`  Sum[cderiv[[i]] x[i] + x[i] M[[i,i]] x[i]/2,{i,3}];`

In[95]:= `Needs["Graphics`Legend`"]`

In[96]:= `Plot[{dist/(0.3 Apply[Plus,guess]),chisquare/Ctempaim},{alpha,0,2},`
`  PlotStyle -> {Dashing[{0.01,0.03}],`
`  Dashing[{0.04,0.04}]},`
`  AxesLabel -> {"alpha",""},`
`  PlotLegend -> {"Distance",  "Chi^2"},`
`  LegendSize -> {0.7,0.4},`
`  LegendPosition -> {1,0}]`

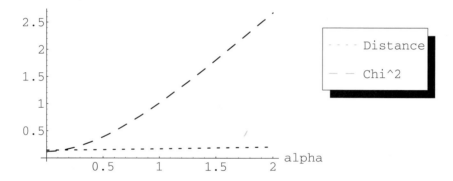

We want to solve the equation $\chi^2 = \chi^2_{aim}$ for α:

In[97]:= `alpharule = FindRoot[chisquare/Ctempaim == 1,{alpha,1}]`

Out[97]= `{alpha -> 0.991411}`

This should give a smaller value of χ^2 than our original guess:

In[98]:= `{initchisq, chisquare /. alpharule}`

Out[98]= `{37.0406, 13.4192}`

What does this value of α correspond to in terms of motion in the direction of the unit vectors?

In[99]:= `{x[1],x[2],x[3]} /. alpharule`

Out[99]= {-4.0124, 2.86657, -0.868464}

This motion corresponds to a distance of

In[100]:= dist /. alpharule

Out[100]= 5.00708

It is best not to allow the distance of any one step to be too large; a useful guide is to keep the distance in the range $0.1 \sum_i d_i$ to $0.5 \sum_i d_i$. Skilling [21] has given a set of rules for coping with the situation in which this bound is exceeded (we have not implemented these rules here). We have now reached the end of the first iteration. We can examine the output:

In[101]:= move = Sum[x[i] finvec[i],{i,3}] /. alpharule;

In[102]:= ListPlot[move + guess, PlotRange -> {0,3}]

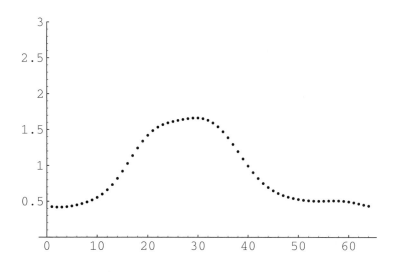

Automate it

The final stage is to iterate several times. We have grouped together all the code in a single function maxentiter:

In[103]:=
```
maxentiter[guess_List,observed_List, Caim_] :=
  Module[{grad,len,vec,initchisqr,initent,M,
    cderiv,sderiv,x,Ctempaim,dist,chisquare},
    maxdist = (0.3 Apply[Plus,guess]);
    grad = {-( Log[guess] + 1), 2 Rt[R[guess] - observed]};
    len  = {Sqrt[ grad[[1]]].(guess grad[[1]]) ],
            Sqrt[ grad[[2]]].(guess grad[[2]]) ]};
    vec  = {guess grad[[1]],guess grad[[2]]};
    AppendTo[vec, 2 guess Rt[R[(vec[[1]]/len[[1]]-vec[[2]]/len[[2]])]]];

    initchisq = Apply[Plus,(R[guess]-observed)^2];
```

```
vec = basisvectors[vec,guess];
M = 2 Map[Rt[R[#]]&,vec];
M = Table[vec[[i]].M[[j]],{i,3},{j,3}];

vecmat = Eigensystem[M][[2]];
vec = Table[Sum[vecmat[[j,i]] vec[[i]],{i,1,3}],{j,3}];
M = 2 Map[Rt[R[#]]&,vec];
M = Chop[Table[vec[[i]].M[[j]],{i,3},{j,3}]];

cderiv = Chop[ Table[vec[[i]].grad[[2]],{i,3}] ];
sderiv = Chop[ Table[vec[[i]].grad[[1]],{i,3}] ];

x = Table[(alpha sderiv[[i]] - cderiv[[i]])/(M[[i,i]]+alpha),{i,1,3}];

Ctempaim = Max[Caim,
               initchisq-2/3 Sum[cderiv[[i]]^2/M[[i,i]]/2,{i,3}]];
dist = Apply[Plus,x^2];
chisquare = initchisq +
        Sum[ cderiv[[i]] x[[i]] + x[[i]] M[[i,i]] x[[i]]/2,{i,3}];

alpharule = FindRoot[chisquare/Ctempaim == 1,{alpha,1}];
Print[alpharule];
distance = dist/maxdist /. alpharule;
Print["Chisquared = ", chisquare /. alpharule];
Print["Distance Moved = ",dist/(0.3 Apply[Plus,guess]) /. alpharule,
        " times maximum"];

guess + Sum[x[[i]] vec[[i]],{i,3}] /. alpharule]
```

Finally, we iterate 10 times from the initial condition and examine the result:

```
In[104]:= aveval = Apply[Plus,observed]/64;
          guess = Table[aveval,{64}];

In[105]:= Do[ guess = maxentiter[guess,observed,0.2^2 64],{10}]
          {alpha -> 0.991411}
           Chisquared = 13.4192
           Distance Moved = 0.857119 times maximum

          {alpha -> 0.565611}
           Chisquared = 5.53051
           Distance Moved = 0.108361 times maximum

          {alpha -> 0.309269}
           Chisquared = 2.79556
           Distance Moved = 0.0252095 times maximum

          {alpha -> 0.279758}
           Chisquared = 2.56
           Distance Moved = 0.000695317 times maximum

          {alpha -> 0.281284}
```

```
Chisquared = 2.56
Distance Moved = 0.000101211 times maximum

{alpha -> 0.281557}
Chisquared = 2.56
Distance Moved = 0.0000152433 times maximum

{alpha -> 0.281692}
Chisquared = 2.56
                         -6
Distance Moved = 1.38643 10   times maximum

{alpha -> 0.2817}
Chisquared = 2.56
                         -7
Distance Moved = 4.35069 10   times maximum

{alpha -> 0.281718}
Chisquared = 2.56
                         -8
Distance Moved = 6.27217 10   times maximum

{alpha -> 0.281723}
Chisquared = 2.56
                         -8
Distance Moved = 2.64104 10   times maximum
```

How does the result compare with the reconstruction of Section 20.3?

In[106]:= ```ListPlot[guess, PlotJoined -> True, PlotStyle -> Dashing[{0.02,0.02}],
         PlotRange -> {0,3}]```

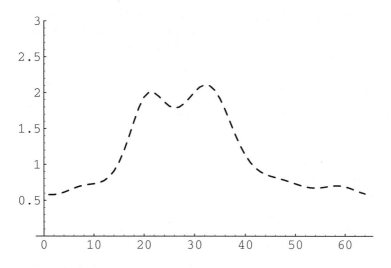

Note that the two peaks have been reconstructed and no spurious peaks have been introduced:

In[107]:= `Show[%,recon, PlotRange -> {0,3}]`

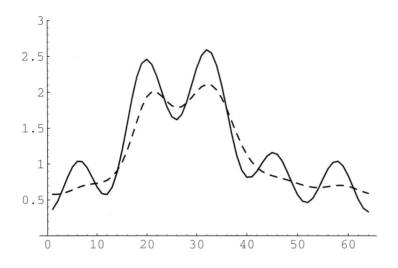

20.4 Summary

In the case study of this chapter, we have used *Mathematica* to reconstruct underlying data from an incomplete and noisy image. At first, we used the `SingularValues` command to find a solution that minimized χ^2. This solution was extremely jagged, and we obtained a much better reconstruction when we introduced a penalty on nonsmooth data. When images are blurred by detector resolution, Fourier techniques may be applied for reconstruction. Using *Mathematica*'s `Fourier` and `ListPlot` functions, we saw that in addition to generating features in the underlying data, other spurious features also appear. Although slower, the maximum entropy reconstruction process that we coded in *Mathematica* does not introduce features for which there is no evidence.

Digital Image Processing

This chapter presents a case study to show how we can use *Mathematica* to implement digital image processing — the process by which, for example, undesirable noise is removed from photographs. *Mathematica* provides an excellent platform on which to demonstrate processing tools and to prototype new ones. An image can be read into *Mathematica*, displayed, filtered in Fourier space, or enhanced by simple list operations in a remarkably compact manner. The material in this chapter would provide, for instance, a valuable tool to allow optics students to create and manipulate their own images effortlessly. The ideas presented here are covered in more detail in *Digital Image Processing* [7], which also contains many references.

21.1 Use of *Mathematica* to View a Digital Image

The technique of digital image processing is usually employed on photographs that have been digitized and stored in a computer. We could have used data of this form for the examples in this chapter, but that would have meant that you would not have been able to try out the examples for yourself. So, we opted to create our own photographic images. The following instruction creates a 64×64 pixel image with 64 levels of gray scale (equivalent to a low-resolution photograph):

```
In[1]:=    gaussdata = Table[Floor[64*N[Exp[-x^2-y^2]]]
                    ,{x,-2,2,4/63},{y,-2,2,4/63}];
```

We can extract a line of this image to ensure that we have only used 64 gray levels:

```
In[2]:=    gaussdata[[32]]
Out[2]=    {1, 1, 1, 2, 3, 3, 4, 5, 6, 8, 9, 11, 13, 16, 18, 21, 24, 27, 30, 34,
           37, 40, 44, 47, 50, 53, 56, 58, 60, 62, 63, 63, 63, 63, 62, 60, 58,
           56, 53, 50, 47, 44, 40, 37, 34, 30, 27, 24, 21, 18, 16, 13, 11, 9,
           8, 6, 5, 4, 3, 3, 2, 1, 1, 1}
```

As expected, all the data lie in the range 0 to 63. We want to display this image with *Mathematica* such that a pixel with gray-scale value of 0 appears completely black and one with a gray-scale value of 63 appears completely white:

In[3]:= `ListDensityPlot[gaussdata, Mesh -> False, PlotRange -> {0,63}];`

21.1.1 Fourier Transforms

Most of the processing that we shall discuss in this chapter relies on performing a Fourier transform of the data. We are fortunate that *Mathematica* supports a function called `Fourier` to perform this operation. Even more fortunate is that it employs an implementation known as *fast Fourier transform* (FFT), which is particularly efficient on data sets whose length is a power of 2. Our data sets are 64 × 64, so they satisfy this criterion.

For display purposes, we would like the output of our Fourier transform (which is a two-dimensional list) to have its low-frequency components located in the center and its high-frequency terms located on the periphery. This description is the opposite to what `Fourier` provides, so we shall define a function that creates a centered spectrum for images measuring 64 × 64 pixels:

In[4]:= `centeredfourier[x_List] := Transpose[RotateRight[`
`                Transpose[RotateRight[Fourier[x],32]],32]];`

We must also make a new definition of the inverse Fourier transform, which inverts one of our centered spectra:

In[5]:= `centeredinverse[x_List] := InverseFourier[Transpose[`
`                RotateLeft[Transpose[RotateLeft[x,32]],32]]];`

In general, the amplitudes of the Fourier spectrum will be complex, so we must take the absolute value before we can display that list. It may also be necessary to fiddle with the contrast to discern any detail in the spectrum. The Fourier spectrum of `gaussdata` provides an excellent example of both of these problems. First, we create the Fourier-transformed image:

In[6]:= `fouriergaussdata = centeredfourier[gaussdata];`

Then, we create, but do not display, a density plot of the absolute values of this spectrum, setting the plot range so that we include all the data:

In[7]:= `truefour = ListDensityPlot[Abs[fouriergaussdata],`
`                Mesh -> False, PlotRange -> All,`
`                DisplayFunction -> Identity];`

The next command creates a similar density plot, but with a smaller plot range:

```
In[8]:=    contrastedfourier = ListDensityPlot[Abs[fouriergaussdata],
                       Mesh -> False, PlotRange -> {0,1},
               DisplayFunction -> Identity];
```

When we look at the two images side by side, we see the advantages of the second approach; with `PlotRange` set to `All`, we resolve little structure in the spectrum:

```
In[9]:=    Show[GraphicsArray[{truefour,contrastedfourier}]];
```

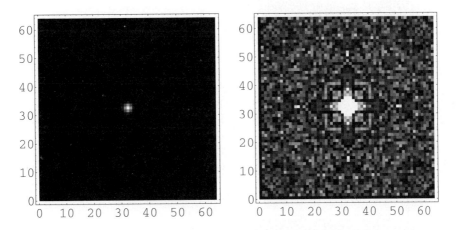

The remainder of this chapter is devoted to the problems involved in touching up images. For instance, an image may have been corrupted by electronic noise or blurred through motion or a fault in the camera. We consider electronic noise first.

21.2 Removal of Sinusoidal Interference

A common source of interference in an image is the presence of other electronic equipment in the vicinity of the detecting equipment. The electronic equipment will emit electronic noise of a particular frequency, which leads to the appearance of bands in the image. Let's simulate a photograph with such noise added. First, we generate interference of unknown frequency:

```
In[10]:=   unknownfreqx = 50 Random[];
           unknownfreqy = 50 Random[];

           interference = Table[4 (Sin[unknownfreqx x + unknownfreqy y]+1),
                       {x,-2,2,4/63},{y,-2,2,4/63}];
```

The image will be a superposition of this interference and the original data. There are now clear bands in the output:

```
In[11]:=   sinedata = gaussdata+interference;

           ListDensityPlot[sinedata, Mesh -> False, PlotRange -> {0,63}];
```

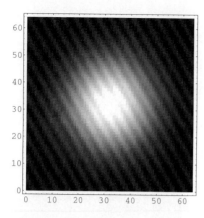

Interference of this type occurs frequently in television transmission. Because its underlying source is sinusoidal, it seems plausible that we could remove the noise by applying a suitable filter in Fourier space. Let's look at the Fourier transform with a suitable plot range:

```
In[12]:=  fouriersinedata = centeredfourier[sinedata];
          ListDensityPlot[Abs[fouriersinedata],
                    Mesh -> False, PlotRange -> {0,30}];
```

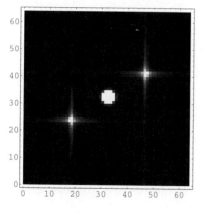

The strong signal in the center is the low-frequency information in which we are interested. The two outlying satellites are the high-frequency noise. We shall apply a simple filtering process of masking out these satellites. Before we can mask out the upper-right satellite, we need a more accurate fix on its location. We zoom in on the square that has corners at (38,45) and (48,50). Note that if you are following this simulation on your own machine, do not be surprised if the satellites are located elsewhere because the frequencies are random.

```
In[13]:=  ListDensityPlot[Abs[ fouriersinedata[[ Range[38,48],Range[45,50] ]] ],
                    Mesh -> False, PlotRange -> {0,10}];
```

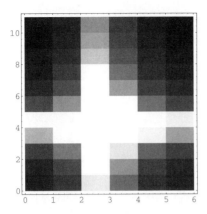

If we replace all the elements in this part of the Fourier transform by zero, we will lose most of the first satellite. A similar process can be used to remove the lower-left satellite (which is symmetrically placed because our data contain real numbers—the symmetry is $x \rightarrow 66 - x, y \rightarrow 66 - y$). We shall use the function MapAt to replace the selected values in the spectrum with zero; use a shorter name for the filtered spectrum if you wish!

```
In[14]:=   filterfouriersinedata =
               MapAt[0 &,fouriersinedata,Flatten[
                   Table[{i,j},{i,38,48},{j,45,50}],1]];
           filterfouriersinedata  =
               MapAt[0 &,filterfouriersinedata,Flatten[
                   Table[{i,j},{i,18,28},{j,16,21}],1]];
```

We can check that the masking has been successful:

```
In[15]:=   ListDensityPlot[Abs[filterfouriersinedata], Mesh -> False,
                   PlotRange -> {0,10}];
```

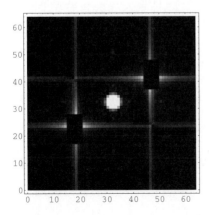

To reconstruct our image, we take the inverse Fourier transform and display it on the screen after removing any small imaginary parts with Chop:

```
In[16]:=   noiseremovedata = Chop[centeredinverse[filterfouriersinedata]];
```

```
ListDensityPlot[noiseremovedata, Mesh -> False,
        PlotRange -> {0,63}];
```

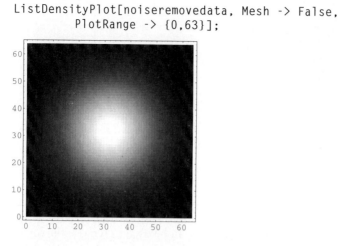

Clearly, most of the noise has disappeared. The interactive masking procedure that we have just followed is a common tool for touching up photographic images. In case you would like to reproduce these results, here are the random frequencies that we obtained:

```
In[17]:=   {unknownfreqx, unknownfreqy}

Out[17]=   {13.3199, 22.1161}
```

21.3 Image Sharpening

Image sharpening is the process by which the boundaries between different objects in a photograph are enhanced. At a boundary, the gray-scale value changes rapidly, or, equivalently, the gradient of the gray scale takes a large value. To enhance the boundaries in an image, we multiply the gray-scale values of the individual pixels by some function of the gradient at the pixel's locations. The most extreme course of action, which we describe here, is to impose a threshold. All pixels where the gradient is larger than this threshold value are colored black; the remaining pixels are colored white. This choice should produce an image of the boundaries only. To demonstrate this technique, we need to generate an image with some objects in it. We shall use a triangle, a square, and some random noise:

```
In[18]:=   triang[x_,y_] := If[y > 0 && y < 2 x && y < 2 - 2 x,1,0];
           square[x_,y_] := If[x>-1.5 && x<-0.5 && y>-1.5 && y<-0.5,1,0];

           objectdata = Table[Floor[63-30*N[triang[x,y]+0.5*square[x,y]+
                              Random[]*0.2]],
                         {x,-2,2,4/63},{y,-2,2,4/63}];

           ListDensityPlot[objectdata, Mesh -> False, PlotRange -> {0,63}];
```

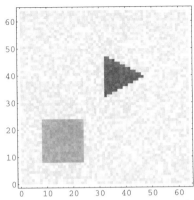

Computing gradients in *Mathematica* is simple! A rigorous treatment was given in Chapter 5; we present a brief summary here. Consider a one-dimensional list representing the values of a function sampled at constant intervals:

In[19]:=   `sinelist = N[Table[Sin[x],{x,0,2 Pi-Pi/50,Pi/50}]];`

To produce a derivative list, we can implement the approximation $f'(x) \approx (f(x + a) - f(x))/a$ by rotating the list and subtracting the initial list:

In[20]:=   `derivlist = N[ (sinelist - RotateRight[sinelist])/(Pi/50) ];`

Everyone knows that the derivative of $\sin x$ is $\cos x$; we can check whether our operation has been successful:

In[21]:=   `ListPlot[derivlist, PlotJoined -> True];`

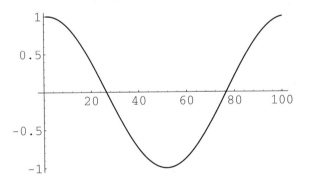

Photographic images are two-dimensional, so we need a concept of the gradient in two directions. We take an average of the squared value of the gradients in the x-direction and y-direction. To rotate the list in the y-direction, we have mapped the `RotateRight` function onto the inner lists:

In[22]:=   `linedata = Sqrt[N[((objectdata - RotateRight[objectdata,1])^2+`
               `(objectdata - Map[RotateRight[#,1]&,objectdata])^2)]];`

Finally, we define a threshold function and map it onto `linedata` to create an outline of the objects:

In[23]:= `threshold[x_] := If[x>10,0,1];`

```
linedata2 = Map[threshold,linedata,{2}];
ListDensityPlot[linedata2, Mesh -> False, PlotRange -> All];
```

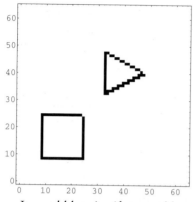

It would be nice if we could superimpose this outline on the original picture. We can do this so simply in *Mathematica*. First, we define a function that returns the original shading for nonboundary points or 0 (that is, black) for boundary points:

In[24]:= `superimp[orig_,bound_] := If[bound == 0,0,orig];`
`Attributes[superimp] = {Listable};`

Setting the attributes of `superimp` to `Listable` allows us to merge `objectdata` with `linedata2`. The function acts on two lists, replacing by zero any element in the first list for which the corresponding entry in the second list is zero:

In[25]:= `superimp[{{a,b},{c,d}},{{1,0},{0,1}}]`

Out[25]= `{{a, 0}, {0, d}}`

In[26]:= `ListDensityPlot[superimp[objectdata,linedata2],`
`                Mesh -> False, PlotRange -> All];`

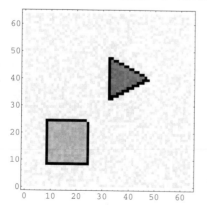

21.4 **Blurring and Deblurring**

Photographs frequently appear out of focus or blurred when they are developed. There are many sources of this phenomenon — a common cause is motion of the camera or the subject. It may not be immediately obvious that motion blur and having the wrong focal plane (out of focus) have any features in common; in fact, they are both linear convolutions and are amenable to the same analysis. With suitable information about how the blurring was introduced, it is possible to restore the image. We can get *Mathematica* to perform this restoration for us, but first we need to create a blurred image. We shall start with a crisp image of the letter "d" and then shall blur it. The following function is a mathematical description of the letter:

```
In[27]:=  chard[x_,y_] := Which[x > -0.0 && x < 0.5 && y < 1.4 && y > -1.2,0,
                          0.1 < (x^2 + (y+0.3)^2) < 0.81 && x < 0, 0,
                     True,1]

          ddata = Table[N[chard[x,y]],{y,-2,2,4/63},{x,-2,2,4/63}];

          ListDensityPlot[ddata, Mesh -> False, PlotRange -> All];
```

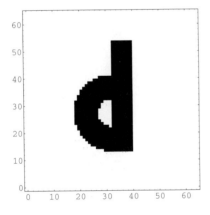

We can imagine blurring as occurring when many slightly displaced images are superimposed, or, equivalently, each pixel in the image is replaced by some weighted average of its value and those of its neighbors. This process has the effect of deteriorating high-frequency information in Fourier space: We can use *Mathematica* to demonstrate this degradation in the high frequencies. First, let's create the transform of the crisp image:

```
In[28]:=  fourierddata = centeredfourier[ddata];

          ListDensityPlot[Abs[fourierddata], Mesh -> False,
                    PlotRange -> {0,0.5}];
```

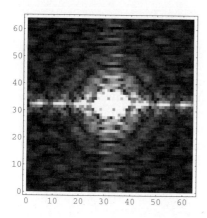

The following instructions blur the image by replacing the gray-level value of each pixel by an average of the local pixel (notice that the high-frequency components of the Fourier spectrum are strongly attenuated):

```
In[29]:=  blurredd = Transpose[Sum[RotateRight[ddata,i],{i,-2,2}]];
          blurredd = Transpose[Sum[RotateRight[blurredd,i],{i,-2,2}]]/16;

          blurfourierdata = centeredfourier[blurredd];
          ListDensityPlot[Abs[blurfourierdata], Mesh -> False,
                    PlotRange -> {0,0.5}];
```

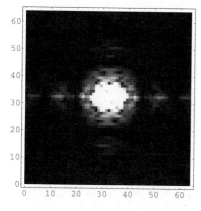

21.4.1 Blurring by Convolution

A more efficient way to implement a blurring process is by directly attenuating the high-frequency Fourier amplitudes, rather than averaging the pixel values. The convolution theorem states that the Fourier transform of the observed image is equal to the product of the Fourier transform of the actual image and the Fourier transform of the detector resolution. First, we generate the detector resolution function:

```
In[30]:=  blur = Table[1/(x^2+y^2+25.0),{x,-31.5,31.5},{y,-31.5,31.5}];
```

```
In[31]:=   Plot3D[1/(x^2+y^2+25.0),{x,-20,20},{y,-20,20},PlotRange -> All,
              PlotPoints -> 30, PlotLabel -> FontForm["Detector Resolution",
              {"PalatinoB",12}]];
```

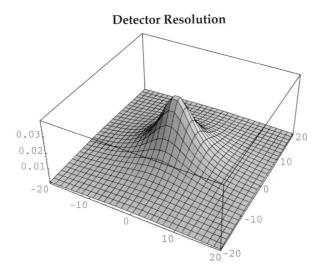

What does the letter "d" look like when we view it with a detector with such a resolution?

```
In[32]:=   blur = Map[RotateRight[#,32]&, RotateRight[blur,32]];

           observed = Chop[centeredinverse[centeredfourier[blur]*
                       centeredfourier[ddata]]];

           blurpic = ListDensityPlot[observed, Mesh -> False, PlotRange -> All,
           PlotLabel -> FontForm["Blurred d",{"PalatinoB",12}]];
```

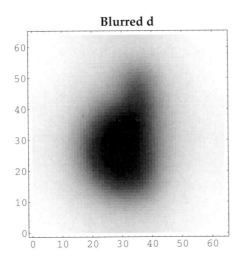

The letter is now very badly blurred — it is hardly recognizable at all. We can improve the clarity of the image if we use color:

In[33]:=
```
ListDensityPlot[observed, ColorFunction -> Hue, Mesh -> False,
  PlotLabel -> FontForm["Blurred d in color",{"PalatinoB",12}]];
```

To restore the original image, we must modify the Fourier spectrum by multiplying with a suitable correction matrix. The question is, How do we determine this matrix? Because the operation of blurring is a linear one, this correction matrix is independent of the image. Consequently, we can use the image of a known source to determine it; a point source is the simplest choice. The problem with dividing by the correction matrix is that this approach does not work when noise is added to the image after the blurring process — for instance, speckles on a photograph:

In[34]:=
```
Needs["Statistics`ContinuousDistributions`"];
noise = Table[Random[NormalDistribution[0,0.0005]],{64},{64}];
observed = observed + noise;
```

In[35]:=
```
conv = centeredfourier[blur];
```

In[36]:=
```
ListDensityPlot[
Re[centeredinverse[centeredfourier[observed]/(0.001+conv)]]]
```

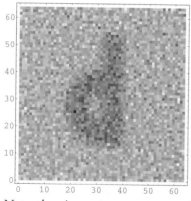

Note that it was necessary to add a small value to the correction matrix to prevent division by zero. The high-frequency components have been so strongly attenuated in the blurring process that the correponding correction is very large. Unfortunately, the same frequencies in the noise have not been attenuated and completely swamp the corrected image. We can avoid this problem by applying the correction to only the low frequencies:

```
In[37]:=    mask = Table[If[(i-33)^2 + (j-33)^2 < 50,1/conv[[i,j]],0],
                    {i,64},{j,64}];
```

```
In[38]:=    recons = Chop[InverseFourier[
            Map[RotateRight[#,32]&, RotateRight[mask,32]] Fourier[observed]]];
```

```
In[39]:=    reconpic = ListDensityPlot[recons, Mesh -> False,
            PlotLabel -> FontForm["Reconstructed d",{"PalatinoB",12}],
            DisplayFunction -> Identity];
```

```
In[40]:=    Show[GraphicsArray[{blurpic,reconpic}]];
```

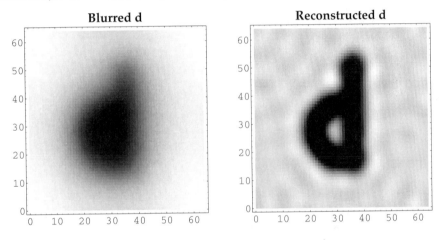

21.5 Summary

In the case study of this chapter, we have implemented a variety of tools for processing digital images. We saw that *Mathematica*'s ability to perform Fourier transforms on two-dimensional data sets allows rapid prototyping of ideas involving manipulations in frequency space. The operations to rotate *Mathematica* lists are invaluable for blurring data, and graphics commands such as ListDensityPlot and ListPlot3D gave an instant visualization of our experiments. The message behind this case study is the strength of *Mathematica* as a prototyping tool for reseachers; it is so easy to try out different possibilities. This feature also makes *Mathematica* an ideal teaching tool.

References

1. Anscombe, F. J. 1973. *American Statistician* 23, p. 17.
2. Broomhead, D. S., and G. P. King. 1986. On the qualitative analysis of experimental dynamical systems. In S. Sarkar, ed., *Nonlinear Phenomena and Chaos*. Adam Hilger, Bristol, United Kingdom.
3. Burden, R. L., and J. D. Faires. 1989. *Numerical Analysis*, 4th ed. PWS-KENT, Boston, MA.
4. Crandall, R. 1991. *Mathematica for the Sciences*. Addison-Wesley, Redwood City, CA.
5. Crank, J. 1984. *Free and Moving Boundary Value Problems*. Clarendon Press, Oxford, United Kingdom.
6. Eisenhart, L. P. 1912. Minimal surfaces in Euclidean four-space. *American Journal of Mathematics* 34, p. 215.
7. Gonzalez, R. C., and P. Wintz. 1978. *Digital Image Processing*. Addison-Wesley, Redwood City, CA.
8. Goodwin, B. W., and A. Wikjord. 1987. Environmental assessments using SYVAC, and environmental and safety assessment for the Canadian Nuclear Fuel Waste Management Program, reports presented at the 7th AECL, EURATOM meeting, Pinawa, Manitoba, Canada, October 1987.
9. Hitchin, N. J. 1982. Monopoles and geodesics. *Communications in Mathematical Physics* 83, p. 579.
10. Jehan, D. A. 1993. *Rare Earth Magnetism*, doctoral dissertation. Oxford University Clarendon Laboratory, Oxford, United Kingdom.
11. Keiper, J. 1992. "The N Functions of *Mathematica*," Wolfram Research technical report. Champaign, IL.
12. Levy, D. 1983. *Computer Gamesmanship*. Century Publishing, in association with Personal Computer World, London, United Kingdom.
13. Maeder, R. 1992. Minimal surfaces. *Mathematica Journal* 2, no. 2, p. 25.
14. Ogawa, A. 1992. The trinoid revisited. *Mathematica Journal* 2, no. 1, p. 59.
15. Press, W. H., B. P. Flannery, S. A. Teukolsky, and W. T. Vetterling. 1988. *Numerical Recipes in C, the Art of Scientific Computing*. Cambridge University Press, Cambridge, United Kingdom.
16. Rawlings, J. O. 1988. *Applied Regression Analysis: A Research Tool*. Brooks/Cole, Pacific Grove, CA.
17. Rousseeuw, P. J., and A. N. Leroy. 1987. *Robust Regression and Outlier Detection*. Wiley, New York.
18. Shaw, W. T. 1985. Twistors, minimal surfaces and strings. *Classical and Quantum Gravity* 2, L113.

19. Shaw, W. T., and P. Grindrod. 1989. Investigation of the potential of fuzzy sets and related approaches for treating uncertainties in radionuclide transfer predictions, report EUR 12499, Commission of the European Communities, Luxembourg.

20. Skiena, S. 1990. *Implementing Discrete Mathematics: Combinatorics and Graph Theory with Mathematica.* Addison-Wesley, Redwood City, CA.

21. Skilling, J., and R. K. Bryan. 1984. *Monthly Notices of the Royal Astronomical Society* 211, p. 111.

22. Stoer, J., and R. Bulirsch. 1980. *Introduction to Numerical Analysis.* Springer, New York.

23. Tigg, J. 1993. *Dynamical Chiral Symmetry Breaking*, doctoral dissertation. Oxford University Department of Theoretical Physics, Oxford, United Kingdom.

24. Tufte, E. R. 1985. *The Visual Display of Quantitative Information*, 5th ed. Graphics Press, Box 430, Cheshire, CN.

25. Wolfram Research. 1992. "Guide to Standard *Mathematica* Packages," Wolfram Research technical report. Champaign, IL.

26. Wolfram Research. 1992. "The *Mathematica* Compiler," Wolfram Research technical report. Champaign, IL.

27. Wolfram, S. 1991. *Mathematica, A System for Doing Mathematics by Computer*, 2d ed. Addison-Wesley, Redwood City, CA.

28. Wozniakowski, H. 1991. Average case complexity of multivariate integration. *Bulletin of the American Mathematical Society* 24, no. 1, p. 185.

29. Yam, P. 1991. Math exorcise, a new algorithm lifts the curse of dimensionality. *Scientific American*, July 1991.

Index